SPACES AND PLACES FOR ART

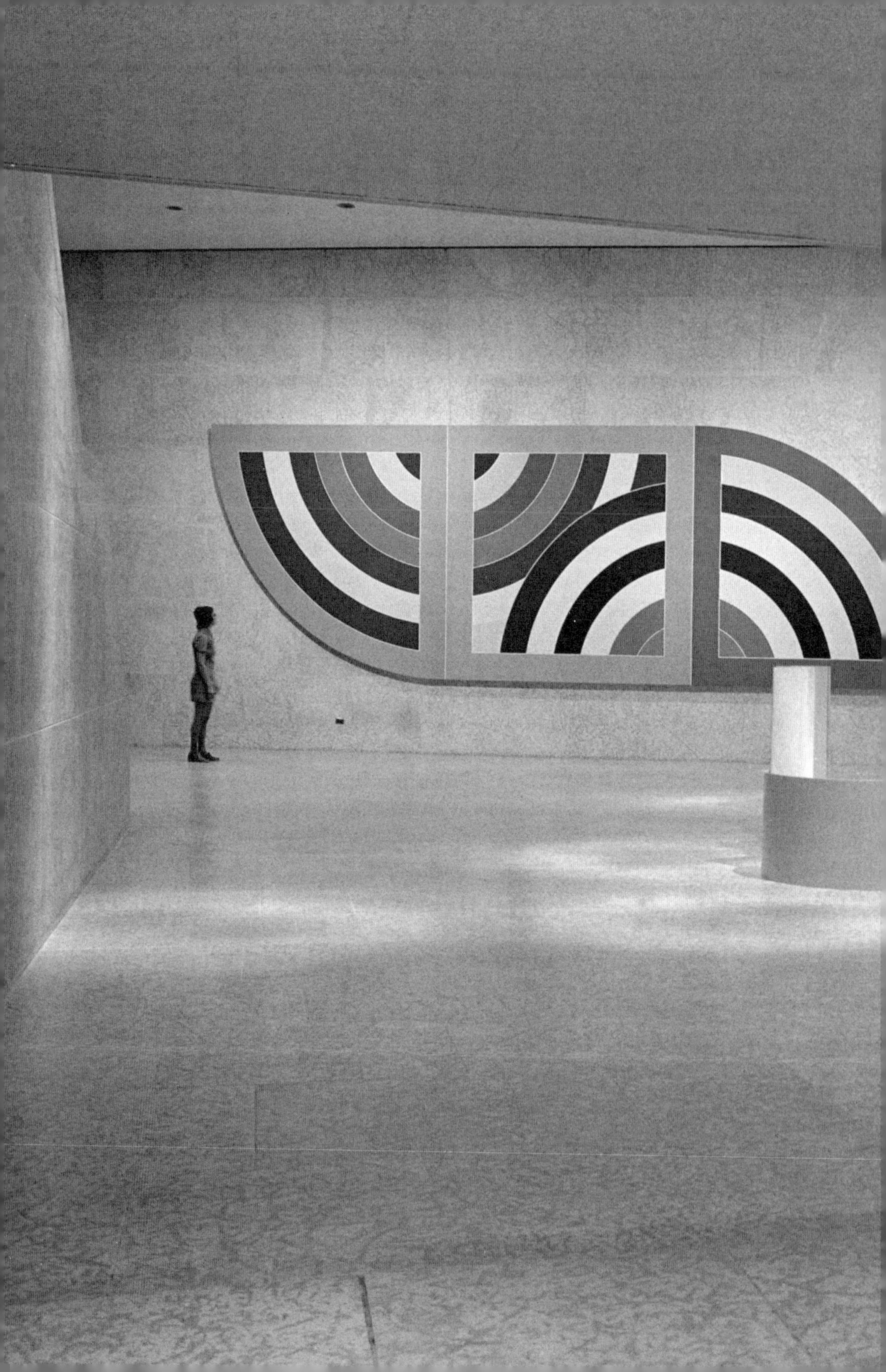

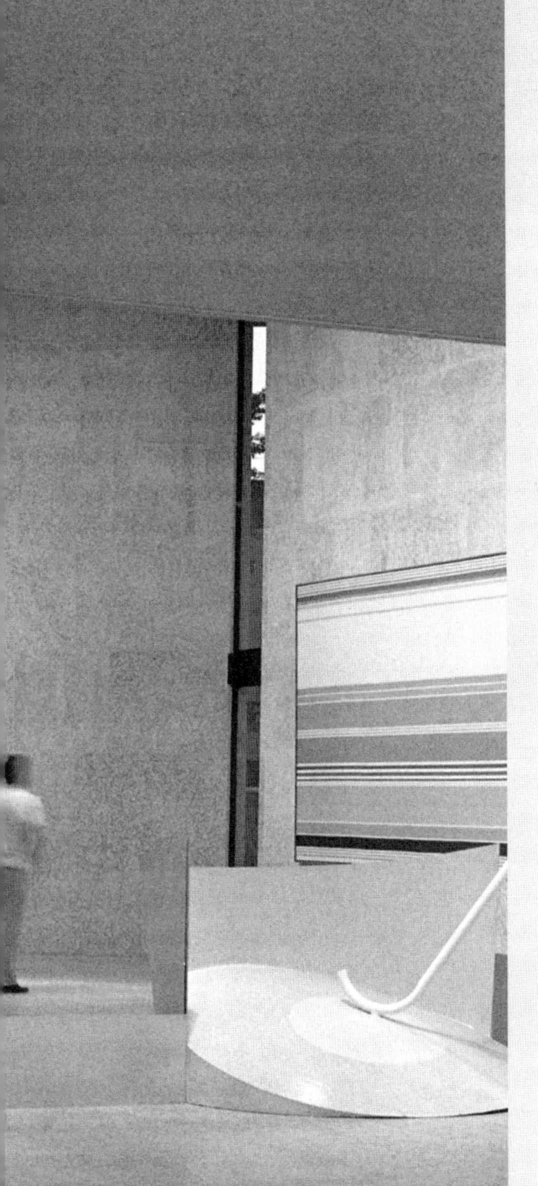

SPACES *and* PLACES *for* ART

MAKING ART INSTITUTIONS IN WESTERN CANADA, 1912–1990

Anne Whitelaw

McGill-Queen's University Press
Montreal & Kingston | London | Chicago

© McGill-Queen's University Press 2017

ISBN 978-0-7735-5031-5 (cloth)
ISBN 978-0-7735-5032-2 (paper)
ISBN 978-0-7735-5067-4 (ePDF)
ISBN 978-0-7735-5068-1 (ePUB)

Legal deposit first quarter 2017
Bibliothèque nationale du Québec

Printed in Canada on acid-free paper

This book has been published with the help of a grant from the Canadian Federation
for the Humanities and Social Sciences, through the Awards to Scholarly Publications
Program, using funds provided by the Social Sciences and Humanities Research
Council of Canada. Funding has also been received from Concordia University's
Faculty of Fine Arts and Aid to Research Related Events (ARRE) Program.

McGill-Queen's University Press acknowledges the support of the Canada Council for
the Arts for our publishing program. We also acknowledge the financial support of the
Government of Canada through the Canada Book Fund for our publishing activities.

LIBRARY AND ARCHIVES CANADA CATALOGUING IN PUBLICATION

Whitelaw, Anne, 1966–, author
Spaces and places for art : making art institutions in Western Canada, 1912–1990 /
Anne Whitelaw.

(McGill-Queen's/Beaverbrook Canadian Foundation studies in art history)
Includes bibliographical references and index.
Issued in print and electronic formats.
ISBN 978-0-7735-5031-5 (cloth). – ISBN 978-0-7735-5032-2 (paper). –
ISBN 978-0-7735-5067-4 (ePDF). – ISBN 978-0-7735-5068-1 (ePUB)

1. Art museums – Canada, Western – History – 20th century. 2. Art – Collectors and
collecting – Canada, Western – History – 20th century. 3. Art and state – Canada,
Western – History – 20th century. 4. Canada, Western – Cultural policy – History –
20th century. I. Title. II. Series: McGill-Queen's/Beaverbrook Canadian
Foundation studies in art history

N908.C3W55 2017   708.11'2   C2016-907358-0
                                 C2016-907359-9

Set in 11/14 Sina Nova with Gotham
Book design & typesetting by Garet Markvoort, zijn digital

CONTENTS

ACKNOWLEDGMENTS

Writing this book has been a twelve-year journey of reading, thinking, archival research, and conversations. I would like to first recognize Catherine Crowston and Tony Luppino – chief curator and executive director of the Edmonton Art Gallery – who back in 2004 were extremely receptive to my idea of curating an exhibition that examined the gallery's collecting activities. They generously gave me full access to the gallery's archives and free reign over how to present that history in the exhibition *Building a Collection: 80 Years at the Edmonton Art Gallery*. This was the show that prompted the writing of this book and I am very grateful for their encouragement of this project. Catherine, now executive director of the Art Gallery of Alberta, continues to be a wonderful conversationalist on all things art and gallery related. Early stages of my research were supported by grants from the University of Alberta, and I would like to thank the Department of Art and Design and the Faculty of Arts for their support and encouragement. The final research and writing was undertaken at Concordia University and thanks go to my colleagues in the Department of Art History for creating such a warm and supportive environment in which to complete the manuscript, and to the Office of the Vice-President Research and Graduate Studies and the Faculty of Fine Arts for financial support.

Throughout this project I have received excellent help from numerous research assistants: I thank Andrea Perechitz, Karl Davis, and Taylor Leedhal for their diligent bibliographic searches, Gwynne Fulton for the sanity-saving image research, and Jessica Veevers for her detailed formatting and reference work. Friends across the country read chapters of the book at various stages of completion and coherence. Thank you for your insights, comments, and reality checks to Liz Czach, Brian Foss, Martha Langford, Sasha Mullally, Diana Nemiroff, Liza Piper, and Julie Rak. For reading the manuscript in various forms over many years and making this a much better book, Lianne McTavish earns my deepest gratitude and appreciation. Thanks FFG!

A book of this kind cannot be written without the incredible work of archivists past and present whose careful management of the most ephemeral of documents facilitates academic work. Thank you to Cheryl Siegel at the Vancouver Art Gallery, Kenlyn Collins of the Winnipeg Art Gallery, Judy Thompson at the Art Gallery of Greater Victoria, Philip Dombowsky at the NGC, Alexandra McEwen at LAC, all the staff at Edmonton City Archives, as well as the many reference librarians across the country who answered my questions by phone or email. My deepest appreciation, however, must go to Cyndie Campbell at the National Gallery of Canada Library and Archives whose knowledge of the NGC's holdings provided the best guidance to unearthing the most appropriate and useful sources. Thank you Cyndie – you make writing Canadian art history possible.

In addition to the above, many friends and colleagues have patiently listened to me talk about this project and have provided information, suggestions, and reassuring conversation. They are Charlie Hill, Brian Foss, Kristina Huneault, Martha Langford, Johanne Sloan, Sandra Paikowsky, Greg Spurgeon, Bill Kirby, Mel Hurtig, David Silcox, Frances Plaunt, Joyce Zemans, Kirk Niergarth, Michelle Jacques, Andrew Kear, and I am sure many others. I would be remiss if I did not also warmly thank the external assessors for their close reading, insightful questions, and tremendous support of the manuscript. Jonathan Crago of McGill-Queen's University Press earns my heartfelt appreciation for his patience and encouragement, as do series editors Martha Langford and Sandra Paikowsky whose enthusiasm for the manuscript never flagged.

Finally – and most importantly – I must thank my partner Danielle Comeau for living with this manuscript for so long. As a Winnipegger, she has been instrumental in helping me think through what "western Canada" might mean, and for over twenty-seven years she has been unflagging in her support of all the things I do. My parents, Pat and Jim Whitelaw, have been equally encouraging of my academic and other ambitions, and likely inspired my life-long interest in museums by taking me to them from an early age. Thank you, Mum and Dad, for your love and your faith in my abilities. I dedicate this book to you.

ABBREVIATIONS

AAM	Art Association of Montreal
AGGV	Art Gallery of Greater Victoria
AGO	Art Gallery of Ontario
AGT	Art Gallery of Toronto
BCAL	British Columbia Art League
BCSFA	British Columbia Society of Fine Arts
CMA	Canadian Museums Association
CMC	Canadian Museums Committee
EAG	Edmonton Art Gallery
EMA	Edmonton Museum of Arts
FCA	Federation of Canadian Artists
MAA	Maritime Art Association
MAP	Museum Assistance Programmes
MMFA	Montreal Museum of Fine Arts
NGC	National Gallery of Canada
NMAG	Norman MacKenzie Art Gallery
NMC	National Museums of Canada Corporation
NMP	National Museum Policy
SAB	Saskatchewan Arts Board
VAG	Vancouver Art Gallery
WAG	Winnipeg Art Gallery
WCAC	Western Canada Art Circuit

SPACES AND PLACES FOR ART

On a cold night in late October 1924, hundreds of Edmonton's citizens made their way to the Palm Room of the city's lavish Hotel Macdonald to view the first exhibition of the newly formed Edmonton Museum of Arts. This inaugural display featured sixty works from local collections as well as twenty-four paintings on loan from the National Gallery of Canada (NGC), all of which, according to press reports, were received enthusiastically by the public. The inclusion of works from the National Gallery's collection was not an unusual occurrence for a new art organization trying to establish its legitimacy in what was still viewed as a relatively remote part of the country: the Winnipeg Art Gallery, founded in 1912 and the only other art gallery west of Toronto in 1924, was similarly dependent on National Gallery loan exhibitions for its ongoing activities, as were the art associations of smaller communities such as Brandon and Moose Jaw. Instituted in 1913, the loan exhibition program was one of the primary means by which the National Gallery was able to overcome the limits of its location in Ottawa and achieve its mandate of building Canadian public interest in the fine arts and promoting the nation's artists. Closely following the passing of the National Gallery of Canada Act in 1913, its director, Eric Brown, justified the establishment of the loan exhibition program as being the best way to demonstrate the quality of Canadian art and to encourage individual Canadians to purchase in that area.[1] Brown also argued that loan exhibitions would ultimately encourage the formation of art societies and institutions across the country, thereby increasing the appreciation and collecting of Canadian art. Commenting on the program in his annual report of 1917–18, Brown wrote, "These exhibitions were all eminently successful, and the rapid increase of applications for them is sufficient evidence of the growing desire for artistic knowledge throughout the country."[2]

The loan exhibitions are just one example of the complicated relationship between the National Gallery and art organizations in western Canada that this book explores.[3] While the loan exhibitions mutually benefitted both the national institution and regional galleries, they also became sources of tension as art organizations in the west sought more influence over the content of the exhibitions and the manner in which they travelled from centre to centre. The National Gallery, for its part, fought to maintain control over the kinds of work that circulated from its collections and to manage the movement of the exhibitions across the country. Over the roughly eighty years covered by this book, art galleries in western Canada both relied upon and resisted the leadership and assistance given by the National Gallery and other federal or federally funded institutions. On one hand, arts organizations in the west needed programs such as the loan exhibitions, which allowed paintings, small sculptures, and works on paper to stay in one location for up to a year at a time, because they did not have enough works in their own permanent collections to put together a significant display of "fine" art. Similarly, grants from the Canada Council providing matching funds for the acquisition of contemporary Canadian art were welcomed from the late 1950s through the 1990s by many cash-strapped institutions in western Canada; these same institutions also benefitted from such federal government policies as the Museum Assistance Program of the 1970s and 1980s that funded the circulation of cultural programs to all parts of the country.

On the other hand, as in much of the region's dealings with federal institutions in economic and political affairs, western Canadian art institutions often chafed under what they perceived to be paternalist federal government policies and a lack of consideration for their particular needs. Out of their frustration with the manner in which the circulation of the loan exhibitions was managed by the National Gallery, for instance, art organizations both large and small, from Winnipeg to Vancouver, organized themselves into the Western Canada Art Circuit (WCAC) in 1944 to have more control over the scheduling of the exhibitions received from the NGC and to reduce shipping costs from Ottawa. But when the improvements in packing and care of the loans promised by the circuit failed to materialize, the National Gallery created the department of Exhibition and Extension Services in 1957 to reassert control over the movement of Gallery collections and other exhibitions across the country. Similarly, when the Royal Commission on National Development in the Arts, Letters and Sciences (a.k.a. the Massey Commission) argued in its 1951 report for the expansion of National Gallery services while maintaining the core of its administrative operations in Ottawa, it was rejecting calls by the BC branch of the Federation of Canadian Artists (FCA) and certain art groups in Alberta for the decentralization of the National Gallery and the dispersal of its collections to the regions. Finally, despite the benefits of being designated Associate Museums during the reorganization of the National Museums in 1972, the reallocation of institutional funding by federal agencies to better reflect the diversity of exhibition spaces and practices occasioned by the increasing number of artist-run centres in the 1970s and 1980s was perceived by many major art institutions in the Prairies as a reassertion of control from "the centre" over the kinds of work that could be seen in the regions. Although each of the institutions considered in this study presents a particular history, broadly considered, the period between 1912 and 1990 was a time of continuous negotiation between federal and federally funded institutions and arts organizations in western Canada and it is these instances of negotiation that *Spaces and Places for Art* seeks to unpack and assess.

—| Arts organizations emerged in western Canada at about the same pace that cities developed in the region, with public galleries usually being formed by societies of either artists or art lovers as soon as some form of support from civic government – whether financial or in-kind – could be obtained. The Winnipeg Museum of Fine Arts (now the Winnipeg Art Gallery) was established in 1912 as a result of the activities of the Manitoba Society of Artists and the Western Art Association (formerly the Winnipeg branch of the Women's Art Association of Canada), and after spending its formative years in the city's Industrial Bureau, it was housed in Winnipeg's newly erected Civic Auditorium from 1933 until its current building opened in 1971; the Edmonton Museum of Arts (now the Art Gallery of Alberta) was established in 1924 by a group of private citizens with the support of the Edmonton Art Club and moved frequently until erecting its own building in 1968; the Vancouver Art Gallery was founded through the generosity of some of the city's leading citizens who raised enough funds for a building as well as a collection of mostly British paintings in 1931; in Saskatchewan, the Saskatoon Art Centre, founded in 1944, afforded meeting and exhibition space to the

Saskatoon Art Association, the Camera Club, and the Archaeological Society until funds and a significant donation of artworks from businessman Frederick Mendel made possible the construction of a permanent building – what would become the Mendel Art Gallery – in 1964; the Norman MacKenzie Art Gallery was finally opened at the University of Saskatchewan's Regina College in 1953, seventeen years after Norman MacKenzie's bequest of a significant portion of his collection and funds for a building; also in Regina, the Public Library's chief librarian Marjorie Dunlop began to organize art exhibitions in the periodicals reading room in 1948 and successfully advocated for the inclusion of an art gallery in the new public library building, erected in 1964; the Art Gallery of Greater Victoria opened in 1951 but the Island Arts and Crafts Society had presented exhibitions in the city since 1910; and while the Glenbow Museum is currently Calgary's principal collecting institution, from 1939 to its sale in 1960, Coste House was home to many of the city's art and theatrical societies, exhibitions, as well as the first site of the Provincial Institute of Technology and Art (what would become the Alberta College of Art and Design). Meanwhile, artists and interested amateurs formed art societies in smaller towns across western Canada, many of which found spaces for exhibition of their members' works in library and community halls, spaces that also displayed travelling exhibitions from the National Gallery or smaller shows organized by art galleries and museums in the regions' larger centres.

In its focus on the relationship between federal institutions such as the National Gallery and western Canadian art museums, this book is not intended to provide a detailed history of any of these institutions; however, key moments and activities of organizations large and small emerge throughout the text. For example, in its analysis of the externally directed operations of the National Gallery between 1912 and 1990, *Spaces and Places for Art* cannot help but map out important aspects of the history of that institution, most of which have not been covered in the existing literature.[4] The National Gallery's role in fostering the development and appreciation of art in Canada has often remained an unquestioned or assumed aspect of its mandate as a federal institution. How the gallery executed this mandate over the years, particularly in its dealings with institutions and organizations outside of the principle centres of Toronto, Montreal, and Vancouver has not received the critical attention that this complicated relationship deserves and constitutes a central aim of this publication. I have already mentioned the loan exhibitions, but the work of the National Gallery to disseminate art to the regions, and in so doing present itself as the primary source of information about art in Canada, went far beyond the loan of artwork and includes funding for children's art classes, reproduction programs, and lectures. My research examines the pivotal role of H.O. (Harry Orr) McCurry, the gallery's second director, in managing the development of art in Canada in the 1930s and 1940s – from the distribution of Carnegie money to galleries across the country in support of art education classes to managing the loan exhibition program and advising directors of emerging galleries and arts organizations across the country. McCurry almost single-handedly shaped the institutional culture of art in Canada from 1930 to his retirement in 1955, but his managerial style led to perceptions that he sought too much control over the development of art in Canada, an accusation that was extended to the National Gallery more generally in assessments about its extension activities. More broadly, the National Gallery's ability to set policy around the circulation of exhibitions to the various regions of the country, as well as its role in giving value to certain kinds of contemporary Canadian art through acquisitions and exhibitions, assures its centrality to any consideration of art in Canada. My discussion of the relationship of this Ottawa institution with arts organizations in western Canada will ultimately illuminate the wider nation-building role of the National Gallery.

If *Spaces and Places for Art* investigates key functions of the National Gallery of Canada, its focus on the relationship between the gallery and arts organizations in western Canada also entails an examination of the formation of art galleries and exhibition centres from Winnipeg west. For the record, this project began as a history of what is now the Art Gallery of Alberta and resulted in the preparation of two exhibitions: *Building a Collection: 80 Years at the Edmonton Art Gallery* (2006), which examined the collecting history of the institution from its formation in 1924 to the present, and *Seeing through Modernism: Edmonton 1970–1985* (2008), which explored the relationship between the art gallery, the fine arts department at the University of Alberta, and alternative exhibition spaces in the city during a period when what was then the Edmonton Art Gallery was particularly interested in acquiring the work of modernist painters and sculptors. While exploring the history of this institution, I was struck by the consonances between the experiences of the Edmonton Art

Gallery and other institutions on the Prairies – for example, the Norman MacKenzie Art Gallery in Regina and the Winnipeg Art Gallery – particularly in their engagements with the National Gallery and in their reactions to proposed policies formulated by cultural branches of the federal government. I have consulted the archives and annual reports of these and other institutions in western Canada, but as a result of my initial research, my knowledge of the history of the Art Gallery of Alberta is particularly detailed and for this reason, *Spaces and Places for Art* draws many of its analyses from the history of the Edmonton Art Gallery. However, I have explored specific examples from other institutions in the region when they better illustrate a larger point. Although this book does not provide a full history of every art institution in western Canada – a task that is woefully needed given the lack of institutional histories of art museums in Canada[5] – I hope that the information included here gives the reader a sense of the specificity of individual organizations. At the same time, I intend my broad focus on institutions in four Canadian provinces to illuminate their common experiences both in establishing themselves in the region and in navigating the requirements of institutions and policies originating from the centre.

—| My decision to emphasize the commonalities of experience of art institutions in western Canada over specific histories also speaks to the way I am thinking about this part of the country and its historiography. When this project was still an analysis of the Edmonton Art Gallery, I quickly realized that such a narrow focus ran the danger of becoming a triumphalist narrative of the prairie museum overcoming the challenges of chronic underfunding, minimal public interest, and relative geographic isolation to occupy its current location in a brand new building with established public programming. There are many such publications documenting the story of "the little art gallery that could" and I didn't want to write another one. My solution, therefore, was to take a broader look at the emergence of art institutions in western Canada, to map out the commonalities in the histories, as well as the differences, and to consider both the networks they formed and how together they negotiated their relationship with powerful forces from central Canada. Although I recognize that such an approach risks erasing or smoothing over the distinguishing features of individual institutions as well as the particular civic and provincial contexts of their formation, the benefits accruing from presenting a bigger picture of shared struggle are invaluable and align with recent writing on western Canada that underscores the strategic value of a homogenous view of "the west." Indeed, historians have argued that following settlement and the establishment of communities at the end of the nineteenth century, "the west" was imagined as a coherent entity built from the institutions introduced and established by British or British-identified migrants to the region and reinforced over the following decades by a federal civil service that oversaw the vast area as a single administrative unit.[6] Such assumptions belie the diversity of the population of western Canada: as Frances Swyripa has convincingly argued in her examination of eastern European immigration to Manitoba, Saskatchewan, and Alberta, any distinctive character ascribed to the region must include analysis of its "peculiar ethno-religious history,"[7] an assertion that can be extended to the necessity of attending to the impact of Indigenous peoples on past and present realities. For their part, western Canadians – or more specifically political leaders and organizations – embraced a unified vision of "the west" that shared many of the characteristics outlined by the federal government, but modified the image to play up the elements of "frontier vitality, economic grievance and political protest"[8] that differentiated the western provinces from Ontario and Quebec. Deployed in the early part of the twentieth century to resist tariffs and elevated transportation costs that favoured central-Canadian manufacturers over western resource producers, revived in the political protests of the 1930s over regional economic disparity and in the 1970s over the National Energy Policy, and alive again in the twenty-first century, the image of a homogenous "western Canada" battling the powerful centre has been wielded by all four provinces, even while underscoring provincial differences. Two editorial cartoons from western Canadian newspapers emphasize the resilience of such rhetorical positioning: in Arch Dale's "The Milch Cow" published in the 16 December 1915 *Grain Grower's Guide*, prairie farmers toil to feed the cow being milked by top-hatted industrialists from Ottawa, Montreal, and Toronto; over six decades later, at the height of western alienation, the *Calgary Herald*'s Tom Innes drew then prime minister Pierre Elliott Trudeau beaming over his obedient children Newfoundland, New Brunswick, Nova Scotia, Prince Edward Island, Quebec, and Ontario under the sign of Unity, as unruly progeny Manitoba, Saskatchewan, Alberta, and British Columbia sulk to the side. As Gerald Friesen argued in 2001, "the strength of ["the west"] lies less in some imagined social unity than in an imagined political force"[9] strategically wielded to rhetorically mark out a position in relation to another imagined region – "central Canada." That Ontario and Quebec have been the political and economic decision makers of the country is evident; that Manitoba, Saskatchewan, Alberta, and British Columbia have largely played subordinate roles in histories of the nation is equally clear – the result of what historian W.L. Morton described in 1955 as the "initial bias" of Confederation.[10] As the six decades following Morton's essay has made clear, however, the history of western Canada is rich and complex, and bears telling in multiple ways, many of which do not rely on the view from Ontario and Quebec. In looking at the specific histories of arts organizations from Winnipeg westwards, I want to think through the *relationship* between so-called central Canada and "the west" as something other than "centre–periphery" or the discourse of a region alienated by a dominant (or dominating) centre.

By invoking the term "centre–periphery" I am purposefully referencing a long tradition of Canadian historiography that relied on the political economy framework of Harold Innis to explain the particularities of the nation's economic and political growth.[11] Briefly put, in texts written primarily in the 1920s and 1930s, Innis argued that Canada's development as a state was shaped by trade systems determined by the country's geographical character rather than by the actions of individuals or organizations. Starting from the centrality of the Saint Lawrence River and the Great Lakes Basin to the fur trade, but expanding to account for the equal importance of the Mackenzie River and the Hudson Bay basin, Innis argued that these river systems were more than trade routes: they determined the flow of power from the economic centres of the emerging nation – Montreal and later Ottawa and Toronto – to the peripheral regions of eastern and western Canada, ultimately resulting in the political structures and relations of power that have come to characterize the modern Canadian state. Innis's focus on the links between geography and economic history and his examination of the inevitability of Canadian political structures make him particularly pertinent to the study of the rise of institutions in western Canada. Much of the tensions that emerge in this study relate to western art gallery directors' feelings of being on the geographical and cultural periphery of the country and subject to the whims of federal institutions. As Edmonton Museum of Arts director Robert Hedley wrote to the National Gallery's H.O. McCurry in 1947, "we

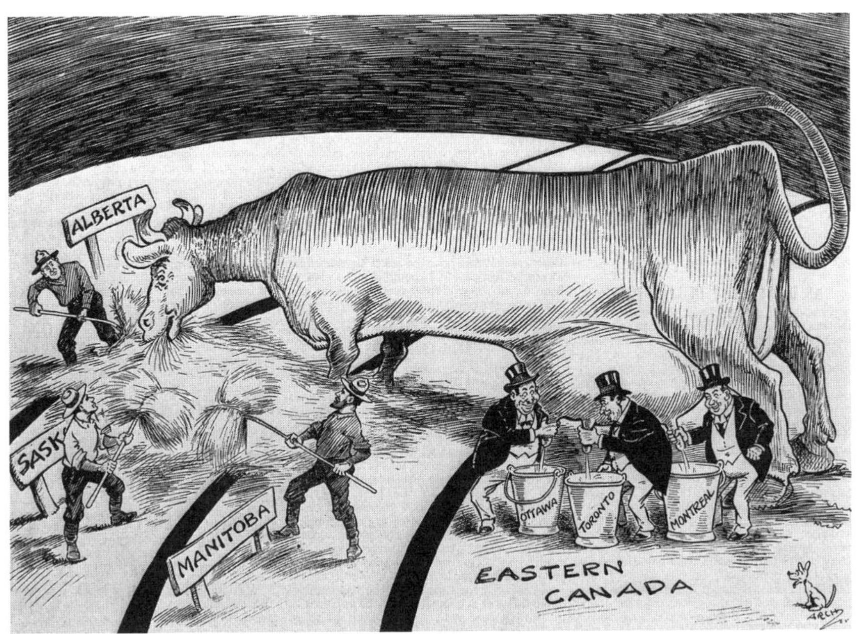

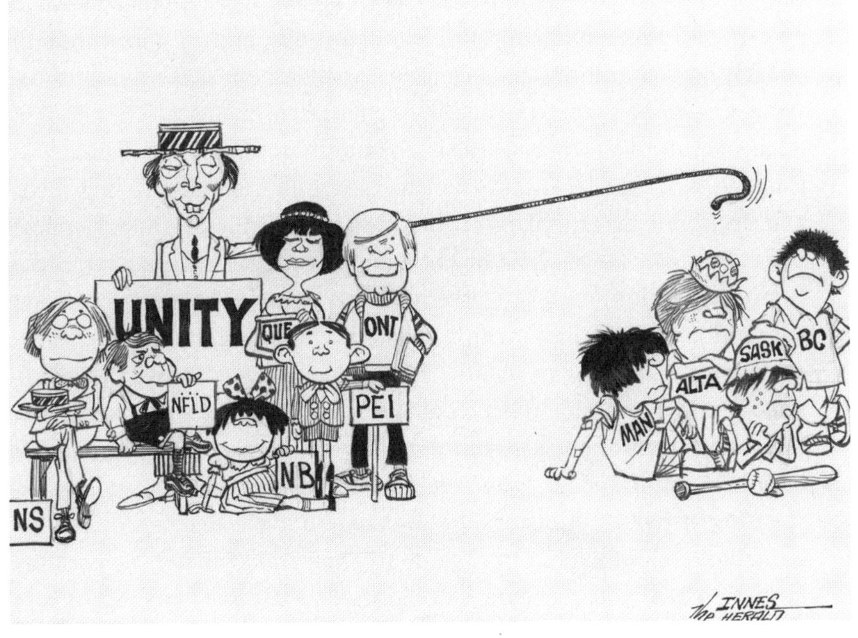

0.1 | Arch Dale, "The Milch Cow," *Grain Grower's Guide*, 15 December 1915

0.2 | Tom Innis, "Family Gathering," *Calgary Herald*, 3 April 1979.

are a long way from Ottawa [and] the West has little influence, relatively, unless for some matter concerning grain or hogs."[12] Both Carl Berger and William Buxton have pointed to Innis's strong distrust of centralization and his recurring interest in the marginalization of the interests of western, Atlantic, and northern regions of the country. Citing Innis's 1930 essay "The Canadian North," Buxton writes that Innis believed that "closer relations between western Canada and the Atlantic provinces ... [would be] a mitigation against the 'blighting influences' of centralization,"[13] a view that resonates profoundly with western Canadian attitudes towards central Canada in the 1930s and beyond. If relations of centre and periphery are often understood in terms of the colonial relations of Europe and Canada, Innis extended that model to explore how such concepts applied within Canadian geographic space.

Innis's more critical exploration of centre–periphery relations is somewhat at odds with his contemporaries – historians such as A.R.M. Lower and Donald Creighton whose environmentalist approach to the writing of Canadian history did little to question the "natural" dominance of central Canada over the less developed regions. This approach shaped studies of Canadian history well into the 1960s, and its imbrication of geographical conditions and economic development as the motor of national becoming shaped the underlying narrative of such classics of Canadian cultural history as J. Russell Harper's 1966 volume *Painting in Canada: A History*.[14] In an effort to escape the nation-building focus and economic determinism of this literature, historian J.M.S. Careless presented his own analysis of the experience of the national with the "limited identities" thesis,[15] essentially an argument for an expanded conception of Canadian identity that would attend to the ethnic, class, and regional markers of identity as themselves constitutive of nationhood. Subsequent historians would add gender, race, and sexuality as areas of identification that required analysis, but Careless's argument – originally published in 1969 – advocated for a more nuanced understanding of Canadian history that was rooted in the lived experience of Canadian communities rather than an overarching theory of national formation that could encompass the particularities of identity across geography and time. Although written some time apart, Careless's appeal to historians to consider investigating the experience of individual Canadians rather than "the deeds of hero federal politicians"[16] shares Benedict Anderson's 1983 proposal that scholars attend to the means through which "nation-ness, as well as nationalism, ... command such profound emotional legitimacy."[17] Anderson's now-familiar description of nations as "imagined communities," to be assessed not by their falsity or genuineness but "by the style in which they are imagined,"[18] has fundamentally changed the manner in which scholars have framed their examinations of the nation. Indeed, for both Anderson and Careless, the move away from broad-based nationalist histories towards the investigation of local narratives and affective experience has provided salutary models for writing particularized accounts of national identity. For historians in western Canada, Careless's injunction that "the true theme of the country's history in the twentieth century is not nation building but region building"[19] was the impetus for the production of numerous publications chronicling the specific history and experiences of communities and institutions that had largely been ignored by central Canadian historians. But what may initially have been seen as an attempt to "break the shackles of the metropolitan thesis,"[20] which sought to inscribe histories of regions within all-encompassing nationalist narratives, resulted in isolated histories of particular regions. One could argue, following Jean-François Lyotard, that these histories are the "petit récits"[21] that together weave a more complex and global picture of the experience of identity in western Canada. However, many of these narratives are so inwardly focused that they do more to contribute to the isolation of these regions from larger "national" histories. The potential downfall of writing a "regionalist history" thus looms large in my account. To take up what I think is the ultimate challenge to Careless's limited identities: can a history of the region ever be anything other than a regional history?

In thinking about this question in my own research, I have come to the conclusion that the way out of such isolationist regionalism is to bring back the centre but to try to destabilize its centrality, if you will. Most art institutions in western Canada could not have survived, and in many cases would not even have existed, had it not been for the loan exhibitions and other forms of support from the National Gallery. That such support was welcomed is evident; but it is also clear from the formation of the WCAC that art institutions in the regions sometimes felt that their best interests were not always the primary focus of such organizations as the National Gallery, and that, indeed, the loan exhibition program was to some extent a public relations exercise designed to cast the gallery as fulfilling its obligations as a *national* institution. By framing this project as an exploration of the *relations* between "Ottawa" and "the West" – rather than as the history *from* either location – I argue that the complexities of each centre's experience or history – the National Gallery's attempts to deliver its programming across the country and the art galleries in western Canada's efforts to produce fine arts programming with little provincial or civic support – function as parallel narratives from which the larger story of museum building in Canada can be woven. The result, I hope, is the production of history from neither the centre nor the periphery – or even a clever reversal of what might constitute the centre and the periphery – but a narrative that attends to the specificities of each as they are constituted in and by their relations with the other.

To achieve this reconsideration of centre and periphery as a framing device for Canadian history, I foreground conceptions of space and place in my analysis of western Canadian art institutions. It is no intellectual stretch to write about western Canada in spatial terms: the story of western expansion as the quest for "the last best west" is a longstanding trope that retains its rhetorical power into the twenty-first century despite the increasing awareness that such expansionism came at the devastating expense of Indigenous people and communities. The history of western Canada in the period under discussion chronicles efforts to occupy space through the building of towns and cities that would become the economic motors of the region and compete with the capitals of Ontario and Quebec. The transformation of spaces from "frontier" to "metropolis" was key to western cities' efforts to assert a sense of place within the national imaginary. These themes play a similar role in writing on Canadian identity and nationhood and I turn again to the writing of Harold Innis to clarify them. Innis's conceptualization of Canada's economic and political growth in spatial terms has already been outlined as it pertains to relations of centre and periphery; his interpretation of Canada's history through an analysis of "the interplay of geographical, technological and economic forces"[22] distinguishes him from earlier historians who focused on the actions of individual men. Innis's interest in the impact of geography on the development of the nation is best seen in his account of the fur trade; however, his later writing on the spatial logics of communications technologies have been invaluable to a generation of scholars keen to think through the impacts of radio, television, and other modes of communication – all industries highly subsidized by successive Canadian governments for their assumed ability to bind a nation together.[23]

Reading technologies as either time- or space-binding, Innis argued that the literal mapping of space that occurred with the fur trade was equally at work in radio and the emergent medium of television; although invisible, the spatial effects of communications technologies were as powerful in constituting the nation as the economic industries that spearheaded the colonization of the country. In her assessment of Innis's writing on current approaches to colonial space, Jody Berland builds on this writing and argues that space is never empty but is rather constituted through material practices. In her words, "Space is neither an empty frontier nor a backdrop for history, but the very subject/matter of historical change."[24] If space is constituted through material practices, then uncovering the development of civic structures in western Canada – including art museums – is key to understanding the experience of this region.

In terms of how I employ these terms in the book, "space" should be understood as the geographical site of individual art institutions and the cities whose identity they worked so hard to create. I am also using "space" to call attention to the physical expanse of art galleries and the room they form for the presentation of art in sites across western Canada. I use "place" to underscore the ideological and affective power of art galleries in the region. While the construction of permanent spaces for art preoccupied towns and cities across Manitoba, Saskatchewan, Alberta, and British Columbia, the aspiration to build an art gallery was inextricably tied with the impetus to establish centres of civilization in what was considered to be the western frontier. The ascription of civilizing values to art institutions has a long history and the business elites of western Canadian cities were fully aware of the symbolic capital that accrued from the establishment of an art gallery in a growing city. As the site of high culture and elite values, art museums provide important opportunities to assess the shifting ideological beliefs in western Canada over the twentieth century and how these values were differently negotiated at different points in time. As boundary-defining institutions, art museums also provide an opportunity to think through the constitution of publics in western Canada over the course of the twentieth century. Initially formed as a means of educating the public and providing guidance to manufacturers for the production of suitable consumer goods, museums quickly became associated with the interests of the business and social elites of western Canadian cities and were instrumental in purveying many of the values of that class to the wider community. The ethnic and cultural background of members of these elites – with a few exceptions largely drawn from Anglo-Ontario and British-born families – provided a certain cast to the organizations' interests, and in the first decades largely mirrored the interests of central Canadian organizations. As western Canadian provinces' senses of identity developed and points of dissension with the centre emerged, the commonality of interests that had characterized the first half of the century began to wane and galleries became implicated in a wider set of negotiations or *partis pris* that positioned the region in conflict with the ideological values of the political centre.

I have largely attended to questions of region in my discussion thus far, but, as noted earlier, the ascription of a common identity to "the west" often belies individual provinces' senses of their own autonomy and individuality. Indeed, the differences between Manitoba, Saskatchewan, Alberta, and British Columbia are many, particularly for those who have called each province home for generations. Beyond topological characteristics – the strong presence of the Canadian Shield in Manitoba; the fields of wheat in Saskatchewan; the plains and mountains of Alberta; and the old-growth forests of British Columbia – the political histories of each province are remarkable for their differences as well as their moments of connection. If Manitoba still references the 1919 Winnipeg General Strike as a touchstone for that province's continued support for labour-oriented governments, Saskatchewan's and Alberta's populist parties whether the leftist-oriented Co-operative Commonwealth Federation or the fiscally and socially conservative Social Credit, have produced populations that remain determined to defend their political self-sufficiency, and to ignore attempts from Ottawa to direct their policies. British Columbia, meanwhile, separated by the Rocky Mountains from the rest of the country, has long seen itself as distinct from the Prairie provinces. Benefitting from extensive cultural and economic relations with the American pacific states, its peripheral status within the Canadian context has been counterbalanced by strong and productive connections to the United States and Asia. Nevertheless, over the course of the twentieth century, these four provinces have found the common designations "western Canada" and "the west" politically useful when seeking to establish their difference from the rest of Canada, and particularly Ontario and Quebec. "Central" Canada, meanwhile, has only fueled the region's feelings of alienation by continuing to ascribe a homogeneity to all four provinces rooted in stereotypes of the untamed frontier. *Spaces and Places for Art* does not attempt to unpack the rhetorical deployment of "the west" from either standpoint; nor does it present a full picture of the history or politics of individual provinces. In its consideration of the histories and activities of art institutions in western Canada from the 1910s to 1990, it relies on the ways that the actors in these histories saw themselves as part of a broad social and economic entity called "the west," and in turn, how figures from Ottawa, in particular, equally viewed them in such homogenizing terms. Institutions across the region rarely pitted themselves against each other as representatives of provincial identities; nor did they engage in any city-to-city battles for preeminence, even in situations – such as Edmonton and Calgary or Regina and Saskatoon – where civic rivalries were otherwise rampant. Rather, as will be seen in the chapters that follow, art institutions across all four western provinces saw themselves as facing similar challenges and banded together, as needed, to form a bulwark against what was often seen as a controlling force from Ottawa.

Spaces and Places for Art in Western Canada

Spaces and Places for Art is broadly organized chronologically beginning with the formation of the first art gallery west of Toronto – the Winnipeg Museum of Fine Arts in 1912 – and ending with the demise of the National Museums Corporation of Canada in 1990. Over the course of the six chapters, various themes are highlighted that draw out both the challenges of establishing art galleries in western Canada and the constant requirement to negotiate relations with federal institutions in Ottawa. The resulting book thus presents an overview of museum building in the region as well as analyses of the relationship between centre and periphery as these were played out through fine arts institutions.

Chapter 1 maps out the context for the arts in western Canada in the first half of the twentieth century and presents capsule histories of arts organizations in Winnipeg, Regina, Saskatoon, Edmonton, Calgary, Vancouver, and Victoria as well as the efforts of select smaller communities to establish art associations and present exhibitions. A key thread running through this chapter is the significance of museum building to the transformation of frontier towns into major cities. The symbolic importance of cultural institutions was predominantly recognized by members of the economic elite who had immigrated to western Canada from Ontario and Britain in the late nineteenth century and who held closely to the cultural values of central Canada. By the 1940s, civic governments also began to see the merits of supporting the arts as they sought to build cities that could compete with the metropolises and establish western Canada as an important economic region.

Chapter 2 builds on the previous chapter's discussion of the struggles faced by emerging western Canadian art galleries by examining the institution with which it had the strongest relationship: the National Gallery of Canada. The NGC's federal mandate ensured that it was the principal conduit for information on and support of Canadian art throughout the country, whether through the acquisition of significant works for its permanent collection, the presentation of Canadian art abroad, or the circulation of loan exhibitions to art organizations across the country. The loan exhibitions program is particularly important in any discussion of the relationship between the National Gallery and organizations in western Canada as these exhibitions enabled emerging institutions with small or non-existent permanent collections to present significant works of art to their communities. Insofar as they also allowed the National Gallery to increase its visibility across the country and to justify its status as Canada's "national" art gallery, the loan exhibitions likewise were integral to the public face of the NGC, but equally enabled that institution to shape the kind of works that would be seen across the country.

The question of power and control appears again in Chapter 3's examination of developments in cultural policy in Canada from the 1930s through the 1950s. If the 1930s can be broadly characterized as a period of centralization in the operations of the federal government, in the 1940s the Canadian art world witnessed the emergence of such groups as the Federation of Canadian Artists whose British Columbia branch, headed by Lawren Harris, sought to diminish the powers of central institutions such as the National Gallery in favour of more local initiatives that would allow for greater participation from and for the community. This chapter culminates with a discussion of the Massey Commission's findings – including the establishment of the Canada Council – and the report's reassertion of centralized national institutions as the primary locus for cultural decision making and activities.

Where Chapter 2 was concerned with the relationship of western Canadian art galleries and the National Gallery in the 1920s and 1930s,

Chapter 4 drills down deeper to examine these galleries' reaction to Ottawa's control over the circulation of art to the west, specifically through an analysis of the Western Canada Art Circuit. Founded in 1944, this network of museums, cultural institutions, and art associations from Winnipeg to Victoria aimed to facilitate the circulation of National Gallery–sponsored exhibitions throughout the region by pooling their resources to obtain better shipping and insurance rates and coordinating more efficient travel routes for the exhibitions. Beyond this largely administrative rationale, participating institutions also believed that the WCAC would encourage the circulation of exhibitions organized by the western institutions themselves and would increase national exposure to artists from western Canada. As I argue, however, such assertions of western independence and self-regulation were met with resistance from the National Gallery, which sought to regain control of the circulation of its exhibitions by forming a department of extension that would oversee the Gallery's relationship with other organizations across the country.

Chapter 5 continues the exploration of centre–periphery relations by examining the manner in which Canadian art galleries sought to professionalize. Although proper practices of museum management had been advocated by the National Gallery since the 1920s, the establishment of the NGC's department of Exhibition and Extension Services in 1957 and its classification of art galleries across the country led institutions to feel the full impact of the pressure to professionalize, a pressure that the National Gallery itself was experiencing from the international museum community. From the 1950s onwards, Canadian art galleries began to hire directors and curators with training in museum management, erect buildings that met professional standards for the display and storage of artworks, and developed management systems and policies that more efficiently structured acquisitions and exhibition programs. These practices went far in raising the profiles of art galleries in western Canada, allowing them to participate on a more even playing field with the institutions in Montreal, Toronto, and Ottawa.

Chapter 6 traces the effects of the 1968 formation of the National Museums of Canada Corporation on art institutions in western Canada. The corporation, which remained in place until the 1990 National Museums Act, was an attempt to rationalize the administration of Canada's national museums (the National Gallery, the Museum of Man, the Museum of Nature, and the Museum of Science and Technology) under a single board of trustees. By 1972 this overt move towards centralization was mitigated by the designation of museums and galleries of a certain size outside of the nation's capital as Associate Museums, a title that was accompanied by operating funds and clear association with the larger institutions in Ottawa. Associate Museum status benefitted the major art galleries in western Canada as the provision of operating funds enabled them to spend other monies on acquisitions. When support to museums changed in the mid-1980s from operation to project funding in response to the increasing number of artist-run centres in Canada, museums across the country – including western Canada – viewed the change as another example of federal control over or interference with the activities of regional galleries. By this time, however, galleries in the region were developing their own areas of expertise and specialization, and with increased funding from provincial art bodies starting in the 1970s, they began to rival the National Gallery in terms of level and quality of programming.

The Epilogue brings the discussion of the relationship between western Canadian art galleries and federal institutions into the 2000s. This can be viewed to some extent as a period of equilibrium insofar that art galleries in Manitoba, Saskatchewan, Alberta, and British Columbia had, by 1990, established themselves as important contributors to the shaping of artistic practices in Canada. While these medium-sized galleries were already viewed as important regional centres, feeding smaller institutions and organizations in their respective provinces, they had also marked out areas of expertise and collecting activities that distinguished them from each other and from the larger galleries in Ottawa, Toronto, and Montreal. Indeed, it would seem that in the 2000s the issues preoccupying art organizations in Canada were tied less to regional recognition – although such recognition could be tied to the recent boom in museum construction – than to the representation of gender, sexual, and racial diversity in acquisitions and exhibitions, and to participating in aesthetic activities that were framed by global rather than national interests.

—| In his 1969 report on the state of art galleries in Canada, written for the Canada Council, Richard Simmins wrote, "the prairie institutions, in spite of some problems which seem insoluble, are among the healthiest and most stable in Canada. There is a brashness, a pride in attempting to overcome a harsh environment which transcends yeasty, effete, intellectual considerations."[25] The director of the Norman MacKenzie Art Gallery from 1951 to 1957, and head of the NGC's department of Exhibition and Extension Services from 1957 to 1962, Simmins was well placed to heap such praise on art galleries in western Canada. While his contrast of the brashness of these institutions with the effete intellectualism of, one assumes, central Canadian institutions, appears to fall into the trap of stereotypes of "the west" as rugged frontier, the sense of struggle and determination conjured by his description resonates with the histories of the institutions themselves. Founded by small groups of committed citizens with little money but big ideas, art institutions in western Canada struggled to achieve recognition from the community and financial support from provincial and federal governments. Yet they persevered in their aim to bring art to growing cities far from metropolitan hubs and in so doing helped build those cities into the political and economic centres they are today. *Spaces and Places for Art* tells that story.

1

KEEN PROPAGANDISTS FOR CANADIAN ART

Establishing Art Galleries in Western Canada

Art galleries in western Canada, as in much of North America, were established through the efforts of varying combinations of artists, businessmen, and women community workers. Artists, whether professional or amateur, provided expertise in matters of the fine arts and were actively involved in the formation of artists' societies in each of the western provinces. Businessmen, if not amateur artists themselves then *amateurs* of art in the classic sense, provided financial backing as well as persuasive arguments to city councillors of the expediency of establishing an art gallery. As Kathleen McCarthy and Dianne Sachko Macleod have demonstrated,[1] however, women were the driving forces behind the creation of many artistic endeavours in North America in the late nineteenth and early twentieth centuries, and the same is true for western Canada. Maud Bowman, founding president and first director of the Edmonton Museum of Arts (EMA), is a prime example of the unflagging efforts and organizational capacities of women to bring dreams of an art gallery to fruition. Originally from Cornwall, England, Bowman immigrated to Canada around 1900 where she met and married David Bowman of Kitchener (then Berlin), Ontario. The family moved to Edmonton and Bowman quickly became involved in the city's cultural organizations, despite the responsibilities of raising five children. Bowman was a member of the Edmonton branch of the Women's Art Association of Canada (WAAC) from its founding in March 1911 until the branch ceased to exist in 1919,[2] and she also served as president of the Edmonton Women's Musical Club in 1914 and from 1919 to 1922. The 1918 annual report of the (national) WAAC noted that the Edmonton branch was working in cooperation with "a local association of the schools and colleges" – likely the Edmonton Art Association, which was comprised of art teachers and instructors from the city's Normal School – to "encourage instruction in art and to arouse artistic feeling among the citizens generally."[3] Like its counterparts in other areas of the country, the Edmonton WAAC arranged for exhibitions by local artists and for the display of loan exhibitions obtained from the National Gallery of Canada (NGC). Membership in the WAAC connected Bowman to a national network of women interested in the arts, while its affiliation with the influential Local Council of Women gave Bowman the political clout necessary to rally support from Edmonton's business-men to establish an art museum. As indicated by the occupations of the founding signatories of the document of incorporation of the Edmonton Museum of Arts, Bowman was able to enlist the support of figures from the realms of politics (John A. McDougall, former mayor of Edmonton), business (John Imrie, managing editor of the Southam-owned *Edmonton Journal*), and the professions (Lucien Dubuc, judge, and R.B. Wells, doctor). Bowman's ties to cultural organizations in the city through the Local Council of Women also gave her access to the Edmonton Art Club whose members, with some persuasion, supported Bowman's plans to set up an art museum.

This pattern of collaboration between members of business and political elites, volunteer women, and artists' clubs in the formation of art museums was repeated in cities across North America. In the United States, the same story underpins the founding of such major institutions as the Metropolitan Museum of Art, the Detroit Institute of the Arts, and the Portland Art Gallery,[4] although these institutions operated with much more money and enough significant donations of works to form larger permanent collections. In Canada, the founding of the Art Association of Montreal (now the Montreal Museum of Fine Arts) in 1860 and the Art Museum of Toronto (now the Art Gallery of Ontario) in 1900, was achieved with the same combination of wealthy patronage, business and political interests, and voluntary labour.[5] The specificity of the situation in western Canada lies in the smaller size of the cities intent on establishing cultural institutions, the largely resource-based economies that shaped the fortunes of its business class, and the diverse demographics of western municipalities that resulted in relatively small audiences for elite cultural activities. Despite these differences, the individuals responsible for establishing art museums across Canada in the late nineteenth and early twentieth centuries shared the same ethnic and cultural backgrounds: they were all of British stock, whether newly emigrated from the United Kingdom or from established families in Montreal and Ontario who had immigrated to western Canada to seek their fortunes; they shared an affiliation with the Protestant faith;[6] they would all be classified as members of the upper or upper-middle classes, and belonged to many of the same national clubs and associations. Along with other civic leaders, these museum founders held a profound belief in the values that built the British Empire, and the loyalty many felt to both Britain and Canada was upheld by what Phillip Buckner and Douglas Francis have described as "a complex web of family, cultural, commercial and professional networks that linked the British in Britain with the British overseas."[7] Given the extensive immigration directly from Britain to all parts of Canada, and secondary migration of British-born from Ontario to western Canada in the early years of the twentieth century, it is unsurprising that the legal, commercial, cultural, and religious institutions that accompanied settlement all had their origins in British society and promoted a largely unified British world view. Although allegiance to political ideologies would be tested in western Canada over the decades, the adherence to Anglo-Canadian cultural values would remain strong among the leaders of western art institutions from Winnipeg to Victoria.

This chapter maps the conditions for the formation of public art galleries in western Canada in the first half of the twentieth century, paying particular attention to the quest for exhibition spaces, the acquisition of works for permanent collections, and the relationship between cultural institutions and all levels of government. The socio-political context of the period in western Canada addressed in the Introduction will be referenced here as it affected the creation and development of public art museums. In the next chapter, I will examine more closely the assistance given by the National Gallery to fledgling art organizations across the country, but in what follows my focus will be the specific challenges facing groups and institutions in western Canada in their quest to bring art to the region. When, in 1929, Ontario Society of Artists president F.H. Brigden characterized Maud Bowman, director of the Edmonton Museum of Arts, as "a keen propagandist for Canadian art in the west,"[8] he could have been describing any of the leaders of arts organizations in western Canada, all of who were intent to ensure that the fine arts was a central feature of the growing cities and towns across the region.

Finding Spaces for Exhibitions: Edmonton, Winnipeg, and Vancouver

The primary challenges of establishing an art gallery in the first decades of the twentieth century were finding spaces in which to exhibit art, and finding art to exhibit. These challenges were faced equally by groups in the major centres of Winnipeg, Edmonton, and Vancouver as well as by enthusiasts in the smaller towns of Brandon, Moose Jaw, and Medicine Hat. As will be discussed in greater detail in Chapter 2, the problem of finding work to exhibit was partially addressed by the program of loan exhibitions developed by the National Gallery to fulfill its national mandate. The larger centres also benefitted, to an unequal degree, from the loan of work from local collectors for special exhibitions, and they regularly displayed paintings and sculptures from local artists' societies and sketch clubs. Space, however, remained an ongoing concern for all institutions as, without dedicated rooms for exhibitions, the principal functions of a museum as a site for the public presentation of art would be impossible. The galleries discussed in this chapter were (and in some cases remain) established and administered by private associations. While the majority of their funding – both cash and in-kind – came from municipal governments, they were not municipal museums. The exceptions are the Vancouver Art Gallery (VAG), whose building was owned by the city but was administered by a registered private organization; the Mendel Art Gallery in Saskatoon, also municipally owned but run by a private board; the Norman MacKenzie Art Gallery (NMAG) in Regina, established as a university museum through a private bequest; and the Glenbow in Calgary, the only institution considered here that was created under a provincial statute. These distinctions are important to remember in assessing the level of funding that galleries received in the first half of the twentieth century: while the current funding landscape in Canada suggests that art institutions have long been the beneficiaries of governmental largesse at the federal, provincial, and municipal levels, history shows that until the late 1940s, the only financial support for art galleries in western Canada, if not across the country, came from municipal governments and private supporters, with the administration of virtually all galleries in the hands of private associations.

The Edmonton Museum of Arts held its first exhibition at the Hotel Macdonald, the city's premier hotel, in October 1924.[9] The scope of this

exhibition was impressive and included over sixty works from local collections, oils and watercolours by members of the Edmonton Art Club,
as well as a selection of paintings on loan from the National Gallery. The
twenty-four works loaned by the NGC included paintings by William
Brymner, Maurice Cullen, Frank Johnston, Laura Muntz, Homer Watson,
and Mary Wrinch. The larger grouping of works from local collectors
ranged from such contemporary Canadian artists as J.E.H. MacDonald,
J.W. Beatty, and W.J. Phillips, to more historical European figures such as
(Adriaen or Isaac) van Ostade and Gerard Dou. The small exhibition by
members of the Edmonton Art Club was accompanied by a display of
war artifacts from the collection of Brigadier-General W.A. Griesbach and
another of "Indian and Eskimo relics"[10] in keeping with the Edmonton
Museum of Arts' belief in the importance of presenting both the fine arts
and objects of historical interest.[11] Reviews described the exhibition as
a great success, and the directors of the new museum recorded their de-
light with the attendance. The reporter from *The Edmonton Journal* made
particular mention of two of the works on loan from the National Gallery: Georges Delfosse's *Maison de Cavelier de La Salle* (1919), which he
described as "a poem in theme, tone, and coloring," and Group of Seven
member Frank Johnston's *Fireswept Algoma* (1920), where he felt the artist
had "captured the spirit of desolation which lies in the wake of the forest
fire until the willow herb grows and transferred it to canvas."[12] Despite
such poetry, the reviewer concluded that Johnston's more modern painting was a work that "few people would care to live with," signalling the
aesthetic conservatism of western Canadian audiences. Further endorsement of the exhibition as a whole came in the form of an editorial from
the *Journal* that underscored the significance of the fledgling museum,
pointing out that "even what pass for the most materialistic cities have
felt the need of such institutions and their creation and development
have been a source of great community pride. Without the opportunity of
seeing fine pictures and fine sculptures, it cannot be said that any city's
educational facilities are anywhere near complete."[13]

For the next four years, the EMA continued to hold an annual fall exhibition at the Hotel Macdonald with a similar combination of National
Gallery loans, works from local collections, and contributions from
members of the Edmonton Art Club. But while the hotel was ideal for the
temporary displays of paintings, it could only be a stopgap measure if
the museum wanted to accomplish its goal of fostering knowledge about

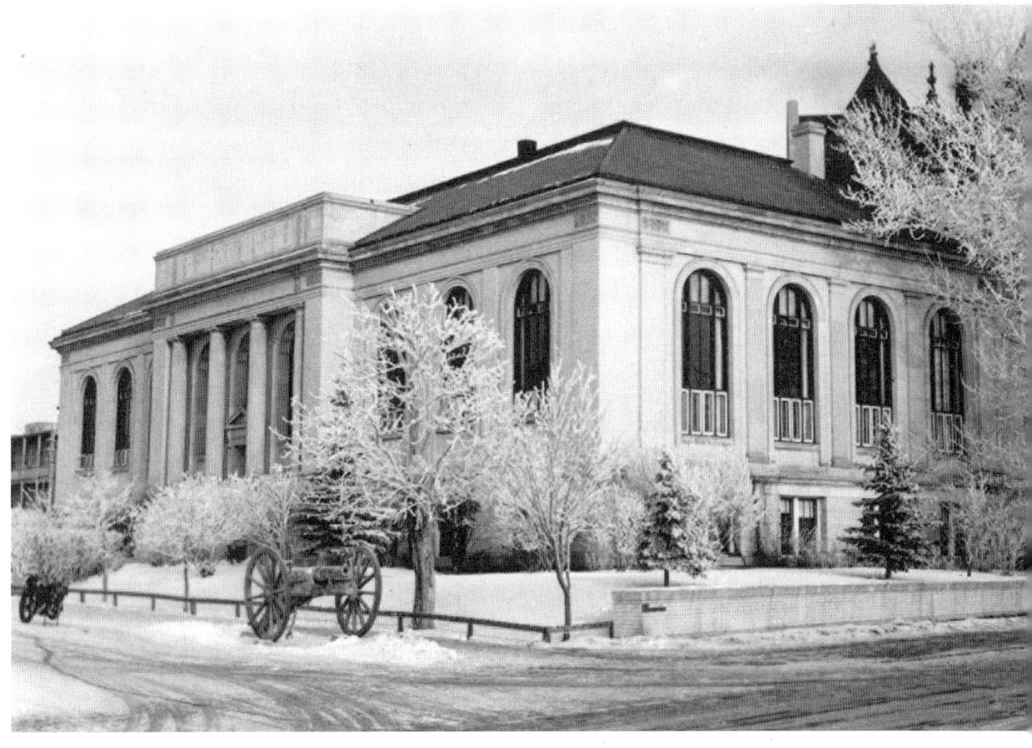

1.1 | Edmonton Public Library, 1940. Built with Carnegie funds, the library was the Edmonton Museum of Arts' first home from 1924 to 1927.

art in Edmonton's citizens. Shortly after the opening exhibition, the EMA was offered the lecture hall of the newly erected Public Library building for its exhibitions,[14] a move repeated in many cities and towns in Canada that had benefitted from funding from the Carnegie Corporation to erect libraries across North America.[15] In 1927, after two years petitioning the city for larger quarters, the EMA moved to a large room on the fourth floor of the Civic Block, which also housed City Hall and the offices of other social and cultural organizations. The Edmonton Museum of Arts remained in the Civic Block for almost seventeen years.

The proposal to establish an art museum in Edmonton was a tough sell in the 1920s. The economic boom and bust cycle of the last decades of the nineteenth century and the first decades of the twentieth century had resulted in both great wealth and enormous poverty in the city, a discrepancy that would only become more evident as immigration of relatively wealthy merchants and white-collar professionals from Britain, the United States, and Ontario was rivalled by an influx of Eastern European farmers displaced by war and famine.[16] The city benefitted from political alliances with the federal Liberal government by being named the provincial capital in 1905 and acquiring the charter for the provincial university in 1907. Yet, despite a population of 54,000 in 1918, few Edmonton streets were paved, electricity and telephone service was sporadic, and natural gas only became available to citizens in 1923.[17] For most residents – some of them living in tent communities near the downtown – the fine arts were of little interest and did not figure in their vision of an improved city. For Edmonton's elite citizens, however, high culture played a central role in their lives as can be witnessed by the formation of the Edmonton Amateur Dramatic Club in 1896, the Edmonton Women's Musical Club in 1910, and the Edmonton Art Club in 1921. Consisting mostly of talented amateurs, many of them women, these groups did much to foster the production of artistic events for the enjoyment of the emerging middle and upper-middle classes and for what they perceived to be the edification of the city's inhabitants as a whole. Throughout the 1920s and 1930s, the EMA's board of trustees blamed the lack of permanent space for the consistently low attendance at the museum and for the minimal number of works acquired through either purchase or donation.[18] The frustration is palpable in the minutes of the 1927 annual meeting when EMA President Maud Bowman noted that the "lack of [permanent accommodation] was causing us to lose valuable material owing to the unwillingness of owners to make gifts while we have no proper place to care for such."[19] While Bowman's address, published in full in *The Edmonton Journal*, was delivered in May, just six months before the move to the Civic Block, the need for more space, preferably in a separate building, continued to dominate the museum council's monthly meetings, and over the next twenty-five years, several attempts were made to secure property and adequate financial support from the city.[20]

Over this period, Edmonton, like all Prairie cities, suffered the economic effects of the Depression intensified by the extreme drought that engulfed the region. Wheat prices in Alberta dropped from $2.31 a bushel in 1919 to $0.77 a bushel in 1922, entailing a profound political shift in the province away from the traditional ruling parties towards the populist agrarian-based United Farmers of Alberta (UFA), which was elected provincially in 1921 and returned a majority of Alberta's seats in the federal election that same year.[21] With a largely rural support base and a strong sense of anger at the federal government for its trade policies – particularly transportation tariffs for wheat and other raw goods – the UFA galvanized a sense of Alberta identity among many outside the cities that, under the Social Credit elected in 1935, generated the rhetoric of alienation that characterized much of the twentieth century. Although receiving little support from voters in Edmonton or Calgary, the policies of the UFA and then Social Credit affected the cities insofar as there was little funding for what were considered cultural frills, and the traditional Anglo-Ontario values that continued to dominate the elites of both cities were at odds with those of the ruling party. Edmonton's population did not grow significantly in the 1930s as most immigrants settled in rural areas, and those fleeing worse drought and depression conditions in Saskatchewan increased the number of unemployed. Nonetheless, new movie theatres were built in the late 1930s, and in 1938 Eaton's erected its new modern department store while the Hudson's Bay Company expanded its existing premises.[22]

In 1944 the museum was asked to leave the Civic Block to make way for a children's crèche and offered rooms in the basement of the Edmonton Motors Building a few blocks from the city centre. The poor ventilation, low ceilings, and basement location, however, were unsuitable, and the museum's council held out for a better space on the building's ground floor, moving in during the late spring of 1945. The rooms in the Edmonton Motors Building allowed for the display of more of the museum's collection of 110 objects than ever before, but council felt that the museum would be better served and would capture greater public interest if it had a building of its own. This would not occur until 1952 when the EMA acquired Secord House, a large mansion in a more genteel part of the city close to the provincial Legislature.[23] Secord House afforded the Museum of Arts space for its permanent collection, rooms for temporary exhibitions and art classes, as well as an office for the director and meeting rooms for local cultural groups. The acquisition of increased square footage, while welcome, was less important than the symbolic capital of a stand-alone building: something that proclaimed the EMA's autonomy and apparent self-sufficiency to Edmontonians as well as to other Canadian art institutions. Such physical autonomy was central to the EMA's establishment of its legitimacy as an arts organization, and

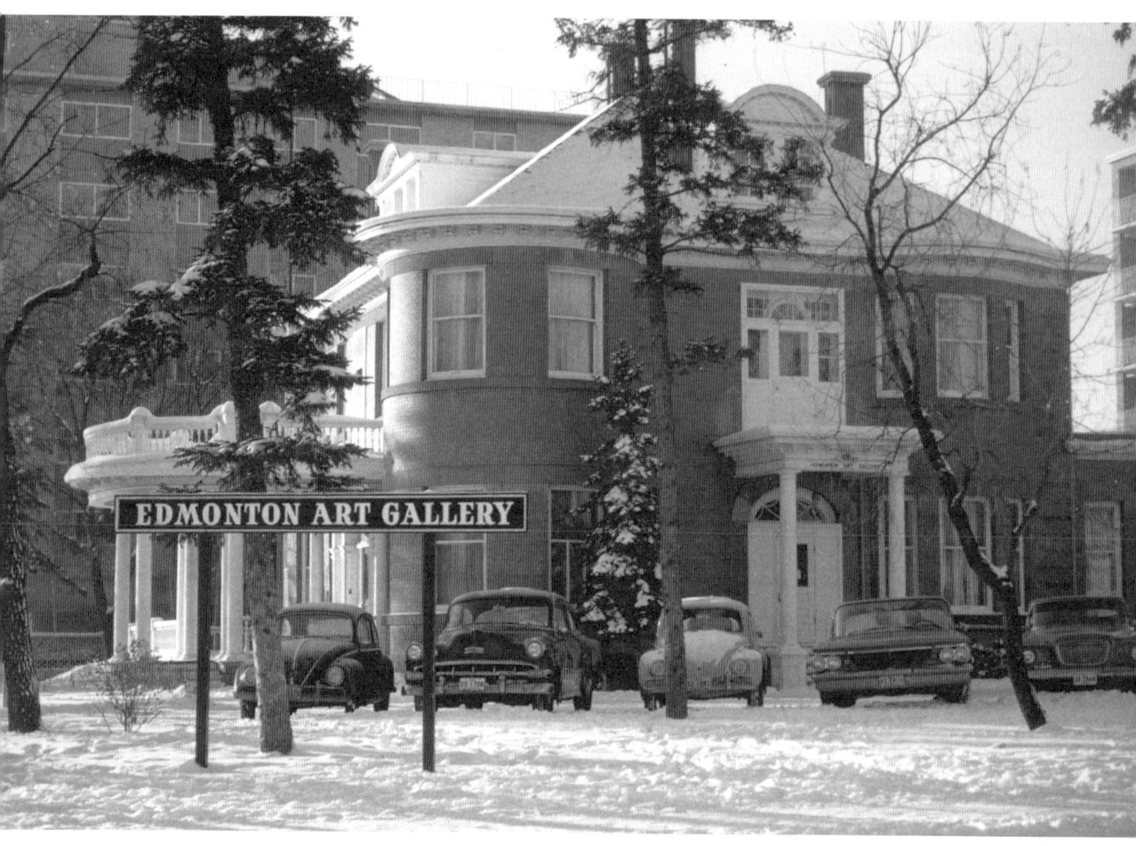

1.2 | The Edmonton Art Gallery at Secord House, c. 1965. Despite less than ideal room arrangements, many old mansions were converted to art galleries in the first half of the twentieth century.

the larger and more attractive space drew more members and donors and increased the museum's stature in the city.

The EMA's story of inadequate housing in temporary or shared buildings would have been familiar to the majority of art institutions discussed in this book. Before the founding of the Winnipeg Art Gallery (WAG) in 1912, the desire for such an institution was expressed by all the city's existing arts organizations. A founding document of the Manitoba Society of Artists proclaimed in 1902 that the principal aims of the organization was the establishment of a Provincial Art Institute, an Art School, and a Municipal Art Gallery;[24] the Western Art Association – successor to the Winnipeg branch of the Women's Art Association of Canada – had been lobbying for exhibition space for its own activities as well as for the creation of a public art gallery and school since its founding in 1907.[25] The erection of the Winnipeg Industrial Bureau Exposition Building by the Board of Trade in 1912 provided the perfect opportunity to develop permanent space for art exhibitions in the city, and the Winnipeg Museum of Fine Arts was officially opened on 16 December with an exhibition of 270 works from the Royal Canadian Academy.[26] The final push to obtain an art gallery came from businessmen who tied space for art to the establishment of Winnipeg as a major North American city. At the turn of the twentieth century, Winnipeg was Canada's third largest city with a population of 136,035 in 1911.[27] Enjoying a degree of economic prosperity due to its central location and status as a major railway hub for both people and goods travelling west and east, Winnipeg was experiencing a building boom that would consolidate its commercial influence and cause the city to be given the title of "Chicago of the North."[28] The erection of major institutions like the library in 1905 and Eaton's department store – opened in 1905 but with three storeys added to the original five by 1910 – underscores the city's prosperity and the desire of its elite immigrants from Ontario and Britain to raise the social and cultural capital of the city and cement connections to political and cultural institutions in the established metropolises of Montreal and Toronto. The businessmen behind the art gallery were the members of the Board of Trade who had formed an Art Committee as early as 1906 and pushed for the construction of the Industrial Building. All of British or Ontario stock – James McDiarmid emigrated to Manitoba from Scotland while W.J. Bulman and George Wilson had come to Winnipeg from Ontario – amateur artists and art collectors, the three business men firmly believed that the new art gallery would remedy the fact that "for many years Winnipeg has languished in comparative darkness so far as the brightening influence of art is concerned."[29] The members of the Western Art Association, who played an equally formative role in the museum's formation, were women from wealthy Ontario families who believed in the civilizing values of culture. While the large number of Jewish immigrants to Winnipeg would come to play an important role in the cultural life of the city, it remained the British and central Canadian-born families that supported the WAG for the majority of its first forty years.

In its first decade, the Winnipeg Art Gallery had an active program of exhibitions that included loan exhibitions from the National Gallery,

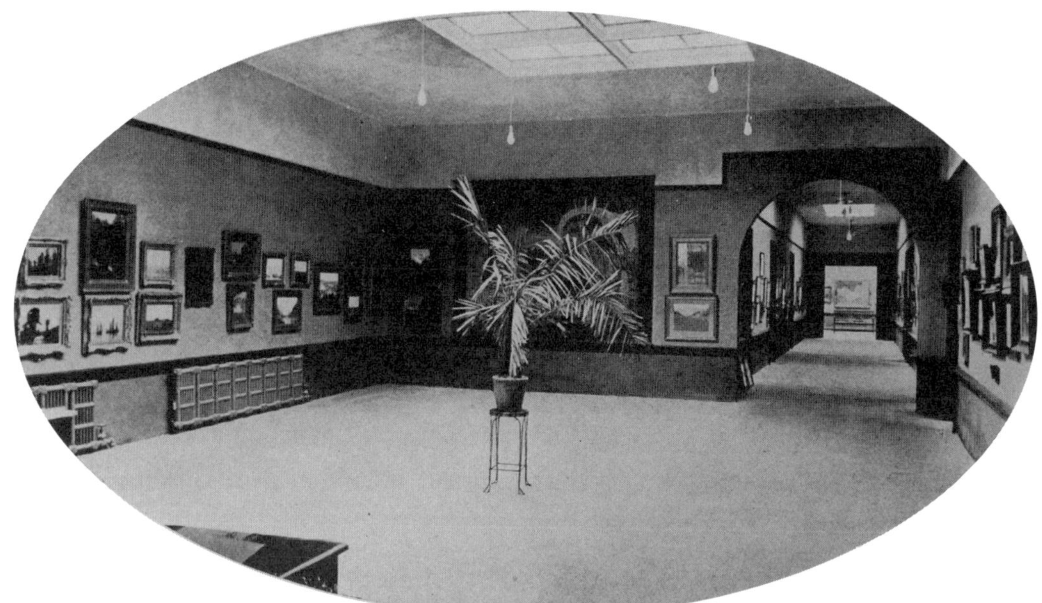

1.3 | The interior of the Winnipeg Art Gallery at the Winnipeg Industrial Building, c. 1912. Hanging paintings in a double row was the convention of the period.

the British Colonial Association, and local collectors, as well as displays of recent work by the Manitoba Society of Artists and other local and regional artists. Unlike the EMA, the WAG hired an artist to helm the nascent organization. Scottish painter Alexander Musgrove was a graduate of the Glasgow School of Art and a vocal member of the Manitoba Society of Artists, and these qualifications made him an attractive candidate to lead both the new gallery and the art school. In 1921 Musgrove left to establish his own art school, and Frank Johnston, a member of the Group of Seven, was hired as both principal of the Winnipeg School of Art and curator of the gallery. The organization was incorporated in 1923 to gain independence from the Board of Trade but it remained in the Industrial Bureau building.[30] In 1925, after reducing its annual grant from $3,500 to $2,500 over the previous two years, the city discontinued all funding to the Winnipeg Art Gallery and School of Art. With no other source of income – a membership campaign had proven to be a dismal failure – the art gallery ceased its exhibiting activities, and the members of the board focused their energies on the continued existence of the School of

Art. Some members of the city's elite rallied, however, forming the Winnipeg Art Gallery Association in August 1926 to ensure the continuing existence of the gallery and to facilitate the occasional donations and acquisitions to the gallery's collection being held in trust by the School of Art. Sporadic exhibitions were held throughout this period through the auspices of Eaton's department store, the galleries of Richardson Brothers art dealers, and the Art School.[31] The construction of yet another city building, this time the Civic Auditorium in 1932, finally provided the Winnipeg Art Gallery with exhibition space: one half of a long corridor-like hall on the second floor, the other half of which was occupied by displays of natural history and the history of Manitoba that would eventually form the Manitoba Museum.[32] A new board was established for the Art Gallery and Alexander Musgrove was once again appointed its curator, leaving Lionel LeMoine FitzGerald, who had replaced Johnston in 1929, as director of the Art School.[33]

1.4 | Winnipeg Civic Auditorium, home of the Winnipeg Art Gallery from 1932 to 1971.

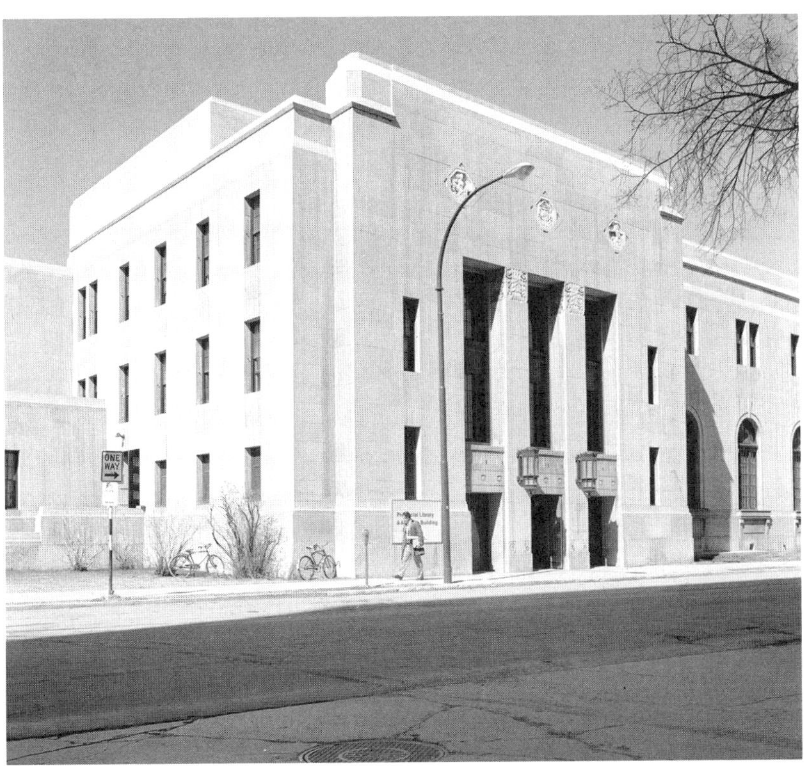

Working out of barely adequate rooms in the Civic Auditorium until the opening of a new building in 1971, the WAG's successive directors used every opportunity to advocate for permanent quarters that would allow the institution to fulfill its mandate as a civic art museum. In the meantime, exhibiting, collecting, and educational activities continued apace but remained hampered by the constraints of the available space. Operating under similar financial and spatial constraints as the Edmonton Museum of Arts, the Winnipeg Art Gallery nonetheless benefitted from the higher number of wealthy citizens living in a city with a longer mercantile past. Their support for their city's art gallery remained unflagging, and they gave generously of works from their own collections to enhance its permanent displays. This stands in marked contrast to the Edmonton gallery whose board members donated sparingly to its permanent collection.

Unlike the galleries in Edmonton and Winnipeg that were constantly searching for a permanent home, the Vancouver Art Gallery opened in 1931 in a purpose-built museum with secured funding for acquisitions. This is not to suggest that the decades prior to the founding of the Vancouver Art Gallery did not share some of the characteristics of the situations in other western cities. A rough, resource-based town at its founding in 1886, by 1889, Vancouver had expanded sufficiently to overtake the provincial capital, Victoria, in population and economic wealth.[34] As the westernmost point of the Canadian Pacific Railway, with access to Seattle and San Francisco markets, Vancouver also attracted numerous British and Canadian companies intent on setting up offices on the west coast.[35] In 1889, a group of amateur and professional artists founded the (Vancouver) Art Association, a group hoping to build an art and historical collection that would "cultivate a taste for art ... in the city."[36] The Art Association held public exhibitions of members' work, conducted art classes, and regularly met to discuss art-related topics. The cause for building interest in the arts in Vancouver was taken up in 1894 by a more broadly based group of leading citizens organizing themselves into the Art, Historical and Scientific Association (AHSA). Based on the British learned society model and seeking to bring a measure of (British) civilization to what was considered an outpost of Empire, the AHSA instigated a program of lectures, discussion groups, and exhibitions, and endeavoured to establish a museum and art gallery that would preserve the province's past.[37] In 1905 it successfully opened a museum on the top floor of Vancouver's Carnegie-funded public library that included the collection and exhibition of artworks as part of its mandate.[38] However, other groups with a more specialist interest in the area would soon take over primary responsibility for developing the fine arts in Vancouver: the British Columbia Society of Fine Arts (BCSFA), established in 1909, and the much larger British Columbia Art League (BCAL), founded in 1920.

The BCSFA was a small group of Vancouver artists who wanted to establish a professional context within which to show their work. Modelled on the Ontario Society of Artists, the organization's founding was fuelled by the feeling of isolation experienced by most artists in British Columbia and the concern that they were "debarred by distance from taking an active part in the artistic institutions of eastern Canada."[39] Never exceeding a membership of thirty, the BCSFA nonetheless held annual exhibitions in rented rooms in the city, establishing itself from 1912 to 1925 on the third floor of the School Board Building.[40] The BCAL differed significantly from the BCSFA in that its membership included representatives from the business and labour communities, in addition to artists, in the belief that lay support would yield financial benefits.[41] Almost immediately upon its formation in 1920, the league began an active campaign to establish a school of arts and crafts as well as an art gallery. Successive applications to the provincial government finally resulted in the establishment of the Vancouver School of Decorative and Fine Arts in 1925, which, under the leadership of artist Charles H. Scott, attracted F.H. Varley, J.W.G. (Jock) Macdonald, and Grace Melvin as instructors.[42] Despite cramped conditions in the top floor of the School Board building, the school flourished, with the teachings of Varley and Macdonald in particular shaping successive generations of British Columbia artists.[43] The BCAL opened its art gallery in 1921 in rooms loaned by the British Columbia Manufacturers' Association. The first exhibition, as at the Edmonton Museum of Arts, consisted of twenty paintings on loan from the National Gallery,[44] as well as etchings from the Graphic Arts Club of Toronto and several paintings loaned directly by artists from eastern Canada. The BCAL Art Gallery would continue in this space until 1928 when financial difficulties forced the league to close its rooms at the Manufacturers' Association; shortly thereafter it found exhibition rooms at the Hudson's Bay Company store, where it remained until 1931.

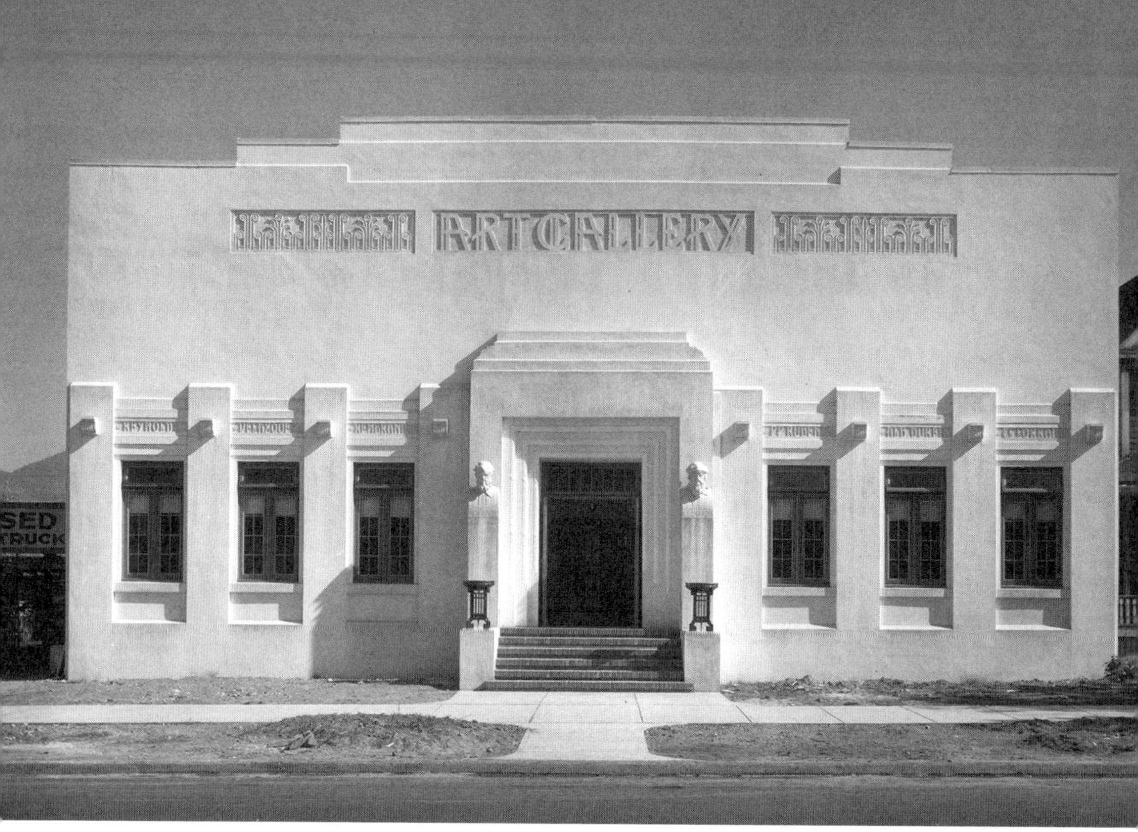

1.5 | Vancouver Art Gallery, 1931. Located on West Georgia Street, this was the first purpose-built art gallery in western Canada.

By that year, a group of leading citizens had successfully lobbied the city government for land, and the Vancouver Art Gallery opened at 1145 West Georgia Street.

The significant factor in the VAG's ability to open in its own building – in contrast to efforts in Winnipeg and Edmonton – was the financial support of members of Vancouver's business community. They realized that such a venture would only be taken seriously by city council and Vancouver's citizens if a purpose-built gallery were erected. In 1925, ten prominent citizens, led by Henry A. Stone,[45] approached the city government with an offer to put $100,000 towards acquisitions for an art gallery if the city would donate land and erect an appropriate building. Successive by-laws presented to city council were defeated, but the group continued to raise funds and pressure elected officials. In 1930, Stone and his colleagues once again approached the city, this time with the promise of $130,000 for acquisitions *and* a building under the condition that the city purchase a site in downtown Vancouver; they were finally successful.[46] The increase in funding undoubtedly sweetened the proposal for city council, but the promise that ownership of the Vancouver Art Gallery and its contents would be turned over to the city and that it would have representation on the governing Art Gallery Association of Vancouver sealed the deal. The art deco building designed by architects Sharp and Thompson opened on 5 October 1931, and western Canada had its first purpose-built art gallery.

The efforts by business and community leaders in Edmonton, Winnipeg, and Vancouver to find permanent spaces for the display of art speaks to a shared desire to provide means of public enlightenment to cities geographically on the margins. The paternalism underpinning such desires is clear, the unflagging belief in the civilizing values of art perhaps most cogently phrased in George Wilson's statement that Winnipeg would be brought from the dark into the light through the building of an art gallery; but such values have supported the building of art galleries throughout the Western world since the eighteenth century. The particularly educational benefits of the art museum was perfected in Britain and can be seen in the founding aims of the South Kensington (now the Victoria and Albert) Museum, later exported to institutions in North America such as the Museum of Fine Arts in Boston, and in Samuel and Henrietta Barnett's civilizing aims in bringing the fine arts to the working poor in the Whitechapel area of London.[47] For the leaders of these institutions, the positive effects of the display of art were assumed to exist, to be felt not only by individuals but also collectively through the increasing aesthetic consciousness of manufacturers who would produce better designs. The founders of the art galleries in Winnipeg, Edmonton, and Vancouver explicitly argued – usually to representatives of city hall – that the public presentation of art would improve the taste of citizens at the same time as it would provide encouragement to industrial design and manufacturing: the economic drivers of emerging cities. In her director's report for 1932–33, Maud Bowman of the EMA argued for the economic as well as aesthetic importance of the museum by asking, "are we to continue to be the dumping ground for badly designed furniture, fabric and clothes from other countries, or are we going to train our own designers who will design for us things of beauty suitable for our needs?"[48] The opening of the Vancouver Art Gallery occasioned similar sentiments from Henry Stone, who underscored the gallery's "far-reaching influence, which

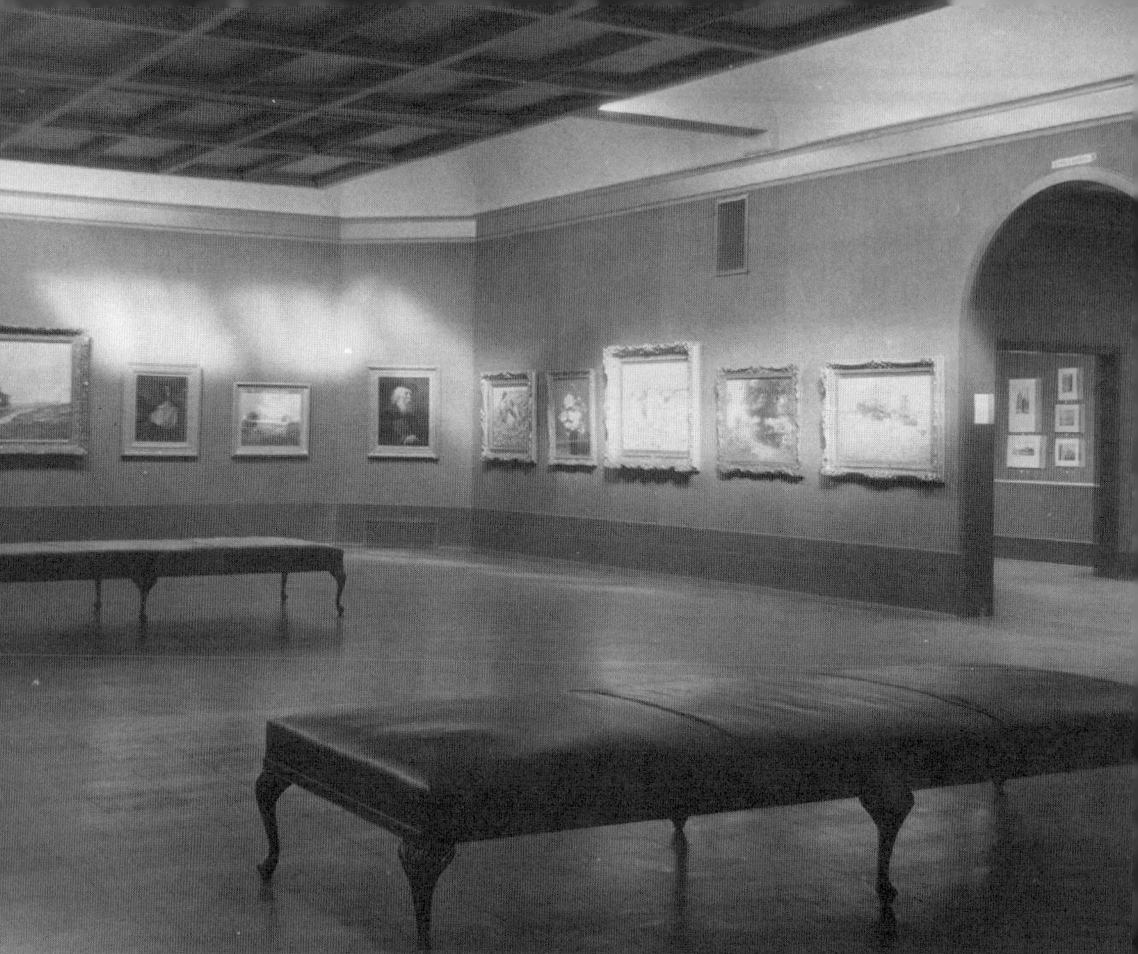

1.6 | An interior gallery of the Vancouver Art Gallery, 1932. The VAG's spacious galleries were favourably noted by Sir Henry Miers and Sidney Markham in their 1931 *Report on the Museums of Canada*.

would bind us all closer in a broader understanding of Art and an increasing happiness in things of beauty both useful and ornamental."[49] The spatial presence of art galleries was thus presented as a fundamental step in improving the image of western Canadian cities, transforming these pioneer spaces into civilized – and civilizing – places.

Regina, Calgary, and Saskatoon: The Advantages of Patronage

Finding physical spaces for their activities preoccupied arts organizations across western Canada, and as the situations of Edmonton, Winnipeg, and Vancouver suggest, funding and the varying levels of civic and community support affected both the growth and the status of art museums. The Vancouver Art Gallery's experience is unique in the 1930s, but the patronage that enabled the construction of a building as well as the formation of a collection was repeated in the 1950s and 1960s in Regina, Calgary, and Saskatoon. The generosity of single patrons whose enthusiasm for collecting, along with the wealth that supported such interests, were instrumental in creating major art institutions in all three cities and mark them as significantly different from Edmonton, Winnipeg, and Vancouver.

The MacKenzie Art Gallery in Regina began with lawyer Norman MacKenzie's bequest of his considerable collection of European and western Canadian paintings and sculpture to the University of Saskatchewan's Regina College in 1936. Accompanied by the promise of funds for the construction of a building to house the collection, the donation provided the kind of "instant" permanent collections enjoyed by Montreal, Toronto, and major cities in the United States that had been fortunate enough to be the beneficiaries of one or more collectors' generosity. An immigrant from Ontario, like many of the figures engaged in the formation of art museums in western Canada, MacKenzie came to Regina in 1893 from Sarnia, having studied law at Toronto's Osgoode Hall. As his practice and wealth grew, he began collecting European and Canadian art in the early 1900s,[50] the reputation of his collection and his connections leading him to be named to the National Gallery's board of trustees in 1925. Active in the Saskatchewan Arts Association, an organization of collectors and laypersons interested in the arts, MacKenzie had long planned to leave a substantial portion of his collection to the city of Regina in the hopes that it would result in an art museum for the city. When the University of Saskatchewan annexed Regina College in 1934, MacKenzie became head of an Art Committee designed to arrange art exhibitions and visiting art instructors to the college, and when efforts by University of Saskatchewan President Walter Murray to secure funds from the Carnegie Corporation for an art gallery generated interest but no money, MacKenzie amended his will to leave both his collection and building funds to Regina College.[51] Despite the significance of the donation and the existence of funds, the economic and political climate in Regina in 1936 was not right for the immediate construction of a gallery, and a building dedicated to the display of MacKenzie's collection did not materialize until 1953, and then only as one room in the new Regina College of Art.

Although the importance of MacKenzie and his bequest to the establishment of an art gallery in Regina is evident, the contribution of other organizations to the development of art activity in the city should not be overlooked. In particular, the activities of the Fine and Applied Arts Committee (FAAC) of the Local Council of Women ensured that Regina's residents received consistent exposure to the work of both fine and craft artists through local and then provincial exhibitions, as well as educational programs. The FAAC's first exhibition in October 1920 was held at Regina College and, drawing from local collections, presented the work of the British and Dutch painters favoured by Canadian collectors of the period, as well as the work of Canadian artists. By 1923, however, the FAAC turned its attention to foregrounding the work of local

1.7 | Norman MacKenzie Art Gallery, c. 1953.

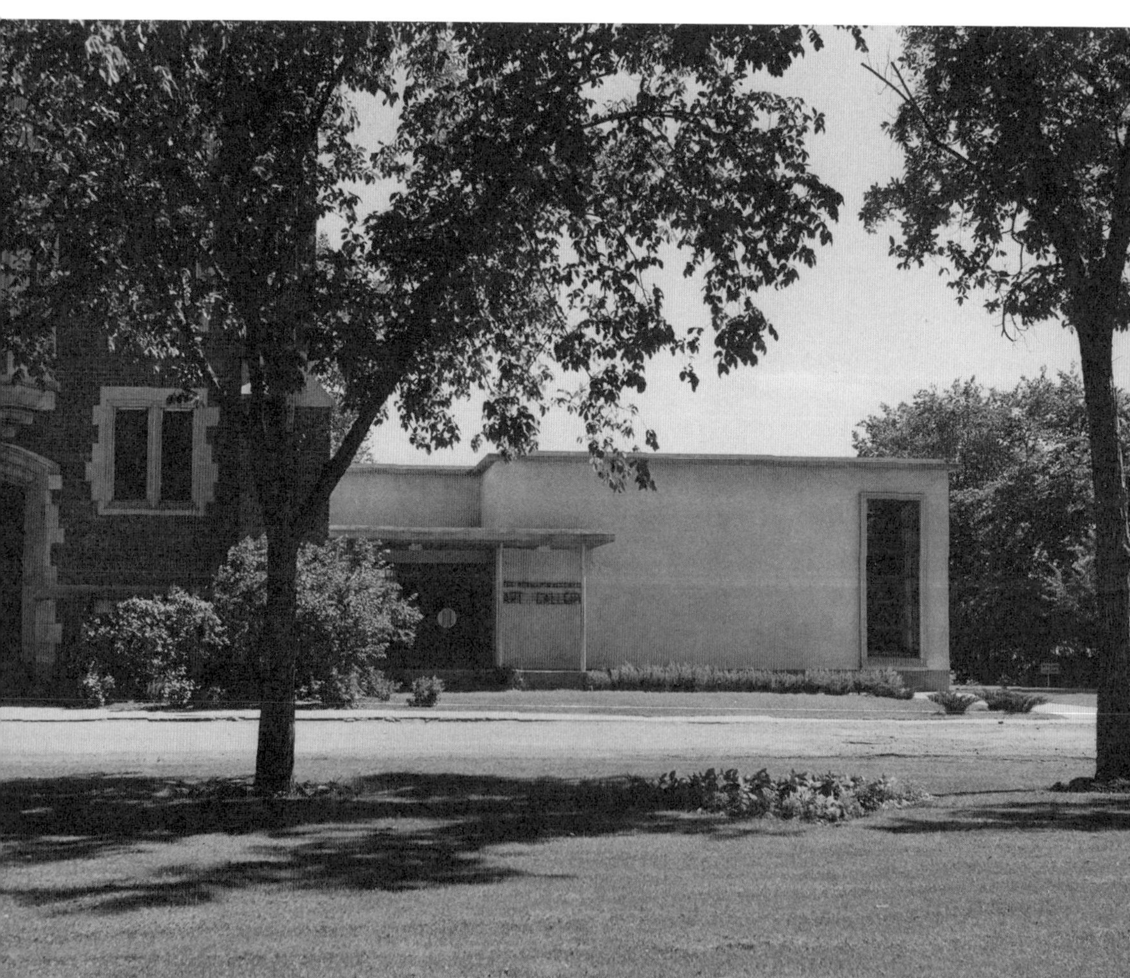

artists through large exhibitions that, despite emphasizing quantity over quality, created significant interest in the visual arts in the province. Throughout the 1920s and early 1930s, the women of the FAAC functioned as a liaison for exhibitions circulating from the Saskatoon Art Club, the University of Saskatchewan, and the National Gallery of Canada. Eager to see an art gallery established in Regina, the FAAC began a collection of Canadian art, with a particular focus on women artists and Saskatchewan artists. The collection of twenty-three works was donated to Regina College in 1936 – the same year MacKenzie bequeathed his own collection – but the majority of the works would remain on display at the Regina Public Library until 1953 and the opening of the Norman MacKenzie Art Gallery.[52]

Before a building was erected to house the art gallery, a number of curators were appointed to care for the collection, starting with artist Augustus Kenderdine in 1936, who was asked to move from Saskatoon where he was a professor of art at the University of Saskatchewan to take over responsibility for the collection and the art course at Regina College; there he was joined by Gordon Snelgrove, who was hired to teach art history following successful completion of his Carnegie-funded doctoral studies.[53] Kenderdine's death in 1947, along with the economic challenges of the postwar period, contributed to a lag in exhibiting activity at Regina College, although local organizations such as the many Saskatchewan branches of the Federation of Canadian Artists organized displays of members' works, and the Regina Public Library began putting on exhibitions of historical and contemporary Canadian art in the late 1940s. Indeed, the exhibiting program of the Regina Public Library took off under the leadership of Marjorie Dunlop when she assumed the position of chief librarian in 1948, although it was her predecessor, Charles D. Kent, who first contacted the National Gallery's H.O. McCurry in 1946 about the possibility of obtaining loan exhibitions for the library.[54] A strong and articulate advocate for the arts in Regina, Dunlop programmed a diversity of exhibitions of local, national, and international contemporary artists and purchased works for the library's permanent collection. By the time planning for a new library building with dedicated space for an art gallery had begun in the late 1950s, Dunlop's programming rivalled that of the larger gallery at Regina College, and in recognition of her contribution, the gallery space was named the Dunlop Art Gallery in 1972 upon her retirement as chief librarian.[55]

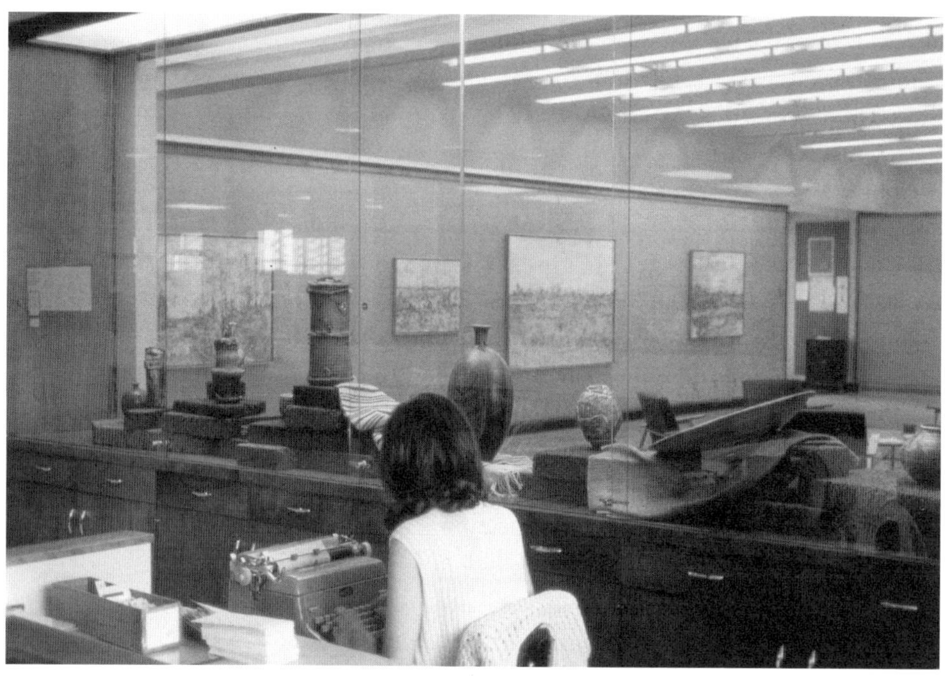

1.8 | Dunlop Art Gallery, view of reception area and gallery, 1970s. The Regina Public Library included art exhibitions as a central part of its programming from the 1950s.

Meanwhile, the 1950 hiring of Ottawa-born artist Kenneth Lochhead as both head of the School of Art and curator of the MacKenzie Collection reinvigorated Regina College and enabled serious planning for a building to house the art school and the gallery. At its opening on 25 September 1953, the one-storey stucco building attached to the school was already considered inadequate to display MacKenzie's collection and plans were underway by the following year to expand the premises. A sign of the Board of Governors' commitment to the NMAG was the 1951 hiring of a dedicated curator, Richard Simmins, whose previous experience as curator at Hart House in Toronto provided some much-needed professional guidance to the gallery's activities.[56] Building on the MacKenzie bequest and the donation from the Regina Council of Women, individual benefactors donated several works to celebrate the opening of the new building, but no purchases were made until 1957 when the newly established Norman MacKenzie Art Gallery Society bought Harold Town's *The Tower of Babbling* (1955) to mark the gallery's expansion. When the painter Ronald Bloore was appointed director of the NMAG the following year, he began a concentrated effort to add to the collection, filling in significant gaps in Canadian art and building a collection of contemporary art by artists in eastern Canada as well as his Regina Five colleagues.[57]

Calgary had difficulty getting a permanent space for the display of art until 1964 when the Glenbow Foundation-Alberta Government Museum opened. Lawyer Eric Harvie had always had an interest in collecting, but when he discovered oil in 1947, his ability to acquire increased exponentially and he quickly accumulated extensive and varied holdings in natural and human historical artifacts. Keen to give back to the province that had afforded him such prosperity – Harvie is often quoted as saying "I want to die broke"[58] – he sought to both bring the cultures of the world to western Canada and showcase the region's own history and culture for the enlightenment and pleasure of the people of Alberta. As he stated at the first meeting of the board of governors of the Glenbow-Alberta Institute in May 1966, he had established and funded the Glenbow Foundation in 1954 with the aim of "researching, assembling, preserving and displaying the history of our Canadian West in its many and varied forms."[59] As a result of Harvie's expansive collecting interests, the Glenbow's displays ranged from natural and human history artifacts from around the world as well as fine and decorative arts from Canada and beyond, but its focus remained the history of western Canada. Before the Glenbow became Calgary's largest museum, the city's artistic endeavours circled primarily around the activities of the Calgary Art Club (begun in 1922 and becoming the Calgary Sketch Club in 1939), the Alberta Society of Artists (formed in 1931 with branches in Calgary and Edmonton), and the Provincial Institute of Art and Technology (now the Alberta College of Art and Design), which employed British artists A.C. Leighton and H.G. Glyde to develop an intensive art curriculum modelled on the British system.[60]

During the Second World War, the art department of the Provincial Institute moved into Coste House, the former mansion of natural gas baron Eugene Coste, which had reverted to the city in 1936 for non-payment of taxes.[61] The twenty-eight-room Coste House quickly became home to a number of cultural organizations in Calgary, including the Women's Musical Club, the Calgary Film Society, and the Alberta Society of Artists whose president, Glyde, was also the head of the Provincial Institute's art

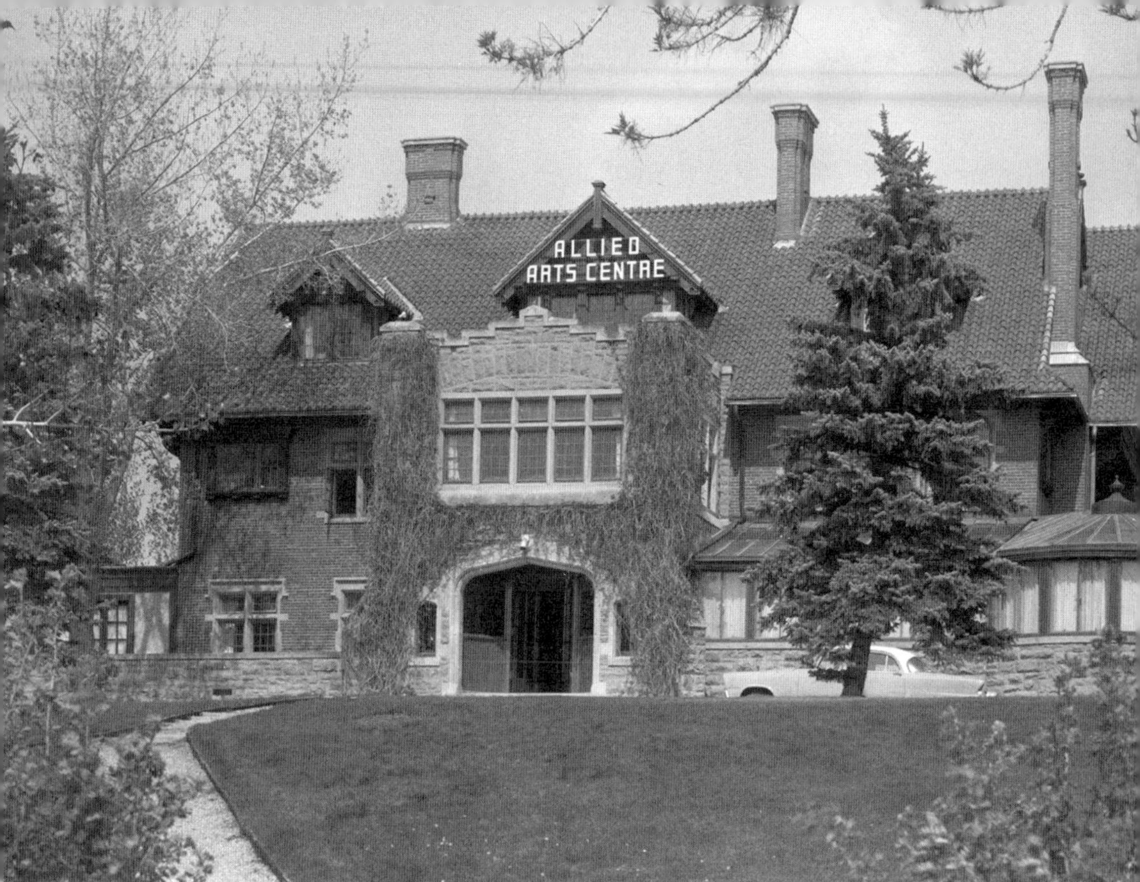

1.9 | Calgary Allied Arts Centre at Coste House, 1956. This former mansion was the city's cultural hub, presenting art exhibitions as well as music and theatre performances.

department. In 1946, with the art department returned to its rooms at the original institute, the newly formed Calgary Allied Arts Council took possession of Coste House and, with the support of the city, established the Calgary Allied Arts Center as a multidisciplinary exhibition and studio space for Calgary's varied arts groups.[62] Archie F. Key, a British-born newspaper editor who would go on to become head of the Canadian Museums Association in the 1960s, was hired as managing director of Coste House. He immediately implemented a program of art exhibitions that included work by the Alberta Society of Artists as well as loan exhibitions from the National Gallery. In 1947 he also became the managing director of the Western Canada Art Circuit (WCAC) (to be discussed more fully in Chapter 4), a position that firmly established Coste House as an important cultural center in western Canada into the 1960s.[63] Like many of the small institutions discussed in this chapter, Coste House faced significant challenges in attracting funding for its activities, and Key focused his energy on obtaining exhibitions that would disseminate art to the community rather than building a permanent collection. As the Calgary *Allied Arts* Centre, Coste House also featured musical and theatre performances that brought the city's visual and performing artists in contact with each other, but the multidisciplinary activities sometimes created conflicts with the centre's art classes and exhibitions.[64]

Coste House nevertheless provided much-needed space for the presentation of the growing group of modern artists working in Calgary, as well as a representative selection of contemporary Canadian art through the exhibitions circulated by the WCAC, ensuring that the city was exposed to regular exhibitions of contemporary art. Informing the collection at the Glenbow, Eric Harvie's taste in art ran to the more conservative

1.10 | First Nations display at the Glenbow-Alberta Foundation, 1961. Mid-century attitudes towards Indigenous cultures are clearly evident in this display of a small portion of Eric Harvie's extensive collection.

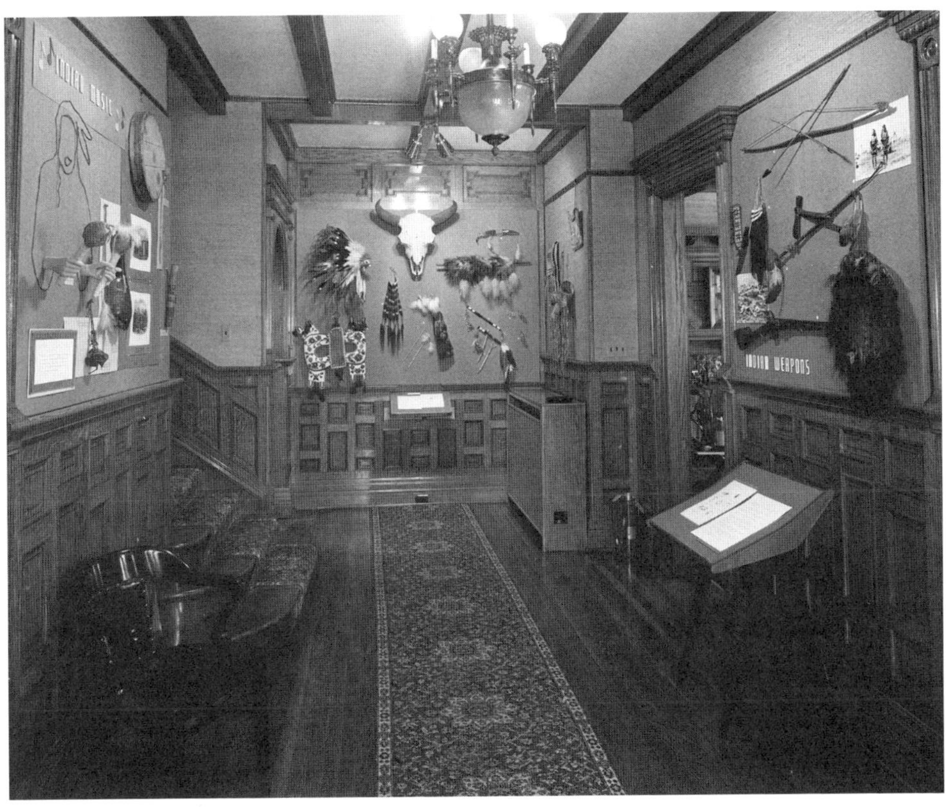

wildlife paintings of Charles Russell and Carl Rungius (the contents of whose New York studio he purchased in an effort to build the most complete collection of the artist's work), and he acquired artworks with a view to how they might animate the historical objects in the collection. With the incorporation of the Glenbow-Alberta Foundation in 1954, Harvie's staff acquired the work of "modern" Alberta and western Canadian artists in an effort to more adequately reflect the cultural production of the region.[65] Objects of First Nations and Métis culture were a strong component of Harvie's collecting, particularly in conjunction with Banff-based newspaper publisher and collector Norman Luxton, and were on regular display at the Luxton Museum in Banff from 1952; such objects, however, were categorized as having ethnographic rather than aesthetic interest and were shown separately from the "fine" art in the collection. In 1964, the City of Calgary gave Harvie the lease to the empty Court House to make his collection accessible to the public, and in return, Harvie donated his collection to the province to mark the Canadian centenary.

Like MacKenzie and Harvie, businessman Frederick Mendel was an avid art collector who wanted to see his fellow citizens benefit from public access to cultural objects. A refugee from Nazi Germany, Mendel and his family moved to Saskatoon in 1940 where he founded what is now Intercontinental Packers Limited. In 1960 the businessman approached the mayor of Saskatoon to discuss the creation of a public art gallery. In the 1940s the city's art scene was animated by the activities of the Saskatoon Art Association (est. 1930) and the Saskatoon Art Centre, established in 1944 on the first floor of the Standard Trust Building in the city's downtown.[66] At its opening, the centre was praised by Toronto-based magazine *Saturday Night* for countering the longstanding opinion that residents of Saskatchewan had "little time for cultural activities and, furthermore, that they are not inclined that way."[67] With its relatively large fireproof space, a vault for storage of exhibition materials, studios for members of the Saskatoon Art Association and the Camera Club, as well as space for archaeological displays and a lecture hall, the Art Centre was viewed as the foundation for the establishment of a cultural centre of the kind proposed in the postwar reconstruction schemes discussed in Chapter 3.[68] Already in place in Saskatoon was the Memorial Art Gallery, established in 1918 at the Saskatoon (renamed Nutana) Collegiate to memorialize the twenty-nine alumni of the school who had died in the First World War. Purchasing one painting for each fallen soldier, the collection

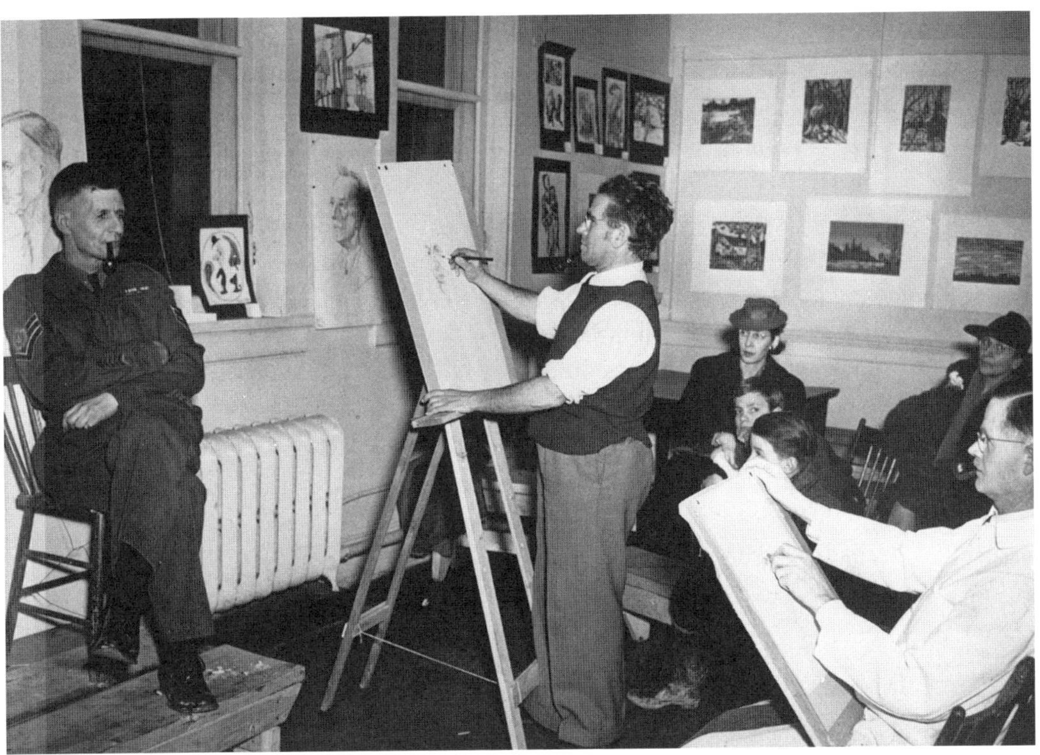

1.11 | Ernest Lindner doing a "portrait demonstration" at the Saskatoon Art Centre, c. 1945.

focused on the work of Canadian artists, most of who were associated with the Royal Canadian Academy or the Ontario Society of Artists, including Homer Watson, C.W. Jefferys, Wylie Greer, and Laura Muntz Lyall. Intent on building the collection further, Nutana Collegiate president Aldis Cameron sought the advice of Eric Brown and corresponded directly with artists with varying success. A.Y. Jackson initially told Cameron that Saskatoon was too conservative for the work of the Group of Seven and refused to send any work for consideration, but he finally relented and in 1927 the school held an exhibition of works that ranged from paintings of academic artists to the more modern works of members of the Group of Seven and some of their Montreal colleagues such as Mabel May and Lilias Torrance Newton.[69] Efforts by Cameron and the members of the Saskatoon Art Club to leverage the interest generated by the Collegiate's exhibitions to convince civic leaders of the wisdom of establishing a modern art gallery in Saskatoon were unsuccessful, particularly with the onset of the Depression, and Saskatoon would have to wait for the opening of the Saskatoon Art Centre for regular exhibitions of contemporary art.[70]

Artist George Swinton was hired as the first curator of the Saskatoon Art Centre for eighteen months between 1947 and 1948, but resigned out of frustration with inadequate facilities and limited civic and provincial government support.[71] The Art Centre reopened in the arcade in the basement of the King George Hotel in 1949, under the direction of Leona Collins. Like many of the other small institutions discussed so far, the Saskatoon Art Centre hosted travelling exhibitions often organized by the National Gallery and circulated by the WCAC, presented the work of local artists, and otherwise functioned as a hub for art activities in the city. Indeed, the very active Saskatoon branch of the Federation of Canadian Artists held both meetings and art classes at the Art Centre and it became an active social and artistic space throughout the 1950s.

1.12 | Saskatoon Art Centre in King George Hotel, 1949. Although situated in the basement arcade of the hotel, this new space was a distinct improvement on the Art Centre's previous locations.

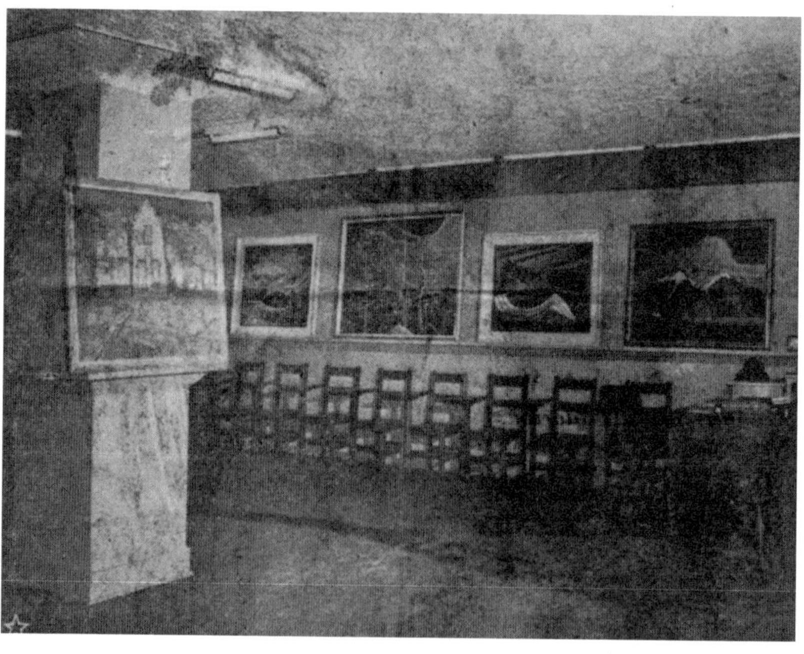

In 1964, with the Art Centre facing yet another eviction from less than ideal premises, Fred Mendel donated $175,000 to the city of Saskatoon as seed funding for the establishment of a permanent art gallery, an amount matched by the provincial government and augmented by the city, which provided land for the erection of a building. The donation was not surprising given Mendel's support of the visual arts throughout his time in Saskatoon, whether through purchases of works by western Canadian artists, funds for the Art Centre, or commissioning local artists to produce murals for his company's buildings.[72] Following the funding of exhibition space, Mendel donated thirteen works by the Group of Seven and their contemporaries from his own collection in 1965, allowing the new Mendel Art Gallery's curator, John Climer, to begin building a permanent collection in earnest.

The individual donations of MacKenzie, Harvie, and Mendel are somewhat unique in the development of art museums in Canada during this period. While individual patronage was crucial to the establishment of many of the galleries discussed so far, particularly for the growth of collections, these contributions of money and time were part of a broader strategy among individuals and business groups who viewed the erection of cultural institutions as a central component in the building of a city, if not a province. In contrast to Montreal and Toronto, where the creation of an art gallery was the expected achievement of a major metropolis, the founding of art galleries in many western Canadian cities was an intrinsic part of the process of confirming the economic viability and legitimacy of a region, and of communities that at the beginning of the century had been little more than trading posts. So while we can argue, along with Anne Higgonet's analysis of the motivations behind Isabella Stewart Gardner's founding of her eponymous museum in Boston, that MacKenzie and Mendel were seeking to assert their personal legacies in founding institutions that bore their name,[73] the particular context of western Canada generates another reading of these acts of benevolence. This reading hinges on seeing such donations as an attempt to establish western Canada as a centre of power in its own right, as a region that could if not compete with, then at the very least hold its own against the more powerful political, economic, and cultural forces of central Canada.

Harvie's aim of "displaying the history of our Canadian West" is clearest in this respect: the founding of the Glenbow-Alberta Institute was just the first of several endowments he established to honour his adopted province, and to bring to it the kind of positive attention he felt it was owed from the rest of the country. Indeed, the scale of the collection as well as its diversity elicits comparisons to other survey museums such as the Royal Ontario Museum, and Harvie's unbridled accumulation, undertaken by agents sent around the globe, underscores his will to build an encyclopaedic museum that would put Calgary on the map. Similarly, MacKenzie's support for art in Saskatchewan – from his establishment of the Saskatchewan Art Association in 1928 to encourage patronage of the province's artists to his ultimately successful attempt to found an art gallery at Regina College – clearly indicates an orientation towards the local over the national, despite his longstanding position as a trustee of the NGC. Mendel similarly sought to repay the community that had welcomed him in 1940, supporting the city of Saskatoon's artists and arts organizations rather than seeking affirmation from more established arts centres in Canada and beyond. In this sense, the Norman MacKenzie and Mendel Art Galleries and the Glenbow Museum are not quite donor memorials in the sense conveyed by Carol Duncan in her analysis of the Frick Collection and the J. Paul Getty Museum: institutions that function as eternal showcases of their founder's collecting obsessions or "surrogate selves."[74] Rather, MacKenzie, Harvie, and Mendel established their museums to fill what they perceived to be a symbolic absence in the cities they called home. The resulting institutions thus showcased their founders' deep-seated belief in the dual importance of culture and community, as well as their conviction that leading such projects was their responsibility as men of wealth and standing. From the discussion of their respective collections, it is clear that "culture" had a different meaning for Harvie than for MacKenzie and Mendel: Harvie was interested in historical objects and artworks that could illustrate that history; MacKenzie and Mendel were keen proponents of the "fine" arts, although taste as well as the historical period during which they were collecting contributed significantly to the differences between the two collections. In all three cases, however, a strong sense of bringing knowledge to isolated cities and the belief in the ability of objects to convey knowledge and a wider view of the world were fundamental motivators to their acts of generosity.

Not just spaces for the display of art, the museums founded by MacKenzie, Mendel, and Harvie were symbols of the changing character of western Canada at mid-century. It is noteworthy that all three galleries opened within a ten-year period. While the NMAG has much older origins in MacKenzie's bequest, it was not a public institution until 1953 when the collection became accessible and programming was put in place. Harvie's gift of his collection to the province may have been facilitated by the donation of a building, but it is also true that Calgary was ready, by the early 1960s, to promote itself as a major city poised to transform its Wild West image into that of a booming centre for industry and investment. The Glenbow's collection of artifacts from western Canadian pioneer life preserved and reified the city's cowboy history, establishing, as Frances Kaye argues, nostalgia for a way of life that was being decidedly set in the past through its memorialization in the museum's displays.[75] The art galleries in Regina and Saskatoon, meanwhile, opened in the mid-1950s and early 1960s because the province of Saskatchewan's economic fortunes were improving due to the diversification of industry initiated by Co-operative Commonwealth Federation programs in the late 1940s and decreased reliance on the agriculture sector. The subsequent Liberal government's encouragement of private enterprise and an increase in public sector jobs in the 1960s introduced significant changes to the demographic makeup of Saskatchewan's cities, provided ready audiences, and increased private funding for art galleries and other cultural activities.[76]

The acts of patronage that established the NMAG, the Glenbow, and the Mendel involved significant outlays of money and gifts of objects. But patronage also occurred in smaller ways at other galleries that had a major impact on their development. The Art Gallery of Greater Victoria (AGGV), for example, began life in 1946 as the Little Centre in an abandoned automobile dealership in downtown Victoria. The association that launched the gallery, however, was established in 1944 as the Vancouver Island branch of the Federation of Canadian Artists whose members were seeking a space to display their work. Severing ties with the federation in 1946, local artists joined forces with supporters of art and culture who wanted to open the aesthetically conservative city of Victoria to more modern art practices – or, in the words of founding member Mark Kearly, "to sweep away the cobwebs, to bring about a wind of change and to open wide the windows on to the wide, wide world."[77] In 1951, the Arts Centre of Greater Victoria – as the Little Centre was renamed – opened in a mansion donated by board member Sarah Spencer. The Spencer mansion, or "Gyppeswick" as it was also known, was not an ideal site for an art gallery, but it had well-proportioned rooms that could exhibit paintings as well as provide appropriate facilities for concerts and other performances.[78] Artist Ina Uhthoff, a founding member of the Little Centre and a strong advocate for the Arts Centre of Greater Victoria, encouraged her former student, Colin Graham, to apply for the position of curator of the Arts Centre, a move that propelled the Arts Centre forward in the breadth of its programming and gave it national recognition as a major arts centre in the region. The limitations of the Spencer mansion as a space for art exhibitions soon became evident but Graham and the gallery's board quickly persuaded several wealthy Victoria citizens to

1.13 | Opening of the Little Centre on Yates Street, Victoria, 1945. The Victoria Branch of the Federation of Canadian Artists welcomed the opportunity to have a permanent space in this former automobile dealership.

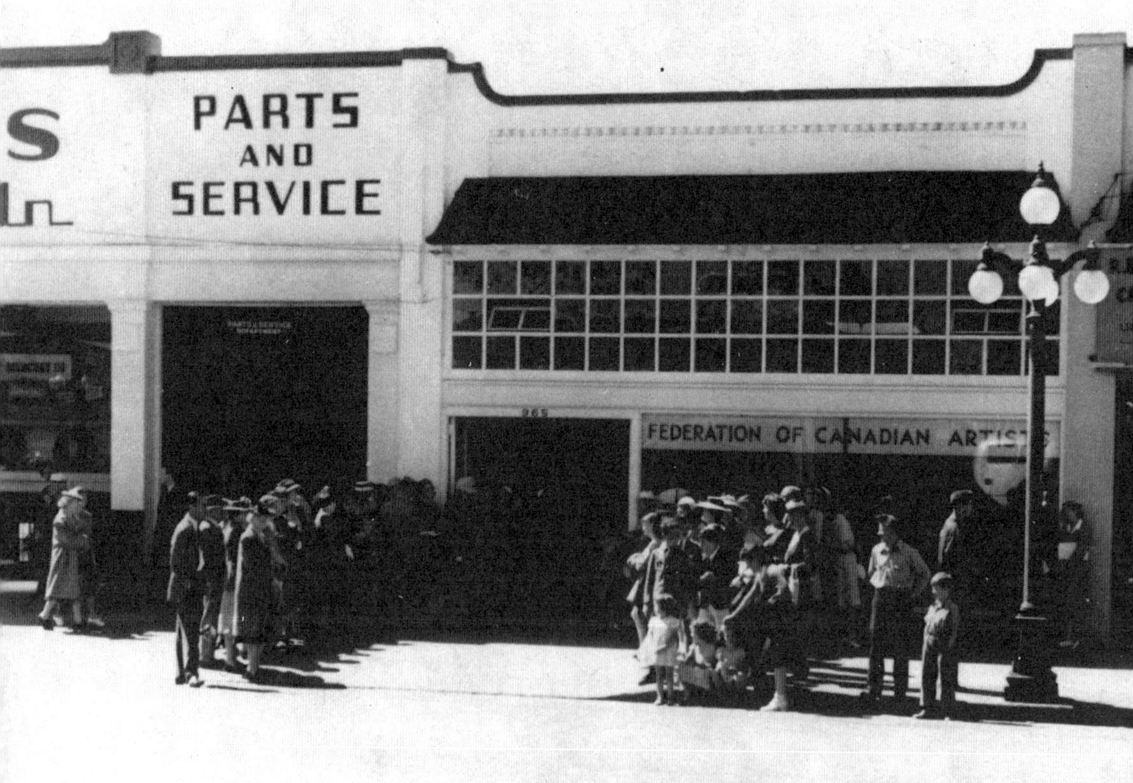

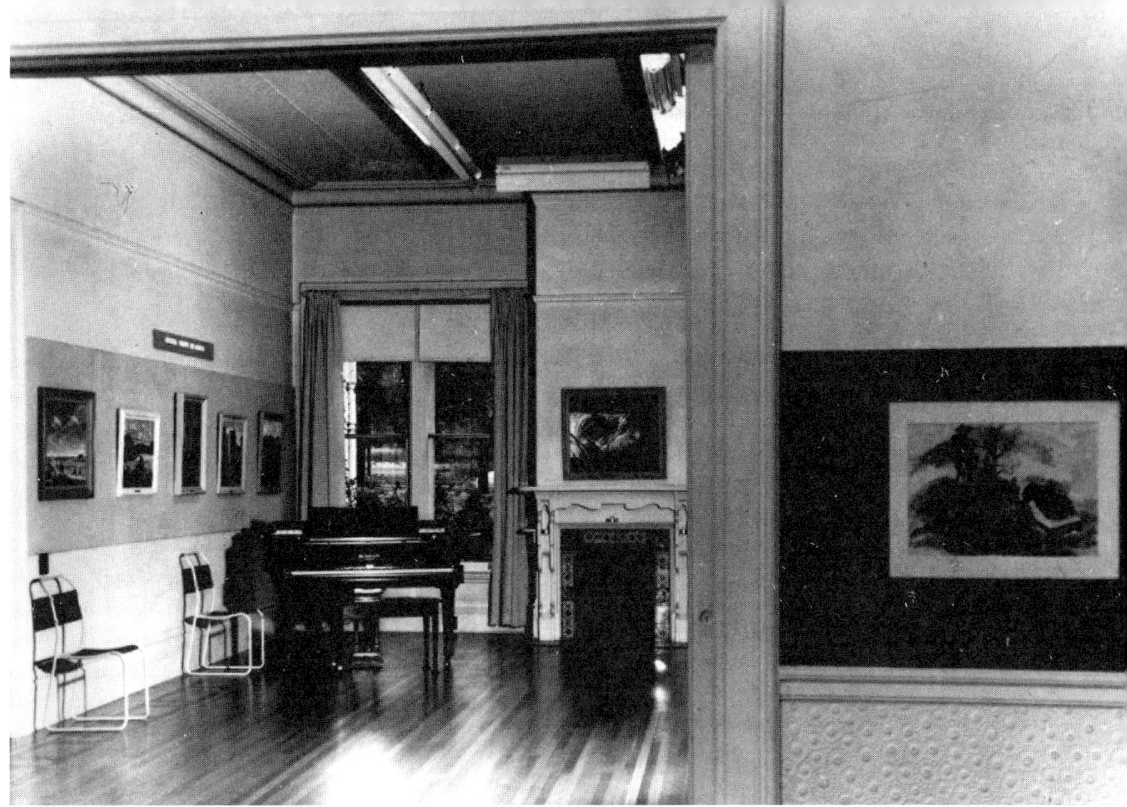

1.14 | Interior of the Art Gallery of Greater Victoria at the Spencer mansion, Gyppeswick, c. 1953.

make significant contributions to the expansion of the gallery, including the building of two fireproof wings in 1958 and 1959 that ensured the AGGV would be able to receive the best exhibitions from the NGC and other major galleries. While relatively small if compared to the donations of MacKenzie and Mendel, the contributions of Robert Ker in 1958 and again in 1969 (along with several friends he strong-armed into contributing) gave physical as well as symbolic credibility to the AGGV, a necessity in the face of the four Victoria area municipalities' ongoing reluctance to fund the fledgling art institution and to recognize it as a civic asset.[79]

Money: A Challenge for Both Big Cities and Small Towns

My discussion to this point has focused on those institutions in major or capital cities for who the building of an art gallery was a visible symbol of that community's economic and cultural standing within a national framework. For smaller municipalities with less economic resources and fewer wealthy citizens, building an art gallery was a dream that few could realize. Centres such as Brandon, Moose Jaw, and Medicine Hat had art associations and societies that held exhibitions of the works of their members on annual or semi-annual bases. Keen to also present the work of professional artists from outside their community, these towns' art associations availed themselves of the loan exhibitions organized by the National Gallery and were the immediate beneficiaries of the exhibitions circulated by the WCAC when that body formed in 1944. As none of these smaller towns and cities had or could hope to have a permanent dedicated display space for many years to come, exhibitions were usually held in a room at the public library, or at city hall, or at some other fireproof building – fireproofing being a condition of any loan from the National Gallery. Small voluntary bodies carried out art programs in these communities, often, as in Moose Jaw, under the auspices of the public library or other large organization. Indeed, it was the librarian, A.H. Gibbard, who first wrote to Eric Brown at the National Gallery in 1916, enquiring about the possibility of getting the loan exhibition then on display in Regina – likely at the summer agricultural exhibition. In his letter, Gibbard described the available space in the public library in some detail, noting its advantages for the display of art works, the excellent lighting, and the presence of staff for security. In an effort to further establish Moose Jaw's credibility, he also noted that the suggestion for the loan came from a Mrs Spotton, who, in addition to being affiliated with the Imperial Order Daughters of the Empire, was a niece of Sir Edmund Walker, chairman of the National Gallery's Board of Trustees.[80] This first application for a loan exhibition was successful and the Public Library at Moose Jaw continued to receive works from the National Gallery for the next three decades, until responsibility for circulating exhibitions was taken over by the WCAC in the 1940s. Other organizations also appear to have been active in Moose Jaw during the period, including the town's branch of the Women's Art Association of Canada (founded in 1929), which assisted in the promotion of the exhibitions held at the Public Library in addition to hosting musical performances. The situation in Medicine Hat was quite similar, with librarian E.C. Warner writing to Brown in 1920, on the advice of Gibbard, that "the [Medicine Hat] library has recently been removed to more commodious premises and I am sure a display of paintings in the Reading Room would greatly enhance the growing popularity of our library."[81] The resulting loan of ten paintings

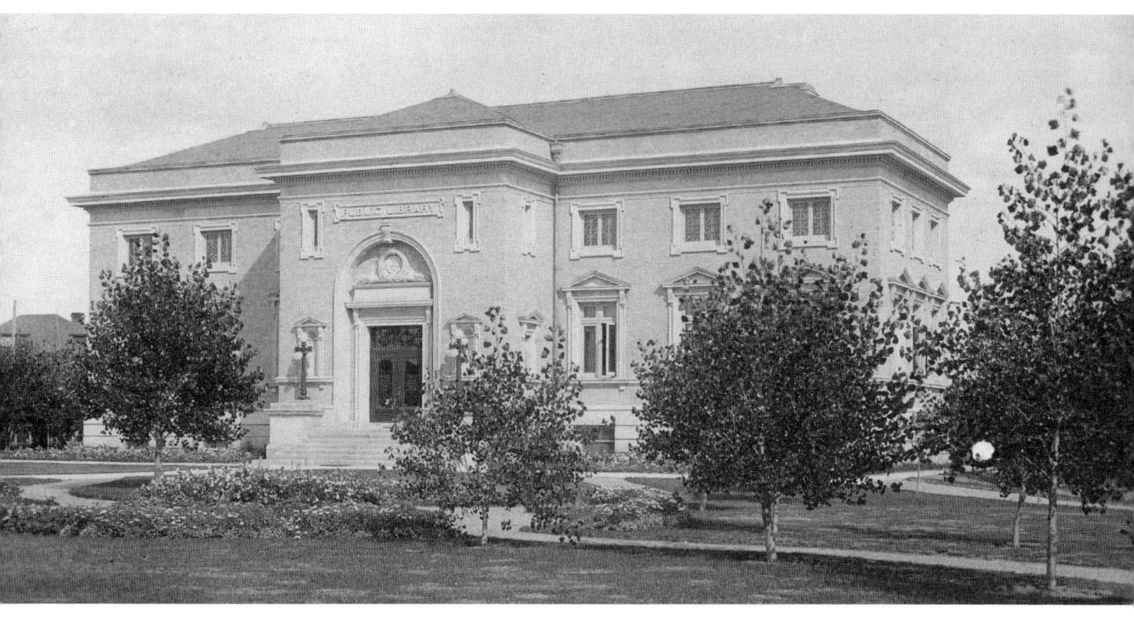

1.15 | Moose Jaw Public Library, exterior, 1916. Although not one of the many Canadian libraries funded by the Carnegie Corporation, the Moose Jaw Public Library employed many of the same architectural conventions.

included works by W.H. Clapp, J.E.H. MacDonald, George Reid, and Mabel May.

Correspondence between the National Gallery and the Brandon Art Club, meanwhile, began in 1922 with a request from the club's secretary for a "traveling Art Exhibit"[82] to be shown in Brandon during the winter. The Brandon Art Club had been in existence since 1907, formed by Henrietta Hancock when she became the director of the Department of Art at Brandon College, and Isabel Sinclair, art teacher for Brandon Schools. Comprised entirely of women members for the majority of its existence, meetings of the Brandon Art Club featured papers on art prepared and delivered by members, usually accompanied by concerts, classes in art and hand crafts, exhibitions of members' works, as well as fundraising activities designed to support local benevolent groups such as the Imperial Order Daughters of the Empire and the teaching of art in schools.[83] In the 1940s, the primary locations for the presentation of the loan collections from the National Gallery were the Public Library and Doig's department store, with Marion Doig, in her role as head of the

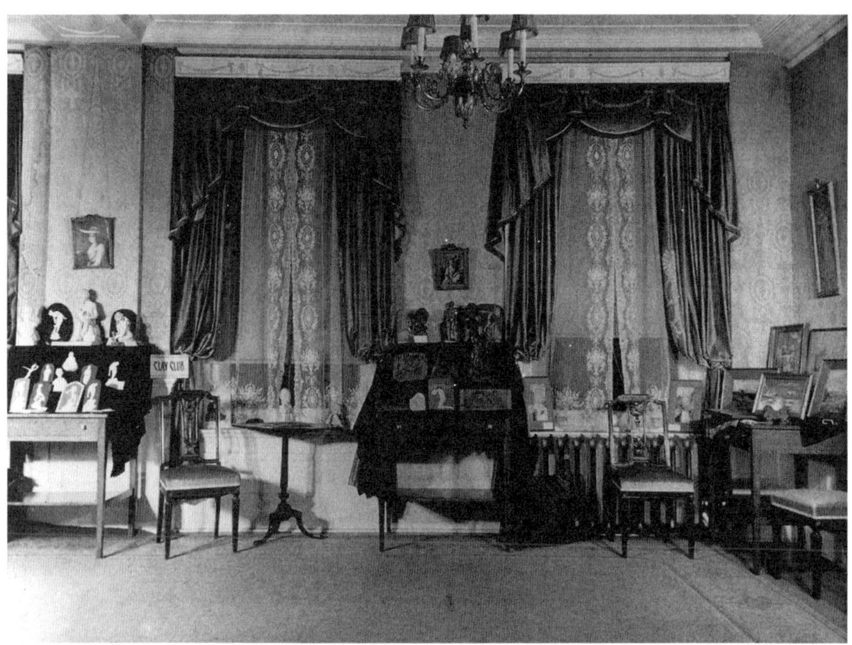

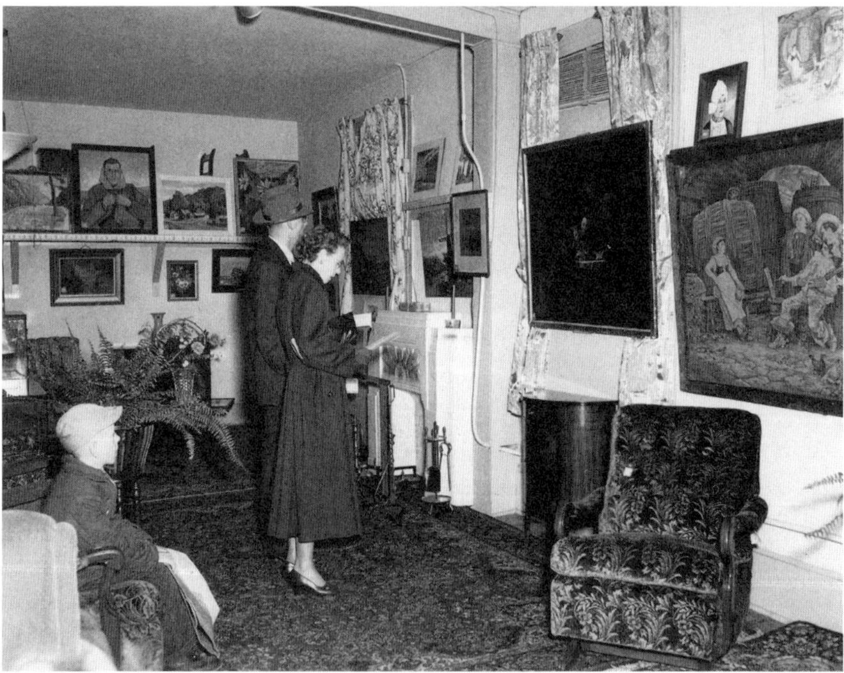

1.16 | Brandon Art Club annual display at the Prince Edward Hotel, c. 1930. In addition to the Clay Club – pictured here – displays of members' work in pastels, weaving, and pottery were also featured.

1.17 | Mc & Mc department store art exhibition, Kelowna, 1956.

Exhibition Committee and president of the Brandon Art Club, in regular correspondence with H.O. McCurry and NGC curator R.H. Hubbard about possible exhibitions and other administrative matters. In April 1950, she wrote to McCurry about the very positive public reception of the four works sent by the National Gallery to Brandon as part of a miniature history of the development of painting in Canada organized by the NGC. The works were displayed in the windows of Doig's department store and lit until 11 o'clock at night. Of the four paintings, Paul Peel's *Venetian Bather* was "very very much admired [and] nobody has complained about it being a nude."[84] Indeed, department stores figured repeatedly in western Canadian towns and cities' efforts to present art as broadly as possible. Members of Kelowna's Teachers Association were the first to inquire about loan exhibitions from the NGC in 1937, and H.O. McCurry responded that while loans could not be made to schools (other than of reproductions), he saw no reason why Kelowna could not benefit from the circulating exhibition program if a publicly accessible suitable facility could be found.[85] Although no NGC loans or exhibitions appear to have gone to Kelowna until 1956, community enthusiasm for art was evident, as can be seen in the catalogue for the third instalment of an annual art exhibition held in the furniture department of Mc & Mc department store that announced itself as "an outstanding exhibition featuring local and international works of merit. Over 100 paintings, worth a King's ransom."[86]

As the examples of Moose Jaw, Medicine Hat, Brandon, and Kelowna suggest, interest in art was as active in smaller communities as in major cities, the players reflecting many of the same aspirations to build up their municipalities through the formation of cultural institutions. Although neither Moose Jaw nor Brandon would establish a permanent art gallery or museum until the 1980s,[87] the efforts of the art associations in both cities over the first half of the twentieth century laid important foundations for the creation of the present institutions. And as the discussion of the early sites for the Winnipeg Art Gallery and the Edmonton Museum of Arts indicates, the size of a community was not necessarily a guarantee that a permanent museum building would be forthcoming. While the WAG and the EMA were able to carve out long-term arrangements for the display of their collections in civic buildings, they were subject to the same degree of uncertainty as to the permanence of their spaces as the art societies in Brandon and Moose Jaw, and had to wait almost as long to see their dreams of a permanent building realized. The common challenge facing all these institutions in the establishment of permanent space and collections was money: Regina, Saskatoon, and Vancouver may have benefitted from the generosity of individual benefactors who provided works of art as the basis of a permanent collection and funding for a building, but the requirements of gallery programming, and plans for expansion required additional funds that were not always forthcoming; Winnipeg, Edmonton, and smaller towns struggled in equal measure to find both gifts of art and funding for exhibition spaces that private donations, memberships, and municipal in-kind support could not always provide. In sum, all art galleries shared money woes, suffering particularly from the dearth of public funds directed towards culture throughout the first half of the twentieth century.

A comparison of the financial situations of art institutions in Winnipeg, Edmonton, and Vancouver is instructive here because of their shared history in the first five decades of the century. While the Vancouver Art Gallery began its life in 1931 with its own building and money left over to purchase paintings, its expansion in 1951 in part to house the bequest of paintings by Emily Carr, left the gallery struggling to pay its operating costs with few funds for strategic acquisitions. The annual reports from the years following the expansion show regular appeals to the city to increase its appropriation so that the VAG could live up to its status as the largest and most vital art gallery in western Canada. Indeed, the 1954–55 annual report approvingly cites an article by the National Gallery's R.H. Hubbard, describing "a creative upsurge [in Vancouver] which is making the West Coast a new centre for the arts."[88] The city responded to these pleas and increased its annual appropriation from $6,450 in 1950 to $10,000 in 1951 and $19,000 in 1953, amounts over and above the funding it provided for the cost overruns on the expansion. Memberships continued to grow during this period, although likely not as quickly as the gallery's management had hoped, and certainly not as rapidly as the much-fêted installation of a permanent display of work by Emily Carr would warrant. The VAG's regular appeals to the province, however, yielded nothing. The art galleries in Winnipeg and Edmonton faced similar problems from the 1930s to the 1950s as government funding – all municipal – remained scarce and only a few individuals made significant contributions to the upkeep of the buildings and the salaries of the staff. After shutting down in 1925 because of the withdrawal of

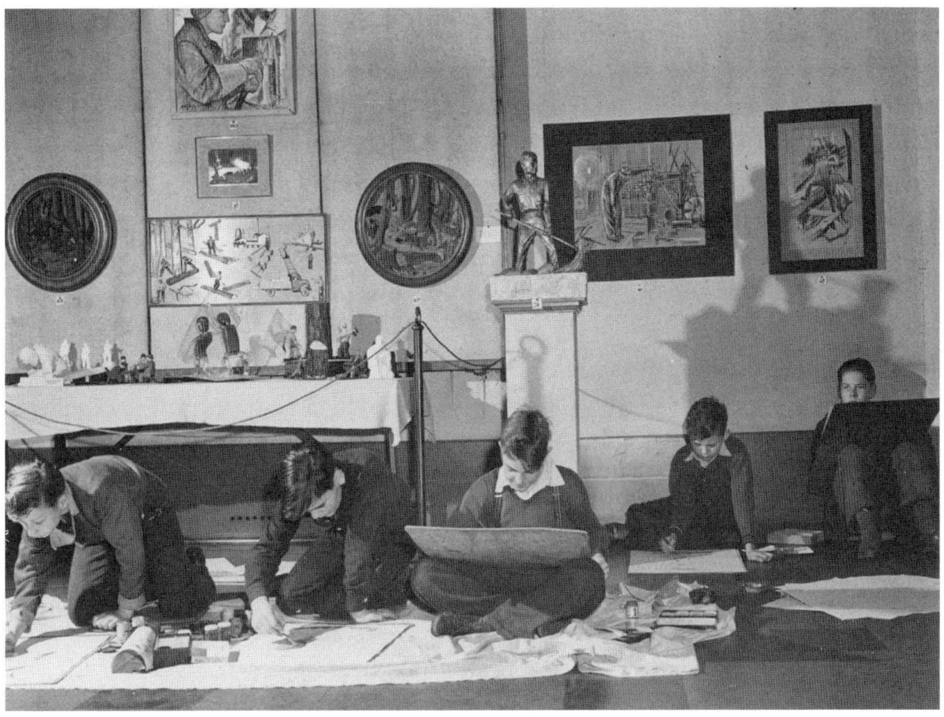

1.18 | Children's art classes at the Vancouver Art Gallery, 1945. Started with funds from the Carnegie Corporation, children's art classes were a mainstay of most western Canadian art galleries.

funding by the city, the WAG was given space in the Civic Auditorium in 1932 along with a small amount of money (roughly $3,000) for annual operating costs. Similarly, the City of Edmonton provided the EMA with exhibition spaces in civic buildings and an annual appropriation that paid for utilities and other services. In 1934, all three galleries received the first of several annual grants from the Carnegie Corporation in New York for children's art classes, a scheme introduced by the corporation and managed by the National Gallery that distributed funds to museums and galleries across the country to further art education. Although relatively small – between $1,000 and $1,500 per year – the grant paid for the salaries of the art teachers, covered much of the materials for the courses, and sometimes left a little for the operating costs of the institution.[89] The Carnegie grants, however, were intended to function as seed money, helping emerging institutions establish art education classes with the assumption that these programs would become self-financing in the short term. Such financial autonomy occurred at both the VAG and the WAG, but despite tremendous interest in the classes, the EMA struggled to make them self-sufficient and continued to appeal for renewals of the grants into the 1940s.

Other government funding was even harder to come by, the governments of all four western provinces unwilling to support cultural endeavours until well into the 1940s. The government of Alberta, for example, provided a grant of $1,000 in 1930 and 1931 but made no further contribution to the Edmonton Museum of Arts or any other cultural organization until 1948 when it awarded $500 to the institution.[90] The Winnipeg Art Gallery faced a similar lack of interest on the part of the provincial government and would not receive a grant from that body until 1956 when $3,000 was made available for extension programs. The British Columbia government was no more generous: the Art Gallery of Greater Victoria's minimal provincial funding was increased in 1957 when the province offered to match allocations by the municipal governments to support a new wing for the gallery to mark the province's centenary. The Vancouver Art Gallery only began to receive provincial funding in 1961: a grand total of $4,000 that constituted less than 14 percent of the amount the city of Vancouver gave annually to the gallery. Only in Saskatchewan would the Co-operative Commonwealth Federation government establish and promote an organization to fund and coordinate cultural activities in the province. Founded in 1948, the Saskatchewan Arts Board (SAB) is often described as the first government art council in Canada and the reason why American art luminaries such as Barnett Newman and Clement Greenberg were enticed to lead workshops at Regina College's Emma Lake facilities in the 1950s.[91] At its founding, however, the SAB was viewed as a means "to make available to the citizens of the province greater opportunities to engage in creative activities … and to establish and improve the standards of such activities in the province."[92] These aims were undertaken by providing both financial and professional support to cultural organizations throughout Saskatchewan, by circulating exhibitions obtained through the National Gallery or the WCAC, and by holding juried shows of Saskatchewan artists from which the SAB made purchases for future circulating exhibitions. Working with an inadequate budget of $4,000 over and above the provincial government's payment of office space and the salary of its staff, including its de facto director

Norah McCullough,[93] the SAB was the primary sponsor of art activity in the province until the opening of the galleries in Regina and Saskatoon. It was particularly effective in its support of a broad range of cultural activities from theatre and music to craft and the fine arts through its assistance to local organizations in smaller communities.[94]

While the SAB is the earliest example of an arts board or arts council in Canada, other western provincial governments in the mid- to late 1940s began to think more systematically about the need to provide financial support to cultural initiatives. Alberta established a Cultural Development Branch under the minister of Economic Affairs in 1946, creating four boards tasked with "the encouragement, expansion, coordination and development of different aspects of the cultural life of the Province" in the areas of music, drama, art and handicrafts, and libraries.[95] The Visual Arts Board began its work in earnest in 1948 and in addition to awarding small grants to promising students for study at the Provincial Art Institute in Calgary, organized circulating art exhibitions to communities in southern and northern Alberta, including two handicraft display trunks that circulated to rural communities throughout the province. By the mid-1950s, a separate board had been created for craft and the Visual Arts Board focused its interests on fine arts, joining the WCAC in 1956. Interest in museums was in place from the establishment of the Cultural Activities Branch, with discussion of acquisitions of objects of historical interest for a future provincial natural and human history museum, but direct funding to museums would come with the establishment of the Provincial Arts Board in 1948. The Edmonton Museum of Arts received $500 from the province that year, an amount that would remain stable until 1952–53 when it was increased to $1,000. Formal recognition of the Manitoba Arts Council was made by the provincial Legislature in 1965 but no members were appointed to the council until 1969. Focusing its support on arts organizations across the province, the Arts Council allocated funds to the Winnipeg Art Gallery in its first year and expanded its programs in 1973 and 1975 to include grants to individual artists, composers, writers, and playwrights.[96] It also made a commitment to supporting the development of cultural organizations in rural and northern Manitoba communities, a direction that significantly benefitted organizations like the Brandon Allied Arts Council, which expanded their activities with Arts Council support in 1974.[97] Financial support for the WAG from the provincial government predated the formation of the Council, with a $3,000 grant awarded in 1956, rising to $6,000 in 1959 and $12,000 in 1960; in 1969, the year the Arts Council finally began its operations, the WAG received $25,000 from the province, $35,000 from the City of Winnipeg, and $75,000 from the Canada Council.

In 1961 *Canadian Art* announced the formation of the British Columbia Arts Board, stating that the aim of this "non-partisan, without political attachment or appointment" organization was "to encourage an interest in the arts, promote production and participation, raise standards, assess the needs and provide assistance where possible."[98] With no money to spend, the Arts Board's initial function was entirely advisory, but the creation of the British Columbia Centennial Fund in 1967, to mark both the national and provincial centennials, entailed a $5 million endowment from which the interest would be directed to major arts organizations and to local community arts councils for further distribution; the principal was increased in 1969 to $10 million and again in 1972 to $15 million. While the province awarded the VAG a small grant of $4,000 in 1961 – significantly less than the $30,000 provided by the city – the Centennial Fund was the most significant generator of funds for both the VAG and the AGGV. For all the major art galleries under consideration here, provincial funding was hard won, and came after lengthy appeals to government ministers and premiers to support the work of these institutions in bringing culture to the citizens. Often couched in comparative language – whether in relation to municipal funding, or as a contrast to the significant funding provided by the governments of Ontario and Quebec – the appeals of gallery directors in Manitoba, Saskatchewan, Alberta, and British Columbia underscored the contribution of their institutions to the growing status and visibility of western cities and provinces, reiterating the belief in the civilizing values of art. Even as provincial funding slowly emerged throughout the 1940s and 1950s, federal funding for cultural organizations other than the National Gallery and the National Museum was nonexistent until the Royal Commission on National Development in the Arts, Letters and Sciences (Massey Commission) deposited its report advocating increased government support for the arts across the country as a strategy for nation building. It would take the formation of the Canada Council in 1957 for any consistent funding to be made available to Canadian galleries, although in its first years, Canada Council funding to organizations was primarily in the form of grants for acquisition – usually matching funds for purchases of contemporary art – and not for the operating funds so desperately needed by so many museums.

The lack of predictable continuous funding in the 1930s, 1940s, and 1950s meant that western Canadian art galleries had to rely on voluntary contributions to carry out their activities. Two primary bodies must be considered in this category: the boards of trustees (sometimes called boards of directors) and the volunteer women's committees. Composed largely of businessmen with the occasional inclusion of artists and other professionals, boards of trustees were primarily governing bodies charged with oversight of the gallery's finances and administration. Before the hiring of professional curators and directors, however, museum boards and councils were much more intimately involved in the day-to-day operations of the institutions they governed than the boards of today: planning exhibitions, running education programs, and actively accessioning works for the collection. The boards of all the galleries considered here were composed of members of each city's business and political elites: figures whose social and cultural values aligned closely with the mandate of the institutions they served. But as Francie Ostrower has observed in her analysis of the composition of the governing bodies of elite arts organizations, boards maintained homogeneity across class lines in an effort to retain a "special sense of identification with the institution,"[99] even as they actively encouraged the expansion of the audiences for those institutions. As a result, art galleries in western Canada – as in the rest of the country – regularly faced accusations of being exclusive social clubs that ignored the (aesthetic) interests of "ordinary" citizens. Such complaints were often taken up by members of city councils concerned with the levels of funding disbursed for "cultural frills" for the city's elites, but the organizations themselves worked hard to counter such perceptions through the inclusion of educational programs and more populist exhibitions.

While boards of trustees oversaw the administration of the organization, women's societies played the often overlooked yet significant role of establishing and maintaining art museums' programs and activities. Formed in the early 1940s in art galleries across Canada,[100] women's committees (also known as women's societies and women's auxiliaries) were given the task of increasing public awareness of and support for the museum. Charting the activities of women's committees during this period and their relationship to the museum's board of trustees, it is evident that while the board was looking for additional financial support, the women saw their role to be much greater than raising funds. Rather, they set out from the start to establish and direct programs that complemented the primary work of the institution while also taking it into new directions. Engaging in any number of behind-the-scenes supporting activities from providing refreshments and creating suitable flower arrangements for openings, to secretarial work and staffing the information desk, women's societies also identified areas where the museum was deficient, and developed programs to fill that gap. Between 1943 and 1970, women's committees of museums expanded art education classes; arranged lecture series and discussion groups; set up art libraries; and with financial assistance from the Junior Leagues of their respective cities, established docent and guide programs that sought to interpret the museum's collection and exhibitions to the broader public. In addition to this educational work, women's groups took care of publicity for museums through their contacts with the editors of the women's pages of city newspapers and their large networks of other women's groups. Responding to the lack of commercial galleries specializing in contemporary Canadian art, the women's committees of the art museums in Toronto, Hamilton, Winnipeg, and Vancouver initiated annual juried exhibitions and sales of original art in the late 1940s that became significant outlets for emerging and established Canadian artists. The "Winnipeg Shows" organized by the WAG's Women's Society sometimes occasioned controversy but were an important source of acquisitions – by the women's society – for the gallery's permanent collection.[101] Other commercial ventures spearheaded by the women's committees include the introduction of gift shops to Canadian museums; the development of art sales and rental galleries (in conjunction with the Junior League); and the establishment of partnerships with local businesses to publicize museum activities. In addition to these public programs, women's committees of all the institutions considered here organized fancy dress balls, tea parties, and rummage sales, the proceeds of which were returned to the institution often for the purchase of works for the permanent collection.[102] From the range of these activities – the majority of which continue to be central public programs offered by North American art museums – it is clear that the unpaid work of volunteer women was key to ensuring that public galleries remained open and active.

Collecting in Western Canada

While the presentation of exhibitions consumed most of the energy of the founders of western Canadian art galleries, the establishment of a permanent collection remained a central mission of them all. As will be discussed in Chapter 2, building a collection was a strong condition of continued participation in the National Gallery's loan program, but more importantly, such a collection ensured both the continuing existence and legitimacy of the fledgling institutions in the region. With limited funds at their disposal, the acquisitions made by many of the galleries in western Canada were haphazard at best. According to the minutes of the 10 March 1925 meeting of the board, the Edmonton Museum of Arts' first acquisition was "the Ernest Brown collection of pictures 'Early days in Edmonton,'" purchased from this local photographer for fifty dollars. Given attitudes towards photography at the time, the purchase underscores the EMA's mandate to collect both objects of fine arts and historical interest, but also signals its eagerness to invest in a permanent collection as much as finances would permit.[103] In the first few years, acquisitions were not particularly numerous, but for the most part there seems to be a certain knowledge of what kinds of work were of the most interest to the museum: works by contemporary painters and sculptors – mostly Canadian, many working in the region, and almost all recommended or supported by the National Gallery of Canada through their loan collections and reproduction programs. For example, in the first five years of the EMA's existence there were three purchases of print portfolios by Walter J. Phillips; Franklin Carmichael, A.Y. Jackson, and Lionel LeMoine FitzGerald all sent works directly to the museum for consideration, resulting in the purchases of works by Carmichael and Jackson. George Reid also sent works for purchase consideration in 1930 and donated a second work when the EMA bought *Dark Canyon* (n.d.). Reid repeated this practice on many occasions, including in 1943 when he sent work to a number of galleries across the country writing that with the forthcoming publication of his biography, he thought it appropriate to have more of his paintings in important collections.[104] Such hopes also underpinned the Group of Seven's almost constant placement of their work in touring exhibitions: while private purchases were expected, institutional purchases were also highly sought after because of the increased public exposure such acquisitions would entail.

If works by contemporary Canadian artists often proved to be the most affordable option for most new museums, the acquisition of European masters remained institutions' holy grail. The Vancouver Art Gallery's possession of a sizeable number of British paintings and sculptures in its permanent collection from the time of its opening was entirely due to the founders' wealth and the ability of major donor H.A. Stone to travel to London to buy works on the gallery's behalf. The first works purchased for the collection were the result of Stone's trip to Europe with artist Charles H. Scott between April and July 1931. Relying heavily on the advice of Sir Charles Holmes, the former director of the National Gallery, London, Stone and Scott[105] focused their purchases on works by British artists in an effort to "faithfully portray as far as was possible the history and development of British art."[106] As Sarah Stanners has demonstrated, the choice of British art as the nucleus of the new art gallery in Vancouver was an indication of the founders' view of the centrality of British values in the project of civilizing and modernizing Vancouver. As Stanners further argues, an interest in British art would remain strong in English Canadian art institutions across the country until the 1970s.[107] Indeed, while the acquisitions made by the Vancouver Art Gallery in its first decade were shaped by the conservative tastes of Stone and of Holmes, who continued to act as the VAG's advisor until 1934, the predilection for collecting British art remained until the 1960s, albeit expanding in scope and approach to include the modernist work of Jacob Epstein, Graham Sutherland, and Ben Nicholson among others.[108] As Karen Finlay has noted, these acquisitions would be influential on the development of painting in Vancouver in the immediate postwar period, evident in the work of such artists as Jack Shadbolt and Gordon Smith.[109]

While British art was the focus of the VAG's acquisition program in the 1930s and 1940s, the gallery's board made nominal acknowledgment of the place of Canadian art in the gallery's activities. Describing the selections in the inaugural catalogue, Stone noted that the purpose of the gallery was to form a collection that would "aim at a history of British and Canadian painting," yet he was quick to acknowledge that while "the first part of this policy ... has been adhered to; the second part – the collection of Canadian works – remains to be made."[110] The acquisition of Canadian art was indeed slow over the following decades: in 1945, the gallery received 157 "choice examples"[111] of work by Emily Carr as part of the Emily Carr Trust, and Lawren Harris's presence on the gallery's Board of Trustees from 1943 onwards ensured that some attention was given to the encouragement of Canadian artists.[112] During this early period the VAG followed the practice of most art museums and hosted exhibitions by local art societies such as the BC Society of Fine Artists,[113] and the BC Artists Annual Exhibition held at the gallery between 1932 and 1968. The

1.19 | Vancouver Art Gallery: Emily Carr galleries with Lawren Harris and Ira Dilworth, 1951. Harris and Dilworth worked together to set up the Emily Carr Trust Collection and to negotiate its transfer to the VAG.

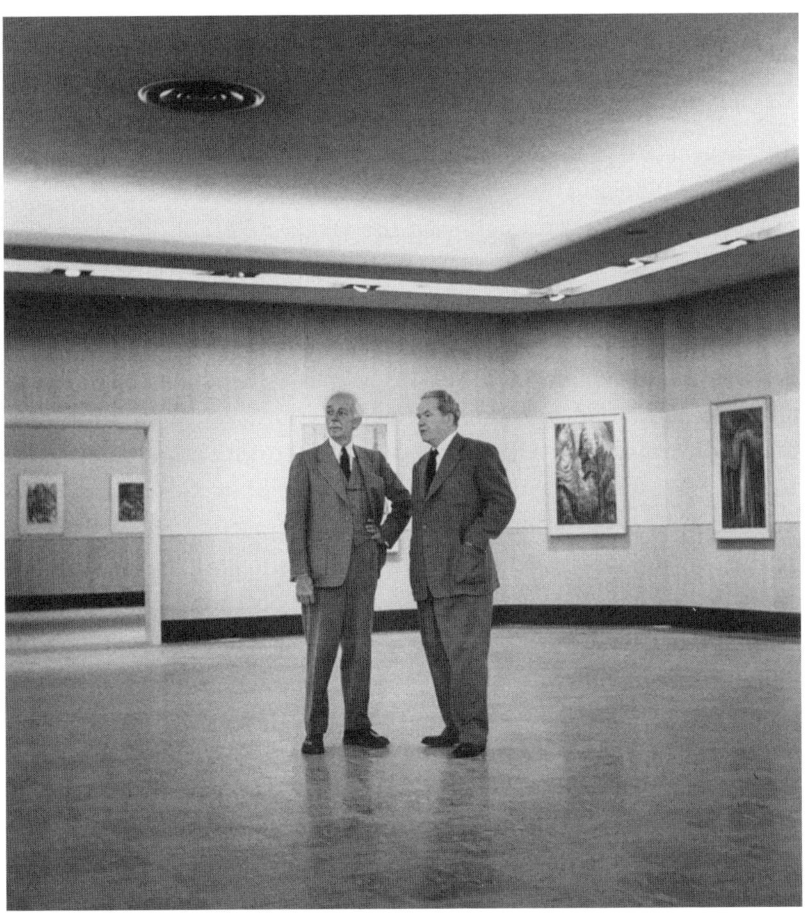

gallery's Women's Auxiliary initiated their very successful Do You Own a Canadian Picture? sale in 1949, establishing a space within which contemporary artists from British Columbia and across the country could present and sell their works. On the whole, however, the VAG would conform to Jack Shadbolt's 1946 assessment of its collecting practices as "the backward yearning of successive boards of directors."[114]

In Winnipeg, meanwhile, the first acquisitions followed the same pattern as described in relation to the Edmonton Museum of Arts: mostly contemporary Canadian artists and some donations – all taking place during the precarious period in the WAG's history when its affiliation with the School of Art connected it to significant artists but the withdrawal of funding temporarily put the gallery's activities in abeyance. In 1933 – the year the WAG re-opened in the Civic Auditorium building – former alderman and MP A.A. Heaps bequeathed twenty-nine paintings of mostly Dutch and British nineteenth-century landscapes, and in 1939, hardware merchant James Cleghorn donated ninety paintings of unequal value by an array of European artists. These provided an important base for the acquisitions made in the 1940s and 1950s both by purchase and by donation. Board president John A. MacAulay was a significant donor in the 1950s, and he strengthened the WAG's collection immeasurably with gifts of works by James Wilson Morrice, Emily Carr, A.Y. Jackson, Fred Varley, and Lawren Harris among others. A systematic collections policy, however, would only begin to be formulated with the hiring of Ferdinand Eckhardt as director in 1953.

The precarious financial situation of the majority of the galleries under discussion here, however, permitted only select purchases; most of the objects that came into galleries' permanent collection were obtained by donations. These can be divided into two categories: those by artists, seeking to have their work represented in collections around the country, and those by individuals or groups in support of the overall goals of the public museum. Works from the first category of donations – those by artists – are in some ways the more intriguing as the process paints a picture of the conditions of artistic production in Canada in the 1920s and 1930s when there were few commercial galleries even in Montreal and Toronto, and artists' societies relied on their annual exhibitions to interest collectors and institutions in buying their work. Organizations and groups such as the Royal Canadian Academy, the Ontario Society of Artists, and the Group of Seven organized travelling exhibitions of their work that they circulated across the country – often with the assistance of the National Gallery. These exhibitions frequently generated sales, if not of the works included in the exhibition then other works still located in the artists' studios. The growth of art institutions in western Canada must have been seen as a boon by artists who perhaps naively assumed that the wealth of these regions would result in a greater number of purchases of their work.[115]

The second category of donations – those by individuals and groups in support of the civic aims of local galleries – deserves equal consideration. Donations of this kind were the initial means through which the majority of institutions developed their permanent collections. As western cities grew in size and the demographics changed to reflect the increasing number of wealthy citizens, art galleries increasingly benefitted from bequests, donations of funds towards the purchase of artworks, or presentations of works to mark significant milestones or the contribution of a particular individual. As voluntary organizations expanded, they too began to offer works of art to their local art gallery, as was the case, for example, with the Fine and Applied Arts Committee of the Regina Council of Women whose donation of twenty-three works to the Norman MacKenzie Art Gallery was featured at the opening of its new building in 1953. Whether it was in the form of major gifts such as the Heaps and Cleghorn bequests in Winnipeg or individual donations of paintings and sculptures by board members and civic politicians, gifts from local art lovers demonstrate the faith bestowed in cultural institutions and their ability to transform pioneer towns into major cities.

In addition to these local groups, national figures and organizations also gave works to museums in western Canada. The members of the Southam publishing family made regular gifts to the museums and galleries in cities in which it owned a newspaper.[116] These donations were likely instigated by H.S. Southam, a major art collector and publisher of the *Ottawa Citizen*. With his appointment as chairman of the National Gallery's board of trustees in 1929, he was active in the presentation of works to select Canadian art galleries, choosing the works to be donated as well as the galleries he felt were most deserving of support. In 1937, Southam and his brothers purchased J.E.H. MacDonald's controversial 1916 painting *The Tangled Garden* for the National Gallery, and then encouraged gallery director Eric Brown to tour the painting to cities across Canada free of charge. *The Tangled Garden* ended up only going to western Canada, but it was greeted with enthusiasm and great interest in every city where it was shown, with the VAG reporting that over 2,200 people came to see the work over the ten days it was on display.[117] In her examination of Southam's collecting practices, Alicia Boutilier has demonstrated that unlike many of his peers, Southam developed a keen interest in making modern art a key component of his collection. After acquiring examples of Barbizon and Hague School paintings in the first five years he collected, by 1929 Southam was regularly travelling to Paris, London, Amsterdam, and New York to consult dealers and buying work by post-impressionist artists at a time when many North American collectors were shying away from such works.[118] His interest in and support of Canadian artists was similarly contemporary, including work by members of the Group of Seven, the Beaver Hall Group – he was particularly fond of the work of Lilias Torrance Newton – and, from the late 1940s, the Contemporary Arts Society and the Automatistes. His donations to Canadian museums reflected his own collecting tastes – he was an ardent supporter of the painter Henri Masson, and paintings by this artist were gifted to museums across the country – as well as his belief that Canadian art should be made available to smaller galleries across the country.

Southam's tastes were unusual, a situation made particularly evident when his donations are compared to those of western collectors. In Regina, Norman MacKenzie's preference ran to European masters, which, according to Timothy Long, he acquired primarily through correspondence with dealers of dubious repute in London.[119] He had little interest in modern art, and when he purchased nineteenth-century works, they tended to be Hague School seascapes or rugged English landscapes. His appointment to the board of trustees of the National Gallery in 1925 increased his exposure to individuals with knowledge of art and expanded his collecting choices significantly. Despite his association with the National Gallery, MacKenzie was not a supporter of the Group of Seven and his tastes in Canadian art were firmly located in the work of members of the Royal Canadian Academy, many of who were personal friends.[120] In Edmonton, Ernest Poole, chairman of Poole Construction Limited, was an avid collector from 1920 as his business expanded from Moose Jaw to Regina and finally to Edmonton. His collection was primarily oriented towards Canadian art and included work by Cornelius Krieghoff, Homer Watson, and James Wilson Morrice, as well as by popular genre painters such as Frederick Verner and the academic artist Paul Peel. His bequest of a portion of his collection to the Edmonton Art Gallery in 1975 – it had been on permanent loan since 1969 – revealed Poole's awareness of the importance of the work of Tom Thomson and members of the Group of Seven, for whom he had a "great fondness."[121] His collection also included work by Emily Carr and David Milne along with antique silver, porcelain, and Asian art, elements of which were eventually bequeathed to the National Gallery and the AGGV. In contrast to many collectors of his generation in western Canada, Fred Mendel's taste leaned towards the European expressionist artists of the early twentieth century he had collected while still living in Hungary. He continued buying the work of such artists as Franz Marc, Lionel Feininger, Marc Chagall, Maurice Utrillo, Serge Poliakoff, and Raoul Dufy, but extended his favour to historical and contemporary Canadian artists from the Group of Seven to Saskatchewan artists Ernest Lindner, Wynona Mulcaster, and William Perehudoff. In Matthew Teitelbaum's opinion, Mendel's collection represents both "a desire to materialize the connection between his lost and present home" and to "broaden ... the contexts in which art is seen and understood."[122]

Art galleries in the western provinces developed permanent collections in a more haphazard manner than might be said about their counterparts in Ottawa, Montreal, and Toronto, and this is due as much to the dearth of wealthy patrons at the founding of many of the galleries as by a lack of knowledge or professional direction by their leaders. As both these institutions and the cities that housed them grew, collecting became more focused and priorities were put in place that guided, more or less formally, the decisions of the "purchase and acceptance" committees that were slowly being established by the 1950s. While the work of regional artists remained a primary focus of purchases made directly by the galleries, donations by local and national patrons provided geographical and historical breadth to burgeoning permanent collections and helped to fulfill founding aspirations to make the history of Euro-North American art available to the citizens of western Canada.

Conclusion

The activities of western Canadian art galleries in the first decades of the twentieth century tell a story of civic aspirations, cultural ideals, and financial struggles. For all the founders of the institutions examined here, the establishment of an art gallery signalled their city's full accession to the civilizing values that characterized the metropolises of central Canada. More than a place to show works of art, museums were symbols of economic prosperity and cultural advancement. No longer the pioneering towns and trading posts of the "Last Best West," the major cities in Manitoba, Saskatchewan, Alberta, and British Columbia sought equal economic and political participation in the nation's affairs with their central Canadian counterparts. Although the museums founded in these cities depended on the services of central Canadian institutions and arts organizations for expertise as well as for the loan of artworks, the galleries in Winnipeg, Edmonton, Vancouver, and elsewhere remained important gauges of western cities' aspirations to equality and autonomy. Over the course of the first half of the twentieth century, they would build their permanent collections, develop exhibition and public programs that attracted visitors and benefitted the public, and seek out donors to help them reach their goals of expansion and increased visibility. The next chapter examines how central Canadian institutions – and the National Gallery in particular – viewed their role in helping build western Canadian art galleries and how they chose to manage these regional institutions' hopes for equality and autonomy. As I will argue, despite western organizations' appreciation of the regular loan of artworks, the relationship with the National Gallery was often fraught with struggles over the power to determine the nature of the exhibitions circulated to the regions, and the degree of control exercised by the NGC over the activities of emerging galleries. Such struggles mirror the relations of power between the centre and the periphery in the political and economic realms so it is no surprise that the complaints of provincial governments over the centralization of power in Ottawa were also voiced – albeit to a lesser degree – by the directors of art galleries in western Canada. These tensions nevertheless continued to characterize the development of art galleries in western Canada throughout the century.

MANAGING THE PERIPHERY

The National Gallery and Regional Museums

As the account of the formation of art galleries in western Canada demonstrates, none of these institutions could have organized the number and variety of exhibitions and programs without significant help from the National Gallery in Ottawa. The National Gallery of Canada (NGC) was founded in 1880 out of a desire on the part of the members of the equally recently established (Royal) Canadian Academy of Arts (RCA) to have a depository for their diploma works.[1] Despite the apparent practicality of this origin story, the formation of a national gallery served a much more significant ideological purpose, functioning as an important symbol of Canada's autonomy from Britain. Much like the RCA was established to ensure professional standards of artistic practice among the country's artists, a national gallery would align Canada with European nations such as England, Scotland, and Germany, which had erected large institutions dedicated to the elevation of public taste and the display of the nation's cultural achievements.[2] As Carol Duncan and Alan Wallach have argued in their analysis of the emergence of public museums in the late nineteenth century, "museums embody and make visible the idea of the state … and those who pass through its doors enact a ritual that equates state authority with the idea of civilization."[3] Although on a much smaller scale than the universal survey museum described by Duncan and Wallach, the creation of the National Gallery of Canada crystallized Canada's economic and intellectual elites' aspirations to bring these highest European values to the new nation. This position is clearly formulated in the gallery's 1920–21 annual report, which outlines the twofold functions of a National Gallery of Art as first, "to build up a collection of the standards of all art, ancient and modern, by which modern standards may be judged and sound artistic education obtained," and second, "to do everything possible for the art of its own country, by purchasing it, exhibiting it and bringing its importance as a national asset and an influence for good before the people generally, and by creating and cultivating in them correct artistic taste."[4]

The National Gallery was not Canada's first major art museum: wealthy businessmen and collectors in Montreal had banded together in 1860 to form the Art Association of Montreal (AAM), and following a bequest of works of art and money for a building from Benaiah Gibb, the association opened an art gallery to the public in 1879 on Phillips Square.[5] Over the first ten years it occupied this building, the AAM's exhibitions largely consisted of rotating displays of its members' collections in the fall, the presentation of contemporary art at the yearly spring exhibitions, and hosting the annual exhibition of the Royal Canadian Academy every three years in rotation with the National Gallery and eventually the Art Museum of Toronto. The AAM further consolidated its influence on the development of artistic taste in the city through the simultaneous establishment of art classes under the leadership of William Brymner, which became the primary training ground for many of the city's major artists.[6] Like the Art Gallery of Toronto – founded as the Art Museum of Toronto in 1900 – and the Owens Art Gallery – established in Sackville, New Brunswick in 1895 – the Art Association was governed by an active board of trustees whose own collecting interests largely determined the institution's direction.[7] As a result, the AAM was closer in approach to American private institutions such as the Metropolitan Museum of Art in New York or the Boston Museum of Fine Arts than to a public museum like the National Gallery whose administration by the federal government ensured that its activities were oriented towards the interests of the nation as a whole.

The distinction between the National Gallery and private associations such as the Art Association of Montreal and the Art Gallery of Toronto is important because it highlights the different mandates and publics of each type of institution. As a federally funded public institution, the National Gallery's remit focused on both serving a national public and encouraging Canadian artists. Its collecting activities reflect this dual responsibility in the efforts to present a complete survey of European art for the enlightenment of the nation's citizens as well as support the formation of a strong Canadian aesthetic practice. In contrast, the AAM had no responsibility to any public other than the local community it sought to elevate, and while it included Canadian art amongst its acquisitions and its spring shows featured contemporary work by Canadian artists, it did not limit its purchases to the work of local artists and was subsequently castigated by figures such as A.Y. Jackson for its preference for Barbizon and Hague School landscapes.[8] In other words, like virtually all museums in the Anglo-American world, both the National Gallery and the AAM saw themselves as improving the artistic tastes of the public, but the NGC had the additional task of building a national public for the consumption of art, and more importantly, answered to the federal government rather than to a group of interested private citizens. As a result, its activities had to reach beyond the confines of Ottawa, if not of Ontario and Quebec, and nurture interest in art across the country. This chapter examines the work of the National Gallery in expanding Canadians' interest in the fine arts, in particular its program of loan exhibitions, lecturers, and slide shows that circulated throughout the country, as well as its role in fostering art education. The loans described in the previous chapter provided the basis for the programming of nascent art organizations across western Canada and, as I argue here, it was the means through which the National Gallery could both serve the national public and assert its status as the premier source of knowledge on art in Canada. This status was confirmed in the 1930s when the Carnegie Corporation of New York directed the funding of art education classes in Canadian institutions through the Canadian Museums Committee (CMC) headquartered at the National Gallery. Although few organizations in western Canada would have been able to survive without the assistance of the National Gallery, this chapter will show that the National Gallery was equally reliant on regional institutions to fulfill its federal mandate and to demonstrate its national reach to international observers. In the end, however, the relationship between the centre and the periphery resulted in the continued attempt of the National Gallery to control the activities of regional galleries and to assert its authority in all matters of art in Canada.

The Early Years of the National Gallery

Established by the Marquess of Lorne, Canada's fourth governor general, as part of his sponsorship of the RCA, the National Gallery was administered by the Department of Public Works and remained homeless until 1882 when it obtained rooms in a building owned by that ministry near the Supreme Court. In 1888 the gallery moved to larger quarters in a building formally housing the *Dominion Fisheries Exhibit* where it was able to present the entirety of its collection to the public. This move was a significant improvement on its former quarters, but the following review from the *Ottawa Daily Free Press* indicates the scale of the enterprise and suggests that the National Gallery was struggling to obtain full support from the government and the public: "The whole collection is now in one room with ample hanging space for it at present, and being alongside the better-known and more popular fisheries exhibit is likely to receive a greater amount of attention from visitors than has hitherto fallen to its lot."[9] During this early period, a close relationship remained between the gallery and the RCA as the latter maintained a certain degree of over-sight over the growing gallery, not least by keeping it supplied with work for its permanent collection through the regular deposit of its newly elected members' diploma works. The first curator, John H.W. Watts, was a member of the RCA, and as assistant Dominion chief architect, was already in the employ of the Department of Public Works. Appointed on a part-time basis in 1883, his four-year term at the National Gallery did not significantly advance the institution's stature, as acquisitions were limited to RCA diploma pictures and a few purchases. In 1897 the position of curator was occupied by another architect in the employ of the Department of Public Works, Lawrence Fennings Taylor. His tenure, however, yielded little in the way of acquisitions or increased interest in the gallery. Indeed, Jean Sutherland Boggs describes attendance at the National Gallery as being just short of 12,000 in 1886–87, reaching a high of almost 23,000 in 1895–96, but declining steadily thereafter.[10]

Interest in the gallery by the RCA continued throughout what Boggs describes as "the years of obscurity" with members of the Academy buying four works for the permanent collection in 1894 and continuing to supply diploma pictures from newly elected members.[11] For its part, the gallery focused its early purchases on works by members of the RCA, including Robert Harris's *A Meeting of the School Trustees* (1885; pur-chased in 1886) and Paul Peel's *Venetian Bather* (1889), purchased in 1895 shortly after his death. A complaint from RCA President George Reid in 1907 about the poor management of the gallery prompted the minis-ter of public works to appoint an advisory arts council to oversee all of

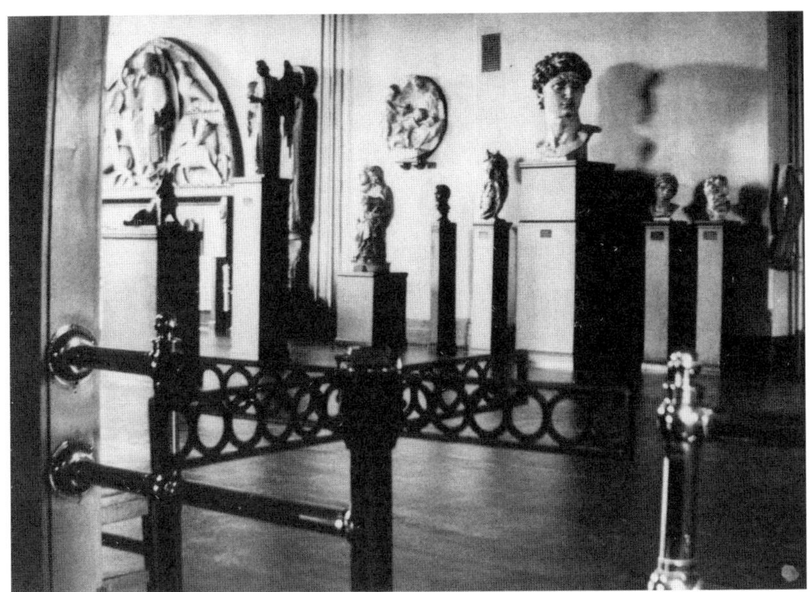

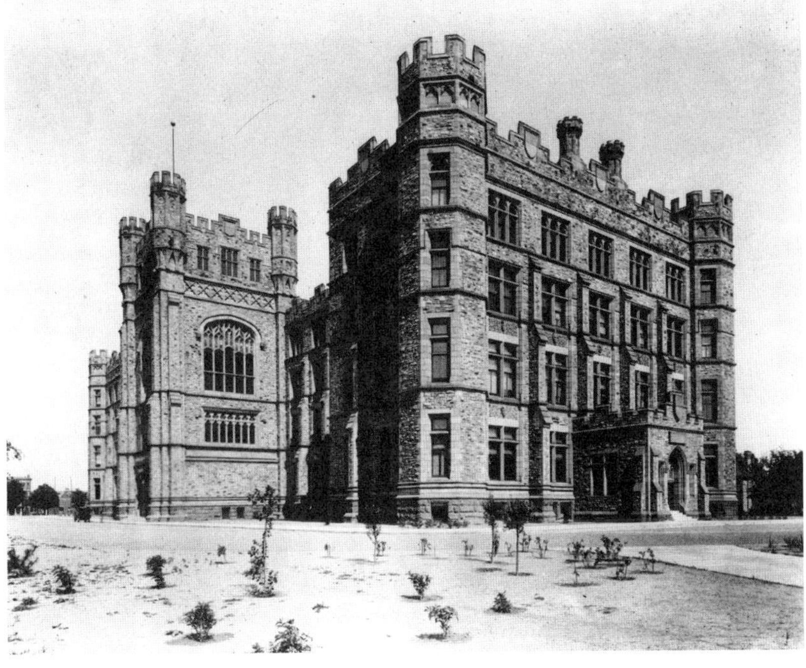

2.1 | National Gallery at the Victoria Memorial Museum Building, interior with turnstiles, 1931. Director Eric Brown installed turnstiles shortly after the NGC moved into the Victoria Memorial Museum Building to enable more accurate visitor statistics.

2.2 | Victoria Memorial Museum Building, exterior 1912. The building was erected to house both the National Gallery and the National Museum.

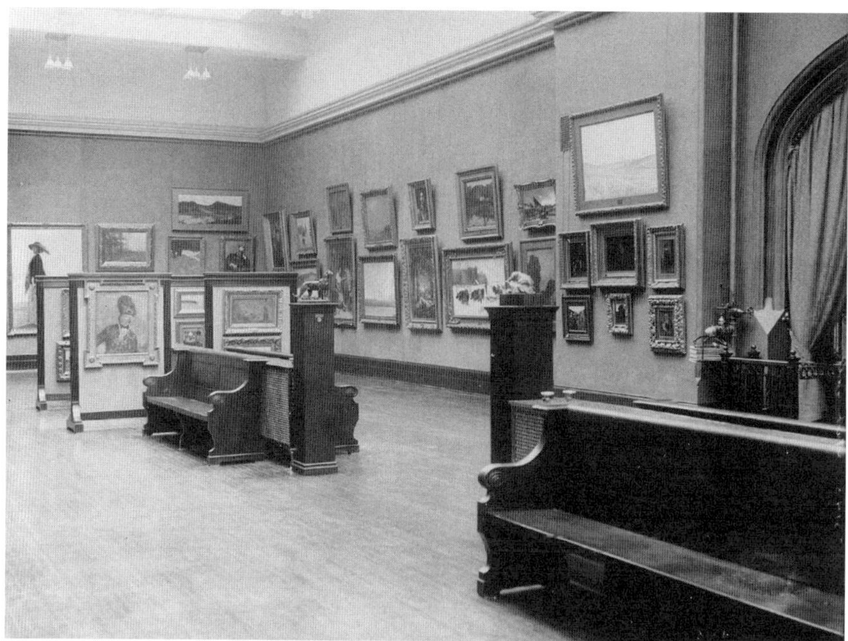

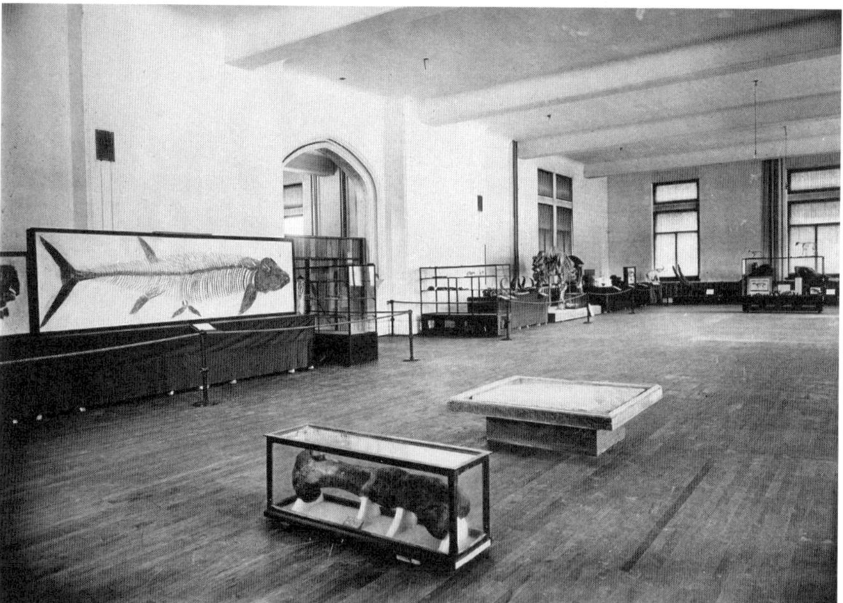

2.3 | Victoria Memorial Museum Building interior, showing the display of the National Gallery's collection, 1913.

2.4 | Victoria Memorial Museum Building interior, showing the display of the National Museum's dinosaur collection, 1913. The museum and the gallery would remain in the same building until 1960.

the nation's cultural affairs including the National Gallery. The order in council that created the advisory board described it as being "composed of gentlemen who have shown their interest in and appreciation and understanding of art as evidenced by their public connection with art associations and their private patronage of art,"[12] and gave a $10,000 appropriation for purchases. The council's first members, businessmen and art collectors Sir George Drummond and Byron E. (later Sir Edmund) Walker, and Senator Arthur Boyer, completely fulfilled these requirements: Walker and Drummond had already demonstrated their expertise in overseeing art galleries – Drummond as president of the Art Association of Montreal from 1896 to 1899, and Walker as a founding member of the Art Gallery of Toronto in 1900.[13] Upon Drummond's death in 1910, Walker assumed the chair of the Advisory Arts Council and hired a recent emigrant from England, Eric Brown, as the National Gallery's full-time curator. Although Brown had an interest in art – his brother Arnesby was a well-regarded British landscape painter – he had no training in gallery management, yet succeeded in impressing Walker when he was hired to canvass for memberships for the nascent Art Museum of Toronto. According to Brown's wife, Maud, on the success of this work for the Toronto museum, Walker asked Brown to go to Ottawa "and bring some order into the affairs of the long-neglected National Gallery," appointing him as both the gallery's curator and his own assistant.[14] The 1911–12 report of the gallery's activities lists Brown's achievements in his first two years at the helm, noting in particular the organization of an ancient casts and modern sculpture gallery; the production of a catalogue listing all the works in the collection; the inclusion of labels identifying works in both French and English; and the installation of turnstiles to better gauge the number of visitors to the gallery. As the report concludes, "Everything possible has been done to make the National Gallery attractive to the public and to fulfil its purpose of usefulness as an educative and pleasure-giving exhibition."[15] By 1913, the National Gallery had moved into the newly built Victoria Memorial Museum Building, which it shared with the National Museum of the Geological Survey (now the Canadian Museum of History); it had obtained a federal charter under the National Gallery of Canada Act; and it had acquired its own board of trustees headed by Walker. This set up would remain in place for almost the next fifty years until the gallery moved into its first independent home in the Lorne Building in 1960.

The 1913 National Gallery of Canada Act clearly sets out the terms of reference of the institution: "the encouragement and cultivation of correct artistic taste and Canadian public interest in the fine arts, [and] the promotion of the interests of art, in general, in Canada."[16] Recording the passing of the act in his report to the Department of Public Works, Eric Brown called for a permanent home for the National Gallery, arguing that it needed "an adequate storehouse for the national art treasures, and a fitting recognition of the native art of Canada which has already done so much for the refinement and true progress of this country."[17] Both statements underscore the nation-building as well as aesthetic aspirations of the institution: the National Gallery would elevate and educate Canada's citizens by acquiring and displaying objects of aesthetic value, and at the same time it would contribute to the development of the nation's artistic production by providing a space where the work of its best contemporary artists could be seen in perpetuity. The consonance of this project with the aims of the Royal Academy is evident. However, relations with the Academy would soon sour as each institution's definition of what constituted "the best" of contemporary Canadian art took a different shape. The RCA continued to look to Europe for inspiration and aesthetic authority, expanding the stylistic range of its membership to include impressionist approaches and the *juste milieu* styles favoured by such figures as Horatio Walker and Homer Watson. The National Gallery, for its part, sought out more identifiably "Canadian" approaches to art-making, and acquired works by emerging Montreal and Toronto artists A.Y. Jackson, Tom Thomson, and Lawren Harris from as early as 1910. As became evident in the 1920s and 1930s, the National Gallery's championing of these more modernist artists put the gallery at odds with some of the more conservative members of the RCA who publicly questioned the gallery's ability and authority to select representative examples of Canadian art for international exhibitions.[18] The criticism directed at the gallery by the Academy and its supporters over the selection process for the Canadian art section of the 1924 British Empire Exhibition at Wembley is frequently described as a turning point in the ascendency of the Group of Seven as Canada's "national school," but it should more accurately be identified as the moment when the National Gallery consolidated its position as aesthetic arbiter in the world of Canadian art. Much of its claim to occupying this position came from the outreach activities it initiated in the first two decades of the twentieth century, which established the NGC as the primary, if not the sole, purveyor of information on and knowledge of the fine arts in Canada. The first of these outreach activities was the program of loan exhibitions it began to send across the country in 1913, followed shortly afterwards by the development of a reproduction program designed to reach an even larger public.

Reaching out across the Country: The Loan Exhibitions

In her invaluable series of essays chronicling the successive reproduction programs with which the National Gallery was involved, Joyce Zemans convincingly demonstrates that by "complementing the Gallery's programme of acquisitions, exhibitions, lectures and articles, [they] influenced the entire country's idea of what was Canadian about Canadian art."[19] Indeed, the program of producing lithograph and silkscreen prints of significant works from the NGC's collection for sale to individuals and organizations in Canada is a key component in the gallery's establishment of itself as the country's visual arts authority. Originally discussed in late 1913 and early 1914 as a companion activity to the loan program, plans were initially made to produce both 5" x 7" prints and postcard-size reproductions, with the prints available for sale by September 1915 individually and in sets of six. In February 1917, Eric Brown sent Moose Jaw's A.H. Gibbard a list of the postcards available for sale from this first reproduction program, which consisted largely of European and English artists (including Caravaggio, Corot, Hogarth, and Millais) and only four Canadians (Cruikshank, Peel, Walker, and Barnsley).[20] The second reproduction program, initiated by A.Y. Jackson in 1927, focused almost entirely on the work of Canadian artists from the NGC's collection and, according to the gallery's report on the undertaking, were intended to "provide an adequate basis for art teaching in the Canadian schools. [They] have, however, proved enormously popular with the general public."[21] Prints were produced in both 8" x 10" and 4.5" x 3.5" formats, the latter also available on thinner paper suitable for scrapbooking, and each print was accompanied by an "Outline for Picture Study" that included the biography of the artist, a discussion of the work, and a lesson plan suitable for use in the classroom. The selection of work for the 1920s reproduction program leaned heavily on twentieth-century artists, including Homer Watson, Horatio Walker, Clarence Gagnon, Tom Thomson, and Group of Seven members J.E.H. MacDonald and Arthur Lismer; by the 1930s the list had expanded to include more members of the Group, including Fred Varley and A.Y. Jackson, as well as James Wilson Morrice. As Zemans's analysis makes clear, the impact of the gallery's reproduction program in establishing a canon of Canadian art firmly rooted in images of the central Canadian wilderness cannot be underestimated: the series included no urban scenes, few peopled landscapes outside stereotyped views of *habitants* in Quebec rural villages, and relied exclusively on the work of artists from Quebec and Ontario. This latter exclusion of work from eastern and western Canada appears to have provoked little protest from those regions despite the fact that the series was heavily marketed to, and adopted by, provincial school boards across the country as an integral component to increasing the Canadian content of public school curricula. Saskatchewan's Minister of Education John Huff was the exception, writing to McCurry in 1933 to request that *The Ferry Trail* by Augustus Kenderdine be included as an example of "a typical Saskatchewan scene, painted by a Saskatchewan artist."[22] The request was unsuccessful but in 1941, a postcard-sized reproduction of James Henderson's *The End of Winter* made the cut.

The power of reproductions to shape Canadians' knowledge of Canadian art can also be traced in the joint program of the National Gallery and graphic art company Sampson-Matthews from the 1940s through the 1960s that produced over one hundred large-scale silkscreen prints that circulated more broadly, from schools and Canadian public institutions, to army barracks overseas during the Second World War. Here again, Zemans's scholarship establishes the pivotal effect of these reproductions in cementing the National Gallery's ability to determine a national aesthetic that continued to privilege the "wilderness ethos" established by Group members.[23] Despite a somewhat expanded roster that included the work of artists from western Canada and the Maritimes, the prints are integral to the historiographical process designed to build a distinctly Canadian art historical narrative that privileged the landscape of the Canadian Shield and the artists of central Canada, supported by the exhibiting activities of the National Gallery. As Zemans notes, the works selected for the gallery-sponsored reproduction programs became the pool from which images were selected for reproduction in magazines, newspapers, and requested for exhibition, influencing the story of Canadian art for generations to come.

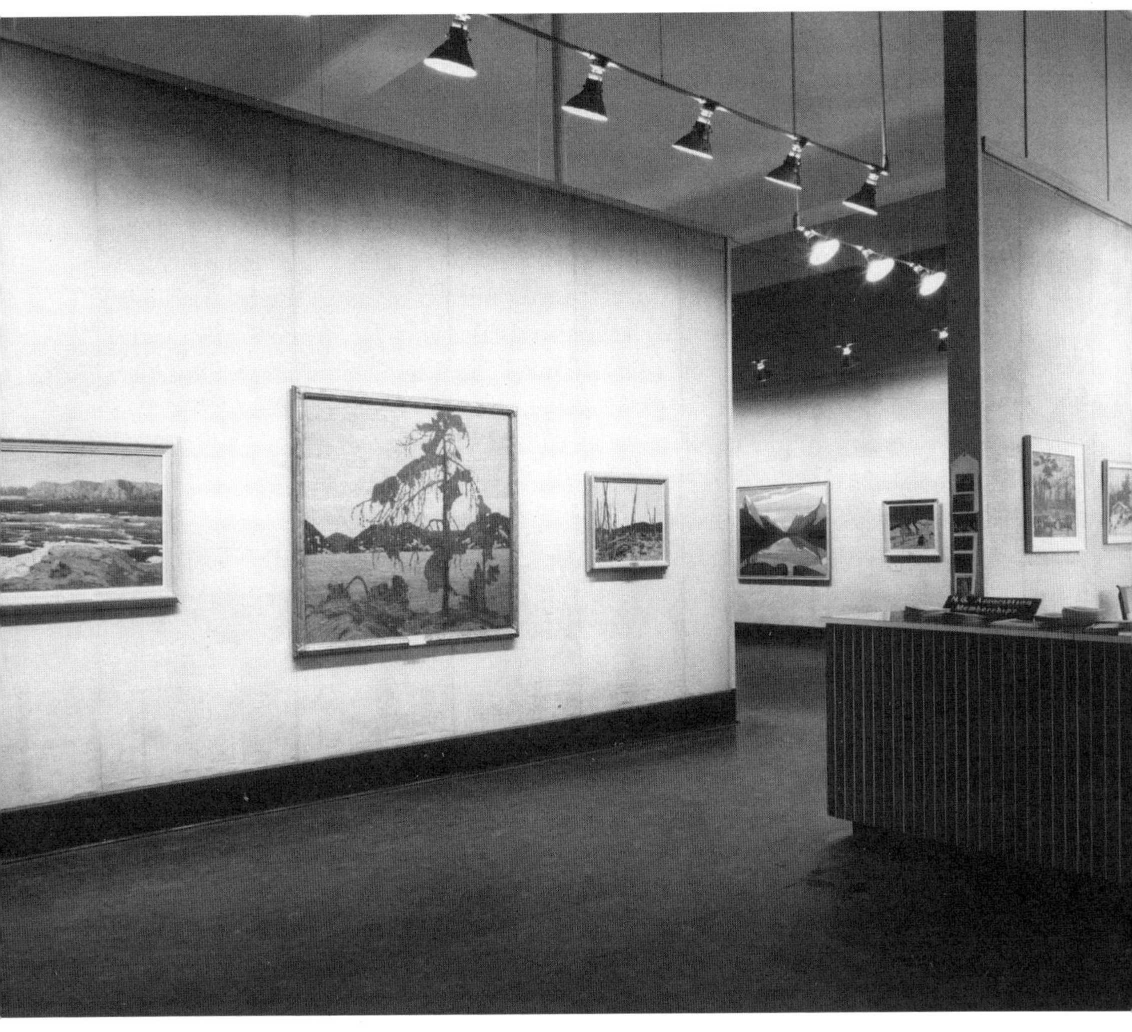

2.5 | National Gallery of Canada, Victoria Memorial Museum Building, entrance and reception desk, 1959. Key works by Tom Thomson and Lawren Harris greet visitors, along with a display of postcards of works from the NGC's Canadian collection available for sale.

Although seen by fewer people, the extended loan of works from the National Gallery's permanent collection was arguably a more important means by which the gallery was able to overcome the limits of its location in Ottawa and achieve its mandate of reaching Canadians across the country. For unlike the reproductions whose scale and medium rendered them more transitory, the paintings circulated throughout the country brought with them the impact and the aura of the original work of art and were highly sought after by groups attempting to establish an art gallery in their community. In 1912 and 1913, letters had been received from members of the Industrial Exhibition Committees of Winnipeg and Edmonton respectively, requesting short-term loans of works for summer exhibitions.[24] The National Gallery refused both requests stating its concerns over the risk to the paintings in transit and the precedent that such a loan would set. There was also worry that even the temporary removal of any works from the NGC's meagre collection would reflect badly on the display in Ottawa. As Brown wrote Sir Edmund Walker, chairman of the Advisory Arts Council in 1912, "The time has not yet arrived when the absence of important pictures would not detract from the value of our exhibition here and this I consider we have no right to do. Also these requests once granted are likely to shade off into others of a more informal and even private nature."[25] By 1913, however, the promise of a National Gallery of Canada Act suggested that a loan program would be a feasible undertaking for the gallery as part of its service as a national institution. Indeed, the report of the Department of Public Works for 1913–14 introduced the loan exhibition program and stated that it would be the best way to demonstrate the quality of Canadian art and to encourage individual Canadians to purchase in that area. It also presented loan exhibitions as a means of encouraging the formation of art societies and institutions across the country and thereby the appreciation and collection of Canadian art.[26] As stated in the 1914–15 report on the activities of the gallery, "It is the policy of the National Gallery in this matter to try to arrange a loan of pictures to any art body in the Dominion which possesses proper facilities for exhibiting them and can meet the moderate expenses of transportation and insurance. By this means, the examples of Canadian art purchased by the National Gallery will circulate throughout the country, and a better understanding of the achievements of Canadian artists will be gained."[27] Interest in the scheme by art associations across the country was immediate, and in 1914, three loan exhibitions were arranged for Winnipeg, Hamilton, and Saint John, featuring between twenty and twenty-five "Canadian and foreign pictures."[28] By the summer of 1917 the loan exhibition program was in full swing with year-long loans set up for Halifax, Sherbrooke, Winnipeg, Moose Jaw, and Fort William (now Thunder Bay), and a set of paintings slated to go to Calgary, Edmonton, Brandon, Regina, Saskatoon, and Prince Albert as part of the Western Canada Fairs Association's summer exhibitions. Shorter loans of drawings, lithographs, and paintings were arranged for venues in Ottawa, Montreal, Toronto, and Vancouver.[29] The NGC's sudden enthusiasm for the loan program was to a large degree occasioned by necessity: in 1916, fire in the Centre Block forced Parliament to find temporary quarters and the National Gallery's rooms in the Victoria Memorial Museum Building were viewed as ideal. With the gallery's removal, the loan program was the only means by which any works from the permanent collection could be seen, and the gallery consequently increased the number of exhibitions it could supply as well as the locations to which it would send pictures.

The criteria for receiving loan exhibitions were clear: the "proper facilities for exhibition" noted in the 1913–14 report specifically meant a fireproof building, display spaces that were consistently monitored, and the presence of an individual with some knowledge of art who could supervise the unpacking and hanging of the pictures. The Carnegie Corporation's sponsorship of library construction across Canada in the 1910s had ensured that most cities and towns in Canada had a stone public library building that more than fulfilled the need for a fireproof building and had spaces suitable for the hanging of medium-sized pictures.[30] Other spaces approved for the display of the loan collections included town halls, industrial exhibition spaces, civic auditoria, and department stores. Members of local art associations, who normally requested the loans, were considered to have enough knowledge to be entrusted with unpacking, hanging, and then repacking the paintings, and instructions were sent with each exhibition to remind those responsible of proper practices. Faith in these individuals was often strained: correspondence between the National Gallery and the various loan recipients are full of admonitions about the careful packing of pictures and the need for constant supervision of the works once on display; return mail featured heartfelt apologies from librarians and art association members for damage to frames or to protective glass incurred during transit or when works were hung. As the loan program grew, the National Gallery began sending out condition report forms that loan recipients were required to fill out and return upon receipt of the paintings. The gallery also requested that the display of loan collections include information about the artist and the works – either through labels or typed lists – gleaned

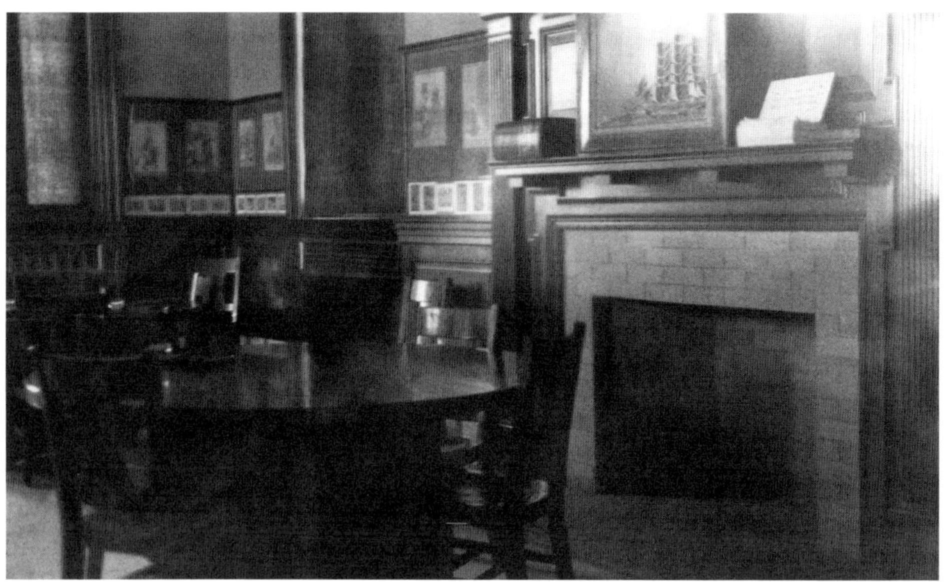

2.6 | Moose Jaw Library, the North Room with display of loan exhibition from the National Gallery, 1913.

from the accompanying catalogues, and that any publicity related to the exhibition was to underscore that the paintings were courtesy of the National Gallery of Canada.

As was seen in Chapter 1, the paintings loaned by the National Gallery were fundamental to the exhibition programs of all the nascent galleries in western Canada, in many places providing the only artworks available for display. Even in a city such as Winnipeg, which had established an art gallery as early as 1912 and had been accumulating works for its permanent collection since that date, the NGC loans remained a cornerstone of the institution's exhibition program for decades and were relied on to present examples of recent Canadian art otherwise unavailable to Winnipeg's citizens and artists. For Brown, this exposure to Canadian art was a key component of the loan exhibitions' ability to fulfill the NGC's mandate to educate the public and to encourage collecting in that area. The success of the loan program was immediate and it continued to grow exponentially over the next decade: in 1917, twelve loan exhibitions were sent to locations from Halifax to Vancouver; by 1929 the gallery was sending 31 loan exhibitions across the country, comprising a total of 2,000 paintings; by 1936, the number of loan exhibitions rose to 101,

an increase of 225 percent from 1929.[31] More significantly for the staff
at the National Gallery, correspondence regarding loan exhibitions increased even more drastically during that period: from 2,598 letters a
year in 1929 to 10,958 in 1935.[32]

The works sent out for loan were predominantly by Canadian artists
and consisted exclusively of two-dimensional works. The artists represented a mix of contemporary figures from all the major artists groups –
the RCA, the Ontario Society of Artists, and eventually the Group of Seven
and members of the Beaver Hall group – with a particular emphasis on
landscape and occasionally portraiture. In addition to the long-term loan
exhibitions it provided, the NGC also facilitated the circulation of exhibitions organized by artist groups such as the RCA, the Group of Seven,
and the Canadian Society of Painters in Water Colour, but its main focus

2.7 | Map of National Gallery of Canada loan exhibitions, 1934–35, from the NGC's
Annual Report, 1934–35.

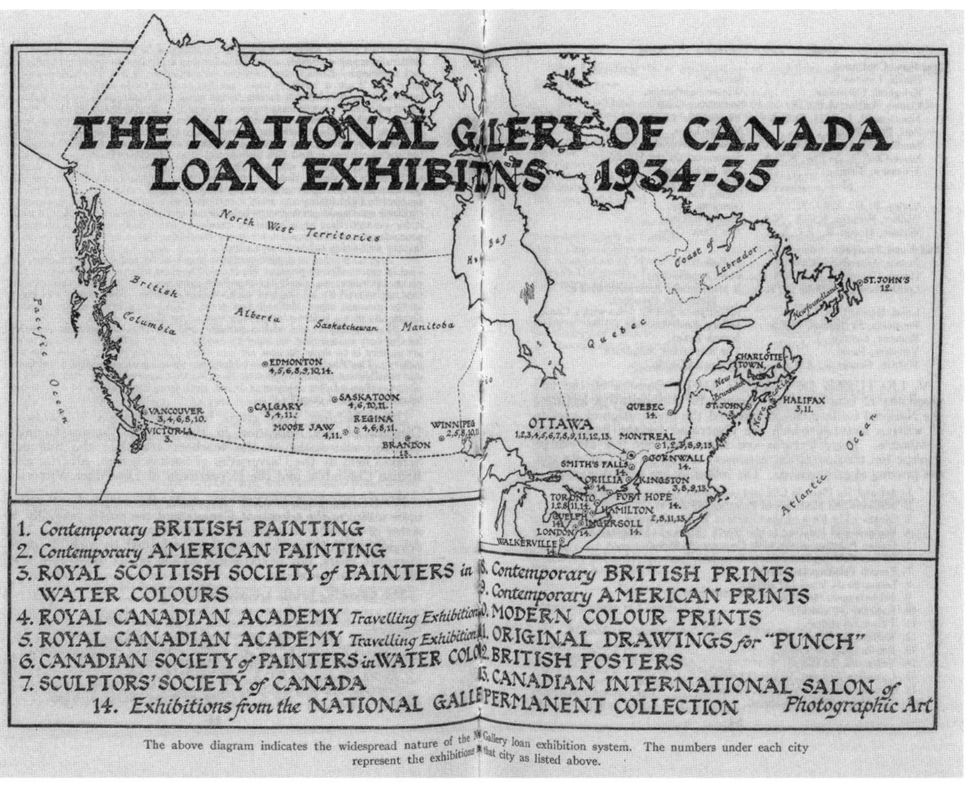

remained the presentation of its own collections. The 1917 loan to Moose Jaw is characteristic of the loan exhibitions, and included work by Frederick Bell-Smith, Archibald Browne, Franklin Brownell, William Brymner (two paintings), Georges Chavignaud, Charles De Belle, Ernest Fosbery, Daniel Fowler, James Graham, John Hammond, Otto Jacobi, C.W. Jefferys, Elizabeth McGillivray Knowles, André Lapine, Arthur Lismer, Laura Muntz, Lucius O'Brien, J.H. Sandham, Owen Staples, and Mary Wrinch. In accordance with the practice of sending primarily medium-sized pictures, the largest painting of the group was F.M. Bell-Smith's *Mists and Glaciers of the Selkirks* (1911) measuring 34 x 50 inches. A sense of the consistency in the kind of works selected for the loan exhibitions can be seen in the list of artists included in the 1925 loan to Moose Jaw, many of who were included in the 1917 loan: Harry Britton, Frederick Challener, Gertrude Cutts, Georges Delfosse, Tudor Hart, A.Y. Jackson, L.M. Kilpin, J.E.H. MacDonald, Manly MacDonald, Valentine Molins, Laura Muntz, Ivan Neilson, Lorna Reid, George Reid, Mary Hiester Reid, Albert Robinson, Percy Woodcock, and Mary Wrinch. And while host institutions attempted to influence the choice of works sent their way – the trustees of the Moose Jaw Library, for example, asked for work by Paul Peel in 1919 – the National Gallery fully controlled the composition of the loan collections, with Brown arguing that "it would be impossible for the various exhibitors of the National Gallery loans to choose their own pictures but when a preference is expressed I always try and meet it as far as possible."[33]

As the National Gallery received more and more requests for loans from communities across western Canada, its staff began to develop a kind of travel itinerary for the exhibitions. The collection of works sent to Winnipeg, for example, would move on to Moose Jaw at year's end, while Moose Jaw's loan would be sent on to Regina, and so on. Such a circuit meant that paintings would be away from Ottawa for years at a time and when the gallery's quarters were occupied by Parliament, such an extended absence was possible. In 1920, however, loan recipients received a letter requesting the return of all paintings so that an inventory and assessment of the collections could be made and the best work retained for exhibition in the newly revamped galleries at the Victoria Memorial Museum Building.[34] Five years later, a full re-evaluation of the loan program was made as the wear and tear on the paintings and the labour involved in organizing and shipping taxed the limited resources of the

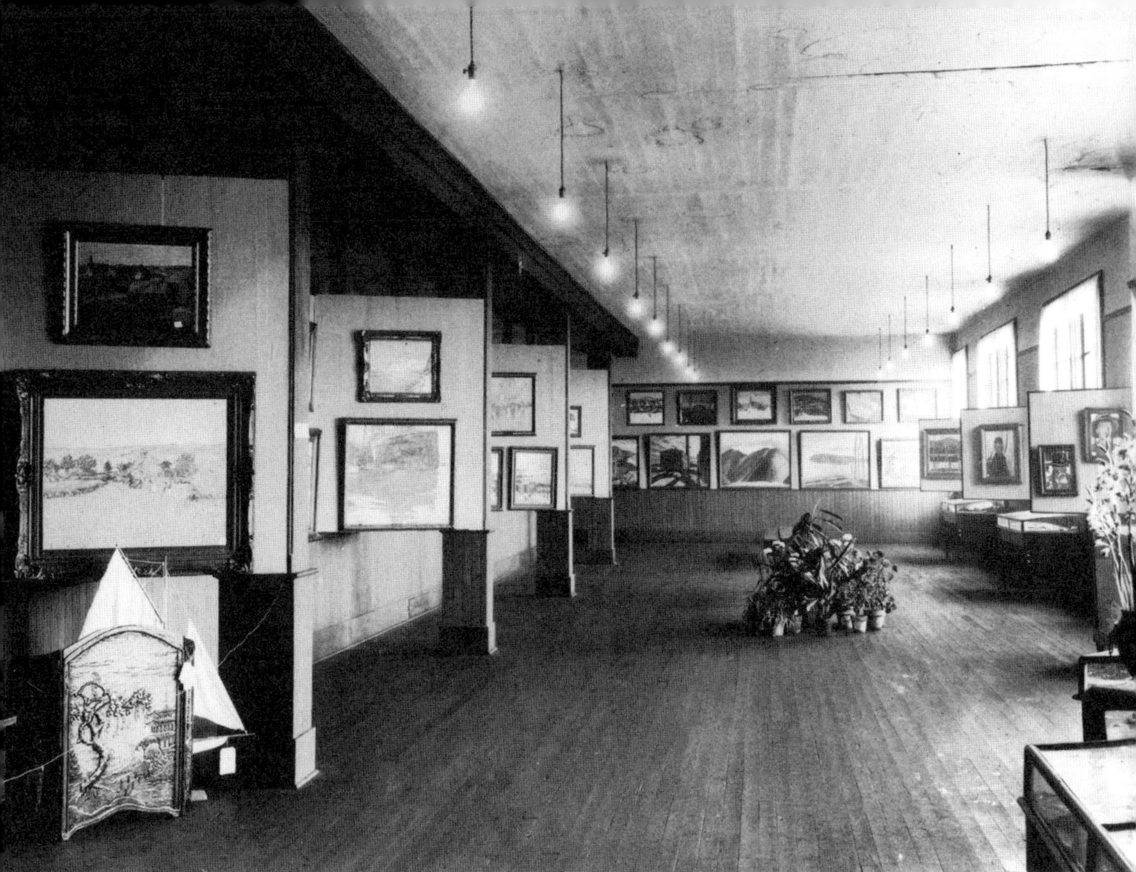

2.8 | John Vanderpant, Loan exhibition in New Westminster, BC, 1928. Loan exhibitions were presented in a range of settings, from provincial exhibitions or fairs, as shown here, to civic buildings such as libraries and city halls.

National Gallery.[35] A survey was sent to all loan recipients requesting information on the impact of the National Gallery loans on local activities. In addition to obtaining data about the number of loans obtained and the nature of the exhibition space, the survey specifically asked whether attendance at exhibitions had increased over the period of the loan program; whether public lectures on art or other exhibitions had been arranged; whether any efforts had been made to build a public collection of art in the city; and finally whether there had been any attempt to interest the municipal government in the art activities of the association. On the basis of the answers to these questions, the National Gallery sought to "estimate the extent to which [its] loans have advanced the cause of art in your locality and to determine the advisability of continuation of the work."[36] Although not explicitly stated in the letter, the inferred question was whether local organizations were any closer to obtaining permanent facilities to house and display works of art. It must be remembered that every exhibition sent to western Canada prior to 1931 was shown in a makeshift gallery in a building erected for entirely different purposes – whether the public library, city hall, or industrial exhibition rooms. Concerned for the safety of its collection, and weary of being the sole supplier of artworks to the nation, the National Gallery wanted to ensure that as many municipalities as possible started building their own permanent collections and creating fireproof and supervised spaces where loaned paintings and works on paper would be secure. In correspondence with A.H. Gibbard of the Moose Jaw Public Library, which had received loans since 1916, H.O. McCurry regularly asked whether the library trustees had given further consideration to the addition of a room for the display of art, as well as whether a proposed scheme to buy a painting a year had yielded any results. Gibbard's silence on the matter indicates that Moose Jaw's city council – in line with other small municipalities – regarded the establishment of an art gallery as a low priority.

The National Gallery continued to be concerned about the reliability of the organizations hosting loans throughout the 1930s and 1940s. While paintings had been lent to all centres in the first years of the program, increased pressure for loans from communities across the country led the National Gallery to restrict loans of works on canvas to larger centres with permanent facilities, and to send reproductions, posters, and prints to smaller organizations. The hiring of Kathleen Fenwick as the gallery's full-time curator of prints and drawings in 1928 facilitated the circulation of print exhibitions and also increased the range of prints from which loan exhibitions could be organized. Reproductions, meanwhile, became an expedient solution to the high number of loan requests as the facsimile collections owned by the National Gallery were extensive and could satisfy the many requests for works by "European masters." Whether it was the loan of paintings or the circulation of reproductions and prints, the National Gallery's annual reports of the late 1920s emphasized the valuable results proceeding from the loan program:

> Not only are the cities and towns who are sufficiently interested
> to secure them kept abreast of the times by knowing what the
> best Canadian artists are doing but local interest is being continu-
> ously stimulated, art societies, associations and schools are being

established and collections started and the condition is being approached at least where Canadian artistic talent can be educated and developed without that departure from the country which so often leads to permanent residence abroad and to the incalculable loss of genius to the country.[37]

The loan exhibitions were thus characterized as having a double effect: on one hand, they exposed the Canadian public to the work of their own artists through the exhibition of original paintings sent by the National Gallery, and at the same time the loan exhibitions were seen to foster local communities' desires to set up their own art institutions that would in turn encourage local artists. Western Canada in particular was seen to benefit from this program: the annual reports as well as correspondence between Brown, McCurry, and the NGC trustees reiterated the necessity of sending paintings to western Canada where the growth of local interest was described as "remarkable" and worthy of as much encouragement as possible.[38] Indeed, while the outreach activities of the National Gallery extended from coast to coast, the less established cities and towns of western Canada seem to have preoccupied gallery staff more than any

2.9 | Mrs R.W. Hawley and Mrs W.A. Wood of the Brandon Art Club putting up a collection of modern French paintings from the National Gallery. Women were central to the circulation of art in Canada, whether as members of art clubs or as active workers in museum auxiliary societies.

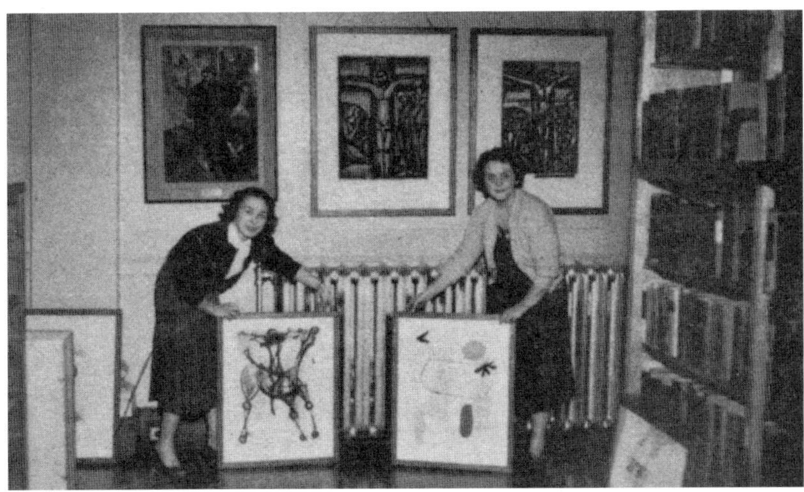

other region, prompting frequent visits of gallery staff and regular mentions of progress in the area in the NGC's annual reports. Although this situation may have had much to do with the region's geographical distance from the national capital, a deep-seated assumption that western Canada remained a pioneering region still in need of civilizing doubtless contributed to the gallery's interests in the area.

The Importance of Personal Contact: Lectures and Tours

The National Gallery's loans were supported by visits from officials and sponsored guests throughout the 1920s and 1930s. In 1921 Eric Brown and his wife, Maud, travelled through western Canada, stopping at Fort William, Winnipeg, Regina, Calgary, Vancouver, New Westminster, and Victoria, and giving lectures on "the progress and strength of native Canadian art and the necessity of becoming acquainted with it and of providing local means for study and the education of artistic talent."[39] By this time, the loan program had been in place for over eight years and Brown doubtless wanted to see for himself the spaces where works from the gallery's collections were displayed. The tour also had an important public relations function in that a visit from such an important figure as the director of the National Gallery served as an indication of the esteem with which the host institution or association was held. In 1922 H.O. McCurry undertook a follow-up visit to Vancouver, Victoria, Calgary, Medicine Hat, Moose Jaw, and Winnipeg. His report to Brown emphasized the success of the loan exhibitions at each of these sites, whether in number of visitors or in the influence on local artists of the work of the Canadian artists on display. McCurry's conclusion underscores the perceived significance of the loan program as well as the work that remained to be done: "The awakened interest throughout the country, largely due to the assistance rendered by the National Gallery is most encouraging. However, it would seem that certain 'follow up' measures be taken from time to time such as lectures, etc., to ensure the maximum of benefit from the exhibition work and to make sure that all loans are fulfilling their purpose."[40]

Brown went out west again in the summer of 1927, this time at the request of Regina-based trustee Norman MacKenzie who wanted to see better representation of western Canadian interests in the nation's capital. The only member of the Board of Trustees from outside Ottawa-

Montreal-Toronto,[41] and with a longstanding interest in forming a museum in Regina (see Chapter 1), MacKenzie was a strong advocate for western Canadian interests and had supported a motion to revise the selection process for the NGC's annual exhibition of Canadian art to regionally located juries of artists. Coming shortly after his appointment to the NGC Board in 1925, MacKenzie's invitation to Brown to encourage interest in art in western Canada by explaining what the National Gallery could do to assist the building of collections by local art societies is a clear indication of MacKenzie's advocacy for the region. His hope that Brown's visit might result in an invitation to representatives of western art societies to meet in Ottawa to discuss collaboration with the national institution also demonstrates his recognition of the central role played by the NGC in guiding the development of art across Canada.[42]

The visit of NGC representatives in the regions was an opportunity for isolated gallery directors and art association presidents to obtain guidance on their activities and support for their endeavours from a trusted source. A sense of this can be obtained from a newspaper account of McCurry's visit to Edmonton in 1931, which described the assistant director's presence as providing "comfort and inspiration for those who labor [sic] in the cause of art in Edmonton."[43] A year earlier, McCurry had been quoted as finding the west "hungry for art and spiritual things,"[44] an attitude he found encouraging in his national work. In these meetings, McCurry would be asked for his advice on installation practices, art education classes, fundraising, and acquisitions. More generally, however, the visits provided the leaders of fledgling institutions the encouragement that they were not receiving from any other source. As funding for permanent buildings failed to materialize for art associations across western Canada, and as money for daily operations from all levels of government remained confined to in-kind contributions of space and utilities, art groups relied on the presence of representatives of the National Gallery to draw attention to their activities and to advocate to the members of the public and city council the importance of art to "cultural progress."[45] The NGC leadership's interest in western Canada is noteworthy, particularly if compared with its relations with other regions of the country. As noted above, Brown and McCurry made numerous tours of cities from Winnipeg westwards and the correspondence with those centres was extensive. While the gallery circulated loan exhibitions to the Maritimes and to smaller centres in Ontario and Quebec, these centres also benefitted from exhibitions from other institutions. In the 1930s and 1940s, Walter Abell's connections through the Carnegie Corporation facilitated travelling exhibitions from the American Federation of Artists as well as from the College Art Association, while Clarence and Alice Lusk Webster's connections to the Boston Museum of Fine Arts and the Royal Ontario Museum ensured significant exchanges;[46] from 1944, the Art Gallery of Toronto circulated small educational exhibitions to centres within a three-hundred-mile radius of Toronto. With art centres of a comparable size in central Canada and a longer history of art education and exhibition in the Maritimes through the Nova Scotia College of Art and the Owens Art Gallery – both established at the end of the nineteenth century – these regions required less support from the National Gallery than western Canada whose arts organizations struggled to find civic and provincial support for many decades. Rightly or wrongly, western Canada was viewed as a region in the process of becoming civilized, its pioneer roots and materialistic outlook dominating central-Canadian perspectives of "the west" well into the 1950s.

For the National Gallery, visits to regional centres resulted in personal contact and reliable information on the situations of organizations with which relationships were largely correspondence based. McCurry's reports on his trips to western Canada in 1921, 1930, 1931, 1935, and 1936 contain extensive discussions of the strengths and weaknesses of the various venues. Of particular relevance for McCurry was the extent to which it appeared that the organizations he visited had built on the gallery's loan program: how much, in other words, they had expanded their own public collections or how closer they were to establishing their own permanent gallery space. This assessment of individual venues' growing autonomy was a key factor in the gallery's future dealings with regional institutions. As the number of requests for loan exhibitions increased, the National Gallery more frequently wrote responses that emphasized the temporary nature of the loan exhibition program, that it was not intended to provide remote spaces with exhibitions in perpetuity, but that rather it was intended to jump-start local collecting, both public and private, if not the creation of a stand-alone or fully functioning permanent exhibition space. The tours, then, were as much a means for National Gallery staff to inspect far-flung venues as they were an opportunity to apply pressure on the leaders of arts organizations as well as on members of civic governments to establish autonomous institutions.

In some cases, however, visits from National Gallery representatives were a means of ensuring that organizations receiving exhibitions were respecting the conditions of the loans, or that potential protests against the authority of the National Gallery were kept in check. In 1930 McCurry was dispatched to Vancouver following complaints from members of the BC Art League over the manner in which works had been selected for the *Annual Exhibition of Canadian Art* organized by the National Gallery. Specifically, members complained that none of the chartered art societies in the province had been contacted regarding the process of identifying works for consideration, and that F.H. Varley, "a newcomer … holding aloof from most of the art societies of the province,"[47] had been given sole responsibility for selecting works to be forwarded to the National Gallery. As a result, the few paintings from the province included in the 1930 *Annual Exhibition of Canadian Art* were not considered to reflect the work being produced in British Columbia. Coming on the heels of concerns over the selections for the 1927 Jeu de Paume exhibition of Canadian art in Paris, which itself had recalled the criticism of the artists included in the 1924 Canadian art section at Wembley (most famously from the RCA, but also from artists in Western Canada who felt completely excluded from the process), McCurry's visit was as much a fact-finding mission as it was a gesture of conciliation to the British Columbia artists. McCurry's report of this trip clearly outlines his perception of the situation: a small professional art association – identified as the BC Society of Fine Arts – incapable of handling the requirements of increased interest in art in the province, and an inadequate exhibition space for the display of National Gallery loans. The exhibition space in question was managed by the larger BC Art League and while its new premises were considered an improvement on its previous accommodations, it was still insufficient for the presentation of paintings from the national collections, particularly when mixed with what McCurry considered to be the less than accomplished renderings of local artists. McCurry's report of activities in Vancouver nevertheless ended with a note of hope for future exhibitions in the province in the form of the proposal by Henry Stone and his associates – many of whom were members of the BC Art League – to build an art gallery able to provide "satisfactory accommodation" for any loan by the National Gallery. In the meantime, McCurry proposed the formation of a western Canadian jury – rather than a single individual – that would be responsible for overseeing the selection of works by BC artists for the annual exhibition. This jury would consist of Thomas Fripp, president of the BC Society of Fine Arts (ironically described by McCurry as "the only important professional art body in British Columbia,"[48] despite his misgivings about the quality of its members' work) and one of the main critics of the 1930 exhibition selection process; Charles Scott, the "very successful" director of the Vancouver School of Art; and F.H. Varley, chosen because of his status as the only member of the RCA in British Columbia. The jury as constituted was accepted by artists in Vancouver – including the members of the BC Art League who presented McCurry with an honorary membership – and the protest against the selection method of works for the annual exhibition was quashed.[49] As will be discussed later in the chapter and the next, the selection process for national exhibitions was particularly fraught for artists in western Canada whose geographical distance from Ottawa often left them feeling overlooked and ignored by the tastemakers of central Canada.

Inasmuch as visits from the National Gallery's director and his assistant were widely sought after from the regions, many organizations were just as pleased to receive experts who were sent across the country by the NGC to give lectures on various art topics. Through the 1920s and 1930s the following, mostly British, figures lectured across western Canada: W.G. Constable, director of The Courtauld Institute, in 1933; BBC lecturer J.E. Barton in 1935; Eric Newton, art critic for the London *Times*, in 1936–37; art historians Stewart Dick in 1928–29 and Julius Held in 1936–37. Carnegie funding also allowed the gallery to send various art education experts to the regions, including Marion Richardson, art inspector for London County (UK) Regional Schools in 1934, Arthur Lismer, head of art education at the Art Gallery of Toronto in 1932 and 1935, and Charles Scott of the Vancouver School of Art in 1935. Although presented as part of the gallery's mandate to bring information and knowledge about art to the country as a whole, the provision of lecturers was part of what W.G. Constable would describe as the important "evangelistic work" of the gallery:[50] a way of advertising and reinforcing the loan exhibition program but an equally central component of the NGC's strategy to assert its national leadership in matters of art in Canada. Even when a lecturer was in the employ of another Canadian art museum, as was the case with Arthur Lismer, for the purposes of the tour, he was consistently presented under the auspices of the National Gallery. For the lectures as much as for the loans, the sponsorship of the National Gallery associated the presence of the art expert with the national institution, functioning as yet another way of keeping the NGC in the public eye.

The gallery was also effective in positioning its other activities to support its status as the primary source of information on art in the country as can be seen in its organization of exhibitions of Canadian art for both national and international circulation. The selections for the Canadian art section of the 1924 and 1925 British Empire exhibitions at Wembley, the 1927 *Exposition d'art canadien* at the Jeu de Paume in Paris, and the *Century of Canadian Art* exhibition at the Tate in 1936 have become touchstones in Canadian art history's narrative of the struggle for power between more conservative members of the RCA and the National Gallery over what works would be selected to represent the nation's art. But these exhibitions were fundamental at the time in underscoring the National Gallery's efforts to firmly establish a *national* aesthetic. As Leslie Dawn has argued in his analysis of the Jeu de Paume exhibition, the National Gallery sought to consolidate the vision of a landscape-based Canadian aesthetic presented in the Wembley exhibitions by increasing the proportion of works produced by artists associated with the Group of Seven in the Paris show and by including a retrospective of the work of Tom Thomson.[51] Despite their presentation outside the country, these exhibitions were visible at home through intense newspaper reporting on their reception abroad and on the controversy that many of them raised in art circles. In addition, the National Gallery ensured the relevance of these international exhibitions to its work at home by including excerpts of reviews in its annual reports and stressing the importance of such events in making Canada and its art better known abroad. Even in the case of the Paris exhibition, where the reviews in the French press were less than laudatory and misread Brown's carefully orchestrated narrative of the autonomous growth of Canada's national school, the portions of the reviews selected for reprint in the gallery's 1927–28 *Annual Report* focused almost exclusively on the few positive comments made about Canada's landscape school and ignored the praise given by Parisian art critics to the work of James Wilson Morrice whose retrospective exhibition had been reluctantly accommodated by Brown at the request of the French authorities.

If the international exhibitions created a positive image for the National Gallery's ability to promote Canadian art abroad, the annual exhibitions of Canadian art held at home between 1925 and 1933 were equally important for asserting the role of the national institution in determining what constituted the best in contemporary Canadian art. Selections for the annual exhibitions were at first made from the annual exhibitions held by the major exhibiting societies such as the RCA and the Ontario Society of Artists, under the assumption that this would be "an exact reflection of the public exhibitions held by the various recognized art bodies."[52] As can be imagined, given the Ontario- and Quebec-centred membership of these societies, the annual exhibitions were not necessarily inclusive of artistic production from across the country. The Board of Trustees amended the selection process for the annual exhibitions in 1929 to "make the exhibition as fully representative as possible of all sections of the Dominion"[53] by establishing artist-based juries to be assisted by the director, and to appoint those juries outside central Canada "where required";[54] but many western Canadian artists continued to feel that the National Gallery was insufficiently familiar with the work being undertaken in the regions as evidenced by the BC Art League's protest discussed earlier. Similar sentiments would be voiced by artists and artist groups in the other western provinces, many of who wrote to the NGC to request assistance in getting their work seen by gallery representatives. For the NGC, the annual exhibitions provided the means to acquire works for its collection, and more importantly, they functioned as showcases for contemporary Canadian art, not only in Ottawa, but nationally. Seemingly ignoring the protests over the selection process – described as "misunderstandings of the work of the National Gallery" – the 1930–31 *Annual Report* emphasized the impact of the annual exhibitions on western Canada in particular, noting their role in stimulating interest in Canadian art among artists and the general public while at the same time observing the need for "assistance and guidance from competent authority on the part of growing art organizations and galleries in Western Canada to ensure the best results from their work."[55] The *Annual Report*'s recommendations to address these concerns included increasing loan exhibitions of contemporary art from Canada, Britain, and Europe throughout Canada, but particularly to western Canada; sending an official of the National Gallery to the region to assist in the selection of works for the annual exhibition; and if possible sending the annual exhibition on tour in all or parts of western Canada for display.[56] The sharp reduction in the gallery's appropriation fund in 1933 signalled the end of the annual exhibitions until the concept was revived in 1953,[57] but as will be seen in subsequent chapters, western Canadian artists would continue to voice criticisms that their work was being ignored by the National Gallery throughout the 1940s and 1950s.

Distributing Funds: The Carnegie Corporation and Canadian Museums

Another significant area of support to regional art galleries from the National Gallery was the allocation of funds. Although it could be argued that the loan program was a form of subsidy for art institutions outside Canada's three largest cities, the National Gallery did not hand out its own funds to other art organizations. Functioning with the smallest of appropriations from Parliament,[58] the gallery was itself in constant negotiations with the Ministry of Public Works to obtain enough money to maintain its exhibition and educational programs and for acquisitions of works for the permanent collection. While these requests for increased funds fell largely on deaf ears at the governmental level, despite the close relationship in the 1930s between H.S. Southam, chair of the NGC's Board of Trustees and Prime Minister Mackenzie King,[59] other organizations were more receptive, specifically the New York–based Carnegie Corporation.

The Carnegie Corporation's philanthropy has already been mentioned in connection to the funding it provided for the construction of libraries in Canada, and along with the Rockefeller Foundation, it had been distributing grants to Canadian educational organizations – specifically libraries and universities – since the early 1910s. Dalhousie University in Halifax, McGill University in Montreal, the University of Toronto, and the University of Alberta in Edmonton received millions of dollars over a twenty-year period to establish departments of medicine, library programs, and extension departments.[60] As Jeffrey Brison argues in *Rockefeller, Carnegie, and Canada: American Philanthropy and the Arts and Letters in Canada*, Carnegie and Rockefeller philanthropic support for culture and education in Canada should be understood less as an imposition of American cultural hegemony than as a recognition of the commonality of cultural values and beliefs among the elites of both countries. Indeed, as Brison's in-depth study shows, in a period where federal government support for research in the sciences and the arts was non-existent, the funding provided by American philanthropic organizations was enthusiastically welcomed and never seen as contradictory to the nation-building aims of Canada's intellectual and cultural elites. That the philanthropic organizations themselves viewed their grants as contributing to the formation of strong national cultures and organizations further underscores the consonant motivations of elites from both countries to, in the words of the founding document of the Carnegie Corporation, "promote the advancement and diffusion of knowledge and understanding."[61] Indeed, the Carnegie Corporation's establishment of the British Dominions and Colonies Fund in 1911 specifically to address the needs of "like" countries outside the United States is a clear indication of the broad support offered by American philanthropic organizations in the first half of the twentieth century.

While postsecondary education had dominated Carnegie funding priorities for the first decade of the Corporation's existence, the appointment of Frederick Keppel as president in 1922 resulted in a broadening of focus to fund organizations with a wider educational remit. In 1923 Keppel instigated a survey of "The Place of the Arts in American Life" that effectively reviewed programs of instruction in art and art history at postsecondary institutions in the United States and Canada.[62] Finding that such instruction was lacking, Keppel initiated several programs that sought to increase the number of courses in fine art at North American universities and train the individuals to teach them. Between 1925 and 1931, fellowships were offered to promising students in the United States and Canada for the museum courses offered at Princeton and Harvard, resulting in what one later Carnegie report described as a "'Who's Who' of the outstanding art historians and museum and gallery directors of their generation."[63] Another program went further in ensuring that the fine arts were taught at the postsecondary level, this time providing funding to select institutions to create art departments or to establish chairs in fine arts. In Canada money was given to Queen's University in 1933 to hire Goodridge Roberts to teach a course in painting, leading to the formation of the Department of Art; the University of Toronto, McMaster University in Hamilton, and Acadia University in Wolfville, Nova Scotia, each received an endowment for a professorship in fine arts, allowing these institutions to bring in leading art historians from Britain (John Alford from The Courtauld Institute to Toronto) and the United States (Lester Longman from Princeton to McMaster, and Walter Abell from Antioch College to Acadia); the University of Alberta received funding to develop an adult education program in the fine arts resulting in the Banff School of Fine Arts.[64] Universities that were not fortunate enough to be endowed with a research chair were nevertheless given support for higher-level art and art history instruction through the Carnegie Corporation's distribution of Teaching Equipment Sets or "art study materials," a massive collection of almost 200 books, 1,800 black-and-white reproductions of works of art, and print and textile samples, which were intended to provide the building blocks for the in-depth study of the art of all periods.[65] With this sponsorship, the Carnegie Corporation saw itself as assisting in the spread of elite cultural values by consolidating a network of institutions that would build high culture in Canada. The list of funded universities reveals that institutions in both the centre and the regions were given support, an approach that can equally be seen in the Corporation's pattern of funding in the United States.[66] As many writers on Carnegie funding have noted, however, while the leaders of the Corporation liked to spread the money to as wide a range of organizations as possible, they also saw the importance and usefulness of a strong central administering apparatus with which they could work on a day-to-day basis. By 1933, the central organizing group in Canada was the National Gallery.

The Carnegie Corporation's interest in museums and art galleries was implicit in its funding of art education programs in the 1920s when it encouraged recipients of its art training fellowships to take Princeton's or Harvard's museum course. The public nature of museum institutions was also fundamental to the Carnegie Corporation's aim to increase public access to education in the arts. In 1931, Keppel invited Sir Henry Miers, president of the British Museums Association, and Sidney F. Markham, British Labour MP and secretary of the same association, to undertake a survey of museums in Canada. Miers and Markham had already undertaken a similar survey in Britain in 1931 and would go on to examine the state of museums in "British Africa" (1932), "Ceylon, British Malaya, the West Indies, etc." (1933),[67] and Australia and New Zealand (1934). Their sixty-three-page *Report on the Museums of Canada* remarked on the poverty of the collections of most Canadian museums and the lack of professional standards in their management and display, and noted the lack of collaboration between institutions with the exception of the extension work by the National Gallery and the National Museum. Miers and Markham also bemoaned the dearth of funding accorded to the majority of Canadian institutions remarking that of the 125 museums in

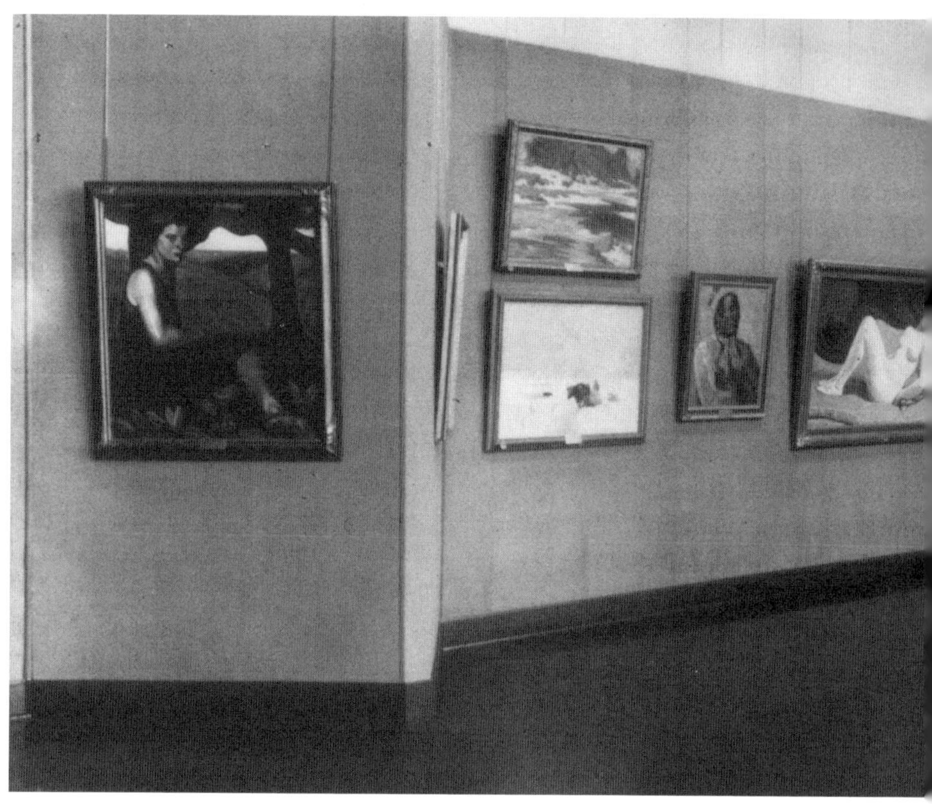

2.10 | Canadian Galleries at the Victoria Memorial Museum Building, 1947. Works by Prudence Heward, Bertram Brooker, LeMoine FitzGerald, A.Y. Jackson, Edwin Holgate, Lawren Harris, and Torrance Newton from the 1920s and 1930s are featured.

Canada, only three had a budget of more than $100,000, while 96 managed to operate with annual expenditures of between $50 and $1,000.[68] Unsurprisingly, the National Gallery received praise for the presentation of its collection, which was considered vastly superior to those of the Art Gallery of Toronto and the Art Association of Montreal. However, the report was emphatic in its view that "taken as a whole, the Dominion provides little to cultivate the appreciation of fine art, and it is a deplorable fact that so many cities of considerable size have nothing to show."[69] In western Canada, the "interesting beginning" made by the Edmonton Museum of Arts was approvingly mentioned as an example of the perseverance of individuals and voluntary associations in the formation of museums in isolated cities, while the newly built Vancouver Art

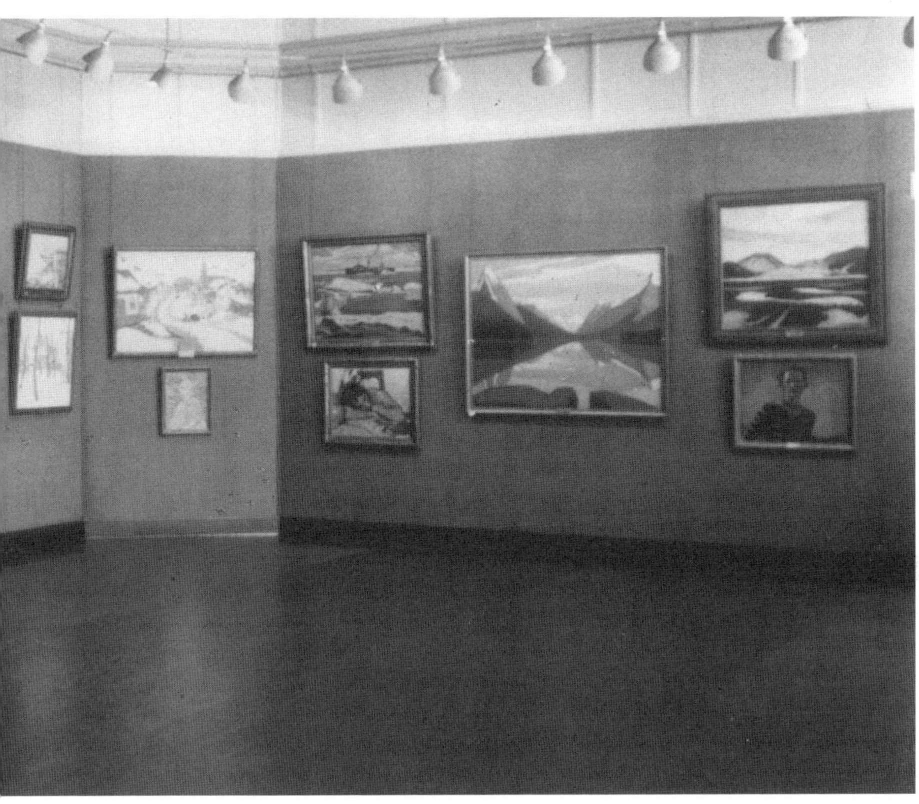

Gallery was cited as an indication of the potential growth of the museum movement in the country. Money and inter-institutional cooperation remained the central barriers to the development of museums across the country, and writing from the perspective of the British context, Miers and Markham made the strong argument that the responsibility for ensuring progress in this field lay with provincial and municipal governments, particularly in the Prairie provinces.[70] On the basis of this report, along with their view of museums as providing the best public exposure to the value inherent in high culture, the Carnegie Corporation directed funds towards Canadian museums.

Carnegie funding began following Eric Brown's request in April 1931 for a $5,000 grant to send NGC–sponsored lecturers on tours of the country, particularly the west, in an effort to "build up an intelligent body of support to these embryo centres of art education."[71] In March and April

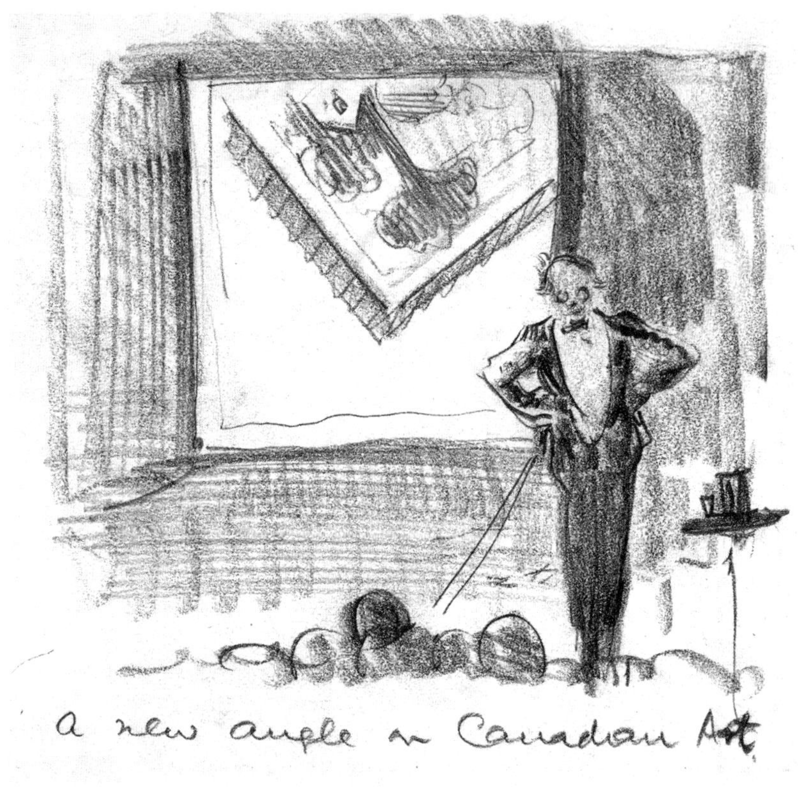

2.11 | Arthur Lismer reflects on his experiences lecturing across the country in *A New Angle on Canadian Art*, 1932.

1932, Arthur Lismer toured western Canada – from Thunder Bay to Victoria – giving talks on such subjects as "The Necessity of Art," "Art and the Community," and "Canadian Painting of Today."[72] The tour was well received by local arts organizations and reinforced the National Gallery's opinion that such visits from gallery representatives did much to support its larger extension activities in the region. By 1933 the Carnegie Corporation provided over $40,000 for art education in Canada, the management of which would be undertaken by the Canadian Museums Committee, a group of men from Canada's elite museum and educational institutions, led by the National Gallery's H.O. McCurry. The members of the committee were Robert Wallace, president of the University of Alberta and future principal of Queen's University; Eric Brown and H.O. McCurry of the National Gallery; Vincent Massey, a trustee of the

Royal Ontario Museum and the National Gallery London; R.W. Brock, former director of the National Museum and a dean at the University of British Columbia; Frank Kermode, director of the Provincial Museum in Victoria; E.L. Judah head curator of McGill University's museums; H.S. Southam, a trustee of the NGC (added to the Committee in 1934); and chairing the committee, Clarence Webster, president of the New Brunswick Museum.[73] The committee ostensibly represented the various regions of the country with members from institutions in central Canada (Quebec and Ontario), the Prairies, British Columbia, and the Maritimes, although given the geographical challenges of meeting on a regular basis, the majority of the decisions were made by an executive committee consisting of Brown, Massey, Southam, and Webster, with McCurry ex officio. As Jeffrey Brison argues, the members of the CMC were selected for their ability to "reproduce and reformulate existing hierarchies of cultural authority"[74] rather than represent the needs of their particular regions. Indeed, their positions within institutions that were invested in the formation of a national culture guaranteed their support for such hierarchies and ensured that the National Gallery would continue to guide the development of museums in the country.

Despite the breadth of membership of the Canadian Museums Committee, it was McCurry who provided direction for its activities: he was the primary liaison between Frederick Keppel, the Carnegie Corporation's president, and the CMC; he selected the members of the committee; and he served as the point of contact for the Canadian institutions and individuals receiving funds. The smaller Executive Committee consisting of Brown, Southam, Webster, and Massey gave McCurry further control over the workings of the CMC and the development of its policies. While placing such a degree of responsibility on one person was a logical administrative decision, that this leadership position was assumed by McCurry rather than the committee's actual chair, Clarence Webster, underscores both the effectiveness of the National Gallery in assuming the status of Canada's foremost cultural institution, and McCurry's own self-presentation as an effective and persuasive leader. As Brison has noted, Keppel favoured a direct connection with a *national* organization, as he was eager to foster clear lines of influence between the corporation and the organization distributing its funds. Indeed, when it became clear that Brown and McCurry were continuing to seek the advice of Sidney Markham on museum matters, Keppel wrote a strongly

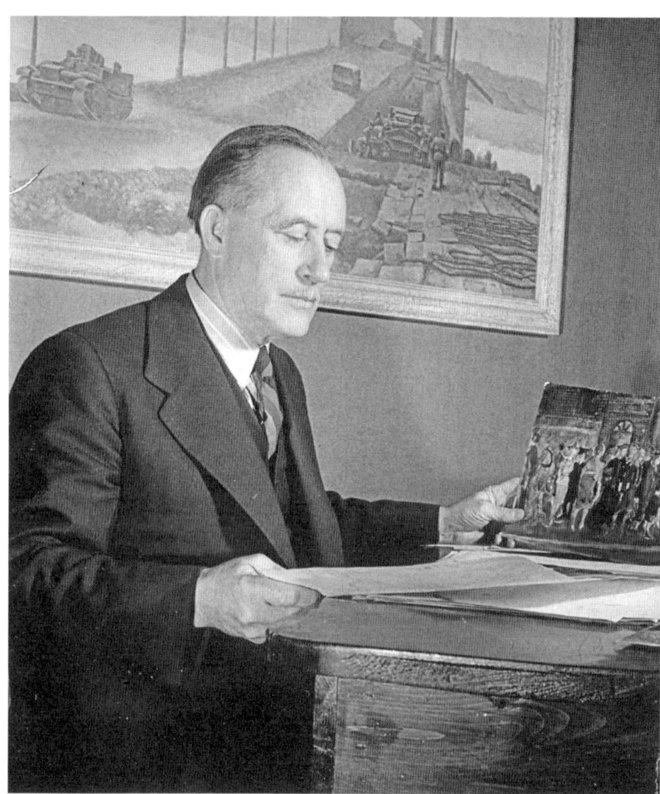

2.12 | H.O. McCurry, director of the National Gallery of Canada, n.d. McCurry holds *London Bus Queue*, a 1945 watercolour by Molly Lamb Bobak; Alex Colville's *The Nijmegen Bridge, Holland*, 1946 hangs behind him (both works now in the Beaverbrook Collection of War Art, Canadian War Museum).

worded letter underlining the corporation's feeling that "initiatives in the Dominions should come from the Dominions themselves" and warning that Markham was being taught a lesson regarding any attempt to control the development of dominion museums from London.[75] The Canadian committee complied and regular communications ensued between Keppel and McCurry. As the de facto head of the Canadian Museums Committee, McCurry held a tremendous amount of influence over the fortunes of art organizations and institutions across the country. In particular, the National Gallery administered Carnegie grants for training suitable individuals for curatorial and other professional museum positions that were instrumental in establishing the careers of such figures as Donald Buchanan and Norah McCullough. The funds also helped solidify the position of already established men like Walter Abell, who was brought to Ottawa with Carnegie money to continue the art education work begun by Arthur Lismer, and to develop the periodical *Maritime*

Art from a regional publication into *Canadian Art*, a major publication with national reach.[76]

McCurry's role as advocate, administrator, and regulator is evident in his correspondence with gallery directors across the country regarding the distribution of Carnegie money for art education purposes. An examination of his correspondence with Maud Bowman in Edmonton underscores both the importance of the money to regional institutions' activities as well as the methods employed in allocating the funds. Like many other institutions, the Edmonton Museum of Arts was first awarded a grant in 1934 to undertake art education classes for children. Over the next four years, the EMA received between $1,000 and $1,500 a year for art supplies, teacher salaries, and lectures on art to Edmonton and surrounding area schools. As with other institutions that received multi-year funding for the development of art education programs, the Edmonton Museum of Arts received money with the understanding that at the end of the granting period, the museum would have a solid program in place and would be expected to find the money to sustain it. As was discussed in Chapter 1, such support was not forthcoming from either the city or the province for any of the Edmonton Museum of Arts' activities. The difficult economic times of the 1930s further exacerbated the institution's financial situation and Bowman's letters to McCurry are filled with pleas for funds to continue the education classes, as well as broader expressions of despair at the thought of how the museum could continue with any of its activities under such adverse conditions.[77] While McCurry did as much as he could to provide financial support for the EMA's overall programming, he was also direct in his counsel when he felt that the museum was not attempting to generate the necessary funds on its own. In 1936, for example, he writes, "Perhaps at this time I ought to pass along warning to the Edmonton Committee that they must not look either to the Carnegie Corporation or the National Gallery for assistance indefinitely. If, after all these years, the Edmonton public does not realize the worth of the Edmonton Museum of Arts sufficiently to support it more effectively then perhaps they ought to be allowed to feel the lack of it"[78] – a warning that Bowman repeated at the next meeting of the museum's board, but to little effect.

Overall, the Edmonton Museum of Arts, like many other galleries, benefitted greatly from the funding given by the Carnegie Corporation. In addition to money for art classes, Bowman received funding in 1937 to undertake a tour of museums in Canada and the United States – from Winnipeg to Minneapolis, Chicago, Philadelphia, New York, Toronto, Montreal, and Ottawa – to observe their art education programs. Her daughter Miriam, one of the EMA's art educators, also obtained funding in 1934 to attend the summer art school at The Courtauld Institute to receive training in modern methods of art instruction. Despite cessation of the Canadian Museums Committee's activities in 1938, the National Gallery was still in charge of a Carnegie-issued grant of $30,000 to "furnish other parts of Canada with exhibitions and appropriate guidance in the development of these activities."[79] From this fund, the Edmonton Museum of Arts received periodic grants of $500 to put towards the activities of its choice. For the most part, the EMA used the funds to continue its children's art classes and to give lectures on art to local schools. Bowman's requests for funds continued – particularly during the war when the already limited civic and provincial funds were redirected to health and social programs – and were further taken up by Robert Hedley when he assumed the directorship of the museum in 1943. Hedley's approach was more systematic than Bowman's impassioned pleas and he voiced a guarantee that "as long as I am Director, we will finance the work at this end."[80] By that time, the Carnegie Corporation's interests had shifted from the arts to the sciences, and the National Gallery was not in a position to do more than distribute what remained of the original Carnegie grant.

In its administration of the Carnegie funds, the National Gallery continued to hone its leadership role in all art-related matters in Canada. Whether it was the selection of individuals to be trained for professional positions in art and museum management, the shaping of art education approaches and curriculum by allocating funds to those museums that best conformed to Carnegie standards, or more generally by being the conduit of information and money between Canadian art institutions and the American corporation, the National Gallery continuously asserted its power in determining the direction and the interests of art in Canada. Although the funding was distributed through the Canadian Museums Committee, the administration of the committee and of the funds was entirely in the hands of McCurry, who, with the increasing absence of Eric Brown on purchasing trips to Europe in the 1930s, came to personify the National Gallery in his voluminous correspondence with gallery personnel across the country. This correspondence shows a high level of personal support provided by National Gallery staff – and

McCurry in particular – to members of regional institutions. The correspondence between Maud Bowman and H.O. McCurry is revealing for the range of issues discussed, and for the degree of closeness between the writers. Bowman evidently knew McCurry personally: she often sends her regards to McCurry's wife, Dorothy – whom she refers to as "my Chile" – and their daughter, and occasionally she slips a familiar greeting to the younger man in her personal letters to him, signing them "Lady B" or "Bobbette." How the two would have developed such a level of familiarity is open to question: neither Maud Bowman nor her husband, David, were of a social or economic class that would suggest travel in the artistic and social circles that would have brought them in contact with someone like McCurry. They did share a faith in Christian Science, a connection that may have enabled the professional relations of two members of the growing museum community in Canada to deepen. It is certain that Christian Science – a faith that in 1921 only had 13,856 adherents in Canada[81] – seems to have had a significant presence within the leadership of the National Gallery, with Brown, McCurry, and board of trustees chairman H.S. Southam all members of the Church. The role of Christian Science in producing a particular view of art or in forming a network of cultural workers in Canada has yet to be fully assessed,[82] but the connection is compelling. Bowman and McCurry rarely refer to their faith in their letters – although Bowman's chronic ill-health prompts her to make reference to visits to the scientist as well as to the doctor – but such a shared commitment is one possible explanation for both the number and tone of the letters exchanged.

Conclusion

The external activities of the National Gallery ultimately served two functions: on one hand, it allowed the gallery to fulfill its mandate as Canada's *national* art museum by making work available to all Canadians, not just those living within driving distance of the capital. At the same time, the selection of which works by Canadian artists would be included in the loan, reproduction, and lecture programs organized by the National Gallery allowed it to consolidate and promote its vision of what constituted Canadian art to emerging institutions across the country. This aesthetic vision had already been revealed in the choice of works for the Canadian art sections at both Wembley exhibitions and for the 1927 *Exposition d'art canadien* at the Jeu de Paume. But it was through circulating art works and information about their study that the gallery effectively determined what would be seen in the regions and, as I argued in Chapter 1, what would become the mainstays of local collections. Although the NGC's influence extended across the country, its efforts were strongest in western Canada where it felt that its impact could be the most significant and need was the greatest. Loan exhibitions functioned to kick-start local collections in the smallest towns as much as in larger centres. Cities such as Vancouver that raised enough funds to erect a stand-alone gallery were praised for their achievements while smaller organizations such as the art association in Moose Jaw were regularly reminded that the loan exhibitions were a temporary measure designed to increase local support for a permanent collection and exhibition space. Despite the sometimes-chiding responses to requests, National Gallery representatives relished their "evangelistic" role as it cemented the institution's authority on art-related matters in the country. The loan exhibitions certainly established the National Gallery as the primary, although not sole, source of artworks available for display across the country. Certainly it was the gallery's mandate as a federally funded organization to circulate its collection as broadly as possible as can be seen in the National Gallery of Canada Act in 1913. But the gallery's extension services – from loan exhibitions, to sponsored lecturers, to reproduction programs – also performed the significant function of establishing the gallery more broadly as the authority on all artistic concerns throughout the country, including the educational programs sponsored by the Carnegie Corporation that were facilitated by NGC connections. Unlike the two other major institutions in operation at the time, the Art Association of Montreal and the Art Gallery of Toronto, the National Gallery was consistently perceived to be the leading expert on artistic matters in Canada. As I will argue in the next two chapters, this position of authority would begin to falter in the eyes of artists and art associations in western Canada in the 1940s and 1950s, resulting in the formation of organizations that sought to wrest control over the circulation of art away from the centre and into the hands of art associations and artists' groups working on the periphery.

FROM KINGSTON TO MASSEY

Developing a Policy for Culture in Canada

A frequent observation about the history of Canada is that much of it can be told through the findings of royal commissions.[1] If this is true, then the 1949–51 Royal Commission on National Development in the Arts, Letters and Sciences, commonly known as the Massey Commission, would be the mother of all royal commissions – in cultural terms what Neil Bradford has described as a "commission on everything."[2] Its report not only set the stage for the establishment of many of Canada's most important national cultural agencies and institutions, but also provided an unparalleled description and assessment of the state of culture in Canada in the late 1940s. The Massey Commission has often been positioned as a watershed moment in the history of culture in Canada, the beginning of what is often referred to as "a coordinated artistic life" in the country: Maria Tippett, for example, ends her account of the history of cultural institutions in Canada with the Massey Commission;[3] communications scholars Jody Berland, Kevin Dowler, and Zoë Druick have returned to the commission's report to assess its resonant stance on cultural protectionism at a continental and international level;[4] federal cultural policy documents cite both its process and its findings as a foundational moment in government support for the arts.[5] At a more prosaic level, the labour that went into the production of the Massey Commission generated important documents that continue to inform our knowledge of culture in Canada; in particular, the 473 briefs submitted to the commission, in addition to the transcripts of the hearings the commissioners held across the country, provide succinct histories of cultural organizations both large and small as well as an invaluable perspective on how these organizations and groups viewed the place of culture in the postwar Canadian context. The manner in which the opinions expressed in the briefs were distilled into the report's overview and recommendations highlights the rhetorical power of policy writing as well as the dominant views of the commissioners on the value of culture as "the spiritual foundations of our national life [and] the foundations of national unity."[6] Close reading of the briefs, however, reveal the disparity between the centralizing approach to nation building advocated by the commissioners and the expression of local and region-specific solutions proposed by many cultural organizations across the country. As western Canadian cultural organizations established themselves and built up collections and programming, they began to seek greater participation in the art activities of the nation on their own terms. So while the Massey Commission's report may be seen as the assertion of culture's nation-building capacity, the decade leading up to it reveals a less than homogenous endorsement of nationalist aspirations by a growing number of cultural organizations.

The growth of art museums in western Canada in the 1940s mirrors the larger expansion of art activities across Canada. Not only was there a significant increase in the number of cultural institutions in all parts of the country, artistic production was becoming more diverse and artists were demanding greater involvement in the nation's cultural affairs. Starting with the 1941 Kingston Conference of Canadian Artists and its spawn, the Federation of Canadian Artists (FCA), followed by the writing of the "Artists' Brief" by members of fifteen art and cultural organizations for submission to the House of Commons' Special Committee on Reconstruction and Re-establishment in 1944, and ending with the Massey Commission's report in 1951, the decade was a period of active debate on the role of culture in Canadian society and the most effective means of supporting it. During the Kingston conference, artists were given an opportunity to express their views about their role in society and how their work could best be supported. While many artists had benefitted from the backing of the National Gallery, others felt that access to such support was based on personal connections to particular individuals rather than evidence of a broad encouragement for the many forms of visual art being produced in Canada. Thus, a primary focus of many of the discussions in Kingston related to forms of government support for the arts beyond what was already being provided by the National Gallery.

Much of this questioning of existing means of funding emerged out of changes in the Canadian art world during the 1930s. The dissolution of the Group of Seven in 1932 is often presented as a new period in Canadian art, with the more geographically diverse Canadian Group of Painters maintaining the group's interest in landscape, while simultaneously expanding its membership to include artists working in portraiture and the figure.[7] Historians of the period also correctly point to increased attention by Canadian artists to their role in society and, indeed, as the effects of the Depression deepened and conflicts erupted in Europe, many artists addressed themselves to the depiction of social ills and political subjects.[8] Despite these changes, the artists most closely associated with the Group of Seven continued to dominate exhibitions and to be held up as arbiters of Canadian artistic production. This position was fostered by the touring exhibitions organized by the National Gallery as well as the reproduction programs it sponsored, both of which emphasized Group of Seven–style depictions of central Canadian landscapes.[9] For western Canadian artists, the "national art" ideology associated with the Group was perhaps felt the strongest in Winnipeg where Lionel LeMoine Fitz-Gerald was principal of the Winnipeg School of Art from 1924 to 1949; but even there, FitzGerald's interpretation of the idea of landscape was highly individualistic and presaged his turn to abstraction at the end of the 1940s. Artists in the Prairie provinces, such as H.G. Glyde, Illingworth Kerr, Augustus Kenderdine, and Ernest Lindner, brought a wide range of influences to their work, producing paintings and prints that were more conservative in style than their eastern and central Canadian counterparts but that reflected their place of production rather than attempting to conform to a narrowly articulated idea of "Canadian" art. And while Lawren Harris might have set up residence in Vancouver in 1940 and played a pivotal role in the development of that city's cultural activities, younger artists such as Jack Shadbolt and B.C. Binning had received training in modernist art practices in Europe and New York, and had little patience for what might be described as Canadian parochialism.

Regardless of approaches to art making, one area of commonality for all western Canadian artists was their physical distance from the centres of Canadian artistic activities and institutions. Feelings of isolation were most often remedied by the creation of local cultural institutions that could support the work of artists in western Canada both financially and spiritually. However, the appeal of broader cross-country networks remained strong for most artists in the west, and as a result they viewed the formation of such national organizations as the Federation of Canadian Artists and the possibility of federally funded cultural initiatives with a mixture of hope that such activities would decrease their isolation from the major institutions in Ottawa, Toronto, and Montreal, but also fear that their local activities would be subsumed into the cultural agenda of the "centre." This chapter reconsiders the narrative of art activity during the 1940s in Canada from the perspective of western Canada, with a particular focus on the tensions between efforts to consolidate the administration of art interests in order to establish a robust national position as evinced most powerfully in the Massey Commission, and the strongly voiced arguments of communities across Canada – and especially in western Canada – to maintain a degree of control over their own aesthetic needs.

The Kingston Conference and the Federation of Canadian Artists

The Conference of Canadian Artists (hereafter referred to as the Kingston Conference) was held in Kingston from 26 to 28 June 1941 under the aegis of the National Gallery, the Carnegie Corporation, and Queen's University, and brought together nearly 150 artists, educators, and museum workers from across Canada. Conceived by its organizer, artist André Biéler, as an opportunity to discuss the technical concerns of painting as well as to consider the role of the artist in society – a topic that was particularly pertinent in the aftermath of the Depression and as the nation entered the second year of its participation in the Second World War – the conference was the first time that such a number of artists from across the country were able to meet. For most scholars, the Kingston Conference is a turning point in the development of Canadian art, where artists debated the role of art in society and organized the first truly national artists organization, the Federation of Canadian Artists. Hélène Sicotte, for example, sees the push for a war art program by conference participants as the catalyst for the development of government funding structures in the 1950s,[10] while Andrew Nurse identifies the discussions held during the Kingston Conference as the beginning of art activism in Canada that was voiced most strongly through the activities of the FCA.[11] The relationship between art and democracy, forcefully articulated by

Acadia University professor Walter Abell was indeed a key theme at the conference, presented both as a philosophical position in the face of the Spanish Civil War and the Second World War, and also in the form of a war art program that would allow artists to usefully contribute to the war effort as well as ease their financial hardship.

Broadly understood by many of the delegates as an investigation into the role of the artist in society, the focus on art and democracy at the conference was buttressed by the presence of several American figures who had been invited to speak about the public art programs developed in the United States in the 1930s. Regionalist artist Thomas Hart Benton's radio address preceding the conference was followed by a longer presentation in Kingston on the importance of experience in the production of democratic art; Edward Rowan, assistant chief, Fine Arts Section of the US Government's Public Building Administration, gave a lengthy presentation on the mural program in federal public buildings and the challenges of producing "democratic" art, which he described as works that spoke to the communities in which they were located. Along with members of the Boston Group of mural painters, the Americans Benton and Rowan were there to present to Canadian artists the benefits of a state-supported fine arts program during times of economic hardship. Specifically, the murals produced as part of the Fine Arts Section of the Public Building Administration, discussed by Rowan and on view in tandem with a pre-conference promotional tour of Canada, as well as work contracted through the Works Progress Administration, were seen by many Canadian artists as the model for a system of government support. Indeed, delegates' demands that the federal government provide such support was voiced in both general terms as the responsibility of a democratic government and more specifically to Albert Cloutier, art director of the Wartime Information Board, during his presentation of the government's proposed war art program.[12]

The strong presence of American artists and administrators might seem odd at a conference that is often framed as a formative moment in the history of Canadian cultural policy, but the financial support of the Carnegie Corporation as well as corporation President Frederic Keppel's personal interest in the event undoubtedly influenced the selection of the speakers. The Kingston Conference immediately followed a conference on Canadian-American affairs at Queen's that was funded by the Carnegie Endowment for International Peace,[13] and the invitation to

Americans to speak to Canadian artists points to the influence of the Carnegie Corporation on the leaders of Canadian art institutions, an influence already made evident in its sponsorship of the Canadian Museums Committee. The corporation's interests extended beyond American–Canadian exchange to the themes that a meeting like the Kingston Conference would explore. Anna Hudson has argued that Keppel's view of "art for society's sake" framed the Carnegie Corporation's encouragement of cultural development in Canada during the 1930s, further arguing that advancing a "social democratic ideal of cultural progress" was a criterion for much of its funding programs.[14] When Biéler returned from a summer teaching trip to western Canada, he presented his idea of bringing together artists from across Canada to Queen's University principal Robert Wallace,[15] who forwarded the idea to an enthusiastic Frederic Keppel.[16] It was at this stage that the themes of cultural democracy and the role of the artist in society were set, mostly likely by Keppel, Wallace, and McCurry. Despite the emphasis on art and society, as Jeffrey Brison has cogently argued, the confluence of Carnegie, Queen's University, and the National Gallery in organizing and setting the agenda for the conference meant that "in the end, the Kingston Conference was a moment of elite consolidation and not of cultural democracy."[17]

Notwithstanding this agenda, Biéler's initial motivation to connect artists from across the country remains an important frame for understanding the discussions that took place at Kingston and has been largely overlooked in the literature. Having just returned from western Canada, Biéler was keen to cement connections with artists he had met both at the Banff Summer School and in Vancouver, where he had subsequently travelled. As Frances Smith notes in her biography of the artist, "he found a complete lack of communication and understanding between western and eastern Canadian artists ... This situation and other impressions of Canada simmered in his mind and were discussed with Principal Wallace on his return to Kingston."[18] In his introductory remarks to the assembly in Kingston, Biéler outlined the goals of this first gathering of the nation's artists: "to get acquainted, to meet each other and thereby to appreciate each other ... [and] to study the function of art in democracy."[19] The question of art and democracy was certainly a significant topic of discussion at the Kingston Conference, and in many accounts of both the conference itself and of the broader concerns of the Federation of Canadian Artists, the question of whether this issue was addressed in any depth

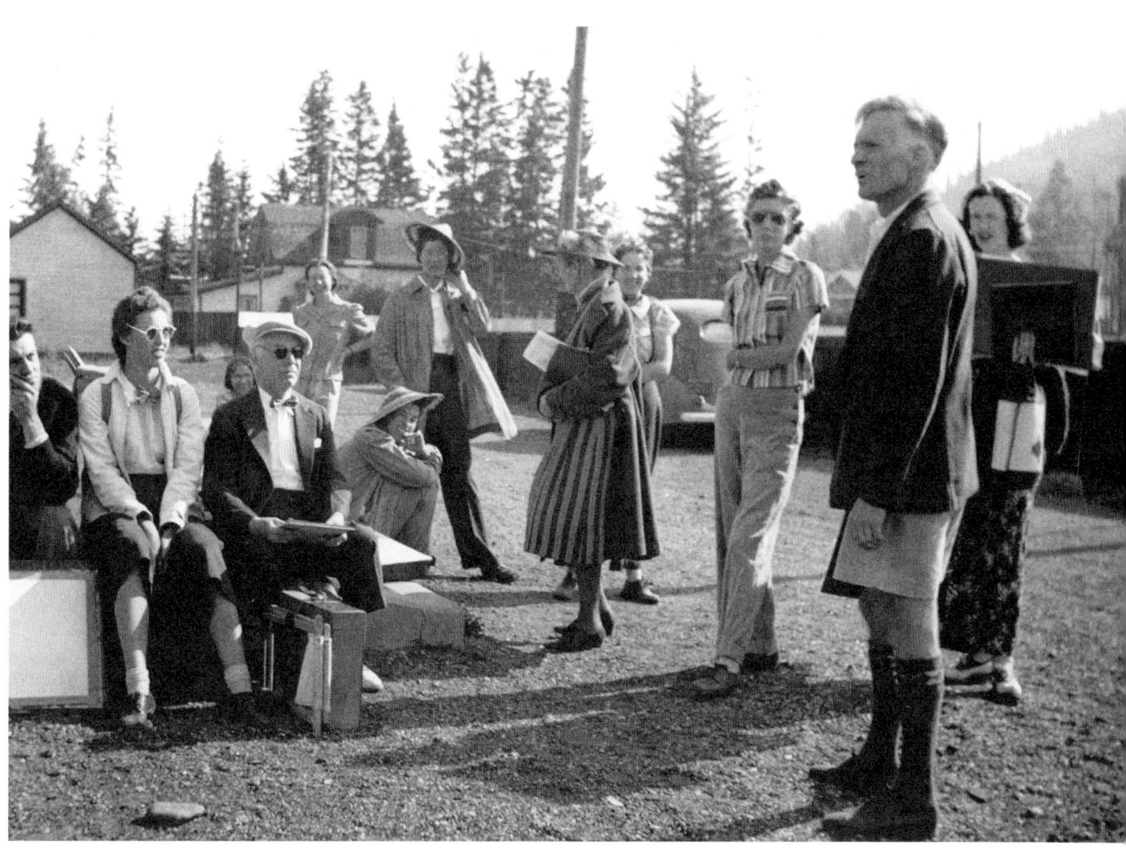

3.1 | André Biéler (right) with a group of students at the Banff School of Fine Arts, c. 1945.

has preoccupied many scholars.[20] I would argue, however, that Biéler's original goal for the conference had greater resonance in the subsequent development of cultural organizations and policy in Canada. While the impetus for artists across the country to "get to know each other" can be viewed as fundamental to the development of art in a democracy, it points even more to the importance of expanding the presence of Canadian art beyond the borders of Ontario and Quebec to the eastern and western parts of the country by creating a broader *network* of artists. The list of attendees is instructive as to the success of Biéler's plan: the familiar figures from Ottawa-Montreal-Toronto were in Kingston, including A.Y. Jackson, Arthur Lismer, Frances Loring, Florence Wyle, and members of the Canadian Group of Painters such as Prudence Heward, Anne

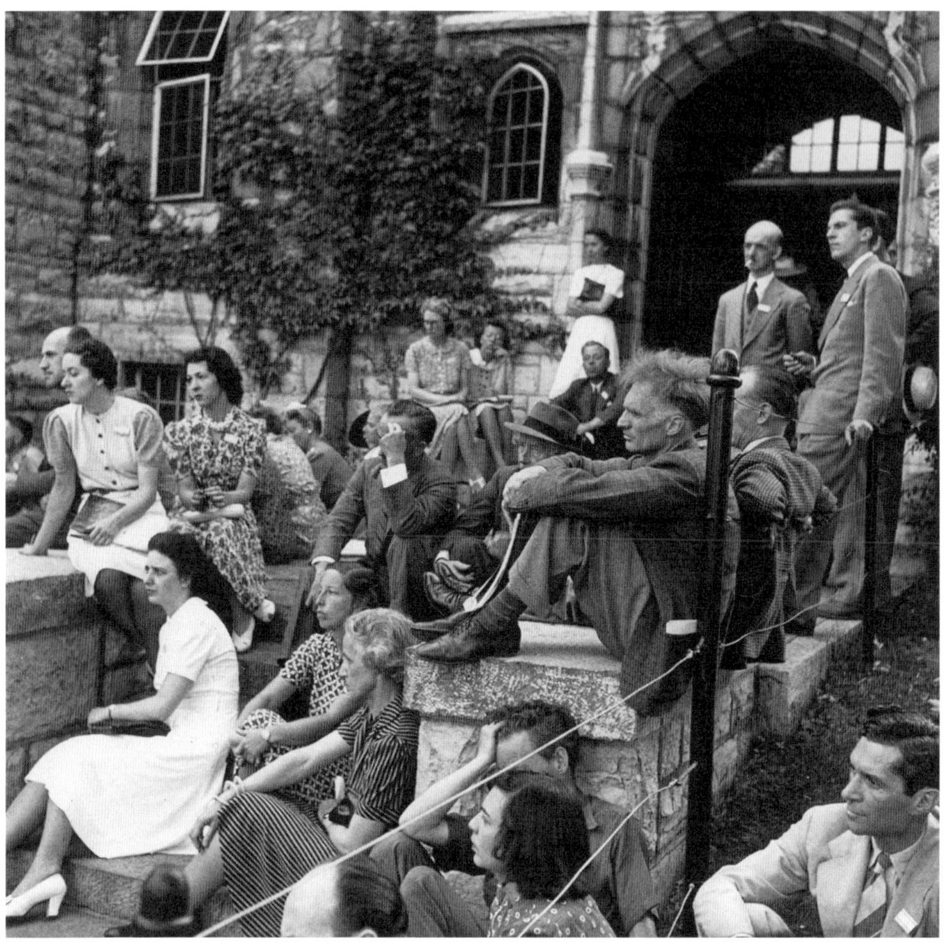

3.2 | Photograph by Hazen Sise of delegates to the Conference of Canadian Artists, Kingston, 1941. Sitting on the steps of the art building at Queen's University, the audience is listening to a presentation by Albert Cloutier.

Savage, Goodridge Roberts, Paraskeva Clark, and Carl Schaefer. Miller Brittain, Jack Humphrey, and Pegi Nicol MacLeod were three of the six artists from the Maritimes in attendance; western Canada was represented by eighteen artists, including Ernest Lindner, H.G. Glyde, Jack Shadbolt, J.W.G. Macdonald, and Alexander Musgrove; ill health prevented Lawren Harris from attending but he sent a letter that was read on the second day and again during late-night deliberations on the final day of the conference. While figures from "central" Canada were clearly in the majority, Biéler's goal of bringing artists from across the country was fulfilled, in part thanks to funds from the Carnegie Corporation that paid the travel of any artist living more than two hundred miles from Kingston, enabling the challenges of artists living outside Ontario and Quebec to be an important point of conversation at the conference.

These issues appeared on the first day of the conference in a discussion of the difficulty many artists faced of getting work seen by exhibition juries and, by extension, the public. Several technical points were made in this regard: the cost of shipping works from western Canada to juries in Ottawa, Toronto, and Montreal; the negative effects of only being able to have one or two works seen by a jury rather than within the context of an entire body of work; and finally the question of frame size, the standardization of which would assist artists in sending their work to exhibitions. While the discussion involved a number of the delegates, the issue of access to exhibitions and of getting work seen was predominantly the concern of artists from western Canada. Ernest Lindner of Saskatoon emphasized the importance of circulating exhibitions between the east and the west so that each part of the country could see what the other part was doing. For Lindner, such an exchange was of particular relevance to art in the west, which he argued "is beginning to develop," but it was also important for artists and the public in the eastern part of the country to see what was being produced in western Canada in order to combat "the feeling that there is a wall against the west."[21] Jack Shadbolt from Vancouver argued that more effort should be made to get substantial numbers of works by individual artists seen in once place, emphasizing the importance of assessing the work of an artist as a whole rather than on the basis of one or two works in isolation. Although as much an issue for artists closer to the artistic centres as for artists on the periphery, the question of context was of particular concern to western Canadian artists. As Lindner noted, "Those in the east do not know what a different country the west is, unless they have lived on the prairies ... I think you might get an idea of the trend of development there if you were able to see a whole exhibition from the west."[22]

Although there was support for this issue from other delegates (Montreal's Louis Muhlstock, for example, suggested that each western province have exhibitions from which work would be selected to send east), ignorance of the very real problems facing artists in western Canada is evident throughout the conference proceedings. Upon a suggestion by

Elizabeth Harrison that rather than sending pictures to juries, the juries could travel to the pictures, the following exchange took place between A.Y. Jackson and André Biéler: "Mr. Jackson: Perhaps the pictures could be arranged on the station platforms. The Chairman [Biéler]: Yes; then, as the train went by, the jury could make its selection."[23] While comical, Jackson and Biéler's comments underscore the lack of understanding of the feelings of isolation with which many artists in western Canada were only too familiar. The exchange also points to the geographic obstacles that hampered the formation of a truly national artistic community. Summarizing the discussion on the last day, Biéler noted that because of its size, Canada could not hope to achieve a "unity of culture" unless the work of artists from across the country were known and appreciated. Picking up on Thomas Hart Benton's arguments from earlier in the conference, however, Biéler argued that an emphasis on regional art – "something which is close to the earth, something vital, which we recognize we are"[24] – could go far to counter the effects of geographic distance and artists' feelings of isolation in different parts of the country. Biéler's appeal to regional aesthetics didn't address the structural challenge faced by artists in western Canada of getting their work seen, and Lindner again attempted to address the issue, this time by proposing a national art magazine along the lines of *Maritime Art* that would expose the work of artists from one region of the country to the others. The problem of geography had been mitigated at the Kingston Conference by the Carnegie Corporation's travel grants, but distance would ultimately be the downfall of any attempt by artists to constitute a national association that could effectively represent the interests of all Canada's regions.

On the last day of the conference, delegates debated late into the night over what resolutions Canadian artists wanted to bring forward as the outcome of the meeting. Resolutions included votes of thanks to officials at the Carnegie Corporation, the National Gallery and Queen's University, as well as a proposal to the Dominion Government to establish a war art program similar to that established by Lord Beaverbrook during the First World War; the creation of an annual juried drawing exhibition that would be national in scope; and a motion urging all universities to establish programs in art history and art appreciation.[25] The major resolution, however, was the decision to create a national body to represent the interests of Canadian artists. Discussion over the nature of this body was heated with opinions divided between those who saw the new organization as a federation of existing art societies and those advocating for an entirely new group that could supersede the aesthetic parameters and political interests of existing art organizations to join individual artists together in a united cause. Lawren Harris's letter, read again during this discussion, clearly advocated for the latter approach: "The time has come when the artists of the country should contribute consciously and designedly to the growth of a more highly socialized democracy. This could best be done, it seems to me, both by forming a nation-wide and inclusive organization and by working through that organization to serve the cultural needs of the Canadian people."[26]

The Continuing Committee, elected from the delegates to address the conference's resolutions and to move forward on the creation of the new artists' organization, consisted of André Biéler (in the chair), Walter Abell, A.Y. Jackson, Arthur Lismer, and Frances Loring – all of whom, with the exception of Abell, were central Canadian artists closely associated with national organizations of the period. The geographical location of the members of the Continuing Committee was directly addressed during deliberations over its composition, with delegates recognizing that there was little sense in appointing representatives from Vancouver and Halifax if the fledgling organization did not have the money to bring them together.[27] Shortly after the conference, and following a meeting of the Continuing Committee, the Federation of Canadian Artists was formed, with Biéler as its first president, and Lismer and Abell featuring prominently in its leadership. In his editorial in *Maritime Art* following the conference, Abell described his hopes for the success of the new organization:

> The last wave of distinctly national consciousness in the field of
> Canadian art was undoubtedly the work of the Group of Seven.
> In symbols inspired by the northern landscape, the group crys-
> tallized our sense of certain spiritual intangibles underlying life
> in Canada today. If one reads correctly the signs of the times, the
> next forward wave, nationally speaking, lies in a consciousness
> of the national problems involved in the relation of the arts to the
> whole of Canadian society. Until these problems are solved, or at
> least on the way to solution, neither Canadian art nor Canadian
> life can reach their full potential stature. Here is a cause which is
> big enough to include all workers in the arts, all types of artistic

expression, and by uniting them in the service of society, to inspire them to their maximum accomplishment.[28]

Abell's aspirational text highlights the challenges the FCA would face over the next decade as it struggled to reconcile the two aspects underlying its formation: giving artists a greater voice in the cultural affairs of the nation, and attempting to ensure that that voice was national in scope. At the first meeting of the national membership held in Toronto in 1942, the FCA's constitution was read, and its underlying commitment to forming a national organization that would bring artists from across the country together was strongly endorsed. As a result of restrictions on travel during wartime, however, FCA undertakings were concentrated in the activities of regional branches established initially in Vancouver and Montreal, but quickly appeared in Edmonton and Calgary, Saskatoon and Regina, Winnipeg, Ottawa, and Victoria. A note in *Maritime Art* in late 1943 suggested the need to amend the original constitution to develop a new governing body that could respond to regional concerns and interests. Indeed, an issue that preoccupied the Executive Committee over the next two years was how to reconcile the active programs and interests of local communities with the larger aims of the national body. While the regional branches wanted to be part of the national organization, they also recognized the challenges of facilitating such a meeting and concentrated their efforts on building an interest in art in their own communities and serving their own membership. Viewing the situation as vice-president of the FCA's Executive Committee in 1944, Montreal artist F.B. Taylor advised Lawren Harris that

> The reg'l [*sic*] propaganda will be governed, as it were, by the nat'l [*sic*] but oriented and pointed to conform to, cater to, the respective provincial problems, scenes. It seems to me that we must have a national matrix even though at this stage our performance is essentially regional. I think you will see what I mean. We must publicly stress our national make-up, foster and build it up continuously, and yet realize that our appeal to prospective members is necessarily largely a local matter. We must show that we are a big concern with particular regional and local opportunities to contribute and serve to common and individualized advantage.[29]

The national executive committee tried to keep each branch aware of the others' activities, as well as of the larger initiatives of the national organization, through regular newsletters, presidential letters to the membership (particular during Harris's tenure), and articles in *Canadian Art*. The latter magazine was a critical tool for the FCA in disseminating information about its activities to its own members and beyond, and the communications possibilities it afforded was a key factor in the FCA's decision to sponsor the magazine as it transitioned from *Maritime Art* in 1943.[30] Balancing the needs of the regions with those of the national organization was of particular concern to the executive in this period as it recognized the necessity of bolstering art activities at a local level while at the same time strengthening the network-building role of the national organization in order to better represent the broader interests of Canadian artists.

Following the news that the Saskatoon Art Association had formed a regional branch of the FCA, President Lawren Harris wrote to the membership noting the importance of building local branches, but also underlining the vital role played by the national organization for all Canadian artists: "we should ... maintain and enlarge our view of the Federation as a National organization striving for a creative comradeship right across Canada; seeking to bring about a spirit of mutual understanding and good will which can do more for the visual arts in Canada than any other agency."[31] The Saskatoon Art Association's decision to become a member of the FCA was further heralded by Harris as an enlightened move that demonstrated the association's commitment to the federation's democratic ideals. Harris's praise of what he described as the Saskatoon Art Association's altruism falls closely in line with the beliefs that characterized his championing of community art centres during his FCA presidency: "The Art Association of Saskatoon is the first Art Association to have seen that it can maintain its own identity unimpaired, remain as distinctive as it always has been, and at the same time become both a part of a great and growing country wide movement in art and make a unique contribution to that movement."[32] Interestingly, in this letter to the regions, Harris maintains the emphasis on the national aims of the FCA – indeed, the national aims of Canadian art – while also affirming the importance of retaining a strong sense of regional identity. In the early years of the federation, this position was not always popular with

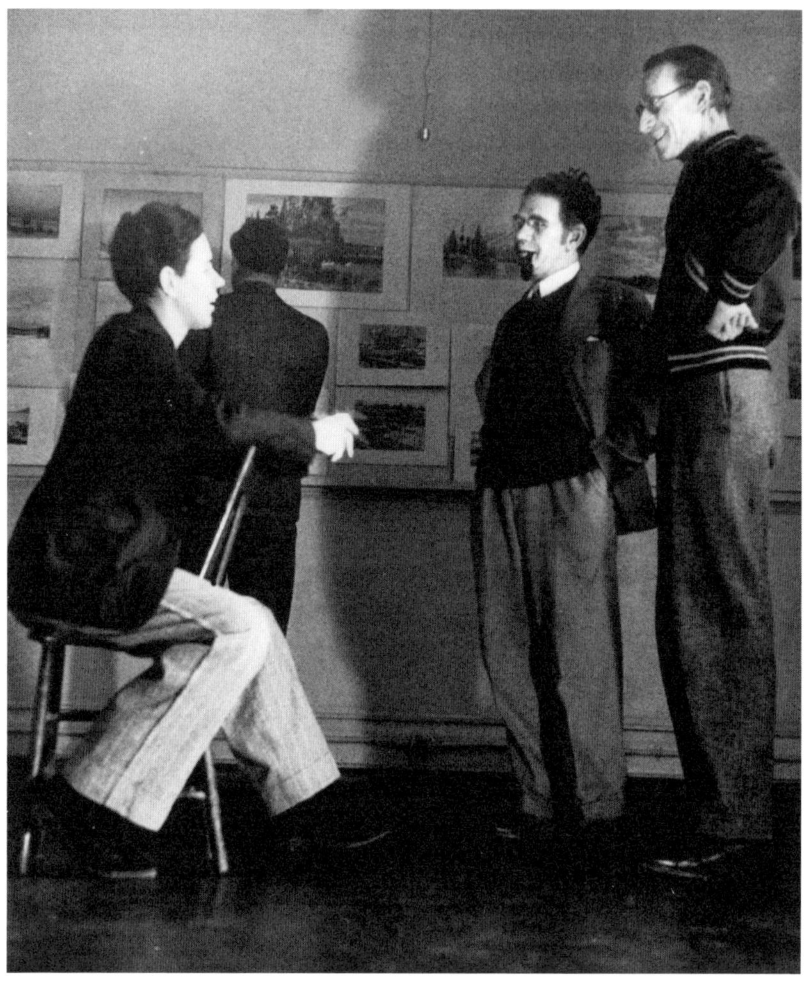

3.3 | Saskatoon Art Centre, with artists Winona Mulcaster (seated), Ernest Lindner, and Robert Hurley, c. 1945.

members who were keen to emphasize the organization's national role; according to Andrew Nurse, Walter Abell complained that the federation was unwilling to direct activities from the centre, instead letting the ideas of regional groups shape the organization's growth.[33] One example of such divergent aims was a petition to the federal government to implement a war art program, championed by then vice-president F.B. Taylor, chairman of the Quebec (Montreal) branch. It was the first major undertaking of the national executive of the FCA as decided at the 1942 meeting in Toronto, but branches outside of Montreal were less enthusiastic about the venture, and despite Taylor's family connections (his brother was industrialist E.P. Taylor, who had a personal relationship with Prime Minister Mackenzie King), the petition did not reach the Prime Minister's Office and the FCA abandoned the project in 1943.[34]

The second major initiative of the FCA was the proposal to create community art centres across the country. A way of invigorating interest in the arts in all Canadian cities and towns, the community art centre proposal was the brainchild of Lawren Harris while he was president of the BC branch of the Federation, but he made it the national association's primary focus on his appointment as the FCA's second president in 1944. Emerging out of the particular challenges of British Columbia's geographical location, the community centre proposal argued that individual towns and regions would be better served by art galleries located in their own communities than by the services of an institution in Ottawa. While it supported and appreciated the National Gallery's loan exhibition programs, the FCA, via Harris, argued that if the national institution's collections could be distributed to centres across the country, it would more effectively fulfill its mandate to bring art to the Canadian public. Community art centres had been a particular interest of Harris's since 1942 and he enthusiastically presented his case in public talks and in print, including in the pages of the Vancouver Art Gallery's *Bulletin* and *Maritime Art*.[35] Once he assumed the presidency of the FCA, Harris used the backing of the national organization to advocate for increased artistic autonomy in the regions. It is therefore not surprising to see that community art centres were enthusiastically supported by the regional branches of the FCA, as well as many regional art institutions, keen to see greater support for art outside central Canada. Indeed, the issue of community centres became a focal point not just for the Federation of Canadian Artists and its attempt to represent the interests of Canadian artists; it also crystallized an increasing concern among artists across Canada over the power held by the National Gallery and its control of art activities in the country. As the following section demonstrates, the case for community art centres underscored the brief presented by Canadian arts organizations to the Special Committee on Reconstruction and Re-establishment in 1944, and became a major point of discussion in the Massey Commission's cross-country hearings and subsequent report. It would also galvanize art organizations across the country that viewed the initiative, particularly when it received support from the federal government, as a commitment to the development of art and culture in the regions.

Region vs. Nation: Harris, Wood, and the Brief to the Reconstruction Committee

At the same time as Harris was promoting community art centres as a remedy for regions' feelings of isolation, several artists' groups and individuals banded together to ask the federal government how it intended to involve artists in its planning for postwar reconstruction. The House of Commons Special Committee on Reconstruction and Re-establishment was formed in 1942 to study the means of facilitating the rebuilding of Canadian society at the end of the Second World War. Chaired by BC Liberal MP J.G. Turgeon and intended to address the economic as well as social challenges that Canada would need to address at the conclusion of the war, the Reconstruction and Re-establishment Committee became a touchstone for many voluntary educational and cultural organizations keen to take advantage of an opportunity to reconfigure Canada's social values following the country's experience through two world wars and an economic depression. As Len Kuffert argues in his study of postwar Canada, "Officially, 'Reconstruction' was about easing the economic and occupational transition to peacetime, but the culture of reconstruction that leapt up around these more pragmatic intentions brought to light questions about the kind of society that Canadians could (or should) fashion once the war ended. Indeed, it gave the question of the state's role in planning for the period a distinctly cultural cast."[36] One vocal advocate on the Reconstruction Committee for the cultural work of reconstruction was North Battleford, Saskatchewan MP Dorise Nielson, who also argued strongly for western Canadians' access to the arts as "their natural right as citizens of this country."[37] Among the cultural initiatives of the period, the "Brief Concerning the Cultural Aspects of Canadian Reconstruction" – or "Artists' Brief" as it became known – gathered some of the foremost cultural organizations in the country and made significant recommendations regarding the fostering of a national culture to support the development of the postwar Canadian economy. The main architect of the brief was Elizabeth Wyn Wood, the Toronto-based sculptor who had already demonstrated her faith in national cultural

institutions through her organization of the counter-petition in support
of Eric Brown and the National Gallery in the face of criticism from conservative members of the Royal Canadian Academy. Contributors to
the Artists' Brief included representatives from the RCA, the Sculptors'
Society of Canada, the Canadian Group of Painters, the FCA, the Canadian Handicrafts Guild, and the Arts and Letters Club as well as the
Canadian Authors' Association, the Music Committee, and the Dominion Drama Festival. As this list suggests, the majority of the participants
were members of national arts organizations headquartered in Toronto
and Montreal, thus contributing to the overwhelmingly nationalist perspective of the final brief. However, sections within the document reveal
fissures in that nationalist narrative. In addition, a prolonged discussion
in the pages of *Canadian Art* between Elizabeth Wyn Wood and Lawren
Harris, by then national president of the Federation of Canadian Artists
but retaining his roots as former president of the Federation's BC branch,
provides an important context for thinking through tensions between
how nation and region figured in proposals for Canada's postwar cultural reconstruction.

The principal strategy of the brief was to encourage federal support
of the arts in Canada by asserting the direct contribution of fine and
commercial artists to the social and economic well-being of the country, and by reminding the government of its role in asserting the centrality of culture in the life of the nation. In this respect, the brief cited
France, Sweden, Denmark, and the United Kingdom as models for government encouragement of culture in support of national growth and
international relations.[38] The authors of the brief identified the federal
government as the source of support for cultural activities, first by setting up a governmental body "for the supervision of all cultural activities";[39] second, through subsidizing the creation of community centres
to provide arts and leisure activities to citizens of all regions of the country; and finally, by advocating a series of strategies and institutions that
would encourage cultural and leisure activities throughout the Dominion. This last objective was also framed as responding to the social needs
of Canadians through housing and town planning schemes, the establishment of parks, and economic incentives for applied and industrial
art production.

The suggested creation of a governmental body tasked with overseeing the cultural affairs of the nation – to be distinguished from a minister

of culture, which many felt smacked too much of the operations of totalitarian regimes – can be clearly linked to recommendations emanating from the Kingston Conference for greater federal support to artists. It was also a key concern of Elizabeth Wyn Wood, perhaps most forcefully articulated in her essay in the February–March 1944 issue of *Canadian Art* entitled "A National Program for the Arts in Canada." Mapping out a ten-point program that substantially overlaps with the final recommendations of the brief,[40] Wood's foremost proposal was the creation of a Ministry of Fine Arts or Cultural Affairs, the establishment of which would be "a vehicle for the accomplishment of all the other items. This is a key point."[41] In Wood's view, echoed in the brief, a central government agency that could provide oversight for the cultural activities of the country was the logical means to ensure the continued development of art making in Canada – by coordinating, for example, the circulation of art, films, and musical and theatre productions to organizations from coast to coast. Such a view reinforced the already existing opinion among many of the representatives that *national* organizations were the most efficient means of fostering a national culture, another objective that underpinned the recommendations of the brief. And this aim should come as no surprise given that the brief was written in response to questions regarding Canada's program for reconstruction, and ties into the "culture of reconstruction" that linked postwar Canadian life to a new democratic ideal of national citizenship.

The second major recommendation of the Artists' Brief was the establishment of community art centres, imagined as local hubs for the production and enjoyment of culture by communities both small and large. As presented in the brief, the centres would receive significant financial support from the federal government, but the communities themselves were accountable for raising at least half of the funds and were responsible for initiating the process and securing support from local citizens. Echoing descriptions proposed by Harris in his 1942–43 publications, centres were proposed in three forms: major centres to be built in large cities, reduced centres in smaller cities, and small centres in small communities. Community centres in the major cities would include an art gallery for exhibitions as well as the holding of art classes, a library, and an auditorium for drama, ballet, orchestra, and other concerts, film screenings, and lectures. For smaller communities, the centre would not only support artistic and cultural activities but would provide a location for social activities and sports. The brief noted, however, that "activities which promote better citizenship and which will enrich the cultural and post-educational life of the community must be the core of the centre's program. Otherwise the hall becomes merely a social and sports hall."[42] Overall the goal of community centres lay in the promotion of culture and national unity, with the arts conceived as the natural means through which such unity could be conceived. That cultural activities would have a social benefit was a given for the authors of the brief who noted that the provision of "citizenship and cultural services" would keep Canada's citizens happy and thus more productive. In particular, the erection of centres in what the brief described as "rural and frontier communities" was seen to be essential to relieving boredom, keeping communities stable and content and less likely to "drift" to larger communities.[43]

The Artists' Brief's community art centre proposal drew enormously from the ideas formulated by Harris, presented in an essay in the Spring 1943 issue of *Maritime Art* and more fully developed in the BC branch of the Federation's "Plan for the Extension of the National Gallery," written by Harris in March 1944. As regional hubs for the arts, Harris envisioned community centres as sites for the local development of cultural activities that would most benefit that community, and as such adjust the centralizing tendencies of national organizations such as the National Gallery of Canada (NGC). Indeed, much of Harris's writings on the subject rest on a critique of the National Gallery and the control it wielded over the dissemination of visual art throughout the country. In the *Maritime Art* essay "The Federation, the National Gallery and a New Society," for example, Harris argued that the NGC needed "to enlarge its idea of serving our people from coast to coast … to visualize and plan and work for a new conception of a National gallery [*sic*]."[44] In order to become what Harris would describe as "a people's gallery," the NGC needed to turn itself into a "distributing agency for works of art of all kinds" by extending its administrative and educational services through the creation of branches of the National Gallery in medium-sized communities, and by increasing collaboration with established galleries.[45] In "The Federation, the National Gallery and a New Society," Harris's criticism of the institution lies less with the NGC's activities: indeed, he praises the gallery's longstanding practice of loan exhibitions as invaluable in showing Canadians the importance of their own artists. Rather, Harris disapproved of what the National Gallery represented: a centralization of power vis-à-vis aesthetic issues and the resulting marginalization of emerging centres on the periphery such as Vancouver.[46]

Harris's advocacy for decentralization stands in contrast with Wood's recommendations for the establishment of a federal ministry for culture and stronger support for the arts from the centre; the series of essays each published in *Canadian Art* as well as the final text of the Artists' Brief are testament to the two approaches to the development of culture at work in Canada. Harris's support for community art centres underlined his strong commitment to the devolution of responsibility for cultural matters to individual communities. As he wrote in 1944, "each centre would be a distributing point for its region, extending its facilities to factories, clubs, schools, and outlying rural districts."[47] In this scenario, national organizations such as the National Gallery, the National Film Board, and the Canadian Broadcasting Corporation (CBC) would function as content providers and central distribution units, with communities determining their programming needs and making requests to the central organizations. In contrast, Wood argued that the successful development of artistic practice in Canada required a central organizing body to ensure both the systematic distribution of resources and the coordination of activities. Under this scheme, communities would necessarily benefit from the leadership and expertise of national institutions and organizations and could then develop their own programming.

The different positioning of these two figures is illuminated in FCA correspondence, particularly between Harris and F.B. Taylor when they were president and vice-president of the national association. Written during and following the preparation of the Artists' Brief, the letters reveal both a personal dislike for Wood – particularly from Taylor – and the struggles over the place community art centres would take in the final brief. The correspondence also reveals the deep antipathy of the leadership of the FCA for H.O. McCurry and what they viewed as the increasing power he was seeking for the National Gallery and its direction of art in Canada.[48] For Harris and Taylor, along with H. Garnard (Rik) Kettle, executive secretary of the national FCA, the community art centre proposal was the first step of a larger plan to decentralize the NGC. Under this plan – considerably more extreme than anything Harris or the FCA had published in *Canadian Art* – branches of the NGC would be established in every major city in the country, and its collection distributed among these regional centres for subsequent circulation within the regions. Interspersed in these letters were discussions of who would assume the editorship of *Canadian Art* with the departure of Walter Abell, a subject of keen interest to the FCA given its sponsorship of the magazine, and the concern of its executive that the National Gallery (viz. McCurry) would use the magazine as a forum to promote its own centralizing agenda. Harris hoped that the primary outcome of the establishment of community art centres was a shift in the relationship between federal institutions and local organizations. If one of the functions of art in Canada was to facilitate "the interplay between the different regions of the country wherein they each find conviction and are helped to shape their own character," then stronger arts institutions outside of the economic centre of the country would only optimize this result.[49]

Despite the significant role played by Harris and the FCA in formulating its proposals, the Artists' Brief to the Reconstruction and Re-establishment Committee was only marginally concerned with empowering regional communities.[50] Like the recommendation that a governmental body be appointed to supervise the development of the arts in Canada, the emphasis in the Artists' Brief was on national institutions and the continued belief that Canada's cultural life would be best served by an organized group at the centre. Even in the discussion of community art centres (and the proposal that these would contribute to the development of an interest in the arts within "rural and frontier communities"), much of the proposed programming was to be delivered by existing national institutions such as the National Gallery, the National Film Board, and other organizations yet to be established, rather than emanating from those centres. There was some dissension amongst the various contributors as to the place given to community art centres in the final brief and the decision to so strongly endorse the proposal was not unanimous.[51] As proposed in the Artists' Brief, then, cultural activities across Canada continued to be directed by the centre despite MP Dorise Nielson's appeal for reconstruction plans to address the specific cultural needs of western Canadians. Such a perspective on the proper means of supporting Canadian culture would similarly underscore the policies proposed in the Massey Commission's report some seven years later. By that point, however, Canada's postwar reconstruction was well underway and proposals for the development of centralized institutions ready to disseminate culture to the regions received much less support from local organizations, at least in western Canada.

The Appeal of Community Art Centres in Western Canada

Of the numerous recommendations of the Artists' Brief, the proposed community art centres dominated the interest and imagination of members of the art community, the press, and city politicians. Reactions to the brief in the press reveal a range of responses. William Arthur Deacon, editorial writer for the *Globe and Mail*, argued that the day the brief was presented might be remembered "as the beginning of co-ordinated artistic life in Canada."[52] *The Toronto Star*, meanwhile, saw the community centre as a potential promoter of national unity in the face of increasing population diversity: "Canada is a 'melting pot' of races and nationalities. Spiritual harmony can more easily be attained when people spend time with each other enjoying music, books and drama, or when they do things which bring out the best that is in them."[53] Newspapers in western Canada, however, were more practical in their assessment of the value of community centres and argued that they would provide much-needed support for the arts in the region – an Alberta newspaper argued that "such culture centres are greatly needed, particularly in the west."[54] But even in these articles, such support was framed as being of benefit to Canada as a whole, leading to a greater sense of national harmony; to wit, the Winnipeg Art Gallery Association's widely reported assertion that "The need of financial support is not so observable in the well-supported galleries of eastern Canada, but in the west any expansion demands support; this it is felt the government should help to provide in the interests and *to the gain of the nation*."[55] What can be gleaned from the above quotes is the differing perspective on the purpose that community art centres would serve. In Toronto (and in editorials published in Montreal and Ottawa as well), the proposed community art centre was a means of extending the civilizing values of "music, books and drama" to all corners of the country. How such an expansion would be accomplished was rarely presented (although one Ottawa paper gallantly proffered H.O. McCurry and the National Gallery as the logical source of any coordinated activity),[56] yet it was clearly assumed that bringing culture to the regions would be achieved by increasing the services of existing national institutions, not by cultivating local cultural production. Western cities, on the other hand, viewed community centres as first and foremost a means of encouraging local talent, and second as an opportunity to expose the local community to works that it would otherwise not get a chance to see. From this perspective, once the cultural life of the community was taken care of, the nation could follow.

How this logic played out in specific communities can be explored through an examination of Edmonton's reaction to the community centre proposal. When the Edmonton Museum of Arts was asked to vacate its rooms in the Civic Block to make way for a children's crèche in June 1944, city council was discussing plans for the development of a city centre scheme accommodating a dedicated city hall building, an auditorium, and other services appropriate for a growing city. As these discussions took place at city council meetings and in newspaper editorials, cultural groups in the city, including the board of the EMA and the newly formed Edmonton Allied Arts (War Services) Council began to formulate their own vision of a civic centre that would include spaces for cultural activities. A lecture in Edmonton by Lawren Harris on the merits of community art centres in 1944 fired the imagination of many museum board members, an enthusiasm that was sustained by the FCA's endorsement and the publication of the Artists' Brief. Following a trip to Quebec and Ontario in August 1945 where he visited the National Gallery, the Art Gallery of Toronto, the Art Association of Montreal, and the London Public Library and Art Museum, EMA Director Robert Hedley stated his preference for a separate building to house the art museum, but also indicated his willingness to have the institution be included as part of a community art centre initiative along the lines outlined by Harris and the FCA. In 1946, Hedley, on behalf of the EMA's board, endorsed a plan for a civic centre that included a three-thousand- to four-thousand-seat auditorium, an extensive area for sports, and a separate wing for cultural activities that would include space for a museum of arts.[57] Despite misgivings of some board members – vice-president Ernest Poole, for example, noted the Winnipeg Art Gallery's unhappiness at being in that city's civic auditorium and cautioned that locating a gallery in a community art centre might bring similar problems[58] – Hedley remained constant in his support for a community art centre type home for the EMA, arguing strongly with representatives from city council for access to all wall space for the display of two-dimensional works as well as the provision of cases for the presentation of handicrafts in any civic centre proposal.[59]

The EMA's discussions were shaped in part by the various plans at the municipal government level to transform Edmonton's downtown core to better reflect the metropolitan aspirations of Alberta's capital. The Dewar plan of 1947 proposed a series of buildings extending from 98 Street to 101 Street that would include a civic centre housing an art gallery; however, a motion to approve an expenditure of $1.5 million for construction was defeated in a December 1947 referendum. In 1950 Edmonton City Council hired an American development consultant, L.E. Detwiler, to come up with another design for a civic centre. In this version, an auditorium and museum were included in the plans, although only a corridor was to be allotted for exhibition space. This plan was also defeated in a citywide referendum. After this second disappointment, the city abandoned its plans for major development in the downtown core and with it disappeared the idea of a community art centre.[60] In 1950 the Edmonton Museum of Arts received word of the donation of a mansion close to the Legislature Grounds, and in 1952 it moved into much improved – although by no means ideal – facilities in Secord House.

The failure of Edmonton to establish a community art centre is not to suggest that the proposal was in itself flawed. Indeed, the model community art centre could be said to be the London Public Library and Art Museum whose success at incorporating a public library, an art gallery, and an auditorium into a single building was widely touted as an indication that multiple cultural activities and institutions could profitably share space. Hedley's visit to London on his 1945 tour of central Canada resulted in great enthusiasm over what director Richard Crouch had been able to achieve there.[61] The EMA director was particularly impressed by the facilities at London, which he described as "the most modern building I saw in the East," with features well worth considering in the construction of any facility in Edmonton.[62] The London Public Library and Art Museum was also highlighted as an example of the potential success of the community art centre idea in the Artists' Brief, and in the pages of *Canadian Art* where Crouch described in some detail the centre's programming and benefit to the wider London region.[63] The London gallery was also praised by the National Gallery in its 1943–44 *Annual Report*, which highlighted the "great contribution" to the community made by the facilities for art, drama, music, and the crafts. Remarkably, the NGC followed its praise of the London initiative by reasserting its own centrality to the development of art in Canada, linking the NGC's activities to the larger aims of local centres: "A system of community art centres, which could only be set up with government aid, would multiply the usefulness of the National Gallery many times, and develop local resources immeasurably."[64] As reports in the press make clear, both civic groups and voluntary organizations saw the benefit of the community art centre proposal: within the context of postwar reconstruction, city councillors embraced the possibility of federal funding for municipal development necessary after the deprivations of the 1930s and early 1940s; cultural groups viewed the promise of funding for the arts – regardless of the shape this might take – as a welcome endorsement of the place of culture in the life of the country. Enthusiastic about the possibility of encouraging the arts in Saskatoon, to give just one example, that city's mayor engaged Ernest Lindner, a member of both the Saskatoon Art Association and the Federation of Canadian Artists to chair a planning committee made up of representatives from all the arts as well as city councillors. But after six months of often-tense meetings between Lindner and city council, the project failed to receive the necessary provincial government support and Lindner's committee was dissolved.[65]

While community art centres failed to take form as the discrete building imagined by the FCA or receive the necessary financial support from all levels of government, many communities developed their own networks and administering organizations to facilitate the coordination of local art activities. In the immediate postwar period this often took the form of municipally based allied arts councils – associations of arts and cultural groups, both professional and amateur, working together to increase popular interest in the arts. Many of these councils were made possible through the initiative of their respective cities' Junior Leagues, voluntary women's organizations that had already been touted as fundamental to the establishment of community art centres.[66] Junior League members had been called to action by the New York Headquarters' 1944 report, *Arts in Our Town*, which strongly advocated for the central role of culture to community development.[67] As a result, Junior Leagues in cities across Canada initiated surveys of existing cultural resources, often resulting in the creation of arts councils that brought together organizations responsible for music, drama, art, and handicraft, and the aim to make these activities more accessible to the broader community. The Community Arts Council of Vancouver was formed out of one such survey in 1946 with the mandate "to increase and broaden the opportunities for Vancouver citizens to enjoy and participate in cultural activities."[68] Although it boasted several important members of the Vancouver art community, such as Charles Scott and Lawren Harris, the Vancouver

Community Arts Council relied primarily on volunteer women to organize activities such as a children's community theatre, a yearly month-long Festival of the Arts, an annual handicrafts festival, and the wildly successful exhibition *Design for Living*, presented at the Vancouver Art Gallery in 1949. Junior Leagues in Hamilton and Winnipeg were also active during the late 1940s in establishing community art projects that contributed immensely to the public presentation of, and appreciation for, culture across the country.

While the community art centres never took the physical form imagined by Harris and the FCA, in locales where such collaboration was essential – predominantly western Canadian towns and cities – the principles underlying these multifunctional art and recreation centres were taken up by voluntary organizations as well as artists and often shaped the broader development of artistic activity in that community. Museums and galleries played a significant role in making culture available to the community, continuing the practice they had championed since their inception. The preceding review of the discussion of community art centres demonstrates great support from artists as well as some city officials who rightly saw such facilities as an important force in the economic development of towns and cities. However, funding was difficult to obtain as neither the federal nor the provincial governments proved willing to set aside funds for cultural activities, each identifying the other as holding primary responsibility for the arts. From the federal perspective, once the national institutions were taken out of the picture, the arts' educational benefits placed them squarely within the domain of provincial funding; the provinces, for their part, wanted to direct their limited funds towards economic initiatives and viewed culture as a luxury whose potential nation-building effects should be managed by the federal government. The tensions between the federal and provincial governments identified by the Royal Commission on Dominion-Provincial Relations (a.k.a. the Rowell-Sirois Commission) in 1940 remained very present throughout the decade, as provinces sought greater jurisdiction over health, education, and social welfare, and the financial resources to enact it. As the Rowell-Sirois report argued, "The Commission's plan seeks to ensure to every province a real and not an illusory autonomy by guaranteeing to it, free from conditions of control, the revenues necessary to perform those functions which relate closely to its social and cultural development."[69]

Such federal–provincial cooperation would have been invaluable for community art centres, which were developed on a tripartite funding model with expected contributions from all three levels of government. As shown in Chapter 1, however, municipal governments were the principal supporters of cultural activities in western Canada with provincial arts boards only emerging at the end of the 1940s and with little funding. Federal funds for culture were equally limited – if not non-existent – although the pressures brought by the Artists' Brief presaged the official review of federal funding for culture that was the Massey Commission. As we have seen, however, the Artists' Brief reinforced the reliance on centralized national institutions for the dissemination of the arts, sidelining the provinces, and leaving municipal governments as the victim of federal–provincial conflicts over responsibility for culture. Arguably, then, lack of funding largely killed community art centres, most of which were reduced to the sports and recreation facilities that the authors of the Artists' Brief warned would result from a lack of broad-based financial support. Community organizations, art associations, and art museums ensured continued cultural activities, but in the same ad hoc and inadequate facilities of the prewar period. Such grassroots activity, however, would remain localized as a centralized approach to the development of culture in Canada was reinforced and firmly established in the recommendations of the Massey Commission.

The Massey Commission in Western Canada

Despite the failure of any centres to be built in the 1940s, the Federation of Canadian Artists, still under the presidency of Lawren Harris, continued to believe that the community art centre idea was key to the development of art across the country and it made this the focus of its presentation to the Royal Commission on the National Development in the Arts, Letters and Sciences when the latter issued its call for briefs in May 1949. Indeed, the FCA's brief to the Massey Commission was virtually identical to the brief it submitted to the Special Committee on Reconstruction and Re-establishment five years earlier, and its calls for a decentralized National Gallery with branches in every major Canadian city became one of the fundamental points of discussion in many of the hearings held across western Canada in the fall of 1949.

From the announcement of its formation on 4 May 1949, the Massey Commission garnered broad interest from arts organizations, community groups, universities, artists, and members of the public. Tasked with examining the activities of federal cultural agencies and institutions in the belief "that it is in the national interest to give encouragement to institutions which express national feeling, promote common understanding and add to the variety and richness of Canadian life, rural as well as urban,"[70] the commission was the first major public enquiry into the state of culture in Canada.[71] Reception of its report ranged from enthusiasm for its strong recommendations for increased government funding for cultural institutions and universities to outright dismissal of its findings as the opinions of "long hairs ... culture vultures ... [and] ... funny little minorities."[72] In newspapers around the country, including western Canada, most positive coverage focused on the report's recommendation that increased funding be found for universities in the form of student scholarships, a proposal that circumvented direct funding from the federal government for education, which remained firmly under provincial control. The proposed Canadian Council for the Arts also garnered support from some corners, although there was an equal amount of concern that such a body would result in too much government involvement in the work of individual artists. The increased funding advocated for the CBC and the commission's unwillingness to endorse a separate regulatory body over the growing radio and television industry incurred the most discussion and criticism in newspapers across the country, bolstered by the opinion of one of the commissioners, engineer Arthur Surveyor, whose dissenting report favourably outlined the argument of private broadcasters that the CBC's control over radio and television effectively constituted a monopoly and encouraged government domination over both the distribution and content of these media. Scholarly discussion of the Massey Commission over the past twenty years has focused largely on the debate over the CBC, situating the controversy over this part of the report as the precursor to the arguments over the development of the Broadcasting Act of 1958 that instituted the Board of Broadcast Governors (precursor of the CRTC) – the independent regulatory body advocated by Surveyor and private broadcasters.

Concomitant with the analysis of regulatory matters, both during the Massey Commission's hearings and subsequently, has been the discussion of one of the dominant themes underlying the Massey Commission report: the threat of American culture and programming to the development of an authentic and distinctive Canadian culture. For many scholars, the report's concern about the damaging effects of soap operas and comic books is but one instance of a more pervasive anxiety in Canadian cultural policy over American encroachment of culture. Kevin Dowler has linked this unease to postwar concerns over national defence, arguing that the commission's plans for a government supported Canadian cultural system as a safeguard against American cultural interests had strong parallels with federal protectionism in economic matters. As he argues, "Culture would provide the bulwark to construct a strong nation with all its critical facilities intact, and to ward off the potentially harmful effects of creeping continentalism in the form of American mass culture."[73] Like the government-funded railway in the late nineteenth century, the CBC and other national cultural organizations encouraged a vigorous national culture that would ipso facto prevent the adoption of unwanted American interests.[74] The second chapter of the report is frequently cited as one of the more pointed critiques of Canada's dependence on the United States in cultural matters: Canada's "lazy, even abject, imitation" of American cultural and educational institutions leads to an unquestioning acceptance of ideas that may be "alien to our tradition" and results in a weak national culture.[75] Quick to concede that American schools and cultural organizations have been invaluable sources of cultural programming, and that Canadian intellectual achievements could not have occurred without the support of US-based organizations such as the Carnegie and Rockefeller Foundations, the report strongly argued that Canadian culture was poorer for its inability to support and thereby foster autonomous and vigorous national cultural traditions. While the dominating presence of American programming was one source of concern, it was the "forces of geography" evident in the sheer size of Canada and the dispersal of its population over great distances that had proven to be a central challenge to the construction and maintenance of a truly national culture. The manner in which culture could transcend geography to build national feeling was a dominant presence throughout the report, particularly in its assessment of how existing and projected national institutions could do a better job of serving communities outside the centre.[76]

The commission's preoccupation with geography, however, did not translate into an interest in regions or regionalism, and the distinction is worth exploring. In the third section of Chapter 2, the report notes that "along with attachment to the whole of the country with its receding distances goes the sturdy self-reliance of local communities. These are separated by both geography and history. In all our travels we were impressed by differences of tradition and atmosphere in regions such as the Atlantic Provinces, the Prairies and British Columbia ... Canadian civilization is all the stronger for its sincere and unaffected regionalism."[77] While it is tempting to read this phrase as evidence of the report's endorsement of distinct regional identities, "regionalism" here appears to signify community characteristics rooted in folk traditions couched in terms of geographical specificity, rather than an understanding of emergent or even resistant regional identities. But as historian Gerald Friesen, among others, has noted, "[the concept of] region should be seen as ambiguous, evolving, and yet capable of expressing ... the lived spatial dimensions of our world,"[78] suggesting that while regions are often viewed as defined geographical spaces, inhabitants of those spaces feel a connectedness to place and to community that exceeds the formal boundaries of a designated region and constitutes a more significant affective relationship than to the nation. For the commissioners – mandated to speak from a national viewpoint, and all proponents of the kind of liberal humanist nationalism analyzed by Paul Litt in his assessment of the Massey Commission[79] – the building of a national culture (or the building of the nation through culture) needed to overcome the challenge of a geographically dispersed population living in the shadow of a major economic and cultural power, to the possible detriment of regional affiliations that might override a commitment to the nation.

This blindness to regionalism had the effect of focusing the commission's discussion of the means to build national culture on the ability of national institutions to respond to the needs of local communities and institutions. The commission's examination of the role of galleries in Canada in Chapter 7 of the report is telling in this regard. This chapter opens with a lengthy discussion of the National Gallery and its role in fostering the development of art in Canada: "Of all the Federal Institutions dealt with in this section the National Gallery has perhaps the most universal appeal, and has certainly achieved the widest contacts with the Canadian public."[80] In the pages that follow, the NGC's role in disseminating Canadian art to the nation is described in terms of its extensive loan exhibition program; the reproduction programs that made low-cost prints and postcards of works from the NGC's collection available to museums, schools, libraries, and individuals; its educational endeavours; production of radio and film programs that brought discussion of artworks to a broad public; and finally the sponsorship of lecture tours by National Gallery staff as well as international art professionals. The report praises such activities for their breadth and quality but notes that their real significance lies in the dissemination of knowledge about the fine arts in Canada across the country and abroad. Key to the success of the NGC's programs, according to the report were its links to local galleries, the discussion of whose concerns and challenges occupied the second half of the chapter. Presenting "on the whole a cheering picture," and supported by both voluntary societies and amateur artists, local galleries were praised for their promotion of the fine arts at the community level and for enabling the National Gallery to extend its reach across Canada. Indeed it is the relationship between the National Gallery and the local galleries that preoccupied the Massey Commission, rather than any work that the local galleries themselves might be undertaking on their own. That the term "local gallery" seems to encompass institutions as large and powerful as the Art Gallery of Toronto and the Art Association of Montreal alongside smaller institutions like the Owens Art Gallery in Sackville and the Edmonton Museum of Arts underscores this focus on the prominent role assigned to the National Gallery in the circulation of art in Canada.

Striking in the Massey Commission's reporting on art galleries in Canada is the mutual interdependence of the National Gallery and local institutions. On one hand, according to the report, local galleries are fortunate because the services of the National Gallery exist. While brief mention was made of initiatives to implement local networks of circulating exhibitions in western Ontario and western Canada, the report emphasized the loan exhibitions provided by the National Gallery that in many instances constitute the majority of the programming of smaller galleries across the country. On the other hand, the report noted that "without the premises of the local gallery and the services of those responsible for them, the National Gallery would be unable to perform ... one of its chief functions, the sending out of travelling exhibitions throughout the country for the benefit of the Canadian people as a whole."[81] A positive spin on this statement is the view that the National Gallery could not effectively do its job as a national institution without the spaces offered by galleries across the country. A more cynical reader might remark that the view of the Massey Commission (and possibly of the NGC itself) is that the dominant purpose of local galleries is to provide space for the presentation of the nation's collection, and to see that work as part of their own mandate to serve their community.[82] Such a view that the aims of the national organization shape the work of local institutions is not surprising in the findings of a commission whose mandate was to evaluate and make recommendations on "the operation and future development of ... federal agencies" such as the National Gallery. The recommendations of the commission further support the centrality of the NGC in the dissemination and circulation of information about Canadian art to the country. Indeed, the report notes that "some groups" – likely a reference to the FCA and the Alberta Society of Artists – had suggested that "branch or affiliated galleries" be established in the provinces to enable the NGC to more effectively carry out its work.[83] As conveyed in the report, these institutions would host semi-permanent displays of the NGC's collection, dispersing the works to the country as a whole and effectively decentralizing the workings of the institution. Quickly dismissed as the unfeasible requests of a minority of respondents, such proposals appear to be mentioned to illustrate the possibility of disagreement about the role of the National Gallery among Canadian arts organizations. Any suggestion of the decentralization of the NGC, once raised, was effectively contained within the nation-building mandate of the Massey Commission by restating the importance of the loan exhibition program of the National Gallery and its effectiveness in disseminating the works in its collection to the broadest number of Canadians possible.

The Massey Commission's re-assertion of the importance of centrally located national institutions belies some although not the majority of responses to both the Commission and its report from the regions. Calls for decentralization such as those voiced by the FCA were heard at various points during the commission's hearings, and resonated with communities that did not feel well served by organizations located in Ottawa. The Saskatoon Archaeological Society's oft-repeated complaint to the commission that the National Museum's claim to be "easily accessible by bus and street-car"[84] was not applicable to its members, echoes a 1949 editorial from *The Edmonton Journal* decrying the commission's emphasis on national institutions:

The royal commission on arts and science will get off to an unfortunate start if as reported, its first concern will be to make the National Museum at Ottawa one of the "world's greatest museums." The great majority of Canadian people don't give a hoot about making the National Museum a world famed institution. Nine-tenths of them will never see it anyway. But they do care a great deal about museum facilities that are available to them. A poor museum that accommodates the maximum number of people is a finer cultural asset than an excellent museum that accommodates only a minimum number of people. Museums are only as valuable as they are seen by the public. Therefore the first business of the royal commission should be, not to promote great cultural institutions in the East, but to insist upon the decentralization of cultural assets so that, in the case of museums, for instance, every Canadian city with more than 100,000 population can have a good museum of its own.[85]

Similar concerns regarding the availability of objects and services were expressed by many of the organizations appearing at hearings in Winnipeg, Regina, Saskatoon, Edmonton, Calgary, and Vancouver in October and November 1949. The *Calgary Herald* announced that "Mediocre art shows and poor service" from the National Gallery had been criticized by Alberta arts groups appearing at the 1 November hearings in Calgary, making specific reference to complaints by James Nicoll of the Alberta Society of Artists and Archie Key of the Western Canada Art Circuit regarding the "inferior works" sent to western art galleries.[86] For many groups presenting their briefs to the commission, a primary concern was that while national cultural organizations might ensure the circulation of culture to the country as a whole, it tended to privilege artists located in central Canada at the cost of developing artistic resources in the regions. The Regina Art Centre Association, representing thirty cultural societies in Regina, recommended avoiding too much centralization of cultural programming. Its brief argued that national development in the arts depended on the activities of local groups across the country and that the only way this could be achieved was through close cooperation between national organizations and societies across Canada whether national, provincial, or local. Furthermore, their brief stated, "there should be no compulsion forcing local groups or agencies to become organic parts of national organizations in order to receive benefits from National Agencies. Money and personnel should not be gathered in large centres where least needed, thus impoverishing smaller centres and rural communities."[87]

Similar sentiments are found in the majority of the submissions to the Massey Commission from western Canada, with groups seeking to navigate the fine line between boosting local culture and making a case for the continuing role and importance of national institutions in supporting activities in the regions. With few exceptions, local groups urged increased funding to national organizations, with the understanding that this would result in both better service to the regions in terms of the distribution of programming, and in enhanced support for regional artists. For some, however, even increased funding would not remedy the inherent inability of existing national organizations to foster cultural development in the country. Wesley Irwin, president of the Alberta Society of Artists, argued before the commission that his association believed that a solution lay in the creation of

> a centralized cultural board existing apart from politics and any
> ideology whether federal or provincial. Anything less – such as
> increased grants to national institutions, the status quo otherwise
> maintained, for example – would be inadequate in spite of the
> excellent work that is being done by them, limited as they are
> by lack of funds and scope to operate throughout the width and
> breadth of the country. These means would be organized through
> a national board.[88]

Ultimately, Irwin would get his wish, as the formation of the Canada Council in 1957 – six years after the Massey Commission presented its report – finally enabled the federal sponsorship for which artists had been advocating since the Kingston Conference.

Made possible by an unexpected financial windfall from the estate taxes of Isaac Walton Killam and James H. Dunn, the Canada Council became the first federal agency to distribute money to individual artists and arts organizations in Canada.[89] Assistance to museums was largely limited to matching funds for the acquisition of contemporary Canadian art and extension services, but this level of support – and the recognition

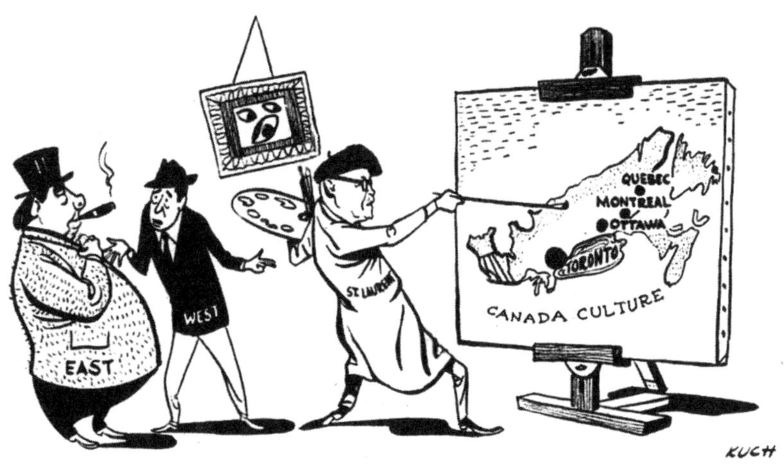

3.4 | Peter Kuch, "Western Canadian: You may like it, but I don't understand this modern art," *Winnipeg Free Press*, 17 April 1957.

awarded to the receiving institution – was enough to encourage many art galleries across the country to continue their activities. The creation of the Canada Council was not without controversy. As with the debate over the central governing arts body amongst the authors of the Artists' Brief, the idea of an arm of the federal government dispensing grants to artists raised the spectre of parliamentary interference in cultural production. For most, however, the Canada Council marked the country's commitment to fostering artistic activity and as such should be actively pursued. Writing in 1954, the dean of arts at Queen's University, C.G. Andrew, compared subsidies for culture to the subsidies for transportation that were being endorsed as necessary for the economic integration of the country, arguing, "We have not hesitated to pay for our political and economic unity and development by the payment of subsidies. We have merely come to recognize the importance of cultural development to the maintenance of political and social unity."[90] For Andrew, the effects of Council funding were not just economic but had the potential to develop a stronger national culture that would encompass both French and English, reduce parochial localism as well as guard against undue American influence. As such, he was closely in line with the overall tone of the Massey Report.

Reviewing the first decade of the Canada Council, however, national unity seemed to be less of a priority than the support of the artist whether through direct grants for research and travel, or to arts organizations tasked with disseminating cultural production to the public – with the latter form of funding of particular relevance to the performing arts. Aware of the eagerness with which arts organizations had been waiting for federal funding, the annual reports of the first years of the council reiterate the message that funding be seen as supplementary to existing support rather than as wholly adequate to cover all costs. It is clear from these first reports that the council wanted to ensure that organizations continue to seek out local funding for their operations, resulting in the frequent repetition of the sentiment that "the more assistance given to creative talent by the Council, the more need of support from other sources to ensure that the artistic gifts we are developing find adequate outlet in Canada."[91] Over 1958–59, the council distributed $65,700 in funding to art galleries, mostly to support extension activities such as circulating exhibitions and lectures, to pay jury expenses for exhibitions, to provide assistance with the publication of catalogues, and to help support children's art classes. In addition, $3,000 was earmarked for purchase awards for paintings, where galleries were given $1,000 of matching funds with which to buy works by contemporary Canadian artists for their permanent collections.[92] A further $12,000 was allocated to galleries to commission sculptures for their public spaces. Only three years after its founding, the Canada Council raised the question of whether its mission should be supporting the best organizations and thereby raising the standards of the arts in Canada, or whether it should be increasing access to the visual arts to as many people as possible. This question pointed less to a debate between fostering excellence and ensuring access, as making the point that the council would not be giving small amounts of money to every artist and organization that made a request.[93]

For art galleries in western Canada, Canada Council funding was a welcome injection of money, however small the amounts. The council's purchase awards were particularly hailed by western art galleries lacking the supply of collectors eager to donate works to their local gallery's permanent collections. For the Edmonton Art Gallery (as the Edmonton Museum of Arts was renamed in 1956), the announcement that matching funds were available for the purchase of contemporary Canadian art enabled the gallery's board of directors to envision greater breadth in their acquisitions. Occurring at the same time that the Edmonton Art Gallery was developing formal accession and collecting policies, access to funds for acquisitions rather than for operational costs was a boon. Funding for program assistance such as the publication of an exhibition catalogue or aid in organizing a special exhibition tended to be directed towards institutions whose activities had already garnered them national recognition. As Assistant Director Peter Dwyer noted in a speech to *Seminar '65*, organized by the Canadian Conference of the Arts, the council's dilemma of whether to "raise or spread" had resulted in the apportioning of greater funds to organizations with demonstrable success: "We have observed that quality in the arts equates with professionalism and that professionalism ... tends to concentrate in the larger cities."[94] Indeed, the major grants to art galleries frequently went to institutions in Montreal, Toronto, Winnipeg, and Vancouver, while smaller disbursements were made to galleries in other cities. Western Canadian arts organizations profited from council funding in equal measure to comparative institutions in other parts of the country, and made good use of the touring programs the council instituted to ensure that Canadian culture was accessible to as broad a public as possible.

Dissemination programs and purchase funds for contemporary art were not the only means through which the Canada Council supported arts organizations. On its tenth anniversary, the council addressed the pressures facing art galleries in its annual report, underlining the difficulties of institutions to adequately address the expanding needs of exhibition, storage, and conservation facilities, also arguing that expanded facilities were required to attract donations of the private collections that had been increasing in Canada since the Second World War. The council also noted that the high demand for curatorial staff was not being met and would require a further influx of funding to induce Canadian scholars to enter the field.[95] The question of capital funding to galleries was taken up by Richard Simmins in his *Report on the Development of Art Galleries in Canada*, commissioned by the Canada Council and submitted in 1969. In that document, Simmins repeatedly emphasized the need for direct funds to art museums as either capital grants or core funding to allow them to better deliver the programs they had been mandated to provide. Writing at the same time that the secretary of state had announced the formation of the National Museums Corporation (to be discussed in detail in Chapter 6), Simmins identified governments – federal, provincial, and municipal – as the principal funders for art museums in Canada. After lengthy consultations with museum personnel and boards across the country, Simmins predicted that memberships and private funding would not be of much assistance in the upkeep of museum programs and further argued that corporate funding was not the panacea that many viewed it to be. Rather, at a time when boards of trustees were playing less and less of a role in the operations of art galleries and not living up to their sponsorship responsibilities, Simmins suggested that the federal government increase its funding and adequately support what he determined to be a flourishing area of cultural development. Simmins's prediction would prove to be accurate and by 1972, Secretary of State Gérard Pelletier announced the National Museum Policy that, among other programs, included capital funds for gallery expansion.

Conclusion

The 1940s and 1950s was a time of major transformation in the landscape of Canadian art, as seen in the multiple approaches to art making that characterized the period as well as the focused attention paid to the role of culture on the development of national feeling. That the country was becoming more visible internationally – from its role in the establishment of NATO to its ascension as a middle power – further underscored the importance of a strong national culture that could serve the projection of Canada abroad. Although such broader political interests were only marginally the concern of Canadian artists, the resulting attention to the support of Canadian art at home was welcomed and heatedly debated across the country. The establishment and activities of such organizations as the Federation of Canadian Artists and the Canada Council for the Arts are key moments in the history of art in Canada, and the debates that resulted from the Kingston Conference, the writing of the Artists' Brief, and the Massey Commission remain central touchstones for the collocation of art and national identity in the country. However, as this chapter has illuminated, such discussions were not entirely in support of a nationalist – or even a national – vision. Regional voices were strong during this period and expressed a fierce loyalty to activities and interests that were taking place on the ground, as it were, alongside an appreciation for the role of national institutions. Such tensions were particularly evident in western Canada where art museums, long indebted for the support they had received from the National Gallery, were beginning to feel that the federal institution was exerting too much control over the activities of organizations on the periphery. The community art centre proposal, first voiced by the BC branch of the Federation of Canadian Artists but then taken up by the national executive, was widely seen in the west as a means of asserting local control and fostering local production. Viewed within the context of a growing political alienation from some western provinces and the broader complaint that Ottawa's distance made it ill qualified to understand the specific challenges of the region, western Canadian art galleries' desires to increase their autonomy from the National Gallery becomes more understandable. As will be discussed in the next chapter, such desires for increased autonomy would result in the formation of the Western Canada Art Circuit, an affiliation of large and small galleries and arts organizations in Manitoba, Saskatchewan, Alberta, and British Columbia that would attempt to wrest control over the circulation of exhibitions in the region away from the National Gallery and allow western institutions to build an exhibition program that more closely fit with the interests of the communities they served.

4

RESISTING THE CENTRE

The Western Canada Art Circuit

As the debate over the merits of community art centres as well as the numerous briefs to the Masscy Commission discussed in the last chapter demonstrate, concerns over the undue centralization of art activities in Canada under the auspices of the National Gallery were voiced by many organizations across the country, and particularly by organizations in western Canada. While the economic and environmental impact of the Depression years were sharply experienced by Manitoba, Saskatchewan, Alberta, and British Columbia, postwar prosperity had increased the population and diversified provincial economies, allowing for the region's renewed sense of itself as a vital participant in the nation's future. Politically, the success of parties such as Social Credit and the Canadian Commonwealth Federation brought a sense of power and regional strength that rattled the traditional Liberal and Conservative parties as their numbers dwindled in western Canadian legislative assemblies. The Massey Commission hearings are telling in this regard as many of the presentations from western Canada – such as those from the Alberta Society of Artists and the Calgary branch of the Federation of Canadian Artists – called for increased support for local artists and organizations, even when such requests were couched as a means of strengthening national culture. Fundamentally, however, western Canadian art organizations did not fully trust central Canadian institutions to adequately attend to the needs of the regions in large part because these actors had not demonstrated that they understood the specificity of local needs nor considered them to be different from the familiar and dominant narrative. In the realm of the visual arts, as western Canadian art galleries built their permanent collections and developed their programs, they became less and less enchanted with the services provided by the National Gallery of Canada (NGC). While the circulating exhibitions, reproduction programs, and lecture tours remained popular services provided by the NGC, gallery directors in western Canada were wont to voice more and more loudly their dissatisfaction with the degree of input and choice they were given in the nature of the programs and exhibitions received. Such complaints were sometimes directed to National Gallery staff but they were more frequently exchanged amongst gallery directors. Recognizing their increased strength as a group, directors of western Canadian art galleries met in 1944 and founded the Western Canada Art Circuit (WCAC). The organization would simplify the work of circulating National Gallery exhibitions throughout the region and encourage individual galleries to develop their own exhibitions for circulation to other circuit members. This chapter explores the activities of the circuit with a particular focus on its self-positioning as a regional organization that could stand up to the organizational might of the National Gallery. In particular, this chapter argues that the Western Canada Art Circuit did more than just facilitate the movement of exhibitions throughout the four provinces, and that it stood as a powerful rhetorical force against attempts by the NGC to retain power over regional galleries. Although it faced a number of challenges in its administration and membership, the WCAC proved to be a forceful voice for western Canada and for a time challenged the NGC to reconsider its relationship to institutions in this part of the country.

Circulating Exhibitions in Western Canada

The Western Canada Art Circuit was formed in Edmonton on June 1944 at the instigation of Robert Hedley, director of the Edmonton Museum of Arts. Bringing together art centres from across western Canada, the WCAC was intended to simplify the circulation of loan exhibitions from the National Gallery to both big and small cities in the region. Original members included the Vancouver Art Gallery, the Winnipeg Art Gallery, the Saskatoon Art Centre, the Calgary Allied Arts Centre, and the Edmonton Museum of Arts. Although a delegate from the city was present at the first meeting, Regina was not one of the original participating centres as it was not known how many exhibits could be accommodated in the available facilities at Regina College and the Public Library.[1] The University of Alberta sent curator J.B. Taylor to the first conference as it had been a regular recipient of loan exhibitions from the National Gallery in addition to those obtained by the Edmonton Museum of Arts, and as the university's fine arts department expanded – particularly with the hiring of artist H.G. Glyde in 1946 – it remained an active member of the circuit.

At the first organizing meeting, delegates emphasized the difficulties they were experiencing in coordinating the movement of exhibitions from one centre to the next, with each centre having to deal directly with the National Gallery. For the individual organizations, staying on top of these arrangements required regular contact with both Ottawa and the centres that either currently had the exhibition or to which it was going. As noted in Chapter 2, the correspondence between H.O. McCurry and heads of various exhibiting organizations in western Canada frequently noted the late arrival of an exhibition from another centre, the careless packing of pictures, and the difficulty of assessing responsibility for payment for the shipping of the exhibitions from point to point. Modelling the new venture on the successful Maritime Art Association established on the East Coast in 1935, members hoped that the WCAC would relieve many of these problems by creating a network of art and artists' organizations in western Canada. The original constitution outlines both the aims of the WCAC and the problems it sought to relieve:

1 To secure the best possible exhibits at a minimum of expense.
2 To work with the National Gallery at Ottawa in its endeavour to bring the best works before the public, from Canadian or other sources.
3 To encourage various groups of artists in Western Canada.
4 To make it possible to have some excellent one-man or two-men, or three-men, exhibits both from the East and from the West, make the circuits when so desired.
5 To so regulate the program that there will be the minimum loss of time in traveling the circuit.
6 Each centre would again be a distributing centre for the region.[2]

Every gallery committed to paying transportation costs on arrival of shipments of exhibitions to their facility; at the end of the exhibition's tour of the western provinces, the total costs of transportation would be tallied and the expenses spread evenly across all the participating centres: in this way, no single art centre would be responsible for a greater share of travel costs. As the suggested agenda for the initial meeting of delegates to form the circuit queried, "is it not possible to organize a Western Art Exhibition Circuit, that various centres joining the circuit may have the very best Art Exhibits possible as well as to encourage home talent at a minimum of expense."[3]

For art centres in western Canada, a formal circuit was the ideal solution to the logistical difficulties of organizing the circulation of exhibitions from the National Gallery. It is clear from the WCAC's constitution that the national institution was still considered to be the primary source of exhibitions for the galleries on the circuit – either by organizing the exhibitions themselves or by facilitating the distribution of exhibitions by such other organizations as the Canadian Society of Painters in Water Colour or the Royal Canadian Academy. Exhibitions from international institutions like the Museum of Modern Art in New York were also much desired and were similarly facilitated through the central organizing services of the National Gallery. Also appealing to the art centres in western Canada was the potential reduction in costs of transportation and insurance resulting from the creation of a circuit. And certainly spreading the costs of touring and insuring the exhibitions over a number of centres, rather than regularly negotiating directly with the National Gallery, was much appreciated by institutions struggling to stay open during the lean years following the Second World War. However, by banding together as a formal body that met regularly to discuss issues of concern to western Canadian galleries, the WCAC was equally invested in the promotion of the region's artists and in creating the conditions for the production of their own exhibitions that could be circulated within the region and nationally.

The National Gallery's reaction to the formation of the WCAC was positive: a confirmation of the success of the gallery's circulating loans program in encouraging interest in the arts in western Canada. This, of course, had been the goal of both the circulating loan and the reproduction programs of the NGC, and the annual reports through the 1940s show that the NGC was committed to continuing this practice since it was key to the claim that the gallery was providing invaluable – and arguably unique – services to the nation.[4] Indeed, at its inception, the

National Gallery appeared grateful to the WCAC for taking over the time-consuming task of organizing the schedule of circulating exhibitions to western Canada, furthermore regarding its formation as instrumental in maintaining the visibility of the national institution in the region. At the same time, McCurry had some difficulty completely relinquishing control of the exhibitions that issued from the gallery. As he wrote to Hedley in 1945, "we at the National Gallery would enjoy very much … to have the Western Conference convene at the National Gallery on some convenient occasion. I think your people would benefit by seeing the 'machine' in operation, and we would get to know each other's difficulties and the possibilities of wider developments."[5] This statement suggests that, in the beginning, relations with the WCAC were viewed as being principally collaborative: a mutually beneficial organization that would coordinate the shipment of exhibitions from the National Gallery to art centres from Winnipeg westward, leaving gallery staff to focus on organizing the exhibitions and the accompanying literature for circulation.

The Western Canada Art Circuit was not the first such organization to coordinate the circulation of exhibitions to a particular region of Canada: an important precedent can be found in the Maritime Art Association (MAA), established by Walter Abell in 1935. Appointed as professor of fine arts at Acadia University in Wolfville, Nova Scotia, in 1928, Abell was instrumental in creating a network of professional and amateur art organizations across New Brunswick, Nova Scotia, and Prince Edward Island.[6] With funds from the Carnegie Corporation, which had already been generous in its sponsorship of Abell's educational activities at Acadia University, he formed the Acadia Fine Arts Club to bring together members of the university and the community who shared an interest in the fine arts. Under Abell, the club organized talks and workshops, developed a picture loan collection, and, in collaboration with Elizabeth MacLeod, director of Mount Allison University's Art School, set about obtaining circulating exhibitions from the College Art Association and the American Federation of Artists. In 1935, Abell and MacLeod expanded their sights and, with the support of the National Gallery, established the Maritime Art Association with the goal to "promote a knowledge and appreciation of art [and] to foster art activities in the Maritime Provinces."[7] The first art association to represent regional interests, the MAA's original membership included a broad range of professional and amateur organizations, including the Acadia University Fine Arts Club, the Nova Scotia

College of Art, the Nova Scotia Museum, the Moncton Society of Art, the Art Society of Prince Edward Island, the Saint John Vocational School, the Lord Amherst and Louisbourg Chapters of the Imperial Order Daughters of the Empire, and Art Clubs from New Glasgow, St Andrews, Newcastle, and Sackville.[8]

Abell and MacLeod viewed the MAA primarily as an interprovincial exhibition circuit, facilitating the circulation of exhibitions throughout the region and reducing costs of presentation for each venue. The association, in the words of Sandra Paikowsky, would also "give more muscle" to regional requests to the National Gallery for loan exhibitions, and would assist existing art groups in the Maritimes to organize and circulate their own exhibitions. As Paikowsky notes, the National Gallery offered both ideological and financial support for the Maritime Art Association through the auspices of the newly formed Carnegie-funded Canadian Museums Committee, with McCurry telling Abell that he hoped the new association would improve the "spasmodic and unsatisfactory" response of eastern Canadians to National Gallery loan exhibitions.[9] In the Maritimes, reaction to the proposed association was overwhelmingly positive, and within two years of its founding, seventeen groups in fourteen cities and towns had joined, a number that would remain consistent for much of the next decade. Member organizations were offered exhibitions, lectures, and a newsletter that gave information on Canadian and international art movements. Abell also harnessed the increasing interest in the fine and applied arts in the region by giving radio talks that were broadcast on the CBC out of Halifax. The most active events sponsored by the MAA during this period, however, were the exhibitions, an average of eight per year circulating through the three Maritime provinces. The majority of these were loan exhibitions organized by the National Gallery, but the MAA–organized exhibitions of local artists – *Paintings by Artists of the Maritime Provinces* – was a popular yearly feature. In line with the MAA's efforts to promote interest in art in the region, Abell wrote extensive commentaries to accompany all the exhibitions, a practice that he felt would "assist in understanding and appreciating the works shown."[10]

National awareness of the work of the MAA was initially achieved through the association's publication *Maritime Art*, founded by Abell in 1940 with funds from the Carnegie Corporation. By 1943, the magazine, along with Abell, had moved to the National Gallery to become *Canadian Art*, with funding predominantly from the NGC and the Federation of Canadian Artists. Federation sponsorship ensured widespread circulation as the magazine was made available for free to members across the country, and as a result the activities of artists from the eastern provinces as well as the MAA itself were publicized nationally. Maritime artists were also recognized throughout the country through another initiative of the MAA, the circulation of exhibitions of East Coast artists to medium and small galleries across the country, including an exchange with painters in British Columbia and the exhibition *Paintings by Artists of the Maritimes* travelling to western Canada in 1939–40.[11] The evident success of the association was doubtless an inspiration to art organizations in western Canada for whom the even greater distances between cities produced a tremendous sense of isolation. For both the MAA and the nascent WCAC, the ability to manage the circulation of NGC loan exhibitions and the potential to develop shows of their own meant a degree of independence from Ottawa. As Paikowsky notes, Abell sent his reports of the MAA's activities both to McCurry and to Carnegie Foundation head Frederick Keppel in order to inform the foundation directly rather than risk it receiving a version filtered through the NGC's perspective.[12] Although a western Canadian version of the MAA was a practical way of establishing an exhibition network to serve arts organizations in the region, the founders of the WCAC likely viewed the symbolic presence of such a network in western Canada to be just as important for securing some form of leverage in its dealings with the National Gallery.

The Early Years of the WCAC

Through the 1940s and into the 1950s, the Western Canada Art Circuit grew as local art associations in all four provinces joined in the effort to secure good quality art exhibitions and to give artists from their communities access to a larger exhibitionary network. By 1949, art organizations in Brandon, Moose Jaw, Prince Albert, Medicine Hat, Nelson, and Kimberley had joined the circuit: some of these had existing relationships with the National Gallery, and all were eager, despite their size, to present art exhibitions in whatever facilities were available. In that year they eagerly welcomed exhibitions such as *Contemporary French Illustration* (organized by the NGC), *Twenty Canadians* (originating from the Dominion Gallery), *Design Down Under* (from the Australian government), and a Lawren Harris retrospective.[13] Meanwhile, the larger and more established galleries in the region continued to build their permanent collections and develop their educational programs, and assumed more of a leadership role in circuit affairs. Headed by a managing director working largely in a voluntary capacity, the WCAC held yearly conferences in a different member city, during which delegates worked out a schedule of exhibitions, and discussed proper packing techniques, display methods, and the kinds of exhibitions thought to be most appealing to the region's residents. Throughout much of this time, the head of the WCAC remained Robert Hedley, who undertook all the organizational responsibilities for the circuit in addition to his work as director of the Edmonton Museum of Arts. Such responsibilities were a heavy burden on the aging Hedley and he eventually resigned as head of the circuit in 1948 at the age of seventy-seven, to be succeeded by Archie F. Key, who headed the Calgary Allied Arts Centre at Coste House. The director's main responsibilities involved acting as liaison among the individual centres on the circuit, and between the circuit and the National Gallery. The former job was largely administrative in nature, coordinating the movement of exhibitions from each point and with the assistance of an accounts manager, tabulating the costs of transportation and insurance so that these were equitably spread across all the centres. This task was frequently complicated by the fact that the small organizations had virtually no money to pay for even minimal transportation costs. This difficulty, along with the fact that many of these art centres also had to find money to rent rooms to show the collections, would remain a concern of the circuit throughout its existence. Liaison with the National Gallery, however, proved to be the more complicated task, as it required negotiating between the needs and particular circumstances of the circuit, and the expectations of the National Gallery around efficiency and the professional handling of its exhibitions.

During these first eight years, membership in the circuit increased from the original five to a high of fifteen in 1949 when the WCAC presented its brief to the Massey Commission.[14] This increase in membership, however, belies the slow physical development of art centres in western Canada. The only organizations with significant spaces for the professional display of fine art remained the art galleries in Winnipeg, Vancouver, and Edmonton. Calgary's Allied Arts Centre at Coste House had a few rooms in a converted mansion where it shared space with most of the city's other cultural organizations; Regina was served by a basement room in the Public Library as well as a small space at Regina College that also held Norman MacKenzie's painting bequest; the Saskatoon Art Centre was situated in the basement arcade of the King George Hotel; and the smaller cities of Brandon, Moose Jaw, Prince Albert, Medicine Hat, Kimberley, and Nelson relied on the rental of rooms in the public halls of civic buildings with few of the minimal requirements for the appropriate display of art.[15] In the face of such constrained exhibition facilities, the need for an organization such as the WCAC in the 1940s is evident. As Edmonton Museum of Arts Director Robert Hedley noted in a 1947 letter to H.O. McCurry, many cities in western Canada had limited facilities or were fledgling organizations that struggled to find and operate the kind of facilities that could adequately host exhibitions of any scale:

> Several places in the West are in the same dilemma or facing the same problem that we did 22 years ago. We had a small room in the Public Library here, which would hold 5 fair-sized pictures. We received five from Ottawa, and made a beginning. Later we managed to get two rooms in the Civic Bloc, later another making a floor space of approximately 1,700 feet. Two years ago we got a place on the ground floor, with about 4,400 feet floor space. This is crowded now and we want one twice as large. Well Victoria, Moose Jaw, Regina, Saskatoon, Prince Albert are in much the same difficulty as we were, in the early days. There is considerable enthusiasm. A start must be made sometime. But I am hopeful that in time troubles will gradually disappear. When we see the almost palatial buildings of Ottawa, Montreal and Toronto, well, we just can hope, and work.[16]

Ironically, during a period when the Edmonton Museum of Arts continued to struggle financially and to face a lack of public interest in its activities, it saw itself as occupying a more advanced position than the organizations in smaller Canadian cities that did not have permanent let alone adequate spaces for the display of fine art. This points to both the largely poor conditions for the presentation of the fine arts in western Canada during this period, and the importance of the Western Canada Art Circuit in bringing exhibitions to a wide array of communities in the region.

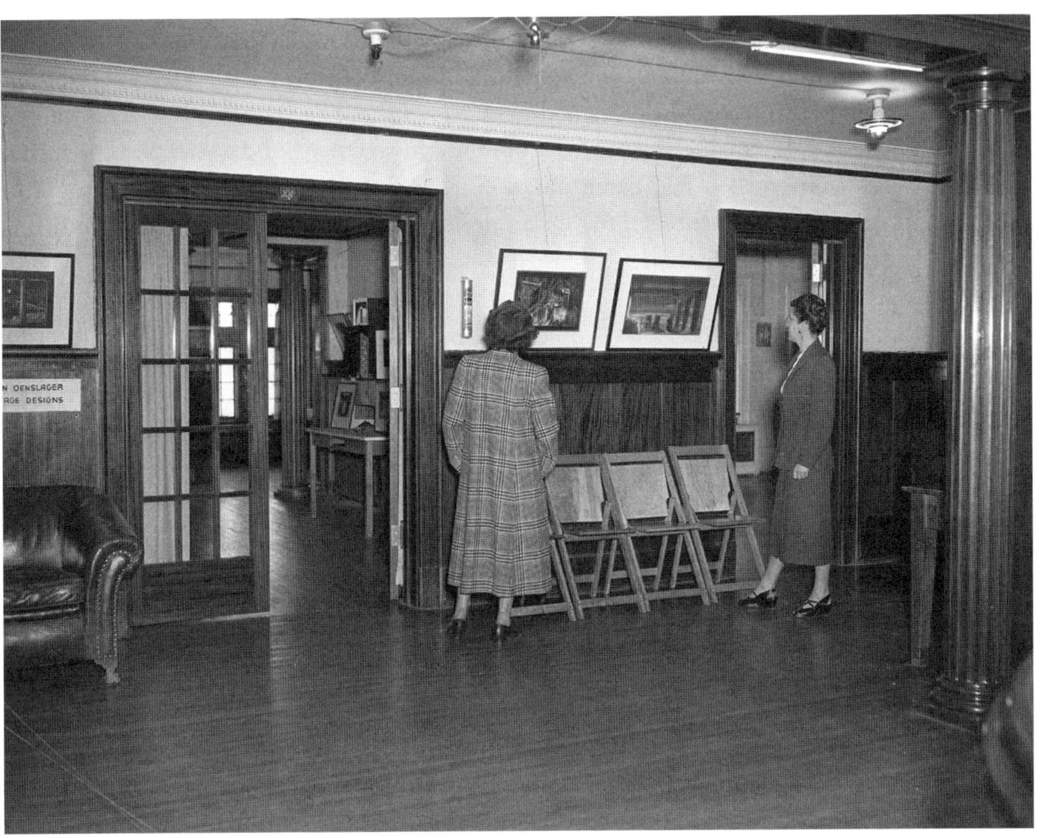

4.1 | Exhibition of stage designs at Coste House, 1961. The Calgary Allied Arts Centre would soon close its doors, leaving the Glenbow-Alberta Foundation as the primary venue for art exhibitions in the city.

Despite the physical constraints facing most of its member organizations, the WCAC managed an impressive program of circulating exhibitions. The majority of the exhibitions came from the National Gallery: either a selection of works from its permanent collection – always one of the more popular exhibitions – or groups of works from such exhibiting societies as the Canadian Group of Painters or the Royal Canadian Academy coordinated by the gallery. Members of these societies sometimes complained that the length of the tours impeded sales of their work, and that the paintings were frequently returned in a damaged state. In a letter to McCurry regarding a WCAC request for a Canadian Group of Painters show in 1947, A.Y. Jackson wrote, "How many sales have been made in the west and the maritimes [*sic*] in the last ten years? About all we get is damaged frames."[17] The gallery also made available exhibitions from organizations outside of Canada, such as the *Look to Your Neighborhood* show, organized by the Museum of Modern Art (1945), and a selection of works from the American Federation of Artists shown in 1951. For their part, member centres of the WCAC organized smaller shows of local artists that could circulate with relative ease (and at less expense) throughout the circuit. Examples of such exhibitions included *The Saskatchewan Federation of Artists* (1952) organized by the Saskatoon Art Centre, and an exhibition of the paintings of Laura Evans Reid organized by the University of Alberta in 1953. Obviously some institutions were more capable of arranging such exhibitions than others; for example, in 1949 the Vancouver Art Gallery (VAG) organized an exhibition of contemporary BC artists, and the Calgary Allied Arts Centre facilitated the circulation of several exhibitions of work by members of the Alberta Society of Artists. The most popular and sought-after exhibitions were historical or representational in style, featuring Canadian (and international) artists working in relatively realist modes and subject matter; frequent requests were made to the National Gallery for works from its collection and for exhibitions of work by members of the Group of Seven and the more traditional artists' societies. In line with this view, there were also complaints about work considered too modern, usually from smaller centres whose views of art (and the role of exhibitions obtained from the circuit) often differed from those of larger cities with longer standing art communities. Circulating shows of art reproductions – of Canadian as well as European master works – were popular with smaller centres and played an important role in the programming of the circuit because they were more affordable and could be shown anywhere.

In addition to giving western Canadians access to a broad range of art exhibitions, an additional benefit to the formation of the WCAC was increased exposure of artists from the region to other parts of Canada – an issue that had been discussed extensively at the Kingston Conference in 1941. One early initiative in this vein was the circuit's organization of an art exhibition from the four western provinces that would tour eastern Canada, as well as its own galleries, in 1946–47. The call for submissions asked artists to "paint pictures of 'Western Life,' or of our expansive plains, our lofty mountains or our rugged coasts," continuing with the assertion that "We may not have a distinctly western style, but we have exceptionally good subject matter. Let us do our best to produce works of art that will reveal the 'aliveness' of the West."[18] As a means of making the region's artists more visible, the authors of the call for submissions elected to trade on existing images of western Canada – many solidified through the paintings and photographs commissioned by the Canadian Pacific Railway in the late nineteenth century to increase tourism to its newly built hotels – to ensure that central and eastern Canadian audiences had a familiar point of entry into the exhibition. Recognizing that a regional style was neither present nor possibly desirable, the organizers opted to focus instead on an image of place that suggested vigorous growth as well as an emerging art scene that was similarly thriving.[19] Presentations of the work of western Canadian artists outside the region did not become the regular event the WCAC had hoped, but in its first two decades the circuit benefitted the region's artists by increasing local public attention for the visual arts through regular exhibitions and producing larger shows that had the potential to travel nationally.

The first setback to the continuing success of the WCAC was the withdrawal of the Vancouver Art Gallery in 1950. In retrospect, this action is not surprising, but at the time it must have been a deep blow to the WCAC and its efforts to establish a strong western presence on the Canadian art scene. Vancouver's decision to quit came as the gallery grew in size and stature under the leadership of Jerrold Morris. In concert with a rapidly growing city and increased support from the civic government as well as the public, the Vancouver gallery expanded its exhibition and educational programs, hired additional staff, and enlarged its facilities, particularly to accommodate the significant bequest of paintings by Emily Carr in 1945. By 1950 the Vancouver Art Gallery had resolved that it could achieve a better quality of programming from associating with larger galleries along the west coast and through direct contact with the National Gallery in Ottawa. As Morris noted in a letter informing circuit director Archie Key of the decision, the VAG had no desire to completely sever ties to all centres in western Canada but rather saw the uneven quality of many of the organizations affiliated with the WCAC as limiting the kinds of exhibitions the circuit as a whole could attract:

> We don't want to belong to any circuit but wish to operate independently, as any established museum should. We are, however, prepared to work fully in cooperation with a small group of

galleries of similar standing in the West, who are [*sic*] interested in obtaining exhibitions of high quality ... The Organization should be a loose one and not named as a circuit. If you ask for a decent exhibition from the East in the name of the Western Circuit you will get nothing – if you ask for a show for Winnipeg, Calgary, Edmonton, and Vancouver you may get somewhere.[20]

Morris's advice had little effect on the organization and running of the Western Canada Art Circuit: indeed the major centres – with the significant contributions of the Saskatoon Art Centre and the Norman MacKenzie Gallery in Regina when those organizations obtained larger facilities in the mid-1950s – continued to band together with groups in smaller cities in the belief that together they could further both the development of artistic practice in western Canada and an appreciation for art amongst the general public. For its part, the Vancouver Art Gallery quickly forged connections with similar-sized institutions in Portland, Seattle, and San Francisco through the US-based Western Association of Art Museum Directors, to which Morris was elected president in 1951 and 1952.

The Challenges of Circulating Exhibitions in Canada

The WCAC was one of five regional circulating organizations that appeared in Canada between 1934 and 1952: besides the Maritime Art Association, there were also the Southern Ontario Art Association, the Western Ontario Art Circuit, and the Northern Ontario Art Association. Both the Southern Ontario Art Association and the Western Ontario Art Circuit were run out of the London Public Library and Art Museum under the leadership of curator Clare Bice, but each had a different mandate and audience. The Southern Ontario Art Association linked the art gallery in London with the Hamilton Art Gallery, the Willistead Art Gallery in Windsor (now the Windsor Art Gallery), and Hart House at the University of Toronto. These four institutions had been operating since the 1940s (with the exception of Hart House whose Art Committee was established in 1922), had been steadily accumulating works for their permanent collections, and all had exhibition spaces – whether in a separate building or in rooms at the public library – that were secure enough to host the National Gallery's best exhibitions. Effectively a loose network of four medium-sized institutions seeking to increase their programming by creating exhibitions for the purposes of circulating them to each other, the Southern Ontario circuit was more interested in sharing resources among the increasingly sophisticated art public of this growing area of the country than in bringing the gospel of the fine arts to small communities in the region. This task was more the purview of the Western Ontario Art Circuit, which provided exhibitions for art groups seeking to establish themselves in such smaller cities as Woodstock, Kitchener, Brantford, Sarnia, Chatham, St Thomas, and Ingersoll. Organized by the London Public Library and Art Museum, the exhibitions featured on this circuit came from the National Gallery, from the London gallery as well as from other sources such as the Ontario Society of Artists and the Canadian Society of Painter-Etchers and Engravers.[21] Meanwhile, the Northern Ontario Art Association was established in 1949 and brought together amateur art groups from small towns in northern Quebec and Ontario.[22] Although initially its concern was to encourage contact among artists from the region, the Northern Ontario Art Association quickly recognized that seeing exhibitions of professional artwork would benefit its members and its director contacted the National Gallery in 1952 with a request for a small exhibition.

While there are differences between the Western Ontario Art Circuit, the Northern Ontario Art Association and the Western Canada Art Circuit – the geographical scale of the regions, the number of larger galleries able to coordinate exhibitions for distribution, for example – they all faced similar challenges that made running them a time-consuming and sometimes frustrating activity. As with many of the member centres of the WCAC, the art associations that participated in the Western Ontario Art Circuit and the Northern Ontario Art Association had little money, inadequate facilities for the display of artwork, and a lack of knowledge of proper packing techniques. The circuits themselves, with their ability to spread out costs of shipping exhibitions over longer distances, resolved some of the money problems; but as Richard Williams, director of the School of Art at the University of Manitoba, complained, there was still an expectation from many of the organizations that eighty-five dollars would yield seven exhibitions a year.[23] Both individual art associations as well as the larger centres appealed to both the circuits and the National Gallery directly for exhibitions that would foster appreciation in the fine arts as well as assist local artists in improving their form. The Northern Ontario Art Association seems to have been somewhat unique in holding an annual juried exhibition of the work of local artists, and frequently requested jury members from larger galleries to come to the area for a few days. The Northern Ontario Art Association also regularly asked for lecture tours by art critics or representatives of the National Gallery as well as for the circulation of films on art – a request the NGC found much easier to fulfill. The lack of consistency in packing remained a constant irritation for both circuit members and the National Gallery as the gallery chided smaller centres for not following the detailed instructions accompanying each case, and circuit members accused the National Gallery of providing inadequate or badly manufactured cases that required constant repairs. In a letter to Alan Jarvis in 1956, Edward Pearse, president of the Northern Ontario Art Association described the challenges of bringing exhibitions to small cities and towns:

> The exhibitions from the Galleries are usually expensive to bring in, and moreover we lack suitable fire-proof housing for them. Conditions vary from bad to tolerable. In Sault Ste. Marie for example, there is a small fire-proof room in the Memorial Gardens – really a hockey arena. In order to view the paintings one must often buy a hockey ticket. Then too, contemplation of the paintings is punctuated by the roars of the crowd. It has it's [*sic*] compensations, for at intermissions the fans pour through the room, and even though they be talking of the last play, are "exposed," at least, to art.[24]

Despite inadequate spaces for display, and a somewhat indifferent public, Pearse's letter demonstrates that the exhibition circulation service offered by the National Gallery (and delivered through various circuits) remained in great demand by small centres across the country. These exhibitions and attendant educational services were the fundamental way that the National Gallery could fulfill its mandate to serve the whole of Canada and not simply those who lived within driving distance of the gallery. However, as demand for exhibitions grew – particularly following the strong recommendation by the Massey Commission that the National Gallery increase its commitment to regional centres – the NGC found it increasingly difficult to fulfill the needs of the various circuits, and indeed often faced competing demands from individual galleries who, frustrated with one aspect of their respective circuit or another, sought to contact the gallery directly for assistance. Undergoing its own shifts in personnel and mandate – including the passing of a new National Gallery Act in 1952, the retirement of McCurry, and his replacement by Alan Jarvis in 1955 – the National Gallery began a re-examination of its loan exhibition program and broader outreach activities in the first half of the 1950s. This included an expansion of its educational activities and services as well as a restructuring of the circulating exhibitions and an evaluation of the regional organizations it serviced.

While the Massey Commission's report was unstinting in its praise for the National Gallery's loan exhibitions and other programs that reached out to the regions, it nevertheless recommended that the NGC expand its board of trustees from five to nine members in order to better represent a diversity of ideas from a broader cross section of the country. With the exception of Robert Newton, president of the University of Alberta, appointed in 1948, and Lawren Harris, who was appointed in 1950, ten years after his move to Vancouver, the NGC's Board of Trustees was overwhelmingly populated by men from Montreal, Toronto, and Ottawa. In December 1951, the new National Gallery Act shifted oversight for the institution from the Ministry of Public Works to the recently created (1950) Department of Citizenship and Immigration. Five new trustees were appointed, including Dorothy (Bobby) Dyde, a collector from Edmonton who would also be named to the council of the Edmonton Museum of Arts later that year.[25] Although the minutes suggest that the majority of the trustees were satisfied with the gallery's activities, Harris and Dyde felt that the NGC could be more responsive to the needs of the regions and worked closely together to develop a more systematic mechanism for the delivery of programs outside Ottawa. Harris had initiated the project shortly after his appointment to the board, initially within the context of improvements he sought to make in the National Gallery's proposal to re-establish its annual exhibition of Canadian painting.[26] Keen to see better representation of artists from across the country, and supported by then fellow trustee Robert Newton, who wanted more artists from western Canada in the gallery's collection, Harris advocated for an exhibition of some sixty works (Newton argued for more) that would be selected by regionally based juries rather than a centrally located committee. After considerable debate regarding how artists would be chosen – representation by population (McCurry's choice) versus a selection of the best work from across the country (Harris's position) – the 1953 *Exhibition of Canadian Art* presented work by seventy-seven artists, distributed fairly evenly across the country's five regions, and chosen by regional juries.[27]

Viewed within the context of his earlier statements about the centralizing power of the National Gallery when he was the Federation of Canadian Artists president, Harris's advocacy of regional juries over the existing practice of having artists send works to a central committee takes up both his commitment to community art centres and many of the arguments made by western delegates at the Kingston Conference about the difficulties of getting their works seen by National Gallery representatives discussed in Chapter 3. Harris's position at that time, it will be remembered, also forcefully argued for the decentralization of the NGC and the creation of "branch galleries" housing parts of its permanent collection. By the time of his appointment to the NGC's board of trustees in 1950, however, Harris had either softened his position considerably, or had become more strategic in his dealings with McCurry in order to ensure better representation of the interests of the regions – and of western Canadian artists – in National Gallery programming. Building on his success in obtaining regional juries for the annual exhibitions, Harris – with the support of Dyde – proposed that the NGC create a department of extension that would coordinate the circulation of artworks to the regions. Harris first suggested the formation of an extension service by the National Gallery in a letter to McCurry in September 1952 where he mentions the proposal he had been working on with Dyde and requests that McCurry add it to the agenda for the upcoming board meeting in October. At that meeting, Harris presented his proposal that a director of extension be appointed, responsible to the National Gallery director, in order "to meet the growing and insistent demands of all parts of Canada for participation in the cultural benefits and services of the National Gallery, pursuant to the recommendations contained in the Massey Commission."[28] Key to Harris's proposal was the hiring of trained personnel who would be able to inspect existing exhibition facilities across the country and assess their suitability for the different types of exhibitions offered by the Gallery. Such an individual would also be able to establish regular communication with regional institutions and be more effective in responding to their needs. Finally, as Harris wrote to McCurry, a man responsible for relations with outside institutions would relieve

McCurry "of the extension details and work"[29] – a situation that Harris would have favoured since it presumably reduced the amount of control exerted by the director.

Interestingly, Harris was not the first to suggest the appointment of staff at the NGC responsible for regional organizations. In the minutes of the 1949 annual meeting of the WCAC, guidelines for the drafting of a brief to the Massey Commission included the resolution "That the National Gallery establish Regional Directors to serve as administrators and/or advisors to groups which have organized country, regional, or inter-provincial exhibition circuits."[30] In subsequent correspondence with the NGC, circuit director Archie Key suggested himself – or another member of the WCAC – as an ideal candidate to convey the needs of western Canadian arts organizations to the NGC. Responding to the WCAC's Massey Commission brief in a memorandum to McCurry, NGC business manager J.K.B. Robertson suggested that the establishment of regional directors or representatives might have merit if handled properly, but cautioned that the timing might not be quite right: "this might be too suggestive of spoon-feeding and contrary to the National Gallery's usual policy of offering services to centres which establish themselves by their own efforts – and presumably have reached a stage of maturity where they do not need constant supervision by a National Gallery representative in the field."[31] Although different from Harris and Dyde's proposal for a department of extension services, the WCAC's recommendation of regional directors at the NGC exemplifies the contradictions in the relationship between the circuit and the national institution. On one hand, the WCAC – and the majority of its member galleries – could not sustain an ongoing program of exhibitions without the support of the NGC's circulating exhibition program. On the other hand, many felt frustration with the control exercised by the national institution over the content and duration of exhibitions, and the continued chastisement from NGC staff over the handling of exhibitions (and what many organizations deemed insufficient instructions over packing of paintings and prints).[32] Despite chafing at Ottawa's control, in the early 1950s the WCAC continued to advocate for increased support from the National Gallery, whether in the form of better exhibitions, financial underwriting of shipping costs, or long-term loans of works from its collection to member centres. In part, such reliance on the NGC was due to the small size and budgets of many of the circuit's member organizations, which would not have been able to survive outside of the WCAC. Larger galleries such as the Vancouver Art Gallery, which left the circuit in 1950, and the Winnipeg Art Gallery, with its European director, established their own relationships with the national institution. But small and medium-sized organizations, including the Edmonton Museum of Arts and the Calgary Allied Arts Centre, without other sources of financial support or significant permanent collections, needed both the expertise and the resources of the NGC to serve their respective communities. So while autonomy was a goal desired by all circuit members, dependence on the National Gallery remained the only option for survival.

McCurry did not explicitly reject Harris's idea of a department of extension at the National Gallery, recognizing that the trustees solidly endorsed the proposal, but he took no formal action to implement any of his suggestions. It fell to McCurry's successor, Alan Jarvis, a man with a longstanding belief in the importance of outreach and adult education programming,[33] to pick up on Harris's scheme and to begin the process of reformulating the NGC's extension work. Shortly after his appointment, Jarvis proposed a meeting of leading art gallery directors, university art professors, and members of the National Gallery's staff and board of trustees to discuss the future of the gallery's education and exhibition services. Held in Vancouver at the University of British Columbia, 15 through 17 August 1956, the conference was attended by representatives of galleries, art schools, cultural foundations, and the CBC, as well as by the directors of the Western Canada Art Circuit and the Western Ontario Art Circuit. The stated aim of the conference, as outlined by Jarvis in his letter of invitation to potential delegates, was "to discuss, and if possible to formulate, some sort of general plans for the future roles of the National Gallery, the smaller galleries and the universities in the cultural life of Canada during the next 10 years ... whereby we may all co-operate more efficiently in future programmes."[34]

The Vancouver conference allowed the NGC to present its proposal for more efficient service to the regions and to hear what members of the Canadian art community expected the National Gallery to do for them. Presentations by Jarvis and by the gallery's assistant director, Donald Buchanan, early in the conference outlined the existing services provided by the National Gallery, including the circulation of exhibitions, lecturers, and publications as well as delivering information on art to organizations across the country. The delegates, drawn from large and small organizations, for the most part concurred with the importance of these services but were concerned that regional institutions – whether in western Canada, the Maritimes, or in smaller cities in Ontario and Quebec – be afforded a greater level of cooperation with the NGC in setting up travelling programs. One point of contention involved the appointment of regional directors by the NGC to act as liaisons between the gallery and outside institutions. While some delegates welcomed such appointments,[35] others felt that any regional representation should come from galleries in the area or better yet, from existing regional circuits rather than an individual unilaterally appointed by the central institution. Not surprisingly, this argument was most forcefully presented by Archie Key, who, building on previous proposals to the NGC that the WCAC be the gallery's western representative, contended that the experience of the circuits was in itself valuable and could more effectively represent the interests of the National Gallery in the regions. This position received the support of both Lawren Harris Jr from the Maritime Art Association and the Art Gallery of Toronto's Martin Baldwin.

Key's reticence to the idea of centrally appointed field officers was very much in line with ongoing power struggles between the WCAC and the National Gallery. Following from his proposal for regional representatives discussed above, by 1954, Key, in his role as chair of the Special Committee on Circuits for the Canadian Museums Association (CMA), further advocated for the creation of a "central clearing house" of exhibitions that circuits across the country could access. Conceived under the auspices of the more neutral CMA, the proposed clearing house would allow for greater cooperation among Canada's exhibition circuits in handling exhibitions from multiple sources, and allow both the circuits and member galleries to maintain their autonomy from the NGC. Writing to circuit galleries across the country, Key argued that the National Gallery should not be called upon to host such a clearing house, claiming that it would place too large a burden on NGC staff, and "would also tend to destroy the initiative of the Circuits and their member galleries."[36] The impending retirement of McCurry and the anticipated creation of the Canada Council shelved any action on the CMA's part, but Key continued to correspond with other circuit leaders about how to better manage relations with the NGC in order to preserve the circuits' autonomy while benefitting from the national institution's collection and administrative expertise. In a 1955 brief to the four Canadian art circuits, forwarded to Alan Jarvis shortly after his appointment at the National Gallery, Key outlined what he perceived to be the function of the National Gallery in relation to the circuits: in addition to the organization of suitable shows for circuit galleries, the NGC was expected to sponsor exhibitions of the national associations, extend loans to smaller centres, as well as assist in negotiations for and shipping of exhibitions sourced from international museums and galleries.[37] Keenly aware that the creation of an extension department at the National Gallery would concentrate power in Ottawa and diminish the authority of the WCAC, and continuing to advocate for the circuit as the gallery's representative in western Canada, Key nonetheless continued to ask the NGC for funds, arguing that the expenses of circulating exhibitions throughout the vast distances in western Canada was a drain on the finances of the large number of institutions in the region and should be financed by the National Gallery as part of its service to the country. Key was not alone in this assessment; in a letter to Jarvis just prior to the Vancouver conference, B.C. Binning praised the work of the WCAC in supplying exhibitions to such a large number of institutions over a broad territory and encouraged the NGC's director to formulate any plans for extension services in such a way that it "not destroy the sensitive and indigenous character of the Circuit as it now exists." Binning further wrote that the future of the WCAC – and arguably all the regional circuits – "is going to depend largely on how the National Gallery acts towards the outposts of the Canadian empire."[38]

In contrast to McCurry, Jarvis was aware of the delicacy with which he needed to approach relations with regional galleries and with the circuits that serviced the smaller centres. By 1956 such institutions as the art galleries in Vancouver, Victoria, Edmonton, Regina, and Winnipeg were well enough established that they could participate in discussions with the NGC around programming on a more equal footing. The smaller centres, however, continued to need the assistance from the National Gallery and along with the regional circuits required the development of an extension service that could work cooperatively with organizations to fulfill their needs rather than dictate these from Ottawa. As Jarvis argued in his opening statement to the Vancouver conference, "How can the National

Gallery use its responsibility [to disseminate Canadian art] for the greater benefit of the whole of the Canadian people without becoming paternalistic [and] without too much centralization?"[39] Jarvis would return to the questions of paternalism and centralization several times throughout the conference without, however, addressing them head on, suggesting that these were questions of appearance rather than a clear indication of the concern he felt over relations of power between the National Gallery and regional institutions. Given the debates around centralization and decentralization that had been voiced throughout the 1940s and 1950s – at the Kingston Conference, in the representations to the Massey Commission and in the commissioners' report, in the platform of the Federation of Canadian Artists – the National Gallery had to tread carefully in its dealings with western Canadian art galleries. On one hand, the circulating exhibitions allowed the NGC to publicly present itself as a national institution, *serving* the people of Canada; its annual reports, however, consistently included statements bemoaning the cost of such service in terms of commitments of time and personnel. Since the Massey Report had made clear that abandoning such activities was not an option, the NGC could only reorganize the terms of that service, consolidating the administration of the exhibitions it circulated and devising a system that would afford it greater oversight over those programs. As the conference progressed, the most effective solution to the gallery's mandated requirement to service the country as a whole was determined to be the establishment of an extension department, with regional directors reporting on the needs of outside galleries directly to the National Gallery. Arthur Lismer's recommendation of "branch offices" of the National Gallery was not taken up by gallery officials in any substantive way, particularly when some of its proponents – echoing Lawren Harris's original proposal for community art centres – suggested that significant portions of the gallery's permanent collection be distributed to institutions outside of Ottawa.[40] Instead, the conference closed with the NGC making few commitments to implementing structural changes to improve relations with regional organizations, and the power of the gallery to determine the development of art in Canada remaining virtually intact. While the decision to hire regional directors recognized the importance of implementing a system of direct liaison between organizations in those areas and the national institution, the nature of the structure – determined by the gallery rather than by the regional organizations – cannot be seen as anything other than a centralization of power in the National Gallery and a continuation of its efforts to maintain the status it had worked so hard to achieve in the 1930s and 1940s.

Late in 1957 the National Gallery established an Exhibition and Extension Services department headed by Richard Simmins, until that point curator of the Norman MacKenzie Art Gallery in Regina. In line with concerns raised at the Vancouver conference that the National Gallery provide officers that could establish closer relations with the west and the east, two additional "field officer" positions were also created. Norah McCullough, from the Saskatchewan Arts Board, was appointed western Canada representative, and Claude Picher, director of exhibitions for the Musée de la province du Québec was installed as eastern Canada representative, a posting that included responsibility for Quebec. The selection of Simmins to head the new extension department is not surprising: originally from Ottawa, he was briefly affiliated with the Hart House collection at the University of Toronto before assuming the position of curator at the Norman MacKenzie Art Gallery in 1951. Throughout his tenure at the gallery he would have become very familiar with the activities of the WCAC as well as forged his own relations with other galleries and organizations in the region. A connection of particular importance was Norah McCullough, who had spearheaded the work of the growing Saskatchewan Arts Board since her appointment in 1948. McCullough's longstanding relationship with the National Gallery – she was hired as an educator to accompany circulating exhibitions to small towns in Northern Ontario in 1946 and then to oversee an art education program in Prince Edward Island[41] – as well as her highly respected extension work with the Saskatchewan Arts Board, similarly made her the logical choice for western Canada liaison officer. Two major tasks awaited the members of the newly formed department: the first was to assess every exhibiting space in the country in order to develop a classification system to help route suitable exhibitions; the second was to deal concretely with the nation's circulating exhibition agencies. Of the existing circuits, the most pressing concern was the Western Canada Art Circuit, although publicly this "problem" was couched within a larger concern about how to address the needs of the rapidly developing interest in art across the whole of western Canada. Working closely together, Simmins and McCullough would become crucial advisors to the NGC's administration on how to address the increasingly vocal concerns of western Canadian art organizations.

The National Gallery Reasserts Itself: The 1958 Regina Conference

If the discussions during the Vancouver conference attempted to address the spectre of the National Gallery's paternalism and centralization, the issue was effectively dealt with some eighteen months later as the NGC organized another conference of representatives of art galleries and art associations, focusing this time exclusively on organizations from western Canada. Held on 12 and 13 April 1958 at the Norman MacKenzie Art Gallery, the Regina conference was a carefully managed affair intended to establish the National Gallery's newly formed Exhibition and Extension Services department as the primary decision maker in the circulation of exhibitions in western Canada, if not completely replacing the WCAC, then wresting control over much of the movement of exhibitions throughout the region. Since its formation in 1957, the extension department had developed a uniform fee structure for circulating exhibitions that included a sliding scale of charges to individual galleries based on population. As described in the NGC's 1956–57 *Annual Report*, the new structure would benefit art galleries in cities with a population of less than one hundred thousand,[42] a doubtless welcome change for the many small centres that continued to spring up all over the country. From its inception, the department took over the coordination of all exhibitions organized by the NGC for circulation, developing a range of shows that catered to the diverse needs of exhibiting centres across the country. Writing in 1958, Norah McCullough described the role of the liaison or field officers as "work[ing] closely with local galleries, ascertaining the types of exhibitions needed and [being] ready to give expert advice on programming and the installation of exhibitions."[43] As this statement suggests, the new approach to circulating exhibitions in western Canada involved direct contact between the NGC and individual galleries regardless of size or characteristic, with circuits playing a secondary role in the department's plans.[44] Indeed, McCullough notes that liaison officers "will attend the meetings of the various regional art circuits to evaluate criticism and suggestions and also to bring the views of the National Gallery to the direct attention of the circuits."[45]

In the months leading up to the Regina conference, tensions between the WCAC and the department of extension were already apparent in correspondence between the circuit's director Archie Key, Extension Director Richard Simmins, and Western Liaison Officer Norah McCullough as Key continued to seek funding for the WCAC and complained about the quality of Extension exhibitions. As Simmins and McCullough prepared the agenda for the conference and discussed which delegates would be invited to attend, their frustration with the demands of the WCAC were evident. As the gallery's western representative and having just completed a tour and evaluation of art centres in the four provinces, McCullough was forthright in her assessment of potential delegates, particularly in terms of where they might position themselves in relation to the WCAC and its erstwhile director, Archie Key.[46] For McCullough and Simmins, the goal of the conference was to establish a more efficient means of circulating exhibitions throughout western Canada. If this could only be achieved through the dissolution of the Western Canada Art Circuit and the creation of a replacement organization that was more in tune with the aims of the National Gallery, neither McCullough nor Simmins would be upset. Indeed, privately, both hoped that the WCAC would be dismantled and that responsibility for managing the local circulation of exhibitions be taken over by the provincial agencies that were beginning to be formed across the country.[47] Indeed, by 1958 Saskatchewan had a well-established arts board (headed by McCullough until her appointment to Extension), and Alberta's Visual Arts Board had been overseeing exhibitions of fine arts to rural communities since 1948. British Columbia and Manitoba had no provincial arts boards, but the Vancouver Art Gallery and the Winnipeg Art Gallery had been steadily expanding their programming activities over the past decade and were ready to take on more responsibility for coordinating the circulation of exhibitions to all areas of their respective provinces.

One of the major concerns voiced by Simmins and McCullough in their preparations for the Regina conference was how to manage Archie Key. It is difficult to parse out the problems of the circuit as an organization from those prompted by personality conflicts with Key himself. The following lengthy excerpt of a letter from Simmins to McCullough is but one example of the imbrication of organization and personality that plagued the WCAC throughout much of the 1950s when the circuit was managed by Key, and is an indication of how this fraught relationship may have precipitated the conference in Regina:

> Norah, I do really feel that we should try and work out the western Canada circulating problem as soon as we possibly can. This region receives more exhibitions and more indirect assistance than any other area in Canada. And, despite the fact that these provinces, considered nationally, are wealthy, there are constant demands for financial support. The Maritime circuit, in which a number of centres really are almost poverty-stricken, has none of the complaints we receive from Key and actually has a surplus of $1700 in the bank. I personally think Key is making mountains out of molehills and that given the opportunity, a lot of the galleries in western Canada would not persist in supporting Key's very violent and emotional attitude. His attitude unfortunately has directly affected our relations with the Coste House itself though not with the circuit, and I am taking immediate steps to rectify the situation.[48]

Simmins's assessment of Key as instrumental in the creation of many of the problems with the WCAC is echoed in much of the correspondence relating to the circulation of exhibitions from the National Gallery. For example, in a letter to B.C. Binning prior to the 1956 Vancouver conference, Alan Jarvis commented, "one of the immediate problems is one of personalities. We cannot really have full confidence in Archie Key and, although we don't want to be unkind to him, we none of us (including Mrs. Dyde) feel we can underwrite the Western Circuit if he is in charge."[49] Almost two years later, attitudes towards Key remained completely unchanged. Nevertheless, as both the preliminary correspondence between Simmins and McCullough and the proceedings of the conference itself demonstrate, a central strategy of NGC staff at the Regina conference was managing Key and attempting to keep the delegates on a track that was more in keeping with the National Gallery's vision of a centrally controlled circulating network. Reviewing the correspondence as a whole, it is true that Key's often-strident advocacy for the WCAC and the combative tone of his letters would have rubbed NGC staff the wrong way. However, his longstanding leadership of the circuit, his support for the many small organizations across all four provinces, and his inexhaustible work to keep both the WCAC and Coste House afloat with minimal backing from private sponsors ensured that NGC staff were consistently made aware of the needs of galleries and arts organizations in western Canada.

Bringing together thirty delegates from large and small art centres from Winnipeg to Victoria,[50] the Regina conference was described as "a meeting of art exhibiting centres and circulating agencies of Western Canada" sponsored by the National Gallery of Canada.[51] Such a description suggests that the primary aim of the conference was to work out problems in the circulation of National Gallery exhibitions in western Canada. But given that the Western Canada Art Circuit had been in charge of such programming for most of the art centres in the west, the underlying assumption by many delegates was that the conference would primarily focus on the activities of the WCAC, either by improving the functioning of the circuit or replacing it with another organization. The desire to dissolve the WCAC was never explicitly stated by Simmins or McCullough, either during the conference or in correspondence. However, Simmins's contributions to the discussions at the meetings, in particular his frequent reassertions of the conference as a meeting of western art centres rather than of the Western Canada Art Circuit, his responses to Key, as well as several strongly worded statements describing the National Gallery's new circulating exhibition policy, were effective strategies to move the conference delegates towards a decision to shut down the WCAC as it was currently run and replace it with a new organization (still called the Western Canada Art Circuit) with different personnel and a new mandate. In light of prior efforts of the National Gallery to assert its control over the development of art activities in Canada, Simmins's attempt to maintain control over the direction of the conversation should come as no surprise.

Simmins's management of the discussion was evident from the first day of the meeting: when conference chair W.A. Ridell, dean of Regina College, asked Key to present the current situation of the WCAC, Simmins interrupted with a request that he be permitted to outline the National Gallery's new exhibition and extension policies. In the presentation that followed, Simmins mapped out the fee structure for circulating exhibitions, the kinds of exhibitions that would be produced for circulation by the National Gallery, security and packing standards expected from galleries, as well as a new classification system for art centres across the country that would determine what kinds of exhibitions could be hosted by which galleries. As a strategic intervention in the proceedings of a conference such a lengthy statement did much to set the tone of the meeting and clearly signalled that the National Gallery had established a policy regarding the circulation of exhibitions (a policy that was presented as a fait accompli) and that art centres in western Canada would be expected to devise a system for circulating exhibitions that fit with that of the National Gallery. Predictably, Key's response was more defensive than conciliatory: after professing pleasure that as circuit director he finally knew "what function and relationship could exist between the Circuit and the National Gallery," Key went on to argue that the primary goal of the WCAC had always been to bring exhibitions to the smallest centres in the region "until such a time as the National Gallery itself could take on that function." He then suggested three possible futures for the circuit: (1) dismantling, with the gallery taking over complete responsibility for circulating exhibitions; (2) the establishment of a new organization for the circulation of exhibitions; or (3) adopting the model of the Southwestern [*sic*] Ontario Art Circuit[52] whereby gallery members of the WCAC would organize their own exhibitions and circulate them amongst themselves.[53]

With these opening salvos, the tone of the conference was effectively set with Simmins reasserting the National Gallery's authority in the production and issuance of exhibitions, and supporters of the WCAC – usually represented by Key, but also taken up by Florence James of the Saskatchewan Arts Board and Lois Lavers of the Medicine Hat Community Art Club – trying to preserve a system (although not necessarily the organization itself) that had facilitated the circulation of art to even the smallest centres in western Canada for almost fifteen years. Such an opposition simplifies the subtleties of the discussion and plays down the genuine concern of all conference delegates that exhibitions continue to be provided for art centres in small and rural communities. As the conference progressed, however, Simmins's antipathy to the WCAC became more apparent as he either pointedly reminded delegates "this is not a meeting of the Western Canada Art Circuit" or objected to proposals for new agencies that resembled too closely the existing make-up and function of the WCAC.[54] When the conference reconvened on Sunday afternoon (the afternoon of the second day) and representatives of the circuit were not able to report on their discussion of a proposal to form a network of provincial circulation agencies, Simmins finally gave voice to his exasperation: "we must have a clear cut decision so that western Canada can be incorporated as part of the national plan as far as the National Gallery is concerned. Postponement is not an option and I would urge this meeting to come to a clear cut and unequivocal decision regarding future operations."[55]

Coming at the end of the two days and followed by a number of similarly emotion-laden comments from other delegates, Simmins's outburst advocated for a move away from the status quo and a commitment from art centres in western Canada to fit into the national system of circulating exhibitions planned by the National Gallery – the "national plan." Following Simmins, Ferdinand Eckhardt, director of the Winnipeg Art Gallery, stated that his previous support for the circuit had now evaporated, and Robert Hume of the Vancouver Art Gallery noted that severing ties with the circuit in 1950 had given the VAG more flexibility in obtaining exhibitions from other sources, including devolving responsibility for circulating exhibitions to smaller centres to provincial circulating agencies or to major regional galleries. The NGC's proposed changes to the circulation of exhibitions in western Canada obviously affected galleries in different ways and, as the proceedings wore on, the impact of the changes were expressed differently by the large and small galleries. For example, many of the larger centres such as Vancouver, Winnipeg, and the NMAG in Regina, did not feel that their programming would be properly served by the kind of exhibitions the WCAC – or any regionally based circulating agency – could provide. They preferred to deal directly with the National Gallery (and each other) in order to obtain first-class exhibitions. In his presentation of the policies of the Exhibition and Extension Services department, Simmins was equally clear that he was in favour of a system that would give the NGC unmediated access to the best, or "Class-A," galleries across the country, leaving the smaller "B" and "C" galleries to deal with a region- or province-based agency for their exhibitions. For their part, smaller centres – the "Class-C" galleries – worried that any changes to the existing system would not assure them the level of attention they currently enjoyed with the WCAC, particularly given the location of its current director in a medium-sized gallery (i.e., Calgary's Coste House). Such concerns seem to have been alleviated by the end of the conference and delegates departed Regina having supported a motion that the WCAC in its current form be dissolved; that all its assets

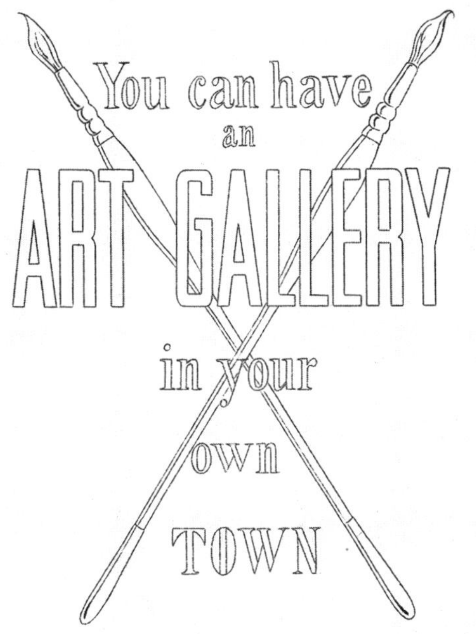

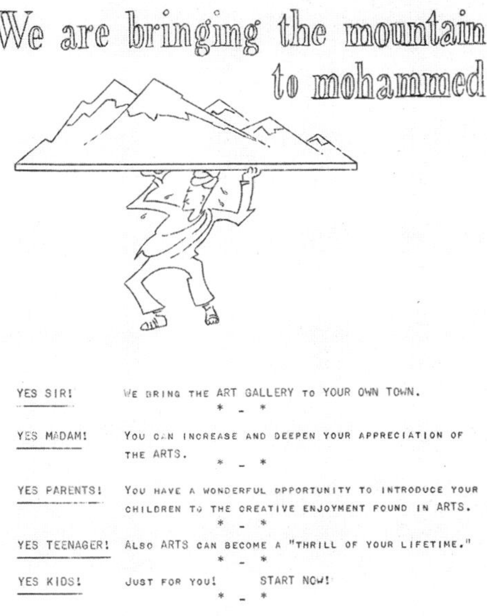

4.2 | Pamphlet issued by the Arts and Crafts Division of the Cultural Activities Branch, Alberta, advertising its circulating exhibitions, 1960.

(and liabilities) be transferred to a coordinating committee made up of representatives from each province's larger galleries and art associations; and that this committee be tasked with the responsibility of gathering information about available exhibitions – from the National Gallery as well as outside sources – and facilitate the circulation of these exhibitions to the smaller centres.[56] In May, a coordinating committee made up of Ian McNairn of the Vancouver Art Gallery, Percy Henson of the Edmonton Art Gallery, Leona Collins of the Saskatoon Art Centre, Richard Williams of the University of Manitoba's School of Art, and Norah McCullough as the western representative of the National Gallery met in Saskatoon and began work on an operating plan that would ensure the continued circulation of exhibitions to smaller western Canadian art centres. In an effort to maintain national and international recognition for the organization, the committee retained the Western Canada Art Circuit name; but

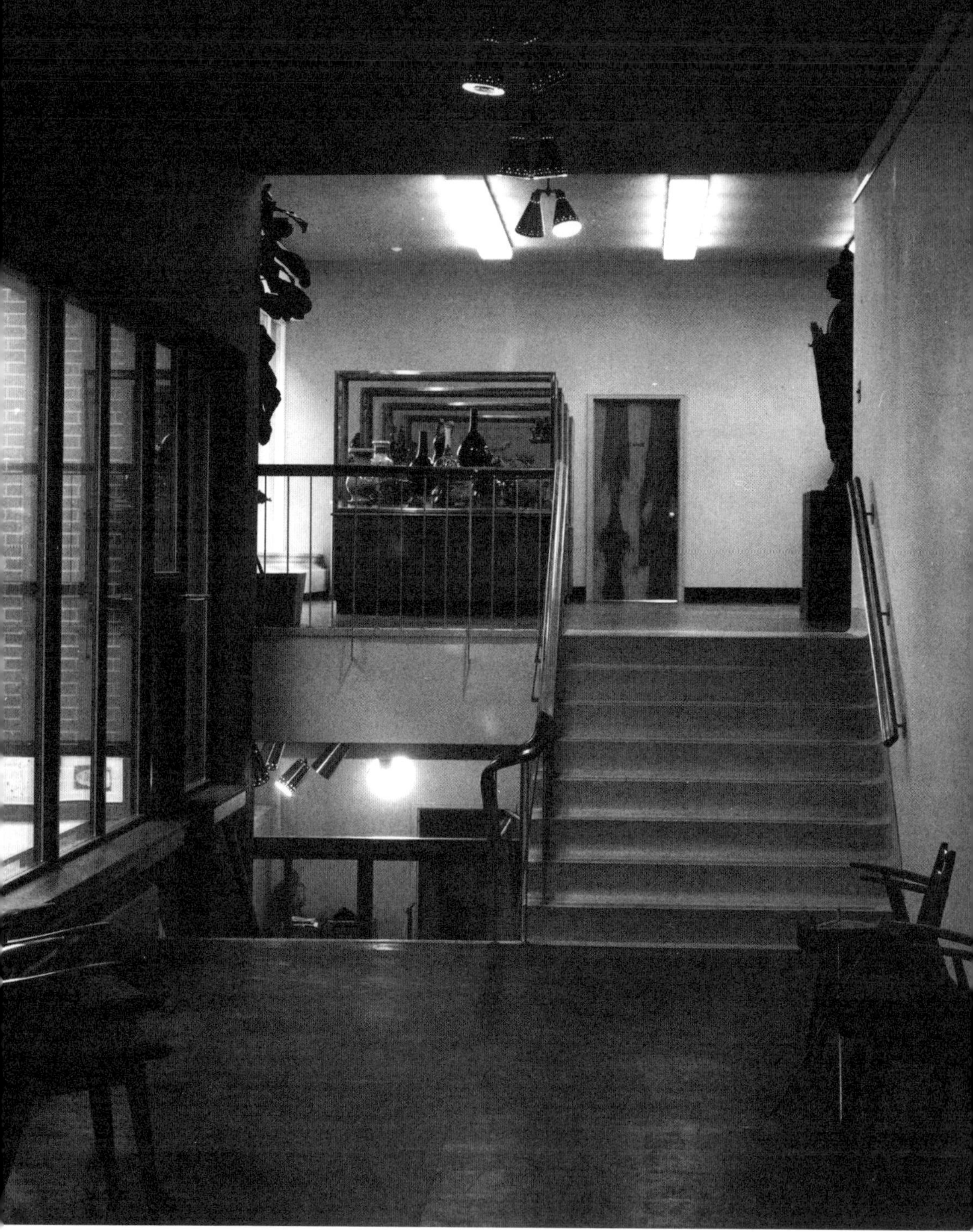

4.3 | Norman MacKenzie Art Gallery interior, c. 1958. The extension by Izumi, Arnott, and Sugiyama increased the display space and improved the flow of visitors.

in its relations with the National Gallery and in its mode of acquiring and circulating exhibitions, it was a wholly different organization, with a coordinating committee consisting of provincial representatives empowered to act for smaller institutions, and to organize exhibitions for circulation throughout each province. In addition, a full-time executive secretary was hired to coordinate the activities of the WCAC and to act as a liaison with staff at the NGC. Minutes from meetings in the years following the Regina conference often echo the financial woes, concerns over packing and the availability of exhibitions that characterized the first fifteen years of the WCAC, but the relationship with Ottawa appears to have improved considerably.

Simmins's frequent refrains during the Regina conference that this was a meeting of the art centres in western Canada and *not* a meeting of the Western Canada Art Circuit, in retrospect, seem disingenuous. The fate of the circuit was clearly paramount to the National Gallery and its supporters, most prominently Hume of the Vancouver Art Gallery, Eckhardt of the Winnipeg Art Gallery, and Glyde of the University of Alberta, all of whom saw the proposed constitution of provincial agencies responsible for the circulation of exhibitions to smaller centres as advantageous to their own desires to deal directly with the national institution. Indeed, the major galleries in western Canada would benefit from a system wherein they would have direct access to the National Gallery and the first-class exhibitions it produced or obtained from external sources. While the Vancouver Art Gallery had withdrawn from the circuit precisely to obtain such unmediated access, the Winnipeg Art Gallery, the Norman MacKenzie Art Gallery, and the Art Gallery of Greater Victoria – all considered Class-A galleries by both the National Gallery and the WCAC – saw the potential inherent in being part of a group of institutions that had links beyond western Canada to the country as a whole. Indeed, in the decade following the Regina conference each of these galleries would achieve a level of growth and program expansion that established them as significant players in the Canadian art world. Meanwhile, both the Edmonton Art Gallery and the Calgary Allied Arts Centre experienced difficulties, partly the result of limited funding for the arts from the provincial government, but also because of a dearth of interest from the citizens of these rapidly expanding cities. The Calgary Allied Arts Centre would succumb to the changing priorities of Calgary during the oil boom of the 1960s and closed its doors in 1969, effectively replaced by the provincially supported Glenbow Museum. The Edmonton Art Gallery successfully erected a new building in 1968, which afforded it Class-A status and access to the National Gallery's best circulating exhibitions. As will be discussed in the following chapter, increased funds and a larger professional staff also enabled the Edmonton Art Gallery to develop its acquisition program and to curate significant exhibitions that toured nationally. Through most of the 1960s, however, it remained a somewhat marginal institution on the national scene.

The provinces' increased responsibility for circulating exhibitions to small centres and communities proved to be a significant boon for the National Gallery's Exhibition and Extension Services department in the 1960s as it could focus its attention on producing exhibitions for medium-sized galleries. This shift also enabled a renewed relationship between the national institution and galleries in western Canada. Contact with what were classified as Class-A galleries was direct and assumed the tone of a conversation if not among equals then between institutions with a shared understanding of professional museum practices. Indeed, the appointment of directors with professional qualifications and/or prior museum experience in the galleries in Winnipeg, Regina, Vancouver, and Victoria could be seen as central to the increased respect accorded these institutions by the National Gallery. Certainly, the Edmonton Art Gallery's decision to hire a "museum man" as director in 1960 – the affable John MacGillivray – is an indication of the increasing importance of professional staff in the establishment of positive and respectful relations with the National Gallery. As for the smaller art centres, the reformulated WCAC's management of exhibition schedules meant that the majority of them had little direct contact with the National Gallery. However, the circulation of exhibitions – whether of original works or reproductions – was an important public relations exercise for the National Gallery and a key feature of its annual reports' assessment of the Ottawa institution's service to the nation: abandoning them was not an option, but taking over such circulation services to all the country's arts organizations was equally impossible. The relegation of responsibility for the circulation of exhibitions to Class-B and -C galleries to provincial organizations thus provided an ideal option for the National Gallery – assuring that on paper at least it was serving the needs of communities large and small across the country, while transferring the logistics of such a program to the provinces.

Conclusion

One of the clear outcomes of both the Regina conference and the creation of provincial agencies that would liaise with the newly formed Exhibition and Extension Services department at the National Gallery was the reinforcement of a hierarchy among museums in Canada. A 1958 Survey of Canadian Art Galleries undertaken by Extension staff Norah McCullough and Claude Picher that divided exhibition centres across the country according to their ability to properly host shows of varying quality effectively organized galleries into strata that determined their relations to the National Gallery and to each other; that the NGC was the author of such a survey further cemented its self-positioning as the key decision maker in the field of Canadian art. Requirements such as fireproofing, professional staff to handle the works, and level of educational programming determined where individual institutions would fit: either Class A, B, or C. Major institutions such as the Montreal Museum of Fine Arts and the Art Gallery of Toronto easily achieved Class-A status, as did the galleries in Hamilton, London, Winnipeg, Regina, Vancouver, and Victoria because of their purpose-built, fireproof facilities. Some surprising exhibition sites, such as the newly built Jubilee auditoria in Calgary and Edmonton, also received a Class-A designation despite what would now be regarded as the lack of security and temperature controls in both buildings. Class-B galleries, meanwhile, were those spaces with a degree of fireproofing and professional support but that could otherwise not support all the exhibitions organized by the National Gallery for circulation. Such facilities included the Edmonton Art Gallery and the Allied Arts Centre in Calgary, both of which were located in renovated houses. One example frequently cited as a rationale for Class-B status was some centres' inability to show an exhibition of contemporary painting from Quebec that featured large-scale works by Riopelle, Gaucher, and others.[57] Class-C gallery classification was given to those centres that were not primarily designated as exhibition spaces. Most of these were found in small cities and towns where the art gallery shared space with the library, the recreation centre, or the community hall. With some exceptions, most of these kinds of spaces were viewed as unsuitable for the safe and proper display of art. As a result of this classification system, galleries developed different relations not only with the National Gallery but also with each other as Class-A galleries created their own informal network by developing exhibitions that could circulate amongst themselves, leaving the B and C galleries to increasingly rely upon the offerings of the National Gallery's Exhibition and Extension Services and such exhibitions as could be obtained from or developed by provincial art agencies. As will be discussed in the next chapter, the development of classification systems along with the construction of new purpose-built museums to house collections and the hiring of trained curatorial staff was an indication of the increased professionalization of art galleries across Canada – a development mandated just as much by the National Gallery's reorganization of its relations with the regions as international pressures to conform to particular museum standards.

BUILDINGS, COLLECTIONS, AND CURATORS

Professionalizing the Art Gallery

The establishment of the Exhibition and Extension Services department signalled a new phase in the development of the National Gallery of Canada (NGC). This transformative period was most visibly marked by the opening of the Lorne Building in February 1960, which enabled the gallery to move out of the Victoria Memorial Museum Building it shared with the National Museum and establish itself in an autonomous space for the first time in its ninety-year history. With five floors of exhibition space, curatorial staff in the fields of Canadian art, prints and drawings, and design, as well as the growing exhibition and extension department, the National Gallery could more effectively assert its status as Canada's foremost art gallery and imagine itself on par with other major North American art museums, albeit with a much smaller budget. While the hiring of staff with art historical training or museum experience had not been the practice at the NGC in its earliest years – both Eric Brown and H.O. McCurry had little more than a cursory knowledge of art at the time of their respective hiring – Robert Hubbard's appointment to the position of curator of Canadian art in 1947 signalled the gallery's commitment to scholarship and conformity to the kind of expertise it was advocating for the staff of regional institutions. With a PhD in art history from the University of Wisconsin and university teaching experience, not to mention being the recipient of one of the Carnegie-funded scholarships allocated by the Canadian Museums Committee, Hubbard was exactly the kind of "museum man" envisioned by the National Gallery's leadership as well as professional museum associations internationally. The selection of Alan Jarvis as the NGC's third director in 1955, however, underlined the

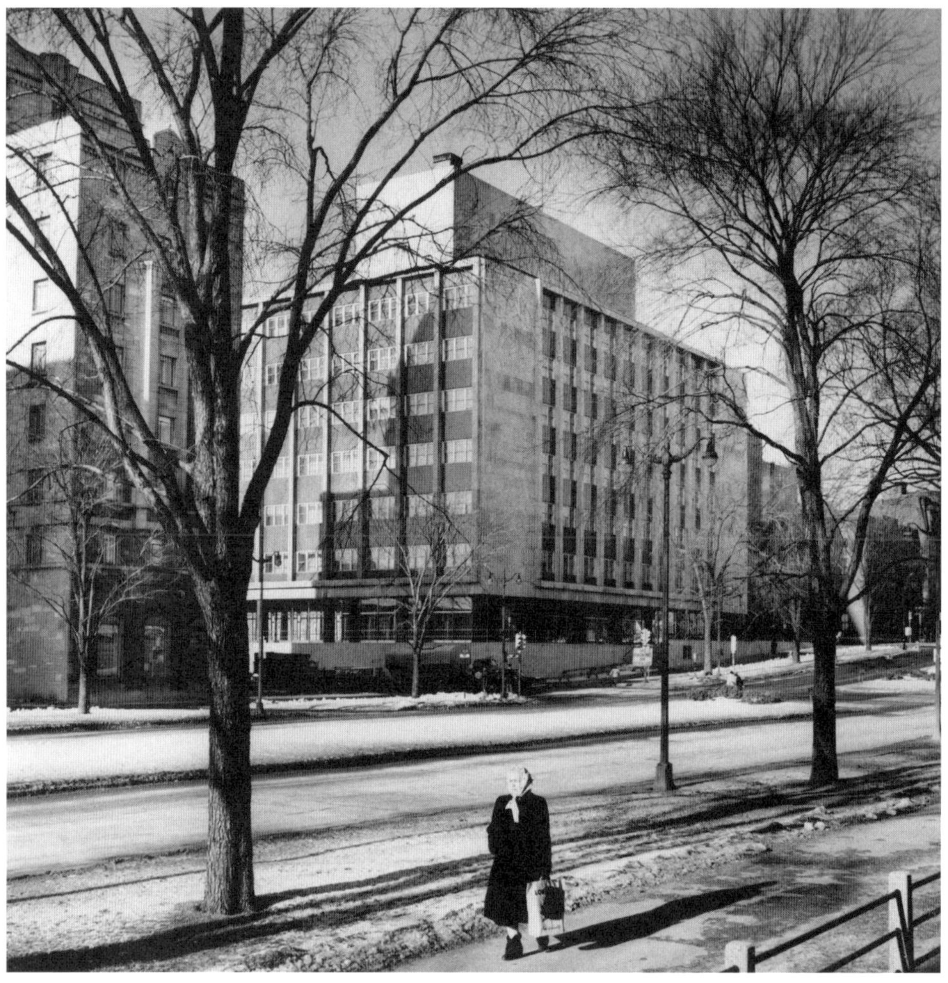

5.1 | The National Gallery of Canada at the Lorne Building, 1960. The NGC remained in these temporary quarters until a new building was erected in 1988.

precariousness of the National Gallery's efforts to conform to museum professional status. As a Rhodes Scholar and personal secretary to the president of the UK's Board of Trade, Jarvis had the cultural authority and personal connections necessary for a successful art gallery director, but his experience in cultural management was limited to short stints in England as public relations officer for the Council of Industrial Design and executive director of the independent film production company Pilgrim Films. Although a sculptor, Jarvis had no knowledge of museum practices or art history, and having lived in Britain for many years, he was unfamiliar with the Canadian art scene. What likely cemented his candidacy was the favourable assessment by Kenneth Clark, at the time director of the National Gallery London. Clark described Jarvis as having "sound judgement in art and considerable knowledge of its history" and further suggested that he would bring "a freshness, energy and administrative ability rare among professional museum directors."[1] As Andrew Horrall has noted in his biography of Jarvis, these credentials were enough for the National Gallery's Board of Trustees.

Although his tenure was relatively short (he resigned in 1960) and marked by controversy,[2] Jarvis was a much more dynamic and forward-looking director than his predecessor, H.O. McCurry, whose lengthy time at the gallery's helm was beginning to wear on its trustees and on others in the Canadian art community. Indeed, it seems that McCurry's background as a career civil servant was never far from the minds of members of the Canadian art world, as is suggested by the title of an article in *Canadian Art* that described McCurry, upon his retirement, as a "Servant of the Arts."[3] Jarvis, meanwhile, was charismatic and well connected, and these personal qualities appear to have compensated for the lack of museum training increasingly expected in leaders of institutions both big and small. Indeed, in other aspects of its organization, including establishing curatorial departments and hiring trained art historians to lead them, the National Gallery was positioning itself more along the lines of major institutions in Britain and the United States for whom specialized training in a subject area as well as in museum practices was increasingly the norm for its staff. In turn, the NGC put pressure on institutions across the country – including western Canada – to adopt many of the principles and structures that would take them from enthusiastic associations of amateurs to professional organizations. At the same time, western Canadian art galleries were working hard to consolidate their status within growing cities by petitioning civic governments for funds to erect permanent stand-alone facilities. Influenced as much by pressure from the National Gallery to systematize its operations as by the recognition of how other institutions conducted their business, art galleries in the west undertook numerous initiatives to carve out space within the Canadian cultural landscape.

This chapter charts the professionalization of art galleries across the western half of the country by examining how different museums responded to the model outlined by the National Gallery and that institution's demands that they conform to standards that were increasingly being promoted internationally. A dominant motif of this discussion will be reading this move towards professionalization in spatial terms, as museums asserted their physical presence and pushed for more recognition of their activities. The erection of permanent buildings is a key manifestation of the desire for art galleries to be recognized as autonomous institutions by occupying physical space, and between 1951 and 1971 new museum structures were built in Vancouver, Edmonton, Saskatoon, Regina, and Winnipeg. However, spatial concerns also underscore other professionalizing endeavours in the gallery, notably the ordering and display of permanent collections, and the consolidation of areas of expertise through the establishment of curatorial departments and the hiring of professional staff. Such administrative moves produce the boundaries that define the activities of the museum as well as its claim to expertise, reinforcing distinctions between amateurs and professionals, between historical artifacts and fine art, and between the public and the experts, thus reifying the disciplinary terrains that constitute the modern art gallery. This shift is neither new nor specific to western Canada. As Tony Bennett argues in *The Birth of the Museum*, the development of disciplinary formations in the late eighteenth century accompanied the emergence of museums in Europe, effectively instituting the transformation of the somewhat haphazard character of the cabinet of curiosities into the taxonomically bound format of the disciplinary museum that we know today.[4] In North America, the disciplinary museum type much discussed in museum studies literature was limited to the major cities of the Eastern Seaboard until well into the twentieth century, while institutions in smaller towns and cities began as incentives to educate the masses, and only narrowed their focus once they were subject to the determining forces of grant monies and the bureaucrats who administered them. As this chapter demonstrates, such a consolidation of interests occurred in western Canada as the directors of museums and art galleries recognized the necessity of conforming to professional standards and disciplined practices if they wanted to participate in a national conversation on art. During the 1960s and 1970s, however, as these institutions grew, such participation can be conceptualized as the active claiming of space, of asserting the presence of art museums in western Canada, and a clear indication of the desire of organizations in this region to control the manner in which they would participate in this conversation.

Training Museum Professionals

The push to professionalization was not just a feature of the 1950s. While the Canadian Museums Committee, discussed in Chapter 2, was primarily a vehicle for the distribution of Carnegie Corporation funds to gallery art education programs, it also initiated a museum training program in 1934 with the specific aim of improving the standards of Canadian curatorship. As described in Chapter 1, the earliest directors and curators of western Canadian art galleries were artists (Alexander Musgrove of the Winnipeg Art Gallery), businessmen (Henry Stone in Vancouver), or community workers (Maud Bowman of the Edmonton Museum of Arts). While all had an appreciation of the arts and felt that the presence of an art gallery was a necessary addition to any city that wanted to describe itself as civilized, none, with the possible exception of painter Musgrove, had much experience in handling art, let alone the competencies required of a museum curator. As a result, such necessary skills as picture hanging, the provision of wall text and other educational material, the packing of works for loan, as well as recording acquisitions were all self-taught. For Canadian museum directors – including those of such major institutions as the NGC, the Art Gallery of Toronto, and the Art Association of Montreal – a main source of information about museum practice were the annual meetings of the American Association of Museums and its publications. Founded in 1906, the association effectively guided the development of museums across the United States and became the locus for debates on both the purpose of such institutions (whether populist or scholarly) and their practices. Publications on museum management, on the proper care of collections, and on visitor behaviour were issued by the association from the 1920s onwards and were widely read by museum staff in both the United States and Canada.[5] *The Museum in America* (1939), a three-volume publication by Laurence Vail Coleman, the president of the American Association of Museums from 1927 to 1958, was held up by the Board of Governors of the Winnipeg Art Gallery (WAG) as necessary reading in 1949 as that institution embarked on a search for a new director.[6] Coleman's *Manual for Small Museums* (1927) was also used by the Museums Association in Britain as a textbook for the museum studies course it launched in 1930.[7]

The Museums Association was also a key influence on the development of museums in Canada. Formed in 1889 to improve the standards and practices of museums across Britain, the association quickly began publishing its conference proceedings and established a journal to disseminate information about professional museum practices. These publications were known to museum workers in Canada, and individuals connected to the association, such as Sir Henry Miers, president, and Sidney Markham, secretary, were often called upon for advice. National Gallery Director Eric Brown was named a vice-president of the Museums Association in 1933 and agreed to address its annual meeting that year, likely the result of the gallery sponsoring Miers and Markham to conduct an assessment of Canadian museums in 1931. Markham in particular would continue to be solicited for advice by Brown and McCurry throughout the early 1930s despite Carnegie President Frederick Keppel's admonition that a "Dominion solution" needed to be found to solve the problems of museums in Canada. As Lynne Teather has shown, while the work of the Museums Association was central to the development of the profession of museum curator, training for curators, particularly within the domain of the fine arts, was more effectively achieved through courses initiated by the University of London's Courtauld Institute. There, W.G. Constable, former assistant director of the National Gallery, London, and professor of art history, established BA, MA, and PhD programs in art history as well as a one-year diploma that included courses for those seeking to enter into museum work. Constable's association with the National Gallery of Canada dated to 1930 when he replaced Charles Ricketts as the gallery's adviser on acquisitions and was otherwise seen as an important "go to" person for museum business.[8] This relationship with Constable resulted in several Canadians being sent to The Courtauld to take the diploma course, often under the sponsorship of the NGC's Canadian Museums Committee.

While the information contained in the publications issued by the Museums Association and the American Association of Museums was certainly useful, it could not completely replace hands-on experience in museums and the teachings of qualified curators – a situation acknowledged by both associations in their establishment of museum courses, often in conjunction with universities. At the National Gallery, the

Canadian Museums Committee instituted a training scheme in 1934 designed to produce "adequately trained Art Gallery and museum personnel to replace, as opportunity permits, the casual, amateur and voluntary assistance with which most of the museum work in the Dominion is carried on."[9] The scheme had two streams: the first was aimed at university graduates preparing to take up work in museums; the second consisted of travel grants to individuals already working in museums who could benefit from further training. Recipients of the first kind of fellowship included Alfred Bailey, Alice Johannsen, and Donald Taylor,[10] all of whom went on to play significant roles in the development of museums in Saint John, Montreal, and Edmonton, respectively. Donald Buchanan was a highly touted recipient of a $1,200 grant and would eventually be invited to head the newly formed Industrial Design Division of the National Gallery before being named the gallery's assistant director in 1956.

The training offered to recipients varied according to their interests but mostly involved a lengthy stay at the National Gallery to observe the workings of its various departments, and either enrolment in the diploma program at The Courtauld Institute in London or full-time graduate study.[11] Studies at The Courtauld in the museum stream had two components: the historical study of works of art and a period of practical study of museum techniques. Describing the program in 1933 to members of the Museums Association, Constable argued that historical knowledge was best acquired at an institution of higher learning; technical knowledge, however, was best learned on the ground, in the museum, as theoretical knowledge of hanging, labelling, and lighting was only valuable when it was put to the test in the production of an exhibition.[12] Fellowships in the second stream of the NGC's training scheme provided significantly less funding and primarily enabled its recipients to take the summer art history course at The Courtauld Institute, or to travel to the National Gallery or other North American and European museums to observe "modern museum methods."[13] Of a much shorter duration – anywhere from two weeks to two months – these grants were designed to expose individuals already working in museums to professional standards and practice in the hopes that these would be replicated in the fellowship holder's own institution. Norah McCullough, for example, was awarded five hundred dollars in 1934 to take the summer course at The Courtauld and while in London to "stud[y] such phases of museum activity as could be related to her work in Toronto."[14] Alexander Musgrove of the Winnipeg Art Gallery received two hundred dollars to observe the educational methods of the National Gallery and the Art Gallery of Toronto in order to develop an exhibition and educational program in Winnipeg.

Although it offered both streams of fellowships, the Canadian Museums Committee valued more highly applicants with advanced degrees who viewed museum work as a legitimate profession. As Lianne McTavish argues in her analysis of Alfred Bailey's tenure at the New Brunswick Museum, the Canadian Museums Committee's training program reinforced the importance of academic training *in conjunction with* hands-on experience in contrast with other programs such as that offered by the Newark Museum under John Cotton Dana.[15] The Canadian Museums Committee's training program emphasized the combination of university education and practical experience in its major fellowship holders with the clear goal of placing them in senior positions in Canadian museums. Sherman Wright, an award-winning graduate of the University of Manitoba, received funding from the Canadian Museums Committee for post-graduate study at Columbia with the specific intention that upon completion of his training, he would take up the directorship at the Winnipeg Art Gallery. Unfortunately, the WAG did not have the necessary funds to hire Wright and he joined the faculty at the University of Manitoba instead. Indeed, with the exception of Norah McCullough and Alexander Musgrove (who already held a position at the WAG), only the recipients of the major museum training fellowships would go on to significant roles in the development of museums in Canada. Overall, the aim of the Carnegie fellowships was to raise the levels of knowledge among the directors of emerging museums in Canada and they did so by establishing clear boundaries between amateurs and those with professional training. Included among the amateurs were artists who were increasingly viewed by museum associations as lacking the necessary skills to oversee the many administrative responsibilities of museum leadership. Reviewing the museum training program funded by Carnegie, the National Gallery's 1935–36 *Annual Report* stated, "It is not generally recognized in Canada that art gallery administration is a highly specialized department of educational work requiring unusual talents and careful training for successful results. The once common belief that practicing artists, successful or otherwise, are qualified to develop and direct art galleries is recognized as a fallacy among educationists everywhere."[16] While continuing to provide funds to some of those artist-turned-directors – and indeed, appointing two of them (Alan Jarvis and Charles Comfort) itself well into the 1950s – the National Gallery strongly advocated for the centrality of museum training at accredited institutions for anyone contemplating a career in a Canadian museum.

In 1934, members of the Canadian Museums Committee pondered the formation of a Canadian version of the American Association of Museums and circulated a proposal to all museums in the country. Despite support for the proposal, it was put on hold until 1939 when McCurry drafted a constitution and by-laws for a Canadian Museums Association whose objects would be "the advancement of public museum and art gallery services in Canada."[17] Unfortunately, the advent of the Second World War prevented progress on the establishment of any museum organization, and it was only in 1947 that McCurry reintroduced the idea to Canadian museum directors attending the annual meeting of the American Association of Museums at the Musée de la province du Québec in May. The Canadian Museums Association (CMA) was duly formed with McCurry as president, Paul Rainville of the Musée de la province du Québec as first vice-president, Clifford Carl of the Provincial Museum of Natural History and Anthropology in Victoria as second vice-president, and F.J. Alcock of the National Museum in Ottawa as secretary-treasurer. A permanent advisory committee was formed at the first official meeting of the CMA, consisting of McCurry; Robert Newton, president of the University of Alberta and a member of the Canadian Museums Committee; and John Dymond of the Royal Ontario Museum of Zoology. This committee was specifically tasked with studying the problems relating to the training of museum personnel.[18] A National Committee for International Cooperation was also formed with McCurry and the National Museum's Marius Barbeau appointed as the Canadian delegation to UNESCO and representing the CMA at the meetings of the recently formed International Council on Museums (ICOM).

The formation of the CMA was an attempt to redress the deficiencies outlined by Miers and Markham in their 1931 *Report on Museums in Canada*, specifically the absence of standards for the display and storage of objects in most Canadian museums, as well as the lack of trained personnel ready to undertake such work. In 1931, Miers and Markham judged only a few institutions to be comparable to similarly sized museums in the United States and Europe, and without exception these were located in Montreal, Toronto, and Ottawa.[19] At the CMA's formation in 1947, reliance for leadership in the association still rested on personnel from the country's largest museums. Indeed, three of the four founding members of the CMA's executive were from institutions that had been singled out by Miers and Markham. Yet the aims of the CMA extended to all museums, art galleries, and heritage sites in Canada, and as with many other Canadian organizations, the association found that geographical distance was an impediment to the creation of a truly national conversation. By 1950, the CMA executive had made the decision to hold a national conference only every second year and to have smaller business meetings in the intervening period. The makeup of the second executive underscores both the problem of geographic distance and the continuing placement of staff from large central Canadian institutions in positions of leadership: Rainville moved into the position of president, and the rest of the executive consisted of individuals from the Royal Ontario Museum, the Art Association of Montreal, and the National Museum. At this second meeting, discussion centred on the preparation of a brief for the Massey Commission strongly emphasizing the need to strengthen the *national* museums in order that they could help smaller museums,[20] alongside the perennial question of how to obtain trained personnel – or how to train existing staff members – in such institutions. In his presidential address at the first annual meeting of the CMA, McCurry underlined the predominant concern of the association regarding training: "plans are under consideration whereby the National Museum, the National Gallery, the Royal Ontario Museum and several of the leading Universities might co-operate to give a comprehensive training course to graduates who wish to enter the museum field. This training scheme if adopted will undoubtedly do much to raise the whole standard of museum work throughout the Dominion."[21]

Concerns relating to the lack of trained personnel underpinned many of the complaints of the National Gallery about how their circulating loans were being handled, and the institutions themselves – particularly those in larger or growing cities – recognized that they would increase their ability to secure better exhibitions from the National Gallery (and improve relations with both that institution and other large art galleries) if they secured a trained "museum man" as their director. The Board of Governors of the Winnipeg Art Gallery, for example, discussed the matter frankly in a meeting on 14 October 1949. In its report on the state of the gallery's budget, the finance committee made a strong argument that a fundraising campaign should not be undertaken without a careful overview of the gallery's future, including a discussion of staffing. It concluded that a long-term policy for the gallery's development could not occur until a director with museum experience had been hired. Despite the friendly relations between the board and the existing director, the painter Alexander Musgrove, the WAG's trustees felt that Musgrove would not be able to develop the gallery into the kind of institution warranted by a city of the size and stature of Winnipeg. The board's description of the differences between the sitting director and the desirable qualities of a good director is telling: the qualities that would constitute the ideal curator consisted of "business aptitude, ability to speak in public, creative ability, a marked inclination to meet the public and be active in community activities, groups, and organizations." In contrast, the existing curator was described as "retiring, non-assertive, non-creative, and inclined to follow the line of least resistance."[22] In 1950, a full year after the board decided to fire Musgrove and begin the search for a new director, Alvan C. Eastman had been hired.

With an MA from Harvard and experience at museums in Boston, Evansburg, and most recently the Pasadena Art Institute, Eastman embodied many of the personal and professional qualities outlined by the board. A graduate of Paul J. Sachs's museum course at Harvard's Fogg Art Museum, he was well schooled in the administration of museums, the management of collections, the installation of permanent collections as well as the best way to approach both private and public funders.[23] Sachs taught his "Museum Work and Museum Problems" course from 1921 to 1948, training a generation of men and women for work in museums as directors, curators, and educators. As Sally Anne Duncan notes, Sachs imparted to his students "the investigative tools of academic scholarship as well as the problem-solving and practical skills of professional management," ensuring that all graduates would have the skills to develop engaging displays and rigorous collections as well as the social and political acumen to effectively communicate with both the general public and potential funders.[24] Eastman began his tenure at the Winnipeg Art Gallery by refreshing the display spaces, painting the walls of the gallery a yellow-green colour that he argued would work well with paintings of any period. He also ensured that objects from the permanent collection were on regular display in the WAG's rooms in the Civic Auditorium and introduced a contemporary gallery that focused attention on artists from

Winnipeg and the province of Manitoba. Most importantly, however, he undertook an inventory of the gallery's collection, organizing it according to whether or not the objects were suitable for permanent display, and securing members of the gallery's women's committee to begin the lengthy process of cataloguing the works in the collection.

Eastman was the first curator with museum training to work in western Canada. Jerrold Morris was hired by the Vancouver Art Gallery (VAG) in 1948, and implemented a number of programs and connections with institutions on the West Coast that would bring the gallery the respect of many North American institutions. However, Morris had only two years of art school training at the Slade in London and had been an engineering consultant in British Guyana and a pilot with the Royal Canadian Air Force before arriving in Vancouver. He proved to be a quick study of museum management practices and by 1952 had been elected president of the Western Association of Art Museum Directors and organized the association's national conference in Vancouver.[25] In Victoria, Colin Graham was lured back to the city of his birth in 1951 to develop the Art Centre of Greater Victoria (renamed the Art Gallery of Greater Victoria in 1955) into a major art institution. Following undergraduate studies at Cambridge, Graham obtained an MA in art at the University of California at Berkeley in 1948 and lectured at the California School of Fine Arts. He was director of education at the Palace of the Legion of Honour in San Francisco from 1949 to 1951, and it was likely this experience that garnered him the position of director of the Art Centre in Victoria. The Norman MacKenzie Art Gallery (NMAG) in Regina established its autonomy from the Art Department of Regina College with the 1951 hiring of a curator, Richard Simmins,[26] a graduate of the University of Toronto's MA in art history, who had previously been suggested by McCurry as a possible curator for Winnipeg and who would be selected in 1957 to head the NGC's Exhibition and Extension Services department.[27] Simmins's appointment as curator, along with the construction of a separate building for the gallery and the art school, marked the University of Saskatchewan's long-deferred commitment to Norman MacKenzie to properly house and care for his collection. The new curator's experience at the University of Toronto's Hart House as well as post-graduate training at The Courtauld were key factors in his hiring and helped him raise the gallery's profile among Regina's collectors and members of the public.

However, despite obtaining a thousand-dollar purchase fund from the university, Simmins was unable to add to the collection and it was only with the expansion of the gallery's facilities in 1957 that Ronald Bloore (paradoxically, an artist), who replaced Simmins as curator in 1958, could begin to systematically build a collection of historical and contemporary art.

Professional qualifications, however, were not a guarantee of a director's success. Despite his efforts to improve the Winnipeg Art Gallery and increase public interest in its activities, Eastman was not considered a good fit and the board began negotiations with Ferdinand Eckhardt, a specialist in museum education with a PhD from the University of Vienna, before Eastman's contract had ended. Eckhardt's experience "popularizing art with the public" at the Austrian State Art Galleries in Vienna, as well as his friendship with one of the members of the WAG's board were important factors in his selection, and the board justified its hiring of a European by noting "the shortage in Canada of persons with the proper training to act as directors of art galleries and the problems which had been encountered by various other Canadian galleries in respect of their directors."[28] True to the trustees' view that "he might possibly become the outstanding Art Gallery Director of Canada,"[29] Eckhardt was a pivotal figure in the history of the Winnipeg Art Gallery and the trajectory of his transformation of that institution from a few rooms in the Civic Auditorium to a major institution in an architecturally significant building is a model for the challenges that faced many art galleries in western Canada during the 1950s and 1960s. During this period, art galleries in the region made concerted efforts to differentiate themselves from their former incarnations. The hiring of directors and curators with university degrees in art history or training in museum work was a marker of professional status necessary for the establishment of an art institution on a par nationally and internationally with other art galleries. The size of the institution was less important than the ability to assert its adherence to standards of professional museum practice as defined by museum associations in Britain and the United States in particular.

The hiring of Eastman and especially Eckhardt in Winnipeg, Simmins in Regina, Graham in Victoria, and Jack MacGillivray in Edmonton signalled that western Canadian art galleries were conforming to the conception of the museum director as having academic training in museum practices as well as experience in the field.[30] This "museum man" – a phrase widely used during this period – points to the clear differentiation being made between the amateur voluntary "keeper," much admired in the nineteenth century, and the "curator/director" with recognized credentials.[31] The gendered nature of the term underscores assumptions of the period that professional museum workers would be male, despite the vital role of women in establishing museums across North America, often serving as their first directors; Maud Bowman of the Edmonton Museum of Arts is but one example.[32] However, a *salaried* woman director of a Canadian museum would not be appointed until 1966 when Jean Sutherland Boggs took over at the NGC, notably also as the first NGC director to hold a PhD. In its usage in the 1940s and 1950s, the phrase "museum man" forges a distinction between the scholar working outside the museum and the curator or director able to translate subject matter expertise to the broader audience of the museum. This differentiation clearly marks out the boundary between those individuals deemed suitable to work within the museum and those to be kept out or displaced, thus underscoring the transformation of the practice of curating into a professional skill understood as both intellectual and practical. This latter distinction, for example, underpins the debate between the president of the American Association of Museums, Laurence Vail Coleman, and Alexander Ruthven, director of the University of Michigan Museum, in the late 1930s: where Ruthven argued that specialist subject matter training was the major skill that museum curators brought to their job, Coleman advocated general knowledge and hands-on experience as key skills for the museum professional and that these skills, moreover, allowed the museum worker to be most effective in reaching the public.[33] As Alvan Eastman knew, Paul Sachs also strongly advocated the importance of knowledge of art in concert with facility in all aspects of museum management, including public outreach. In the 1950s and 1960s, as more universities offered graduate degrees in art history and as the Canadian Museums Association regularly published articles and editorials on the importance of training for museum workers, Canadian art galleries raised their expectations for the qualifications of staff at all levels. Such expectations were cemented in the founding of the Canadian Art Museum Directors' Organization in 1964 "to promote professional standards for art museum directors in Canada" and became increasingly important as funding for museum activities from provincial and federal governments increased substantially in the 1970s.[34] As Perry Rathbone noted in an essay for *Canadian Art* in 1960, expectations of museum directors were high: "The new museum has produced the new director … Larger and more complex staffs require him to be a skilful personnel director; popularization and competition with rival cultural organizations force him into the role of a public-relations and publicity expert. Technological advances have revolutionized ideas of display: the director becomes a showman. He presides over an amazingly complex building; he must know its anatomy, whether it is the new television wiring or the old skylights with their perennial leaks. He must be a writer, a talker, a fund-raiser."[35] Training to become this new museum director came in part through university and hands-on training, but the expansion of museum programming and raised public expectations required a new kind of professional. As much as qualified "museum men" were pursued during the 1950s and 1960s, the boundaries between professional and amateur would be most visibly reinforced through the erection of stand-alone buildings that symbolically marked the separation between general knowledge and the specialized knowledge held in and managed by the museum.

Building New Art Galleries in Western Canada

When Eckhardt arrived at the Winnipeg Art Gallery, he found "nothing of extraordinary excitement": a small collection of objects mostly consisting of gifts from "people who wanted to 'clear their attics,'" some Canadian paintings, and some historical European works of doubtful provenance.[36] Although never explicitly stated, Eckhardt's aim was to grow the WAG into an institution with a permanent collection and exhibition program comparable to other North American institutions. In his annual reports, Eckhardt described the gallery's activities in relation to those of institutions in Ottawa, Toronto, Montreal, and Vancouver. His main frustration often seemed to be with the people of Winnipeg and their apparent lack of commitment to the institution. As he noted in 1956, "the citizens of Winnipeg don't realize the importance of having a good permanent collection of art. They have not felt the need to risk a considerable amount of money in building up an institution which will

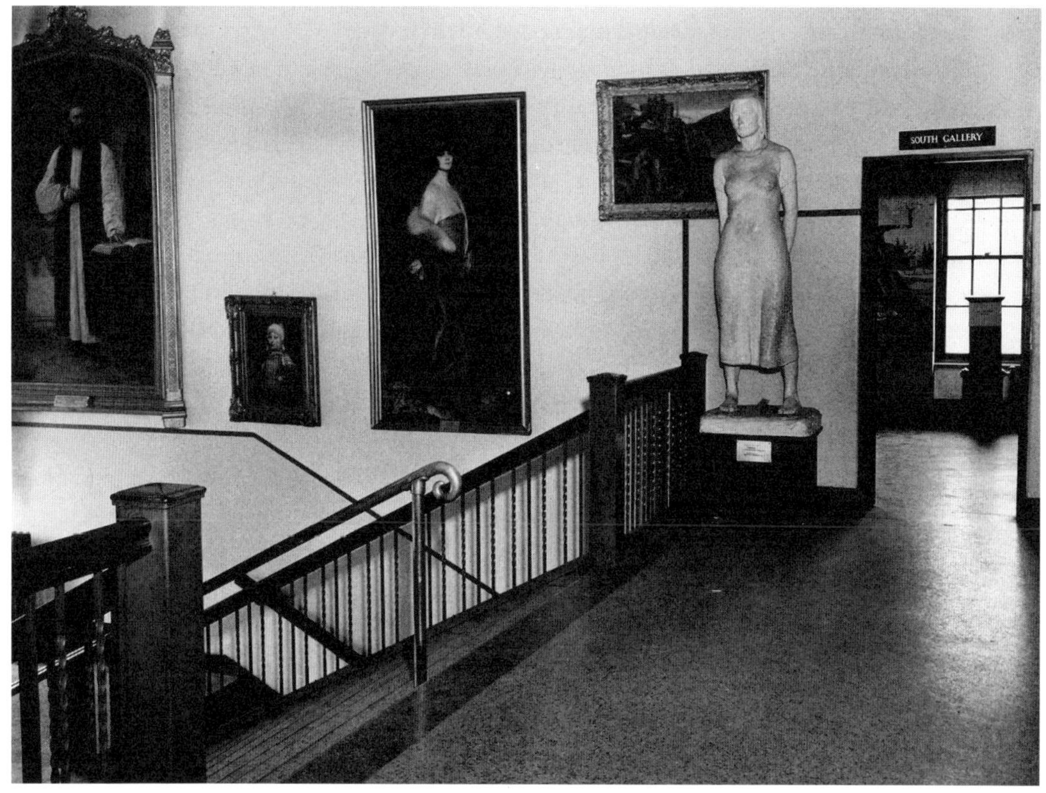

5.2 | Interior of the Winnipeg Art Gallery in the Civic Auditorium, 1958. The painting behind Elizabeth Wyn Wood's sculpture, *Linda*, is by English artist James Clarke Hook and is part of the A.A. Heaps Collection.

influence the cultural level of their city and they have not realized how wonderful it would be for them to erect a lasting memorial in the heart of their community."[37]

While specifically referencing the development of a permanent collection – an endeavour he quickly started to rectify with the help of such Winnipeg collectors as John A. McCauley and Alexander Purves – the main obstacle to Eckhardt's success was the lack of a dedicated art gallery building. For virtually the entirety of his tenure at the WAG, Eckhardt and the gallery's board would negotiate for space outside of the Civic Auditorium. Over a fifteen-year period, sites would be proposed, alliances with other arts groups encouraged, and pleas to municipal and provincial governments made to secure a multi-purpose arts centre. Finally, in

1967, the board purchased a triangular plot across the street from the auditorium and launched a competition to find an architect for a stand-alone art gallery. The building, designed by local architect Gustavo da Roza, would open to much praise on 25 September 1971 and fulfilled board president – and head of the School of Architecture at the University of Manitoba – John A. Russell's admonition that the building

> be dignified and impressive, yet inviting; it should not be a tour-de-force or overpowering, nor should it be dull or pedantic; it should be dynamic and alive, avoiding the clichés of modern or historic styles; it should be neither a "box" nor a "Guggenheim"; yet it should have the simple elegance of the former and might have the sculptural quality such as the latter has ... Above all, the building should have a character, an architectural expression, which immediately conveys the impression that it is an art gallery – one designed especially for its location and, therefore, in harmony with as well as complementary to its neighbours and immediate environment.[38]

These words aptly describe the sentiments behind the building boom of art galleries in western Canada as institutions across the region sought to erect distinctive structures that would call attention to their growing autonomy and presence in the Canadian art world. As Russell and Eckhard fully understood, even if such autonomy had not been achieved, a new building with architectural character would convey that impression most effectively. Prior to the construction of the WAG, new buildings – or significant extensions to existing buildings – were opened for the Vancouver Art Gallery (1951), the Norman MacKenzie Art Gallery in Regina (1953 and 1957), the Art Gallery of Greater Victoria (1958), the Mendel Art Gallery (1964), and the Edmonton Art Gallery (1968). While Calgary's Allied Arts Centre had moved to new premises in 1959, it finally shut down in 1969, by which time art exhibitions in the city had been taken over by the Glenbow Foundation whose multidisciplinary museum opened in 1966.

The quest for a building by all the galleries discussed here was linked to the symbolic value of a permanent structure. For those galleries that had long been struggling with inadequate space in rented and often makeshift accommodations, the prospect of a purpose-built edifice was

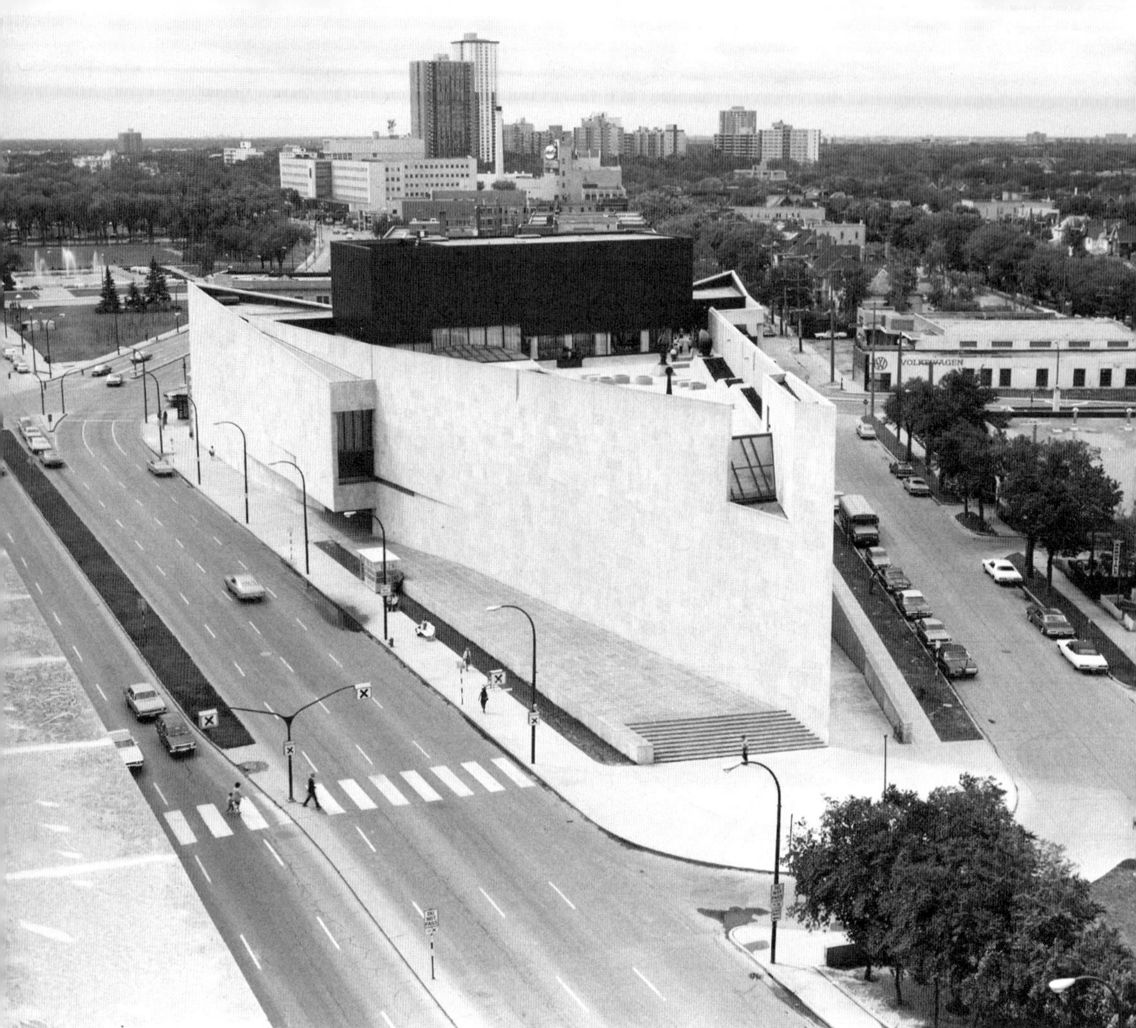

5.3 | Winnipeg Art Gallery exterior c. 1971. Described as "the prow of a ship cutting through difficult waters," the new building quickly became a Winnipeg landmark.

a dream that was constantly reiterated at annual general meetings and in the press. For these organizations, a permanent building brought the promise of increased donations of works for the permanent collection; better loan exhibitions from national and international public and private collections; and the expectation of increased funding from both the city and provincial governments. In Edmonton the need for a permanent building was voiced from the beginning of the founding of the Edmonton Museum of Arts Association in 1923, and as the institution moved from building to building over the course of its first three decades, it linked its lack of funding from the province and limited private donations to its poor image as a seemingly unstable organization in rented quarters. In 1952, the museum moved into a former mansion bequeathed to it by members of the pioneer Secord family. The four-thousand-square-foot Secord mansion was typical of many stopgap measures for museums in Canada in the 1940s and 1950s as too-large houses were converted into display spaces;[39] indeed, the Winnipeg Art Gallery was offered a similar opportunity in 1954 when lawyer G.H. Aikins bequeathed his home to the gallery in the hopes that it would provide improved accommodation for the collection from the rooms then occupied in the Civic Auditorium. Many members of the WAG's board were tempted by the offer, but Eckhardt viewed the house as too parochial for the signature building he envisioned for Winnipeg. Eckhardt's views were supported by W.G. Constable, newly installed as director of the Boston Museum of Fine Arts from his previous position at The Courtauld Institute, whose statement damning the practice of converting old houses into art galleries during a lecture tour of western Canada was widely reported in the press.[40] For the Edmonton Museum of Arts, Secord House was a distinct improvement on the rooms it occupied in the former Edmonton Motors Building, and the prospect of a stand-alone building provided the museum with an opportunity to convey an image of self-sufficiency and strength. Despite extensive redecoration and remodelling, however, the domestic architecture of Secord House did not provide appropriate space for the exhibition of works of art – particularly the larger modern paintings being produced in the 1950s and early 1960s. In 1962 Mrs Abigail Condell bequeathed six hundred thousand dollars to the Edmonton museum for the construction of a new building as a memorial to her son, and the board of directors began negotiations with the city to locate a suitable site. Construction began in 1967.

The new museums built between 1951 and 1971 all made use of the vocabulary of international modernism to assert their presence in the civic landscape. Although responsible for an addition to an existing building rather than a completely new construction, in 1951 Ross Lort replaced the original art deco façade of the Vancouver Art Gallery with a concrete and plate glass walled entrance more in tune with the International Style featured in many Vancouver buildings of the period. Inside the extension, gallery spaces were open and square, with artificial light used throughout. In a memo to the VAG's board prior to the opening of the extension, curator Jerrold Morris outlined his recommendations

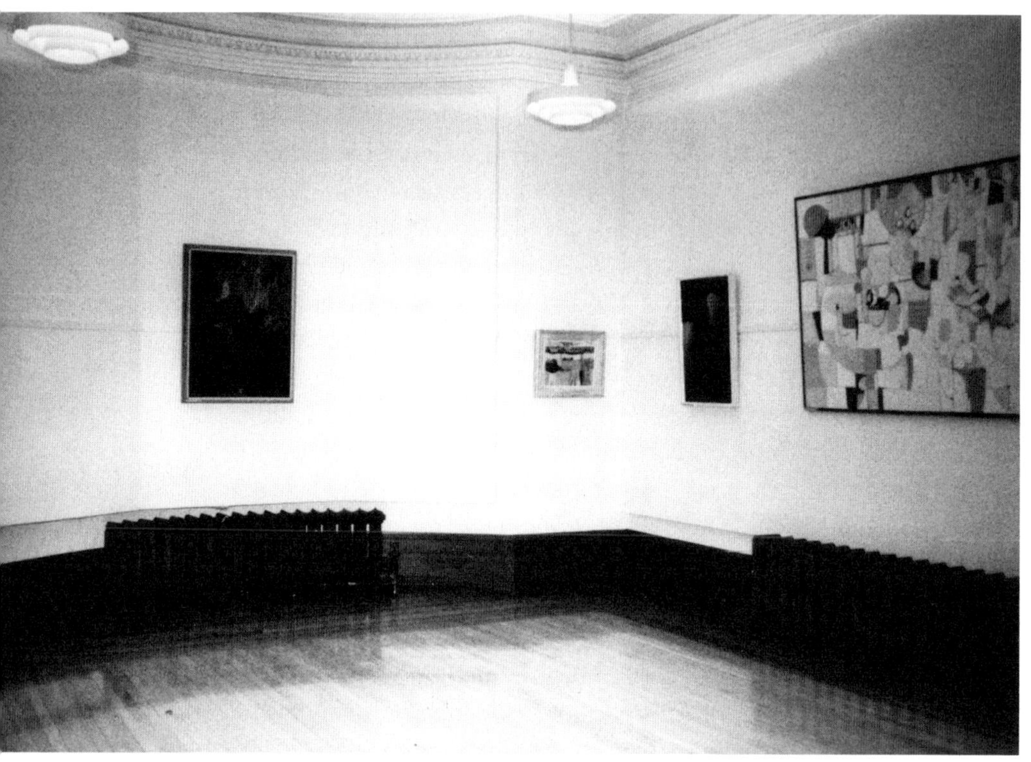

5.4 | The Edmonton Art Gallery, view of a gallery at Secord House, c. 1958.

for display strategies that would make the gallery "a warm and pleasant place to visit."[41] These included creating a more engaging environment by varying wall colours in individual galleries and employing different hanging and lighting strategies; breaking up large exhibition spaces with sculptures and potted plants to alleviate museum fatigue; and making judicious use of commercial display methods by presenting related material to enhance the understanding of the art on display. Examples of such methods included the presentation of Indian masks and influential works of art in the new Emily Carr Memorial Gallery, and the discrete incorporation of labels and other didactic material. Morris also advocated variety in temporary exhibitions and encouraged board members to think positively about displays of small sculpture, decorative arts, ceramics and textiles as well as ethnographic material in order to interest a much wider public. Hoping to broaden the audience for the art gallery's programs, Morris also suggested playing recorded music in some of the galleries at lunchtime (an experiment he had already conducted two years earlier) and opening a tearoom.[42] In making these recommendations, Morris was building on the ideas of Louvre curators Germain Bazin and René Huyghe whose writings were published in *Museum* and other periodicals devoted to the profession. Although couched more in terms of increasing the gallery's audience than in professionalizing its activities, Morris's memo nonetheless underlines an increased awareness of the importance of thinking critically about methods of display and uses of didactic material. As he argues in the concluding paragraph

5.5 | The refreshed modernist façade of the Vancouver Art Gallery (Ross Lort, architect), 1951.

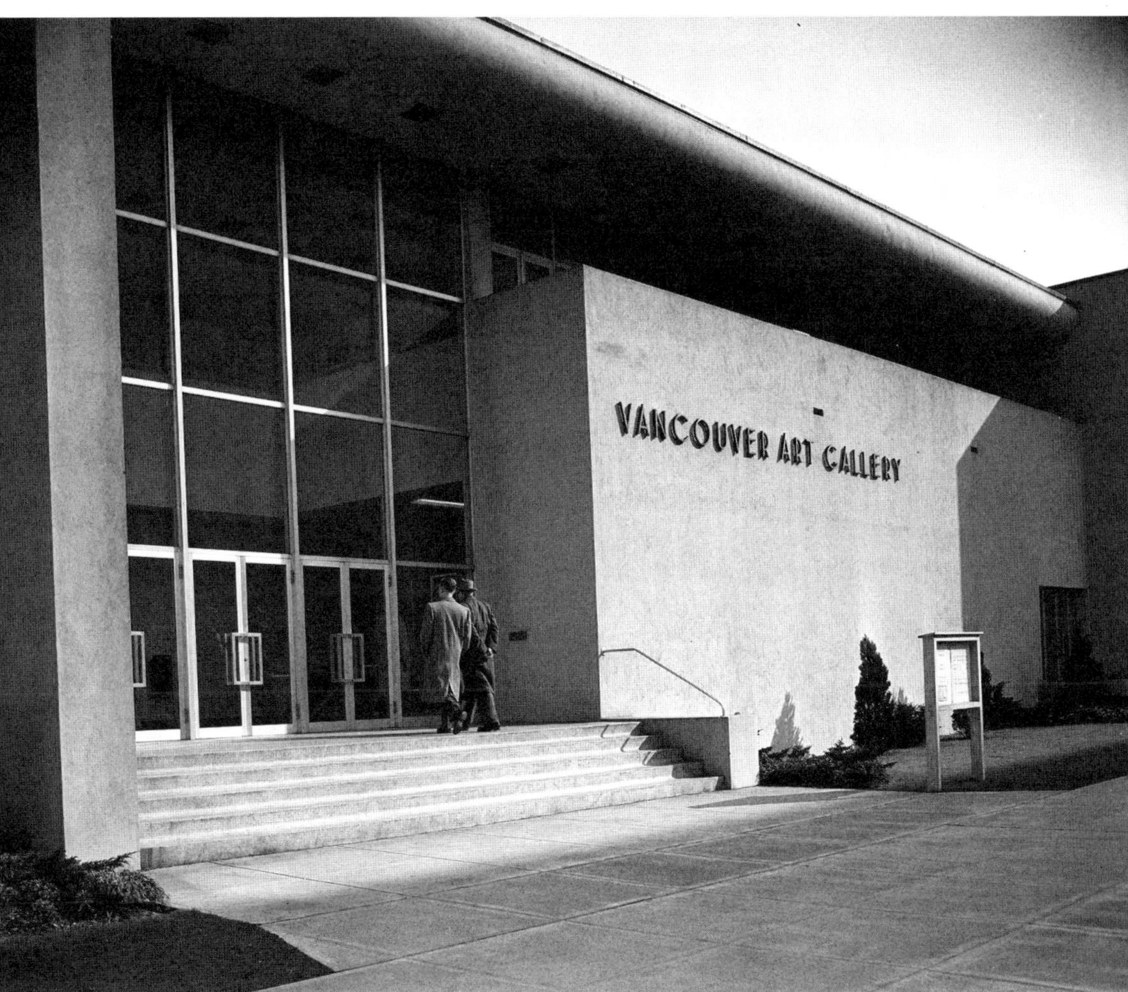

of this document, such means would elevate the standing of the gallery in the eyes of both the public and various levels of government and increase its visibility nationally and internationally:

> Picture now a building with a well-kept boulevard, a bright foyer with a well-equipped sales desk where books and reproductions are available. Inside the visitor may expect to find our older paintings displayed in an interesting manner and well catalogued and labelled; the Emily Carr collection on display; in the older section of the building a temporary exhibition of current interest and perhaps a show of pottery or glass. A feeling of warmth and colour everywhere, of varied interest, livliness [*sic*] and welcome. Tea after the Gallery tour: sometimes music. Such an institution will build its own public and will be valued by our citizens and admired by visitors. Then we shall really begin to serve Vancouver and attract adequate support without having to be constantly fighting for it.[43]

Responding to the announcement of the plans for the new extension, *Canadian Art* determined that the new VAG would emerge as "the most modern art gallery in Canada," and this was certainly the aim of the gallery's leadership.[44]

Similar aspirations for increased status and visibility underscore the new constructions and additions to art museums across western Canada. A new building, designed by local architect F.H. Portnall, was completed for the Norman MacKenzie Art Gallery in 1953, and while not as spectacular as the VAG addition, its square footprint and clean lines signalled its embrace of the modernist art practices with which it would soon become closely associated. An extension in 1957 by the architectural firm of Izumi, Arnott, and Sugiyama created a structure on four stacked levels, expanding both the gallery and the art school, adding space for the display of the permanent collection and temporary exhibitions, and accommodating the services needed to support a modern museum (reception area, business offices, and receiving and packing workshops).[45] In 1960, Fred Mendel's announcement of a $175,000 donation to the city of Saskatoon to build an art gallery, launched a national design competition. Regina-born architect Alan Hanna, of the Winnipeg firm of Blankstein, Coop, Gillmore, and Hanna, won the competition with a concrete and

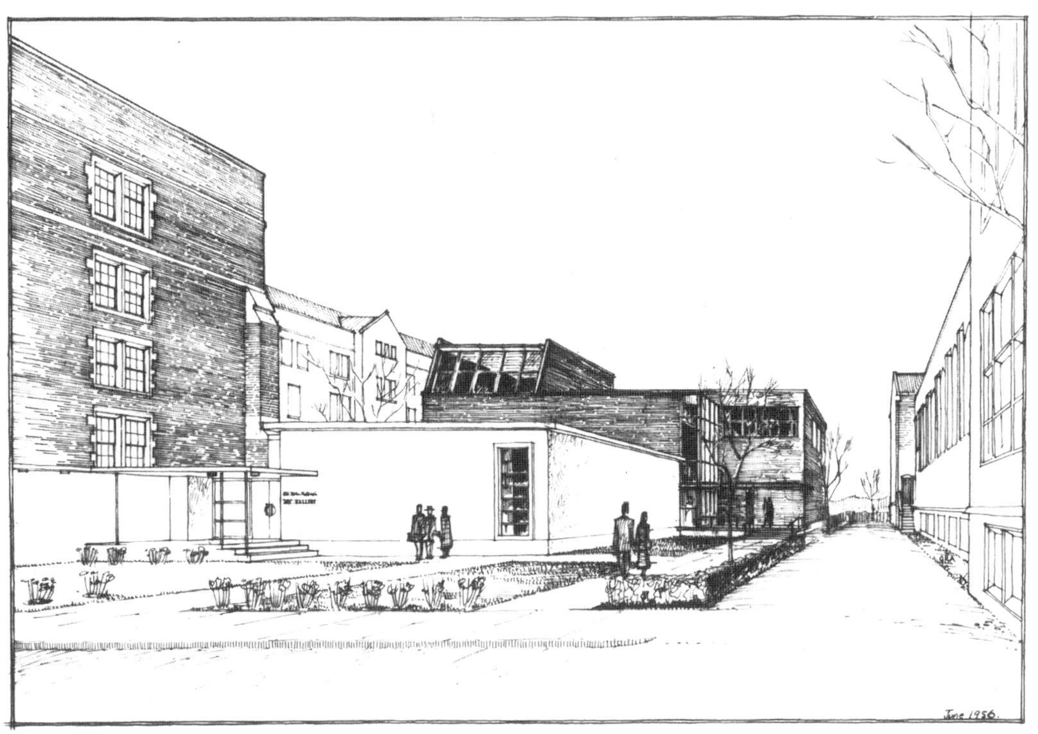

5.6 | Norman MacKenzie Art Gallery, sketch for the extension by the firm of Izumi, Arnott, and Sugiyama, 1956.

glass structure that privileged the smooth circulation of visitors through the exhibition galleries while creating a series of windowed resting points permitting views of the South Saskatchewan River. Working in a mode similar to his teacher Louis Kahn, perhaps best known at the time for his design of the Yale Art Gallery, Hanna used a saw-tooth roofing system to bring natural light into the galleries and created pathways that naturally returned viewers to the conservatory at the front of the building.[46]

A similar turn to modernism can be found in Edmonton. In 1964, the Edmonton Art Gallery finally secured private and government funding to begin planning its own new building, obtaining the services of Richard McLanathan, as recommended by architect Philip Johnson, as a planning consultant.[47] The resulting building, designed by local architects Don Bittorf and Jim Wensley and erected in the downtown core of the city, was a concrete rectangle with few windows but expansive

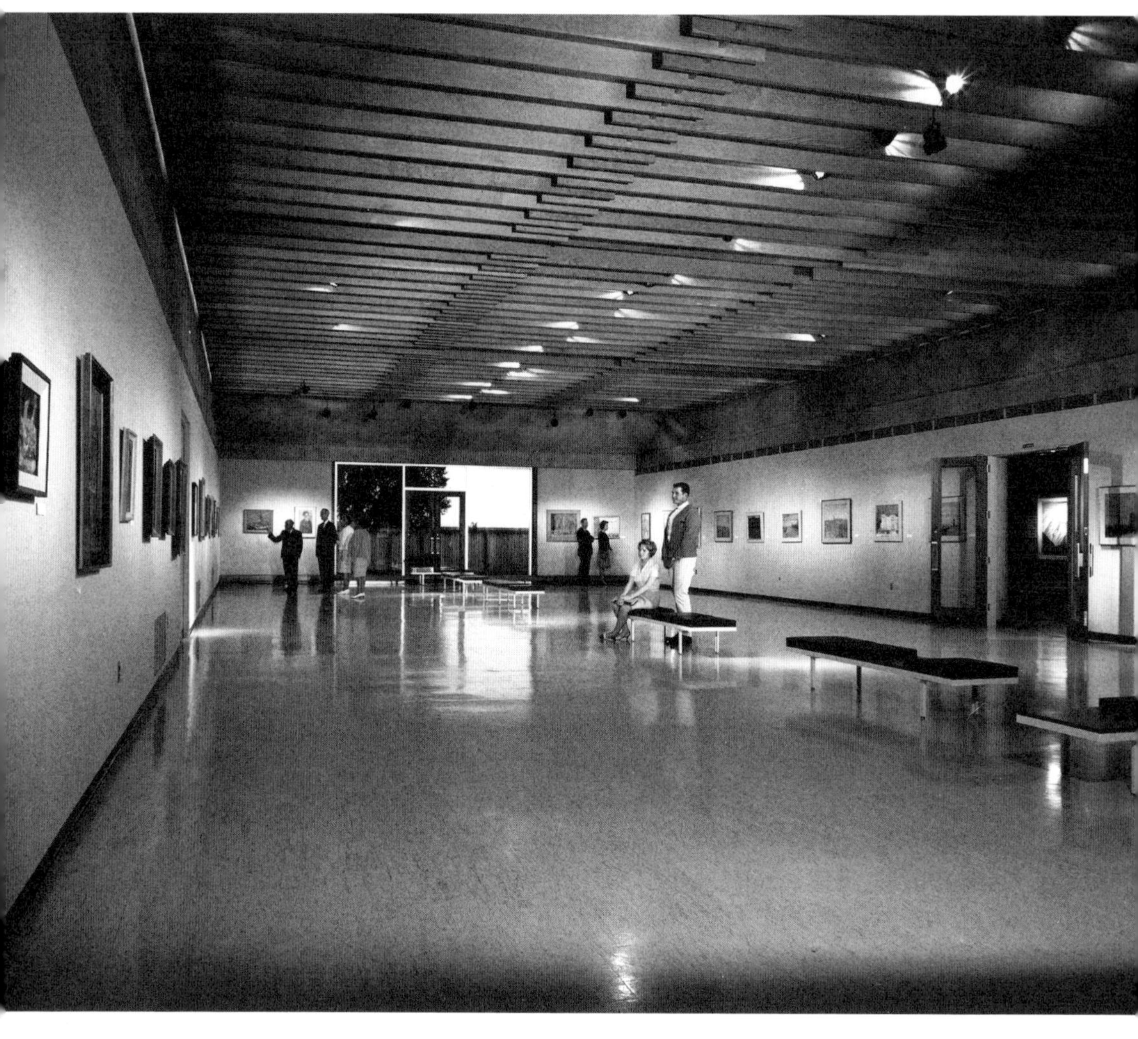

5.7 | Mendel Art Gallery and Civic Conservatory, interior view, 1964. The large number of windows throughout the building permitted restive views of outside.

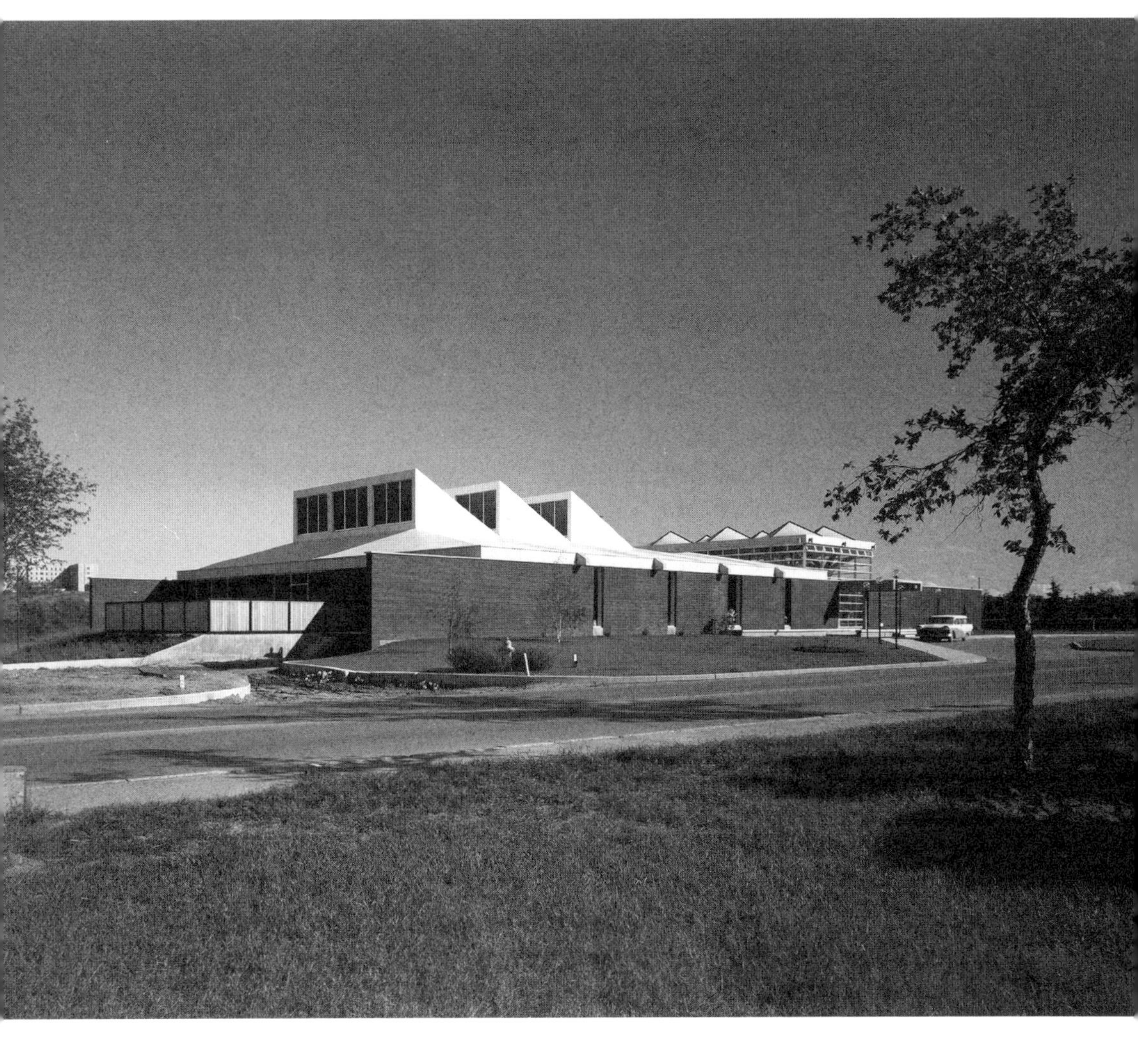

5.8 | Mendel Art Gallery and Civic Conservatory, 1964. Architect Alan Hanna's saw-tooth roofing system is clearly visible.

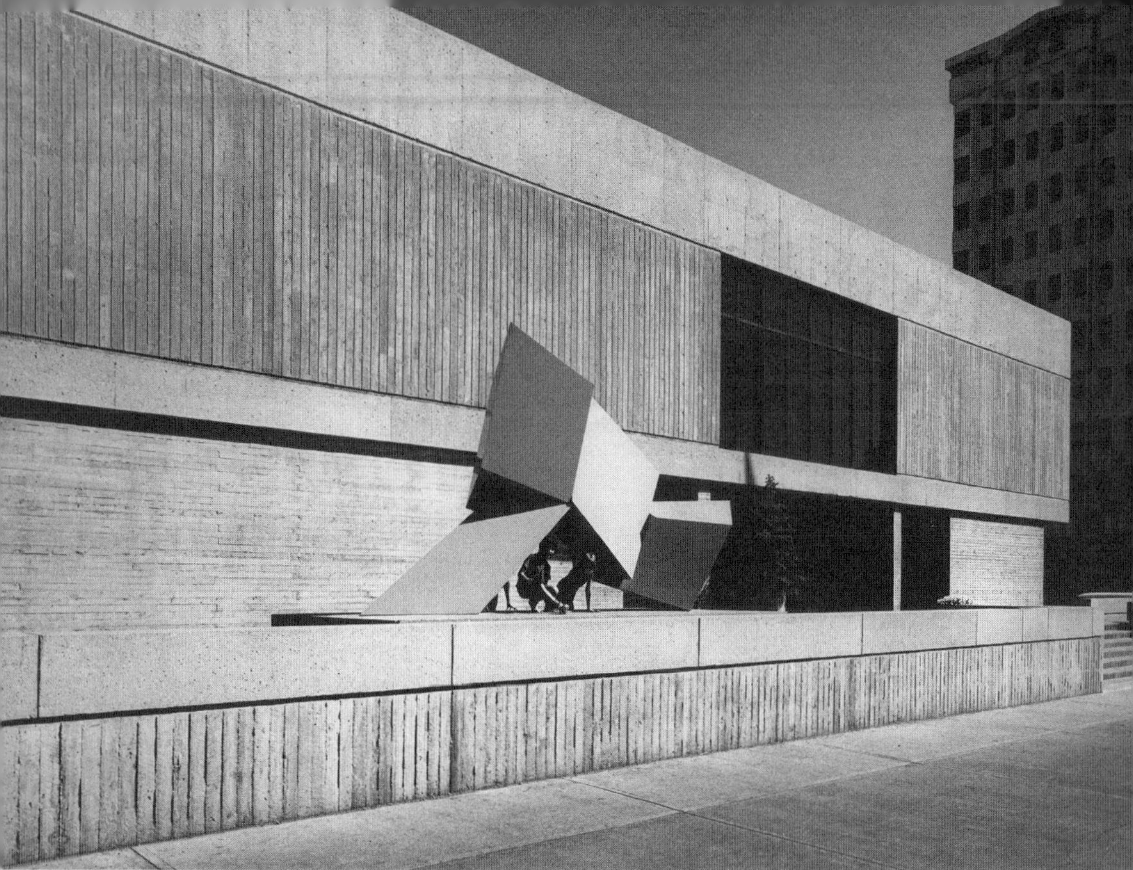

5.9 | The Edmonton Art Gallery (architects Don Bittorf and Jim Wensley), 1972. James Rosati's sculpture *Edmonton* (1971) was commissioned for the new building.

interior gallery spaces. Described by NGC curator Pierre Théberge as the finest gallery building in Canada, the facility marked a new direction in the EAG's programming with the hiring of curator Karen Wilkin and director Terry Fenton, who, with strong support from the gallery's board, embarked on an ambitious collecting program that established Edmonton as a centre for contemporary modernist painting and sculpture.[48]

The Winnipeg Art Gallery's building similarly was designed by local architect da Roza after a major international competition. Like the EAG and the Mendel, the building employed the vocabulary of international modernism to imprint itself as a vibrant, cutting-edge institution. Writing about Winnipeg's built environment, architectural historian Serena Keshavjee argues that the explosion of modernist architecture in that city – as well as in major centres across the country – was the result of the Centennial era's attempts to present Canada as a progressive country.

This sentiment was intensified in Winnipeg as the city marked celebrations of not only the centennial of Canadian confederation, but also the centenaries of the founding of Manitoba in 1970 and of Winnipeg itself in 1974. All three events brought funding for monumental projects to symbolize the city's coming of age, and a modernist style was the unanimous choice of government and institutional boards to convey Winnipeg as "an up-to-date, thriving city."[49] Mirroring the triangular lot on which it was built, and often likened to the prow of a ship cutting through difficult waters, the WAG's new building embodied the ambitions of its director and board of governors for the institution to have a more influential role in the development of art in Canada and to compete on a more equal basis with major institutions in Montreal, Toronto, Ottawa, and the United States. The hiring of Eckhardt, a man with both technical and subject matter expertise, had been a first step in accomplishing such recognition; a new and architecturally significant building was the second. And while the collections of both the WAG and the EAG may not have

5.10 | Winnipeg Art Gallery lobby, c. 1971, with paintings by Frank Stella and Kenneth Noland.

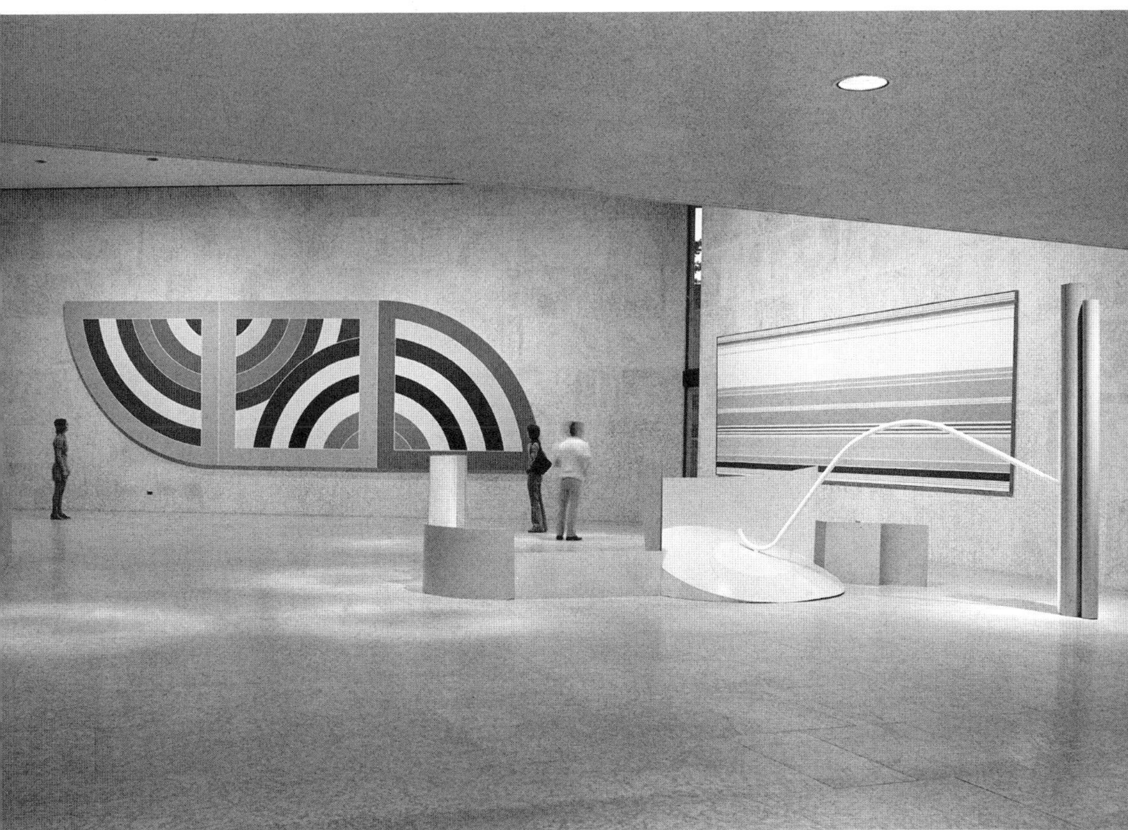

been immediately bolstered by the construction – indeed, *Time* magazine described the new Edmonton Art Gallery as "beautiful but bare" due to the lack of objects on display,[50] and both institutions faced financial deficits in the wake of the new construction forestalling the purchase of new works – the new buildings were clear indications of their leaders' aesthetic ambitions, and the growing role they sought to play in the Canadian art world.

The push to construct new buildings was not prompted solely by a desire for increased recognition from the local community and valorization by members of the art world. The National Gallery's evaluation of the facilities of art museums across the country prompted by the formation of the NGC's Exhibition and Extension Services department forced many museums to more actively engage in a program of facility revitalization and refurbishment. As discussed in Chapter 4, the classification of art centres across the country into A-, B- and C-class facilities was undertaken in order to better place the gallery's touring exhibitions.[51] Class-A galleries were fireproof, had twenty-four-hour security provisions, and were staffed with knowledgeable personnel who were able to supervise the unpacking, hanging, and storage of works on loan from the National Gallery or other institutions. The Vancouver Art Gallery was a clear example of a Class-A gallery with its dedicated concrete building that could be securely locked outside of opening hours, security staff on duty during the day, and a curator, a business manager as well as a preparator on staff to handle all exhibitions. The Winnipeg Art Gallery was also considered a Class-A gallery, its dedicated rooms in the fireproof Civic Auditorium building regularly patrolled by security guards and its well-respected director able to handle even the most challenging exhibitions.[52] Despite having its own building, the Edmonton Art Gallery was listed as a Class-B gallery in 1958, largely because of the condition of its galleries and concerns that Secord House's wood-frame construction did not meet the fireproofing standards of the national institution. That the Edmonton gallery did not have what the National Gallery considered to be a professional director – Jack MacGillivray would only be hired in 1961 – was a further concern of Extension staff in its assessment of the EAG's ability to handle large exhibitions of original artworks in 1958. To address its inability to receive important travelling exhibitions from the National Gallery and elsewhere, the Art Gallery of Greater Victoria embarked on an aggressive fundraising campaign in the mid-1950s to build

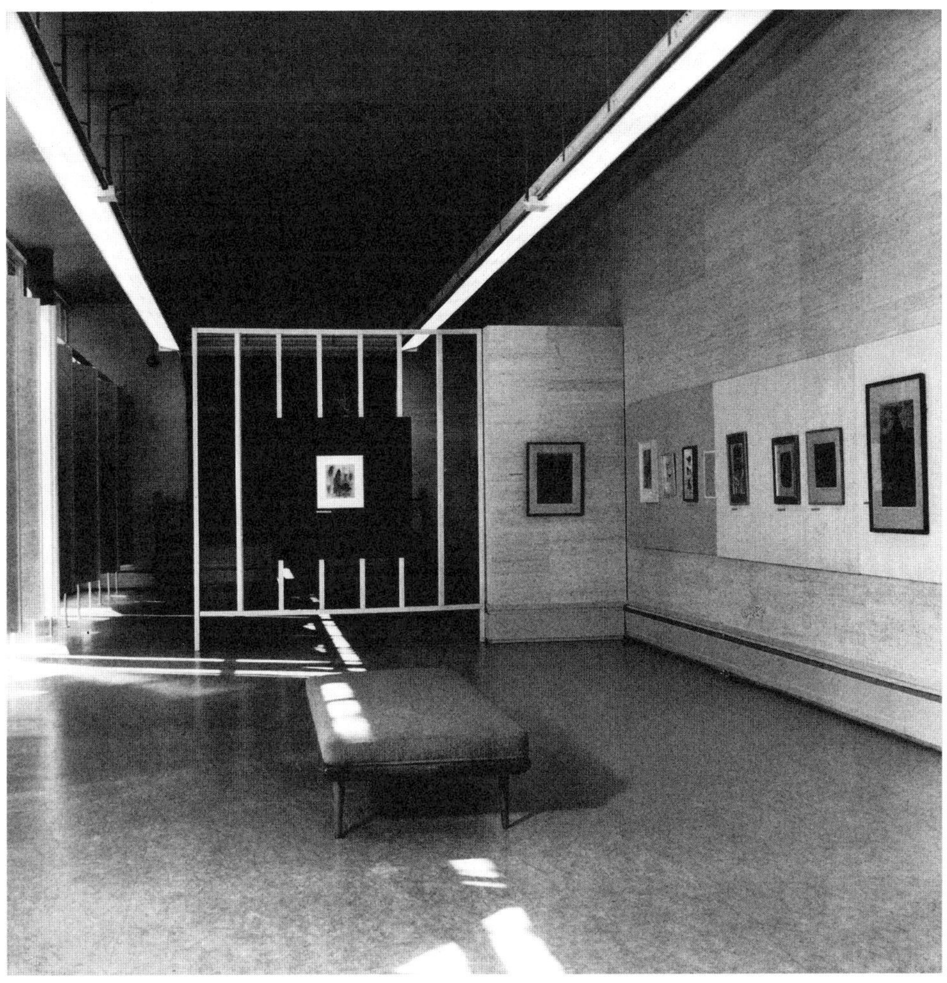

5.11 | Art Gallery of Greater Victoria, Ker Gallery c. 1959. The louvered panels on the left could be adjusted to create more light in the gallery or closed completely to provide more hanging space.

a fireproof addition to the Spencer mansion, resulting in the construction of the Centennial wing opening in 1958. Other organizations that fell into the B-class category included the Calgary Allied Arts Centre at Coste House, the Regina Public Library, and the Saskatoon Art Centre – the latter two eventually addressing this status through building schemes.[53] Although the Extension department's classification of Canadian art galleries was initiated as a means of establishing which exhibitions would tour to which organizations, the assessment reinforced a hierarchy of value among the museums with the Class-A galleries seeing themselves as members of a higher tier of museums that included not only the National Gallery but also the Art Gallery of Toronto and the Montreal Museum of Fine Arts. Class-B galleries, meanwhile, felt shortchanged by the classification and had to work harder to establish positive and productive relationships with institutions that they considered their equals.

Classifying and Cataloguing: Ordering Museum Collections

A less visible but no less central facet of professionalization that occurred during the 1950s and 1960s in galleries across Canada was the systematic processing of collections and the development of acquisitions practice and policies that conformed to the standards advocated by the American Association of Museums and its British and Canadian counterparts. Not surprisingly, such classification occurred when organizations hired curators and directors with museum training, and the development of best practices was significantly aided by publications such as the *Handbook for Museum Curators*, issued by the Museums Association in the mid-1950s and made available to Canadian Museums Association members at a reduced price.[54] Shortly after his arrival at the Winnipeg Art Gallery, Alvan Eastman undertook an inventory of the permanent collection. In a memo dated 24 November 1950, Eastman reported to the board that the gallery had 163 oil paintings in its collection, of which 122 belonged to two collections on permanent loan to the institution. Of those 163 works, the director identified 34 as unsuitable for exhibition and he consigned them to "dark storage" in the gallery's vaults. While not suitable for display in the gallery, a further 12 paintings were thought to be useful to publicize the gallery in store windows, banks, and schools.[55] As part of the inventory, Eastman also classified the collection alphabetically by artist, and began the process of making a card catalogue, assigning an accession number for each work and listing the collections chronologically by the year in which each work was acquired.

The cataloguing program undertaken by Eastman appears both obvious and elementary to twenty-first-century eyes, but in many Canadian museums, such practices were slow to develop. For many institutions, including the National Gallery, records of acquisitions were written out in ledger books until well into the 1940s. Former registrar Greg Spurgeon notes that the National Gallery implemented a card system in the late 1940s or early 1950s when Dorothea Coates became the gallery's first registrar.[56] This card catalogue was not comprehensive as it did not cover all works in the collection and had to rely on the information that had been previously recorded in the ledger books. In addition, the development of new collecting areas such as photography, introduced at the gallery by James Borcoman in 1967, sometimes resulted in a balkanization of records and a delay in their integration into the larger catalogue. Object files – expanded records that documented provenance, condition, as well as the loan history of every object in the gallery's collection – were introduced by Ella McLaren when she came to the National Gallery from the Art Gallery of Ontario with Director Jean Sutherland Boggs in 1966. As early as 1941, Alice Putnam Breuer, associate director of the Mills College Art Gallery in Oakland, California, had described the duties of museum registrars as "keeping an acquisition book, a loan record, a disposal record, and attendant duties" and her presentation to the members of the American Association of Museums is rich in detail about the mechanics of such detailed record keeping.[57] Breuer went on, however, to note that the work of the registrar was much more complex and often involved infinite tact and patience as she [*sic*] frequently had to mediate between public and curators, curators and artists, and between collectors and museum representatives. In most museums with limited staff, Breuer noted that the tasks of registrar and curator frequently overlapped and were often undertaken by one individual. Outside of the major centres in Canada, however, the thorough cataloguing of objects, let alone appointment of registration staff, did not take place until the late 1960s and early 1970s. Nancy Robertson (later Dillow) made the creation of object files a priority upon her appointment as director of the Norman MacKenzie Art Gallery in 1967.[58] The Art Gallery of Greater Victoria did not have a registrar until 1974 when Ian Thom took up the position. In his report to the members of the museum's board on the challenges facing the institution in the early 1980s, AGGV Director Roger Boulet made a particular point of noting the sporadic character of collections management until the appointment of a registrar: "registration had, until 1974, been haphazard and erratic, undertaken by what staff there was when more pressing activities did not require their attention."[59] Virtually every other art museum in western Canada faced similar time pressures on their equally limited staff.

For the majority of Canadian art museums still lacking a curator let alone a registrar, collections were known through memory and through the periodic lists drawn up as inventory for insurance purposes. Pressure to improve standards increased from the Canadian Museums Association, which awarded associate status to those institutions who met professional criteria, as well as from the National Gallery, which refused to loan works to institutions that it felt did not have adequate human or physical resources to care for objects. As a result, even institutions with limited professional staff embarked on the process of producing a thorough record of the works in their possession, often in conjunction with an assessment of the collection as a whole. At the Edmonton Museum of Arts, this process was driven by the appointment of Dorothy (Bobby) Dyde to the museum's council in 1952 and her almost immediate designation as chair of the newly formed Selection and Exhibition (later Acquisition) Committee. This role was a natural fit for Dyde whose own art collection was extensive and whose personal connections with important figures in the Canadian art world far exceeded those of any other member of the Edmonton museum's board.[60] Indeed, the same year she joined the EMA's board, Dyde was appointed to the Board of Trustees of the National Gallery of Canada, a position that would further contribute to her ability to take on the organization of the Edmonton museum's collection.

Within the first few months of her appointment to the Selection and Exhibition Committee, Dyde and her board colleagues met several times to examine the museum's collection of works "with the view of eliminating unsuitable pictures and to organize the collection to meet the standard of high merit worthy of our organization." Commenting on the overall quality of collection, the committee remarked that many of the works had entered the collection "without due consideration as to their artistic merit" while others "were accepted for sentimental reasons."[61] In response, the committee divided the existing collection into categories according to whether they were suitable for exhibiting; had artistic merit but were in a medium that would be more effectively stored in portfolios; were good enough to be sold or loaned but should not remain in the collection; and those pictures that were of poor quality or of no artistic value. Any proceeds from the sale of unsuitable works or from the frames of works destined for portfolio storage would go into the Picture Reserve account from which future and doubtless more appropriate works would be bought for the EMA's collection. Other museums undertook similar assessments of their collections.

Upon his arrival in Winnipeg, Ferdinand Eckhardt divided the WAG's collection into "Grade A" works that would be shown in the permanent collection and loaned only on request of major art centers; "Grade B" works that might be kept for loans to schools and other institutions interested throughout the Province; and "Grade C" works that should be sold.[62] Writing in 1971, Eckhardt would look back on this period as the start of a systematic collecting program that included the establishment of a purchase and acceptance committee in 1954 and a redirection of the collection from the acquisition of primarily Canadian art "to a more universal [goal] with an international level, [which] matched the exhibition policy of the new director" – Eckhardt himself.[63]

The absence of aesthetic criteria in most collecting programs of the period can be explained by the fact that many Canadian museums in the 1950s were still trying to establish themselves and were concentrating on amassing objects rather than assessing quality or formulating a collecting strategy. Even larger institutions such as the Montreal Museum of Fine Arts and the Art Gallery of Toronto had relatively unformulated acquisition policies at this time. In their 1958 survey of Canadian museums for the CMA, American academics Carl and Grace Guthe commented on the absence of collecting standards in many of the institutions they visited over the summer of 1957. In their view, many museum workers were "sincere enthusiasts convinced of the necessity of assembling and preserving objects," but because of a lack of training and outdated ideas about the function of the museum, they were unable to formulate the kinds of policies and procedures necessary to produce compelling displays and programming that could connect the institution to its community.[64] Although the Guthes' assessment was primarily directed at local history and generalist museums, their observation that the lack of professional knowledge in the accumulation and presentation of objects had a negative effect on public interest in museums applies to all the institutions considered in this book. Led by "sincere enthusiasts" at both the director and the board levels, the Edmonton Museum of Arts was, by 1952, in desperate need of clear guidelines for the acquisition of objects for its permanent collection. Reliant up to that point on infrequent donations from local collectors, gifts by artists, and the occasional presentation of work from a collector of national stature (see, for example, the gifts from the Southam family in the 1920s and 1930s discussed in Chapter 1), the EMA had little money for purchases and no collecting focus. The council minutes of May 1945 record the resolution that the museum acquire "at least one picture per annum" – hardly what can be described as an active acquisition program. The overview of the collection undertaken by Dyde's Selection and Exhibition Committee in 1952 constituted the first step in a long process of evaluating the museum's haphazard collection and bringing a modicum of order to it.

More than a cataloguing of the collection needed to occur, however, if western Canadian museums were to increase their stature nationally and internationally. Institutions needed to develop acquisitions policies that would guide systematic and strategic expansion of the permanent collection. In January 1953, with the newly renamed Acquisition Committee still under Dyde's leadership, the Edmonton Museum of Art's Council met to consider an amendment to its by-laws, effectively formalizing the process through which objects were brought into the EMA's collection. Most notably, the amendment insisted that a written valuation of "any works of art or historic relics" be made, as well as a statement as to the authenticity of the gift or purchase, before council could accept it into the collection.[65] In terms of a formal policy, the amendment to the institution's by-laws was not a revolutionary recasting of the museum's existing practices; however, it did establish an acquisitions process more in line with professional museum practices. Writing in the Museums Association's *Handbook for Museum Curators* series in 1956 – a series popular with Canadian museum directors and curators – Trenchard Cox, director of the Victoria and Albert Museum, advised his readers to maintain a policy of "quality first" but to temper overly high ambitions with careful selection of works that could build up a representative overview of the history of art: "in general, it is better to resist the temptation to acquire an indifferent work by a world-famous master rather than an interesting and representative example of the work of a less well-known man."[66] When it came to gifts, Cox invoked the importance of a curator's diplomatic skills in all such negotiations, advising that the continued goodwill of local supporters required giving an honest appraisal with as much genuine sympathy as possible. At the root of Cox's manual, however, was the recognition that while every museum "possesses a quantity of pictures and other works whose quality is now deplored,"[67] the job of the curator – or in the Canadian context, of the director tasked with curatorial functions – was to evaluate current holdings and deploy them as creatively as possible, and then determine an appropriate focus for the museum and begin to build a quality collection; in other words, to develop acquisition policies that would enforce selection of only the best objects available.

Other galleries were also implementing acquisition policies and processes around this time. Following his appointment in 1951, Norman MacKenzie Art Gallery curator Richard Simmins noted the limitations of his budget and focused his energies on an extensive exhibitions program that showcased the work of Saskatchewan artists and strengthened connections with the community. Under Ronald Bloore, director from 1958 to 1966, the NMAG collected heavily in the area of contemporary Canadian art, with Bloore seeking to ensure "cross-pollination ... of east and west" through the acquisition of works from artists working out of Ontario, Quebec, and points east.[68] When Nancy Robertson (later Dillow) became director in 1967, she brought experience as co-ordinator of Extension Services at the Art Gallery of Toronto as well as training in museum studies and art history. Robertson introduced a more focused acquisition plan that built on the strengths of the NMAG's collection. As a result, she pursued works on paper, particularly from nineteenth- and twentieth-century Europe, as an aid to teaching and as background for contemporary works; Robertson also continued the practice of acquiring contemporary Canadian art, with a particular focus on artists from Saskatchewan.[69] However, the acquisitions policy drafted under her leadership retained the breadth of scope of the previous two decades and specified only that the gallery collect original works of art – primarily painting, sculpture, and works on paper – and that aesthetic quality be the primary criterion. A focus on western Canadian art and European art of the nineteenth and early twentieth centuries was only formulated in 1982 under the direction of Carol Phillips.[70]

The development of acquisition policies in the 1960s points to Canadian museums' growing concerns with developing professional management practices and establishing well-defined collections that would allow differentiation from other institutions. The necessity of formal registration and cataloguing was underscored with the federal government's introduction of the National Museum Policy in the early 1970s that included the development of a National Inventory that would make information about objects in Canadian public collections more easily accessible. By 1976–77 funding was available to museums to hire registration staff with the understanding that participation in the National Inventory was a condition of funding. Acquisition policies also became urgent requirements as curatorial staff numbers grew and gallery directors' jobs became more concerned with administrative matters and navigating the increasingly complicated funding landscape. Acquisition policies with clear collecting directions assisted communications between curators and the director, and between the director and the institution's board of trustees. Focused acquisition policies (or guidelines) also allowed institutions to specialize in certain areas, making them more appealing to potential donors. By the late 1970s and early 1980s, several western Canadian art museums identified and built on existing strengths in their collections: the WAG, for example, choosing photography and Inuit art as two key areas for concerted development; the NMAG retaining an emphasis on western Canadian artists; and the EAG building its collection of American and Canadian modernist painting and sculpture. In the relatively small market of western Canada, such differentiated specializations were useful in minimizing competition between galleries for patronage. Most galleries relied extensively on donations from collectors and corporations in their home city and province, but as the art market exploded, gallery directors began to look further afield and a unique and established area of collecting focus was an advantage in the pursuit of potential donors.

Specialization took many forms from the 1950s through the 1970s. The 1953 amendment to the Edmonton Museum of Art's by-laws discussed above did more than simply point to the recognition that quality control was central to the forward movement of the EMA. The statement that "works of art [and] historic relics" be subject to review prior to acquisition underlined that historical objects remained part of the museum's collecting mandate.[71] From its inception, the EMA had received gifts of objects of historical and ethnographic significance. "Emily Murphy's chair" entered into the collection as late as 1950, a gift of the Edmonton Press Club; the museum was a regular recipient of Aboriginal and Inuit objects from a number of explorers and adventurers who made northern Alberta home;[72] and the minutes of the 13 February 1945 council meeting note that the EMA's collection of stuffed birds was to be indefinitely loaned to the University of Alberta. Occasionally, these objects were put on display, as for example in the first exhibition held by the museum at the Hotel

Macdonald where these "Indian and Esquimaux curios" generated much public interest. By the mid-1950s, however, there was little room for the exhibition let alone storage of these collections and the EMA made overtures to other institutions – including the nascent Glenbow-Alberta Foundation in Calgary, which had expressed interest in the museum's Inuit objects – to see if they could transfer them. The dispersal of the EMA's collection of Indigenous objects can be understood from several viewpoints. Aesthetic attitudes of the period rarely considered work by Indigenous artists as "fine art." Even if found in art gallery collections, such objects were not displayed with the permanent collection unless they provided context for the art on display – as can be seen in the Vancouver Art Gallery's plans for its new Emily Carr Memorial Gallery in 1951[73] – or if they were presented in a separate space devoted to objects of ethnographic or decorative interest – as in the "Museum" of the Art Association of Montreal where honorary curator Cleveland Morgan presented ceremonial objects from the Northwest Coast and Inuit carvings alongside French Canadian paintings and wood sculptures.[74] Internationally, occasional exceptions to the view of objects of Indigenous expressive culture as ethnographic artifacts can be found in such exhibitions as the Museum of Modern Art's 1941 *Indian Art of the United States*, which, as Jackson Rushing argues, used highly aestheticized display techniques to highlight the formal affinities between Indigenous and modern art.[75] In the main, however, works made by Indigenous creators were under the purview of anthropologists and ethnographers and their exhibitionary institutions: if the Edmonton Museum of Arts wanted to focus its collecting activities on the "fine" arts, it would have to divest itself of any objects in its possession that was not within such disciplinary boundaries.[76]

For the EMA, the policing of these boundaries became easier when the institution decided to change its name to the Edmonton Art Gallery in 1956. Although the appointment of an advisory committee to oversee the development of a provincial museum in Alberta – what would become the Royal Alberta Museum – was only struck in 1958, discussions of such an institution had been circulating since 1947 and the EMA's board was concerned that would-be donors felt that the word "museum" signalled the institution's acceptance of objects of any kind.[77] With the opening of a natural history museum on the horizon, and faced with the lack of storage space for non-fine art objects, the EMA's board voted unanimously to change its name in the hopes that the attendant symbolic capital would clarify the purview of the institution and generate increased donations. And donations were forthcoming: throughout the 1950s and 1960s, the Edmonton Art Gallery – along with virtually every other art gallery in the country – received works from the estate of Toronto art dealer Douglas Duncan; the EAG also received donations from Toronto businessman and philanthropist Robert Laidlaw, as well as extended loans (and some donations) from Max Stern's Dominion Gallery in Montreal.[78] Throughout the decade, acquisition policies continued to be developed and collecting focuses refined. The category of the fine arts, which had been so strongly asserted with the de-accessioning of work by Indigenous creators, was tested again with debates in several institutions over the acquisition of fine craft (in 1973 in Edmonton and in 1976 in Vancouver) and photography. While craft remained excluded from most art gallery collections in western Canada (and in Canada generally) despite major exhibitions from the 1960s onwards,[79] photography became part of several permanent collections beginning with the National Gallery, which in 1967 tasked James Borcoman, then an education officer at the gallery, with starting a collection that would map the history of photography from its origins to the present.[80] The Edmonton Art Gallery's board was typical of many art galleries when it questioned the appropriateness of acquiring photographs in the early 1970s. By 1977, however, extension curator Douglas Clark, with the assistance of fellow photographer Hubert Hohn, used the two-thousand-dollar allocation to begin building the collection of largely documentary photographs the gallery became known for. WAG director Roger Selby was supportive of photography and introduced the medium into the collection as a means of supporting local practitioners in the late 1970s.[81]

Conclusion

Although art galleries in Winnipeg, Regina, Saskatoon, Edmonton, Vancouver, and Victoria had limited funds at their disposal to build their collections, they nonetheless understood the importance of maintaining the objects already in their possession, and of developing a systematic record of these, if they wanted to encourage future donations. In the wake of increasing calls for greater professionalization in Canadian museums, throughout the 1940s and 1950s, the institutions discussed in this chapter began to systematize their activities, whether it was hiring directors and curators with art historical and/or museum training, cataloguing permanent collections, developing an acquisitions policy, or erecting a building that overtly signalled their symbolic capital and influence. Some institutions, such as the Edmonton Museum of Arts, consolidated their acquisitions. Such consolidation was not uncommon for the museums and galleries in smaller Canadian centers, many of which had been formed as general interest museums designed to broadly educate the population through object-centred displays of a wide range of material. In many such cases, objects documenting the history of the region shared space with First Nations quillwork, "ethnic" embroidery, and paintings. As money became available from various sources to fund the activities of these institutions, a new level of professionalism became a condition of funding, and bodies – such as the Canadian Museums Association – were established to monitor the performance of museum directors, curators, and soon educators. While professionalism is inherently tied to the practices and performance of individuals within a particular field, its side effect is invariably a careful delineation of institutions along disciplinary lines.

Existing on the geographical periphery of the country in relatively young cities, western Canadian museums recognized the importance of adopting professional practices to aid in their development. While much of the pressure to improve standards came from organizations such as the National Gallery, which made fulfillment of certain criteria a condition for the loan of original artworks, institutions in western Canada themselves sought to hire trained staff, build appropriate galleries, and develop collections policies in order to increase their status nationally and internationally. By the beginning of the 1970s, many of the institutions discussed in this chapter – the Vancouver Art Gallery, the Edmonton Art Gallery, the Norman MacKenzie Art Gallery, and the Winnipeg Art Gallery – had all the components of a major museum program in place, including highly developed acquisition policies, curated temporary exhibitions, education programs, and the professional staff to make it all happen. Over the next two decades, changes in funding structures at the federal level would further level the playing field allowing so-called "regional" museums to develop more equal relations with institutions in central Canada.

6

THE PERILS OF
DECENTRALIZATION

Federal Funding and Art Museums in Western Canada

The museum landscape in Canada was transformed during the 1970s and 1980s by significant increases in funding at the federal and the provincial level and the emergence of policies and strategies that shaped the role of museum institutions both large and small. The development and implementation of the National Museum Policy (NMP) in 1972, as well as changes in the policies of the Canada Council in the 1980s and the emergence of provincial arts agencies as major funders of museum activities throughout these decades, ensured that more money was available to institutions across the country. All the galleries under discussion in this book experienced tremendous growth during this period, increasing their program offerings, and in many cases doubling their budgets and the number of professional staff. As a result of this expansion, galleries in western Canada developed more autonomous and well-defined identities with regard to the publics they served, as well as in their relations with other art museums in the country. Much of the growth in budgets and programming was determined by the new funding opportunities provided by the NMP, a complete overhaul of museum policy in Canada that brought the four national museums together under a single corporate structure and created a national network of Associate Museums and National Exhibition Centres (NECs) in order to more effectively circulate the objects of Canada's human, natural, and cultural heritage across the country. As this chapter will show, museum directors and boards, on the whole, were pleased to receive funding for operations, buildings, and exhibitions from the federal government; but the strings that accompanied those grants – often determining the nature and content of activities that could be funded – were resented and sometimes resisted. In addition, the rhetoric that attended the National Museum Policy grated on many institutions, whether this rhetoric was in the form of the idealistic principles of democratization and decentralization that shaped the original presentation of the policy by Secretary of State Gérard Pelletier, or in the purported equalization of institutions across the country through the proclamation of Associate Museum status to both regional and federal museums. Taking up the larger theme of space and place with which this book is concerned, the National Museum Policy had the dual effect of *centralizing* power in Ottawa by concentrating administrative control of all programs within a central National Museums secretariat, while at the same time elevating the status of certain institutions in the provinces by designating them as Associate Museums and funding them accordingly. Although not the original intent of the program, the end result of the National Museum Policy was to diminish the authority and programming capabilities of the four National Museums in Ottawa and raise the national visibility of regional institutions. This chapter examines the shifting landscape of museums in western Canada in the 1970s and 1980s. In particular, it considers the effect of increased federal, provincial, and civic funding on the growth of museums during these two decades, and the impact of such significant increases in government support on the activities and the identities of art institutions. If the story of art museums in western Canada up to this point has been one of struggle for survival and the assertion of autonomy vis-à-vis the centralizing authority of the National Gallery, the events of the 1970s and 1980s would complicate this narrative by providing enough funding to allow western museums an unprecedented degree of independence while simultaneously shaping the institutions' programming focus. Although "democratization and decentralization" were the buzzwords of these decades, Canada's regional museums increasingly found themselves trapped by the desire of federal funding agencies to control the allocation of funds and influence the programs for which these funds could be used.

Democratization and Decentralization: A National Museum Policy for Canada

As the story of museum development in western Canada has shown, direct government support to art institutions was virtually non-existent for much of the twentieth century. Civic governments provided some monies to art galleries, primarily through in-kind assistance in the form of subsidized building rentals and utilities; by the 1950s, most provincial governments had created arts boards that distributed limited funds to cultural events and institutions. With the significant exception of the Canada Council, whose formation in 1957 resulted in matching funds for acquisitions and subsequently exhibition assistance, federal agencies and institutions largely ignored art museums in Canada, except for the National Gallery, which had been awarded an annual appropriation since its founding. This changed in 1967 when the Pearson government implemented the National Museums Act. With this act, the department of the secretary of state brought together the National Gallery and three other designated National Museums (the National Museum of Man, the National Museum of Natural Sciences, and the National Museum of Science and Technology) as the National Museums of Canada Corporation (NMC) under the governance of a central board of trustees. In the words of the act, "the purposes of the Corporation are to demonstrate the products of nature and the works of man, with special but not exclusive reference to Canada, so as to promote interest therein throughout Canada and to disseminate knowledge thereof."[1] In her presentation of the act to Parliament on 30 November 1967, Secretary of State Judy LaMarsh described the creation of the National Museums Corporation as a largely bureaucratic move designed to rationalize the administration of the federal government's museal institutions, thereby saving costs but also relieving the directors of the national museums of the responsibility and routine of dealing with administrative matters.[2] Taking its cue from the management of the Smithsonian museums in the United States, the Canadian government argued that taking control of the administration of the national museums would both create efficiencies by consolidating many of the museums' common administrative activities and allow individual museums to focus on the presentation of their collections to an audience that was increasingly envisaged as national.

From a broader perspective, an important impetus for the creation of the NMC was the federal government's desire to establish a more coherent national policy on culture and to have greater oversight over the institutions tasked with bringing culture to Canadians. Indeed, equally significant precedents for the creation of the NMC can be found in Gordon Sheppard's *Special Report on the Cultural Policy and Activities of the Government of Canada*, published in 1966 when he was special consultant on the arts to then Secretary of State Maurice Lamontagne.[3] Sheppard's report advocated for greater coherence among the various cultural programs of the federal government and dovetailed neatly with the cultural activities then being developed to celebrate Canada's Centennial.[4] The Royal Commission on Bilingualism and Biculturalism (Laurendeau-Dunton Commission), established in 1963 and issuing its six-volume report between 1967 and 1970, also contributed to a climate where the federal government recognized the importance of culture in the social development of the nation by instituting policies such as the Official Languages Act of 1969 that promoted national bilingualism, including the need for all federal services and documents to be available in both French and English. Further underscoring the centrality of culture in Canada's self-imagination, the Trudeau Liberals responded to the recommendations of the Bilingualism and Biculturalism Commission by proposing a federal multiculturalism policy within a bilingual framework, establishing a multiculturalism directorate within the Department of the Secretary of State in 1973.[5] The value placed on the role of culture in a democratic society – with culture understood to be the products of high art as much as populist and ethnocultural traditions – clearly underpins these federal initiatives and falls neatly in line with the argument of the Massey Commission almost twenty years earlier that federal cultural institutions should be shored up in order to strengthen national identity. The shift that occurred in the interim was the increasing role of the state in cultural affairs, largely through the aggressive introduction of policies that would effectively manage the production, dissemination, and consumption of cultural products. Although not specific to Canada – numerous cultural studies scholars have examined the governmentalization of culture in Britain and Australia[6] – the development and maintenance of cultural practices and organizations in this country since the 1970s can be characterized by what Clive Robertson has described as the "administrations of art and culture."[7] Indeed, while the influx of funds that accompanied the formation of the Canada Council, the NMC, and the provincial arts boards was enthusiastically welcomed by cultural producers, the constraints of conforming to the terms and conditions of granting agencies led to expressions of frustration from gallery directors fearing that their autonomy in developing programing for their institutions was in jeopardy. As this chapter describes, the greater involvement of the federal government in cultural funding resulted in the staff of many Canadian museums rethinking their programming in order to conform to funding criteria. More broadly, however, the federal government's consolidation of cultural funding through the NMC meant structural changes that reflected the broader shifting policy positions of the federal government as a whole.

The establishment of the NMC cannot be fully understood outside of the far-reaching effects of the recommendations of the Royal Commission on Government Organization (the Glassco Commission). Established in September 1960 by the Diefenbaker government to "inquire into and report upon the organization and methods of operation of the departments and agencies of the government of Canada," the commission was tasked with identifying those areas where the government could better achieve "efficiency, economy and improved service in the despatch of public business."[8] The resulting July 1962 report included, on one hand, recommendations for greater centralization of services in those areas such as purchasing and printing where there was unnecessary overlap or duplication. On the other hand, the Glassco report advocated the decentralization of operations and administration to individual government departments and agencies in order to achieve greater efficiency and accountability in management practices. The broader orientation of the commission's recommendations has often been distilled in the phrase "let the managers manage,"[9] indicating the influence of private sector models that gave greater autonomy and decision-making power to individual departments within the larger organization. This phrase, however, also underscores the continuing power of government – namely Parliament – to influence institutional directions, a degree of oversight into the workings of cultural organizations and institutions that would characterize the next thirty years of Canadian government operations. As political scientist James R. Mallory noted in 1979, while a sense of greater authority over the day-to-day management of core aspects of departments came to characterize the federal government of the 1960s, central agencies such as the Treasury Board and the Civil Service Commission were able to accumulate greater power under the new regulations and effect more control over aspects of governmental culture.[10]

The Glassco Commission's recommendations for efficiency and economy in the delivery of public services clearly informed the decision to create the National Museums of Canada Corporation and to implement an administrative structure that ensured more direct involvement of the federal government in the activities of the national museums. The Office of the Secretary of State – the ministry responsible for cultural matters since 1964 – conceived of museums as primarily educational institutions, and sought to tie them and their programming to the nationalist aims that characterized the lead-up to Canada's centennial.[11] The increase in the number of federal museums from two to four enabled the Secretary of State to identify and define four key areas where it could provide support for educational activities: fine art, human history, natural history, and science and technology.[12] In 1956, the National Museum of Canada (itself an outgrowth of the Geological Survey) had been divided into two branches: the National Museum (to be renamed the National Museum of Man in 1968), dedicated to the collection and display of objects relating to Canada's human history; and the National Museum of Natural Sciences, devoted to natural history. Both branches remained in the Victoria Memorial Museum Building along with the National Gallery, which was slated to move to the Lorne Building in late 1959. During this period there was also much discussion over the possibility of opening a museum dedicated to the nation's contributions to science and technology drawn from the collections of the National Museum. In 1967, the National Museum of Science and Technology (now the Canada Science and Technology Museum) opened in what were to be temporary premises in a warehouse on the outskirts of downtown Ottawa.[13] Shortly following the decision to form this fourth national museum, the Pearson government announced the implementation of the National Museums Act and the consolidation of the four national museums as the National Museums of Canada Corporation led by a secretary-general who reported directly to the secretary of state. Each institution retained its own director, and the National Gallery managed to hold onto an advisory body – renamed the Visiting Committee – although this was a largely new group of figures replacing most of the trustees who had previously overseen the gallery. From an administrative point of view, the corporation's single board of trustees (made up of twelve individuals representative of both regional and disciplinary diversity, as well as the director of the Canada Council and the president of the National Research Council) enabled Canada's cultural heritage to be viewed as a coherent whole rather than as fragmented entities, and thus closely aligned culture to the nation-building goals of both the Pearson and the Trudeau

Liberals. The appointment of a secretary-general reporting directly to the secretary of state ensured that a single figure oversaw all activities of the federal museums, guaranteeing that each adhered to the larger cultural message of the federal government. As became apparent to the directors of the National Museums, the new reporting structure established with the NMC altered their relationship to the minister, and threatened their authority to make decisions regarding the directions their institutions would take. In particular, directors were concerned with the power of the secretary-general and of the board of trustees, whose members' experience and knowledge, while suitable for an advisory role, did not extend to the administration of museums. Despite such lack of qualifications, the role of the new board included making appointments and approving purchases, much to the dismay of the directors of the federal museums.[14]

Following the announcement of the NMC, the directors of the four museums expressed fears that the administrative consolidation that accompanied the creation of the corporation would result in greater governmental interference and threaten the arm's length principle that governed the Canadian state's role in cultural affairs. The National Gallery was most affected in this respect as the National Gallery Act, which had governed its activities since 1952 was repealed,[15] replaced by the National Museums Act, which stated that "all property, rights, obligations and liabilities of the National Gallery of Canada ... shall be deemed to be the property, rights, obligations and liabilities of the National Museums of Canada."[16] Richard Glover, director of the human history division of the National Museum, cited the Museums Act as one of the reasons he decided to resign from his position in April 1967, arguing that the policy negatively affected the autonomy of the federal museums directors and, through them, all professional staff.[17] As Douglas Ord has noted, Jean Sutherland Boggs felt personally betrayed by the creation of the NMC as it effectively diminished the autonomy and the authority she held as director of the National Gallery of Canada. For Boggs, subsuming the National Gallery within the larger structure of the NMC erased much of the hard work undertaken by the institution to establish collecting and exhibition programs, and it further diminished the gallery's increasingly positive international reputation. She publicly wrote of her concern that with its incorporation into the National Museums of Canada, the National Gallery's policies would be "under review and the purposes which guided it for 55 years ... could be reshaped." Her mission would be "to

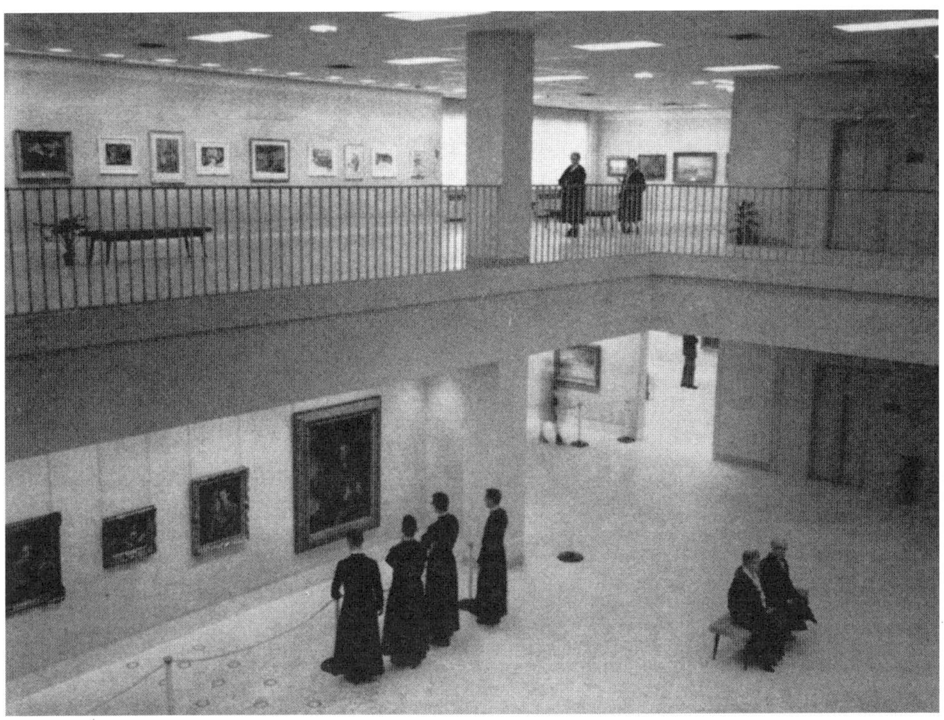

6.1 | The NGC's exhibition galleries on the 4th and 5th floors of the newly opened Lorne Building, 1960.

keep the spirit of the old legislation a reality"– in other words, ensure that the arm's length relationship the NGC enjoyed with the federal government remained in place.[18] Boggs's statement to the Senate Standing Committee on Finance in May 1967 further summarizes her feelings about the impact of the new act and the organization it established: "The gain is for the other museums ... The advantages for them under the new act, we possess already."[19] Boggs was essentially correct in her assessment of the relative benefits of the National Museums Corporation: for the younger institutions such as the National Museum of Science and Technology and the National Museum of the Natural Sciences, membership in the NMC provided a measure of visibility and access to funds that had not been available to them during their tenure as branches of the National Museum. Despite the misgivings of its former director, the National Museum of Man was able to increase its focus on establishing itself as an important site for research on and display of artifacts relating to Canada's human history during the first few years under the corporation. Meanwhile, the National Gallery maintained access to a sizeable portion of funds (certainly more than any of the other national museums) that gave it if not a certain degree of autonomy, then the ability to conduct business as usual in its collecting and exhibiting programming.

Reaction to the corporation from the Canadian museum community was favourable. Writing in the *Calgary Herald*, Archie Key commended the federal government for its action and for assisting the national museums to bring its services "to the outports and outposts of the nation."[20] Articles in the Canadian Museums Association's bimonthly *Gazette* were neutral in tone, reporting rather than commenting on the implications of the new legislation for either the federal museums themselves or their counterparts outside Ottawa. A slight exception to this view, however, might be found in an article from May 1968 that emphasized the administrative benefits of the National Museums Corporation, going so far as to suggest that such an amalgamation would make the individual institutions "more attuned to the modern challenges facing museums today."[21] The CMA also strongly endorsed the inclusion of an Education and Extension division – part of the Administrative Services Branch of the Corporation – that would bring the national museums' collections beyond the institutions' walls to the general public. Education had, of course, been a central aspect of all the museums' activities, but as discussed in Chapter 4, extension activities had been particularly well developed by the National Gallery, and the CMA was quick to highlight that making travelling exhibitions a service of all the national museums was a crucial component of the corporation's program of making the national collections more accessible to the public.[22] Such support for the corporation may have encouraged the decision under the National Museum Policy in 1972 to give a significant annual grant to the Canadian Museums Association for training and professionalization initiatives.[23]

In March 1972, the Secretary of State Gérard Pelletier expanded his vision of the nation-building role of the NMC by introducing the National Museum Policy, whose main goal was to ease the circulation of objects of natural and human heritage across the country. That the corporation's existing education and extension branch was not up to the task was already evident in an article signed by Pelletier for the Canadian Museums Association *Gazette* in 1971, which stated, "The National Museums are making worthy efforts to exhibit their collections outside of Ottawa and to expand their activities on a national level, but these efforts encounter difficulties that we shall have to go to work on."[24] To address such difficulties, the NMP established structures that would facilitate the dissemination of objects from the National Museums across the country: formal links were created with select Canadian museums in all ten provinces and by establishing exhibition centres in smaller cities and towns in order to form a nation-wide network of cultural institutions that would enable both the physical and the intellectual circulation of the national heritage. The designation of certain institutions as Associate Museums was intended "to even out existing disparities in museum collections, activities and standards between one part of the country and another," giving particular recognition to those institutions with collections of regional if not national importance, an experienced director and professional staff, and display space for both permanent and temporary exhibitions.[25] Five to ten Associate Museums were to be designated in the first year of the policy's operation, with the final tally reaching twenty-one by 1973, a number that included the four federal museums, termed "Associate Museums" to diminish the appearance of a hierarchy between museums in the centre and those in the regions. National Exhibition Centres, meanwhile, were non-collecting institutions located in small to medium-sized communities, "remote from collections of national significance."[26] Key to the policy's aim to disseminate Canada's cultural heritage, the NECs were envisaged as receiving centres for travelling exhibitions from the national museums and from the Associate Museums in their regions. All the western Canadian art galleries discussed so far were designated Associate Museums with NECs established in Brandon, Leaf Rapids, Estevan, Swift Current, Moose Jaw, Medicine Hat, Langley, Hazelton (the 'Ksan Historical Village), Castlegar (the Kootenay Doukhobor Historical Society), and Kelowna.

Beyond the establishment of a network of brick-and-mortar institutions through the Associate Museums and NEC programs, the components of the National Museum Policy addressed collections management, program assistance to existing institutions outside Ottawa, and strategies to ensure the display of national collections in small and large centres across Canada. Funding was allocated for the training of museum workers, for emergency purchases of objects of national importance that might be taken out of the country, and to assist museums in cataloguing the objects in their care. A number of other initiatives were instituted to support the work of museums across the country and to assist in the management of existing collections, including the establishment of the Canadian Conservation Institute and the National Inventory of Collections. Finally, national reach would be achieved through the establishment of a National Loan Collection – essentially a set of prints and ethnographic objects designed for display in public places such as shopping centres, schools, exhibition centres, and smaller museums,[27] and the construction of mobile museum units or "Museumobiles" – large trucks containing displays that would criss-cross the country. Taken together, the components of the National Museum Policy constituted an expanded vision of how to make cultural heritage as accessible as possible, a vision that ran against the more conventional idea of the museum as the storehouse of the nation's culture, with its accompanying aura of authority and central location. Indeed, Pelletier introduced his new museum policy by stating, "one must erase the traditional notion of stagnancy that comes to mind when one hears the word 'museum,' and instead try to envisage a modern and dynamic instrument of initiation to culture"[28] – hence the emphasis on a network of cultural venues and programs that would bring culture to communities and in ways that would make it more physically and intellectually accessible.

In the eight-page pamphlet issued by the Department of the Secretary of State in 1972 and circulated widely, the National Museum Policy is outlined as "a programme of decentralization and democratization for Canadian Museums ... to better distribute those cultural resources which are obtainable through Canadian museums, both national and regional, to the end that the greatest possible number of Canadians be exposed to our national heritage."[29] In the 28 March 1972 speech at the Glenbow Museum in Calgary that formally introduced the new policy, Pelletier explained democratization as "increasing access to the products of cultural activity for all taxpayers, not only for a select group as has been the case in the past. Since this concerns the use of public funds, it would be unfair to promote cultural activities that are reserved for the happy few."[30] Decentralization, meanwhile, was defined specifically in relation to Canada as "an active battle against vast distance in order to make our cultural symbols available to all Canadians no matter where they live,"[31] a statement that echoes the Massey Report's references to the impact of "forces of geography" on access to objects in national collections. The guiding principles of democratization and decentralization shaped the funding

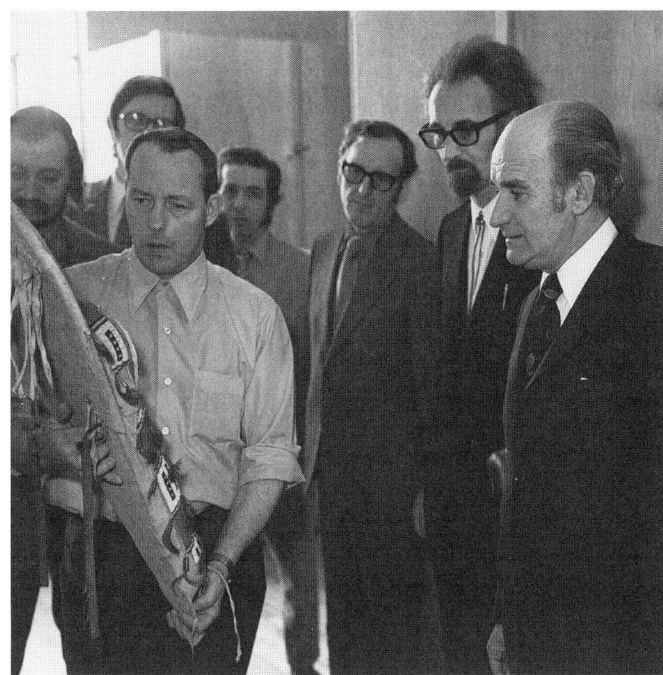

6.2 | Secretary of State Gérard Pelletier examines a cradle board at the Glenbow Museum in Calgary following his announcement of the National Museum Policy, 28 March 1972.

programs implemented under the NMP, with the vast majority of the grants being directed to existing organizations for activities that facilitated the circulation and exchange of objects and exhibitions both nationally and regionally. Introducing the policy in Calgary, Pelletier hoped to underscore the decentralizing aims of the government's approach to culture by announcing such a major venture outside of "the centre,"[32] but Pelletier's emphasis on a decentred approach was also evident in his Calgary presentation when he asserted that his vision of the government as "the contemporary patron of the arts" did not entail any kind of direct intervention in cultural production. Dismissing criticisms that he was positioning himself as a "cultural czar," Pelletier aligned Canada's commitment to cultural funding with similar initiatives by "the governments of the Western World," highlighting the country's longstanding parliamentary tradition of maintaining the autonomy of all cultural agencies as an indication that the secretary of state had no power in determining the content of Canadian culture.[33]

The twin principles of democratization and decentralization had been central components of Pelletier's statements on culture and cultural policy since his assumption of the post of secretary of state in 1968. In the third volume of his autobiography, *L'Aventure du pouvoir, 1968–1975*, he wrote that his first self-imposed task as secretary of state was to outline his vision of the role of culture in the life of the nation. Three major lines of thought emerged out of that process: (1) that the national heritage had to be more accessible to all social groups, not just the elite – the principle of democratization; (2) that national culture not be concentrated solely in Ottawa, but that it be accessible to people across the country in their own communities – the principle of decentralization; and (3) that it was the task of government to support cultural initiatives but not to interfere or direct programming – the principle of arm's-length funding.[34] Although we can question the accuracy of such a retrospective narrative, it is telling that Pelletier starts this third volume of his memoirs with such a clear statement of the centrality of democratization and decentralization to his view not just of culture but of his role as secretary of state. Such a view falls closely in line with the ideals of the just society on which the Trudeau Liberals gained power in the late 1960s, and writing some twenty-five years later, it is evident that Pelletier's assessment of his contribution was still strongly linked to the values of participatory democracy and cultural diversity that underpinned the early years of the Trudeau government.[35] The strong administrative centre at the core of both the NMC and the NMP are also characteristic of the Trudeau Liberals' desires to emphasize federalism and direct the activities of the nation.

Equally revealing of Pelletier's thinking during this period is his explicit linking of the principles of democratization and decentralization to the work of André Malraux during his tenure as France's minister of cultural affairs in the 1960s. For Pelletier, Malraux's championing of "Maisons de la culture" (houses of culture) outside of Paris was a model for encouraging and supporting cultural production outside of the capital city, and for ensuring that culture was not solely a privilege of the elite but was available to all classes of society. In this last point, the former secretary of state was somewhat mistaken: while Pelletier lauds Malraux for placing the Maisons de la culture "en milieu ouvrier" (in working-class neighbourhoods),[36] Herman Lebovics notes that the majority of Malraux's cultural centres were attached to existing institutions, most of which were well-established theatres with a committed public made up largely of the new middle classes.[37] While Malraux's Maisons de la culture may have been less anti-elitist than Pelletier imagined (or remembered) them, their ability to spread France's cultural riches beyond Paris to the "regions" was most certainly the blueprint for Pelletier's vision of a national network of cultural institutions. As Pelletier wrote to Boggs in January 1972, shortly before the announcement of the NMP in Calgary, the circulation of the national collections was "an essential part of a complete network of museum centres in Canada, because it is designed to reach the public outside the museums – in the National Exhibition Centres, shopping plazas, recreation centres, schools, factories, department stores, etc. ... We feel it is essential that art find its way into the smoke-filled factory or the disadvantaged districts, even at the expense of its gradual deterioration."[38] Despite Pelletier's evident enthusiasm for Malraux's initiative, he declined to follow Quebec's decision to create a ministry of cultural affairs in 1961;[39] Quebec's network of Maisons de la culture, however, modelled to some degree on the French institutions, would only emerge in the 1980s.[40]

As multidisciplinary arts centres with facilities for theatre productions, film screenings, art exhibitions, record and book libraries,[41] Malraux's Maisons strongly resembled the community art centres envisioned by Lawren Harris and the Federation of Canadian Artists in the 1940s, discussed in Chapter 3. And the idea of bringing components of the national culture to the people that underpinned Malraux's vision was very much in line with Harris's hopes that the community art centres would end up housing, for extended periods of time, select objects from the National Gallery of Canada, effectively decentralizing the collections of that national institution for the benefit of all Canadians. As a federal minister – and one of the "three doves" of the strongly federalist Trudeau regime – Pelletier had no interest in permanently dispersing the national collections across the country. However, it is clear that with the National Museum Policy – a policy subtitled "A Programme for *Canadian* Museums" (my emphasis) – Pelletier sought to take responsibility for the dissemination of culture away from the geographically restricted purview of the four national museums by expanding the means through which the national heritage would circulate. Indeed, whereas the National Museums Corporation, in its original configuration, included a division of Education and Extension that organized travelling exhibitions and educational programming from all the National Museums collections, both the number and kind of circulating exhibitions, and the places they could be seen, expanded exponentially under the National

Museum Policy. From the Museumobiles and the National Loan Collection to the establishment of new National Exhibition Centres in small communities, physical examples of "the national heritage" would tour farther and to more places than ever before. Through these means, "decentralization" would be implemented, from the centre to the regions, and within regions from the Associate Museums to the more peripheral NECs. The establishment of so many tools to facilitate decentralization required a greater degree of oversight and management than hitherto, rendering the administrative role of the Department of the Secretary of State much more evident. It quickly became apparent that the system built on the strongly articulated principal of decentralizing museum collections would ultimately result in the centralization of power in Ottawa: a situation that would eventually lead to the downfall of the both the NMP and the corporation itself.

For the four national museums, the implementation of the National Museum Policy was even more of a disaster than the original formation of the corporation. To begin with, the reporting structure as well as the large staff needed to oversee the multiple programs introduced by the expanded corporation resulted in additional bureaucracy that taxed the resources of the national museums.[42] The hiring freeze in the civil service that followed almost immediately on the implementation of the NMP did nothing to alleviate the stress of greater responsibility for a growing number of programs while having little control or authority over how those programs would be run. Indeed, upon her resignation of the directorship of the National Gallery in 1976, Jean Sutherland Boggs blamed the bureaucracy of the NMC as a principal factor in her decision to leave.[43] Similarly, the next director, Hsio-Yen Shih, after threatening to quit on numerous occasions, finally left the post in 1981, less than a year after the gallery's centenary celebrations, citing the overwhelming bureaucratic red tape under the National Museums Corporation that limited the director's power and decision-making responsibility over the operation of the institution. Shih additionally blamed the inadequacy of the Lorne Building to house the national art collection, and an appropriation fund that was nowhere near adequate for the development of a national art collection,[44] as reasons for her departure from the gallery. Many of the problems cited by the disgruntled directors of the National Museums had already been noted by the corporation, which argued that the solution to issues such as bureaucratic red tape, difficult access to funds, and other administrative problems would lie in the formulation of a different set of rules governing cultural organizations that would take into account their distinctness from other government agencies.

While the increasing weight of the new bureaucracy was the predominant reason for frustration with the National Museums Corporation, the federal museums also felt as though they were being treated as storehouses for the less wealthy or well-endowed institutions in the regions. Certainly, the principle of decentralization was not just a commitment of the four national museums to disseminate their holdings outside Ottawa: the Associate Museums were equally given the task "to expand their work at national, regional and local levels; to encourage the exchange of their collections; and to continue to improve facilities and services."[45] However, the corporation's annual reports clearly place the burden of decentralization on the national programs and institutions – whether the travelling exhibitions or the Museumobiles – whose very premise was based on taking objects "hidden away in the equivalents of basements and attics" of the National Museums, then "dusted off and sent out for display to the people who owned them."[46] For the National Gallery, whose extension activities had undergone significant changes over the previous fifty years, management of travelling exhibitions continued much as it had since the establishment of the Exhibition and Extension Services department. In an assessment of what was soon to be renamed the "National Programmes," the gallery's 1972–73 *Annual Review* underlined the greater sophistication expected of exhibitions circulated by the National Gallery during a period when the number of art galleries in Canada was growing and funding for exhibitions was being directed to those institutions by both the NMC and the Canada Council, at the expense of the federal museums. Reviewing the situation, the *Annual Review* noted that regional institutions were less reliant on the extension services of the National Gallery for their programming, and that, in turn, the National Gallery was developing circulating exhibitions in collaboration with curators from regional institutions. Despite this spirit of greater exchange, many of the more sophisticated exhibitions entailed new problems for National Gallery staff: the increased costs of shipping larger shows; the need for curatorial and preparatory staff to travel with the exhibitions to ensure proper display; and greater pressure on interpretive and publication staff to produce didactic material that would engage an increasingly media-savvy public. The National Museum Policy provided funds in the

1972–73 fiscal year for two additional preparators – one coordinator of extended loans and one photographer for the national programs – but such measures could not alleviate the criticism of the director of the Western Canada Art Circuit that "a growing number of artists and gallery people in western Canada have become disenchanted with the extension services of the National Gallery and with the decline in contact with the National Gallery staff during the past few years."[47] As the analysis of western Canadian museums' responses to the NMP will show, the new funding provided by the federal government to those institutions to develop their own programming was viewed as both a blessing and a curse with galleries benefitting from the increase in continuous funding, while chafing at the restrictions that such funding entailed.

Associate Museums and Western Responses to the National Museum Policy

For most institutions outside Ottawa, being named an Associate Museum was enthusiastically welcomed as it brought a stable source of increased funding for programming as well as improved status vis-à-vis the federal institutions.[48] In his annual report of 1973, Ferdinand Eckhardt announced the Winnipeg Art Gallery's designation as an Associate Museum and stated that such an appointment clearly indicated the NMC's view that the WAG was "one of the first [i.e., foremost] art museums in Canada."[49] He further characterized the National Museum Policy as "a most ingenious and vitalizing program" that would greatly improve the circulation of artworks throughout the country.[50] In contrast, the Vancouver Art Gallery resisted applying for associate status until it had fully considered the implications of such a designation for its own autonomy. Associate Director Doris Shadbolt argued at the April 1973 meeting of the gallery's board that the new museum policy was too conservative, while a few months later Director Tony Emery advised the board to defer its application as he felt it constituted a compromising step for the gallery.[51] The Vancouver Art Gallery nonetheless became an Associate Museum in time to receive funds for the 1974–75 season. Canadian museums had many reasons to accept Associate Museum status: in 1972–73, the first full fiscal year of the policy, the corporation had $4,366,461 available for distribution to designated museums and exhibition centres outside of Ottawa, with $1,547,593 of that going to institutions in western

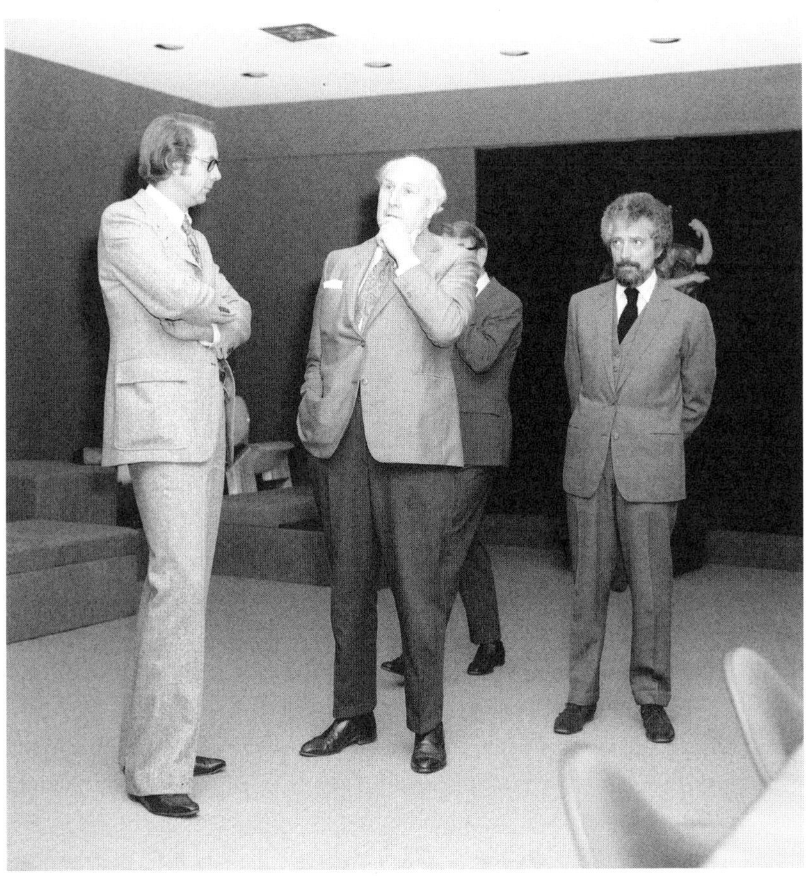

6.3 | Secretary of State James Faulkner (*left*), Winnipeg Art Gallery Director Ferdinand Eckhardt, and National Museums Corporation Secretary-General Bernard Ostry, at the Winnipeg Art Gallery, c. 1973.

Canada.[52] According to the corporation's *Annual Report*, half of these funds went to capital projects while the rest supported the training and extension projects designed to fulfill the democratization and decentralization principles of the National Museum Policy.[53] Institutions received money to fund a range of activities and operations: the Mendel Art Gallery, for example, received a total of $390,000 in capital funding from the NMC between 1975 and 1977 to add 9,000 square feet of exhibition, office, and storage space to the gallery. Additional funds of $93,000 were received in 1976 to pay the salary of four extension staff who were hired to organize the Mendel's expanding circulating exhibition program and to conduct guided tours and educational activities.[54] Experiencing financial difficulties after the opening of its new building in 1971, the WAG benefitted from an annual core grant of around $180,000 to pay for the curatorial, education, and extension services positions appropriate to its new stature and mandate as an Associate Museum.[55] For an organization with an annual budget of close to $550,000, the money provided through the NMP was a welcome relief for the WAG, allowing it – along with other similarly funded Associate Museums – to begin imagining an expansion of activities and the development of long-term plans for growth.

National Museums funding had the added benefit of encouraging provincial governments to increase their disbursement of grants to museums, often exceeding the grants provided by the NMP. Manitoba's Arts Council, for example, created in 1965 but only able to distribute funds from 1969, supported the WAG's activities from its first year of operation. In 1971–72 that support amounted to $39,000 and by 1980 total support from the provincial government had risen to $814,000 a year. Alberta's Culture Branch, for its part, began putting money towards the activities of the Edmonton Museum of Arts in 1947–48 – a small $500 annual allocation that by 1973 had increased to $25,000. The Canada Council was an important source of money for exhibitions and special activities, a situation that benefitted Associate Museum directors who could draw from both sources to fund a range of activities. In 1975–76 the Norman MacKenzie Art Gallery received $23,000 from the Canada Council and $75,929 in core funding from the NMC to support circulating exhibitions in Regina and beyond; the Winnipeg Art Gallery received $150,000 in core funding from the NMC, along with $130,000 from the Canada Council; and the Edmonton Art Gallery benefitted from $115,000 from the Canada Council and $85,000 from the NMC in core funding despite some concerns from the corporation with the institution's apparent difficulties in implementing a circulating exhibitions program. In awarding the funds, the NMC's Consultative Committee noted that funds should be renewed with a small increase over the previous year "in the light of the [EAG's] enthusiasm and also given the large hinterland it serves."[56] As Richard Simmins noted in his assessment of the Associate Museums program in 1977, "Both Canada Council and the National Museums are aware of the *overlap game* played by many art museum directors, and the *syphoning principle*, where project funds are deliberately spilled over into operating expenses."[57] And indeed, many of the Associate Museums took advantage of the multiple sources of funding available for exhibitions and extension programs to ensure that they could support as many activities as possible. The solution, according to Simmins, was for the federal agencies to better delimit the kinds of activities organizations could fund; but a more accurate assessment would see that such double dipping was a way for Associate Museums to manage the constraints that the NMP programs imposed on museums, requiring them to service smaller institutions in their respective regions rather than attending to the care and management of their own collections and delivering programs for local audiences.

In 1976, the NMC reorganized its granting structure by introducing the Museum Assistance Programmes (MAP). Designed for implementation in the 1976–77 fiscal year, the change was prompted by the federal government's austerity measures in the face of rampant inflation, as well as by a recommendation from the corporation's consultative committee that a reorganization of the administration of the NMC's national programs to more effectively support the corporation's decentralizing mission was in order. Indeed, in announcing the shifts in program structure, as well as the creation of three new assistant secretaries-general in the areas of finance and administration, programs, and communications, the NMC's *Annual Report* argued that "in seeking to make do with less in a time of inflation and recession, the National Museums have not abandoned their major policy objectives of decentralization and democratization."[58] Where previously funding was distributed by type of institution – for example, to the Associate Museums, the National Exhibition Centres, the mobile museum units – under the revised Museums Assistance Programme, grants were made for specific services or operations. In the new structure, the key funding areas were core-funding assistance, capital assistance, special activities assistance (which included registration assistance), and training assistance. Core funding was now available only to Associate Museums (excluding the four federal museums, which received appropriations directly from the federal government) and to National Exhibition Centres, and aimed to provide "continuing operational support for public programming"[59] – in other words, a base of funding for the day-to-day activities of the institutions. In 1975–76, the total core-funding budget of the NMC for the Associate Museums was $2,362,500; $443,500, meanwhile, was available for operating costs for the National Exhibition Centres, a relatively small amount to be distributed among the twenty-three centres then in operation.[60] While ostensibly designed for public programs – particularly the extension activities at the core of the NMP – the core-funding category was elastic enough in its definition to be used by institutions to assist with operating costs. For the Edmonton Art Gallery, for example, this base of support was fundamental in that it paid for salaries and other maintenance costs, leaving other funds – such as monies raised by the gallery's Women's Society and private donations – for acquisitions.

Of the three other categories of assistance available through the Museums Assistance Programmes, Capital Assistance was the most generous, disbursing $2,442,849 in 1975–76 and a further $2,470,800 over the following three years. Available for "financial and technical assistance to museums and other related institutions for capital projects that improve their public programming and bring more people to their displays,"[61] capital grants were used by museums to extend exhibition spaces and to help with infrastructure costs accompanying the expansion of their programming activities. The Special Activities Assistance and Training Assistance funds were designed to provide financial and technical help to museums to develop new displays and travelling exhibitions, and to contribute to the training of museum professionals either through grants to postsecondary institutions to develop degree courses in museology, to museum associations, and to individual museums for internship programs. The funding obtained by the Edmonton Art Gallery in the 1977–78 fiscal year offers an example of how the grants were distributed. In that year, the EAG received $55,000 in core funding, most of which was allocated to extension programs; $159,500 in capital assistance to help build a new wing for the gallery; $6,700 in registration assistance to help catalogue the gallery's permanent collection; and $44,600 in special activities assistance to help with the production of *Certain Traditions*, an exhibition of recent Canadian and British painting organized to coincide with the Commonwealth Games held in Edmonton in 1978. The previous year, the Art Gallery of Greater Victoria (AGGV) secured over $550,000 from various MAP funds, including $142,500 in core funding, $6,500 in training assistance, and $405,500 in capital assistance to renovate two of its larger exhibition galleries and for much-needed repairs to the Spencer mansion. The benefits of Associate Museum status were evident: the regular influx of considerable funding that permitted increased exhibition capacity, expanded and ameliorated facilities, and additional

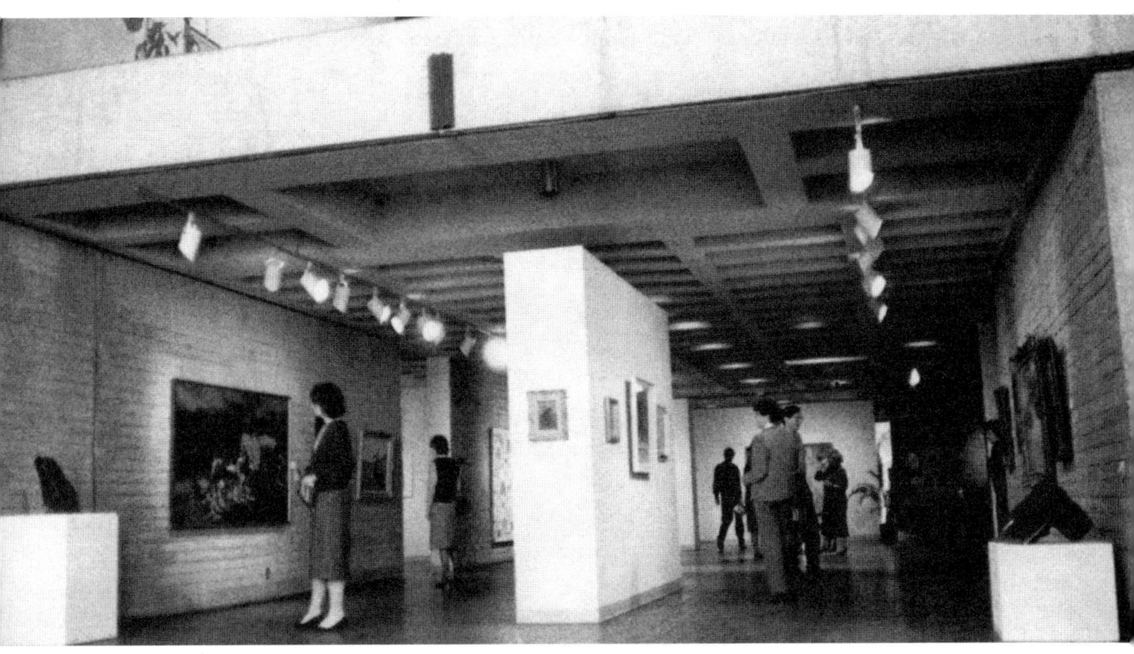

6.4 | The Edmonton Art Gallery, interior gallery view, 1984.

personnel. The fortunes of Associate Museums were also bolstered by the increasing funds they received from the Canada Council and from provincial arts boards. With annual budgets increasing by over 500 percent in many cases between 1970 and 1980, the advantages of Associate Museum status for many institutions was clear.[62]

After several years under the NMP, however, the Associate Museums began to complain about the obligations entailed by the program's funding; in particular, institutions were concerned that core funding was being provided primarily for extension services geared to the National Exhibition Centres and the smaller museums in their regions. Some of the institutions designated Associate Museums did not have extension departments at the time of their appointment and had to quickly get up to speed when the money arrived. Others found that the criteria accompanying the funding required them to expand their extension services, often at the cost of in-house programming – specifically conservation, interpretation, and research on their own collections; art galleries in particular found that the ambitious temporary exhibitions that they hoped to circulate interprovincially were overlooked in favour of smaller shows that could circulate regionally. At a meeting of Associate Museum directors in October 1976, a discussion of the "role and function of the Associate Museums" revealed that many institutions had not been in either a financial or a professional position to undertake the breadth of activities expected of them at the time of their appointment; having used their core funding to ready themselves for the task of delivering extension programming, they now found themselves unable to undertake the fundamental work of collecting and exhibiting institutions. As Glenbow Director Duncan Cameron warned in a letter to NMC Secretary-General Ian Christie Clark in 1978, decisions to fund the national programs could not come at the cost of the essential functions of the museum. Taking particular aim at two prized decentralizing projects of the NMC, the Museumobile and the Discovery Train, Cameron wrote that the train "was an expensive venture that had nothing to do with museums, museology, or the mandate and established policies of the NMC as [he] understood them."[63] Rather, he argued, funding should be redirected to the core functions of conservation, research, and collections management. Other criteria of the NMC programs in relation to circulating exhibitions were also seen as constraints on museums' abilities to deliver their services, especially in western Canada where conditions of federal funding, such as bilingual catalogue texts and exhibition labels, were an expensive burden on many institutions. The Edmonton Art Gallery's director Terry Fenton described some of the challenges he faced in organizing *Certain Traditions* in 1978, an exhibition for which the gallery had received extensive federal funding: "It becomes apparent that NMC funding is a curse as well as a blessing. Their insistence that organizing galleries charge no fees to participating galleries disrupts the marketplace. It also means that organizing galleries are unable to recoup production overruns by charging participants. Their insistence upon fully bilingual catalogues (not just translated inserts) even when exhibitions do not travel to French-speaking areas creates an additional expense and complicates catalogue productions enormously."[64] Similarly, in 1980 the AGGV's director Richard Boulet noted that while the gallery benefitted enormously from the capital funding it received to enhance its exhibition spaces, the dominance of extension services in the NMP's delivery of its decentralization and democratization principles resulted in a dearth of programming for the gallery's own spaces that had been so generously funded by the same organization.[65] The federal museums were similarly burdened by the emphasis on extension services, voicing concerns about the impact of travel and less than professional handling on objects in the national collections, and struggling to manage caring for its own collections as well as program exhibitions for national circulation. For museums in Ottawa and in the regions, the policy to democratize and decentralize the national collections by increasing travelling exhibitions was not considered a success.

The dissatisfaction with the emphasis on circulating exhibitions was part of a larger frustration with the centralizing power of the NMC. If the designation of Associate Museum brought with it the recognition that an institution had reached a high level of professional development, any autonomy that might accompany such status was obviated by the decision-making authority accrued by the NMC. Richard Simmins presciently identified this authority in his description of the programming arm of the NMC as "the Fifth National Museum," writing that it had become "the most powerful museum without walls on the Canadian scene."[66] Responsible for the assessment of grant applications as well as disseminating the funding for all the NMC programs, Simmins argued that the Programmes Branch "has become much more than a centralized unit administering programs under a set of arbitrary guidelines. It is rather a complex force, dynamically involved in determining the general directions of development, especially of the smaller Associates, for decades to come."[67] And indeed, as the branch responsible for disseminating funds to most museum and cultural institutions in the country – including the National Museums and those exhibiting institutions that were neither Associate Museums nor National Exhibition Centres – the Programmes Branch had an astounding degree of power to set the cultural agenda of the nation. The Associate Museums voiced their frustration that their knowledge of regional and community needs were being ignored in favour of the NMC's ambition to develop a national museum policy. Expected to work with the four national museums and to serve their own regions, Associate Museum directors complained that they were never invited to participate in policy development, and argued that only the regional institutions could present a meaningful picture of the needs of the region. As one museum director stated in 1977, "I am concerned with the awesome power of the federal agencies though I am realistic about how much I need them. But the National Museums does not have a clear understanding of the museum field … policies were written

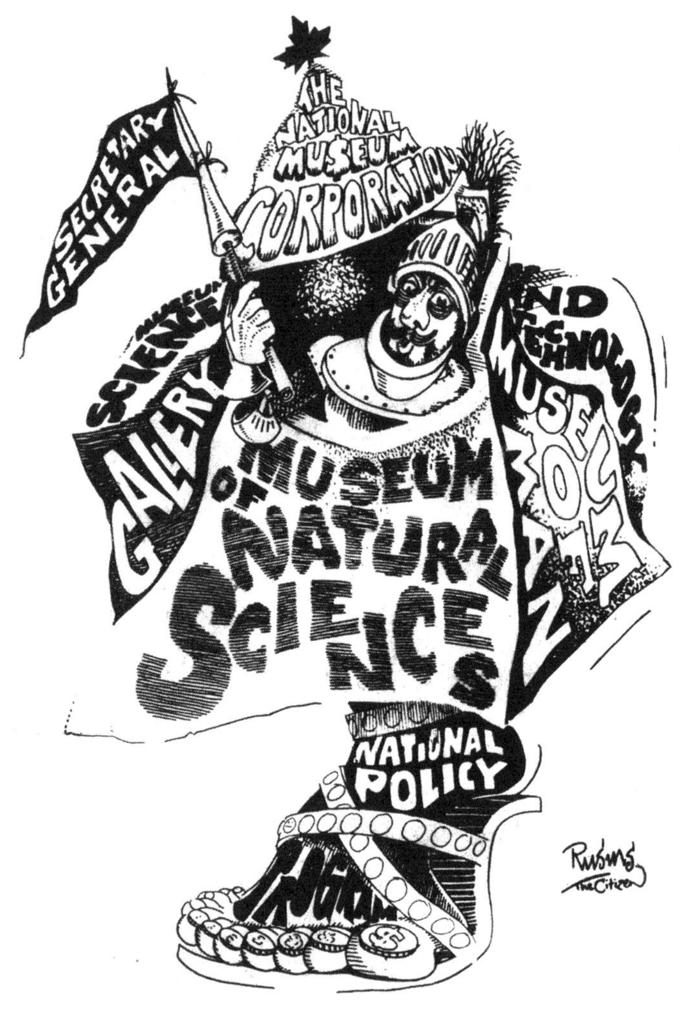

6.5 | Rusins Kaufmanis, editorial cartoon, *Ottawa Citizen*, 1 April 1977. The National Museums Corporation's inability to extricate itself from its own bureaucracy was evident by the late 1970s.

on the run ... surely you have seen the strong anti-federal feeling that exists outside of Ottawa?"[68] Other directors complained that they were consistently being forced to conform to the nation-building project of the corporation. After almost a decade, and in a manner reminiscent of the WCAC's complaints about the power of the NGC, museum directors

across the country resoundingly criticized the principles of democratization and decentralization with which both the NMC and the NMP had
been launched as centralizing and authoritarian. As Simmins astutely
noted at the end of his 1979 report on Associate Museums, "Most of the
Associates want a voice in formulating the national policies that affect
them; true self-determination is one of the prime goals."[69]

Indeed, by 1978, federal aid to museums was in trouble. A nationwide
recession resulted in financial restraints across the federal government
and the NMC's overall budget was reduced by $600,000. In 1979–80 not
only was the NMC's funding envelope further reduced by $4.9 million,
the federal public service cuts of two percent affected the corporation's
ability to provide funding assistance at existing levels.[70] The financial
demands on the corporation and the general climate of fiscal restraint
made the NMC's Board of Trustees realize that it needed to undertake a
major policy review – the first since the formation of the corporation –
and the Policy, Planning and Evaluation Group was formed. The resulting
document – *A National Museums Policy for the 80's* – reviewed, sometimes critically, the achievements as well as the failures of the NMP. In
particular, the report acknowledged that the haste with which the policy
was formulated might have contributed to the lack of preparedness of
many Associate Museums to assume their roles as regional exhibition
hubs, and the creation of a network of National Exhibition Centres that
could not be suitably financed by federal funds. Statements in *A National Museums Policy for the 80's* also recognized that the NMP's focus
on travelling exhibitions and extension services might have resulted in a
failure to attend to the primary aim of museums to collect and preserve.
Nevertheless, in outlining proposals for revising the NMP, the document
reasserted the importance and contribution of the corporation in preserving and promoting Canada's natural and cultural heritage: "As a national
agency, concerned with the national interest and a national public, the
NMC has assumed a national perspective. Its role and responsibilities,
drawn from its national character, reveal and reflect national interests
and priorities, not to the exclusion of regional identities, but rather in a
way intended to enhance them and thereby to present the full scope of
Canadian culture and tradition to all Canadians."[71]

The solution proposed by *A National Museums Policy for the 80's* to
maintain federal support for museums across the country while addressing Associate Museums' concerns about federal interference, advocated

for continued federal funding of both the National and the Associate Museums and management of the national programs by the NMC, with an emphasis on greater collaboration with provincial funding bodies, a shift that mirrored broader government efforts to improve federal–provincial relations.[72] In addition to increasing cooperation with the provinces, the National Museums Corporation leadership refocused its attention from the democratizing and decentralizing principles of the original National Museum Policy to finding suitable accommodation for the National Museums.[73] Writing in the 1981–82 *Annual Report*, NMC Board of Trustees Chairman Sean B. Murphy indicated that while the commitment to the national programs would continue at the existing rate, the priorities for the corporation over the next decade would be accommodation of the national collections, and improved management and conservation of their collections. Reflecting on the legacy of the National Museum Policy and the National Museums Corporation's past and future role in supporting Canadian museums, Murphy wrote,

> The National Museum Policy of 1972 entrusted to the NMC the mandate of translating federal policy into national programmes and services by assisting museums across Canada in preserving their collections and increasing the accessibility of those collections. The corporation's activities over the past decade have reflected the importance it attaches to such a responsibility. In that time, the Board has approved 1,354 grants to institutions across the country for a total of $76,149,809. However, during a period of increasing austerity which began for the NMC in 1979, the Board of Trustees realized that although the Corporation was well prepared for expansion, it was less prepared to respond to reductions in resources. The time had come for the NMC to turn its attention to the stewardship of its own collections in Ottawa.[74]

After more than ten years, the NMC had overextended itself in its ambitious efforts to build and support a national network of museum and exhibiting institutions, while art museums across the country had grown tremendously due to the influx of federal funds. One of the major faults of the program lay in the over-bureaucratization of the NMC and the erection of an unwieldy reporting and managing system that complicated the distribution of funds and accumulated power to the figure overseeing the corporation as a whole – the secretary-general. Indeed, while Gérard Pelletier may have stated in his 1972 announcement of the NMP that he was not establishing himself as a "cultural czar," successive secretaries-general, tasked with overseeing all the activities of the NMP, wielded the kind of power and oversight that belied the principles of democratization and decentralization at the core of the policy. While the *National Museums Policy for the 80's* document attempted to address the problems of centralization and bureaucracy that plagued the NMC, it came too late to reverse its existing operations, or to prevent its eventual demise.

The 1980s: Reviewing Cultural Funding from the Centre to the Margins

For art institutions in western Canada, the problems facing the National Museums Corporation were only an issue insofar as they affected the distribution of program funding and the amounts allocated. The increased bureaucracy that accompanied the grants process was time-consuming for all institutions, and the criteria that accompanied federal funding – such as the need for bilingual catalogues noted by the Edmonton Art Gallery – was a general subject of complaint. Yet, compared to preceding decades, the financial picture for most regional institutions was bright. Core funding from the NMC underwrote a significant portion of Associate Museums' operations; additional funding from the Canada Council for exhibitions and special projects was actively applied for; and contributions from provincial governments continued to increase over the 1970s and into the 1980s. Public funding to the AGGV in 1978–79, for example, included $97,000 from the NMC, $120,000 from the Canada Council, $84,000 from the BC Cultural Fund, and $60,000 from the civic governments of the greater Victoria region – accounting for almost 85 percent of the AGGV's total budget of $426,000 for that year.[75] Similar figures can be found in the budgets of the art galleries in Edmonton, Winnipeg, and Regina. Indeed, a key characteristic of the context for the development of art institutions in the 1970s and 1980s is the expansion of the number of organizations and the diversity of programming that they undertook. Government funding programs were the key engines of this growth, at the municipal, provincial, and federal levels. The Canada Council played a particularly important role as the agency's longstanding commitment to the support of individual artists opened it to the artistic explorations of the late 1960s and early 1970s and the artist-run exhibition spaces such activity generated. This was as important in western Canada as in other parts of the country, as the expansion of regional museums through NMC funding lessened their interest in supporting local art practices.

As art historians have noted, the explosion of artistic production in the 1960s and 1970s is closely tied to the emergence of new exhibition and production spaces and to the new sources of funding for such experimental activity.[76] What would shortly be designated as artist-run centres emerged out of artists' frustration with the conservatism of traditional art galleries and their rejection of the mainstream attitudes towards art that these institutions represented. A notable exception to this disregard was the Vancouver Art Gallery whose support of the artist collective Intermedia included hosting performances at the gallery during lunch hours and integrating its activities into the gallery's extension programs. Significant support for innovative art practices and organizations in other regions came from the Canada Council, whose mandate at the beginning of the 1970s was increasingly attuned to experimentation and self-expression. Intermedia received a $40,000 grant in 1967–68 for "a workshop adaptable to any experimental requirement,"[77] a venture touted in that year's *Annual Report* as earning the council international attention. In 1970, Montreal's Graff Galerie received $9,000 – an amount far below the $200,000 awarded the Montreal Museum of Fine Arts but close to the $10,000 given to the Norman MacKenzie Art Gallery; A Space in Toronto obtained its first funding in 1971, and by 1974 was the recipient of amounts equivalent to what some of the smaller Canadian art museums were allocated. By 1977, artist-run centres across the country were receiving various levels of support from the Canada Council for everything from special projects to core funding for operating costs – an indication of the value placed on their activities and their contribution to contemporary Canadian art. Reflecting on the first grant to Intermedia, Vancouver artist Ed Varney, in a 1983 interview with Diana Nemiroff, argued that the award was an attempt to rectify the agency's lack of knowledge of activities in western Canada: "they've always been worried about western representation … It was a way of putting money into Vancouver without necessarily giving out a whole lot of individual grants."[78]

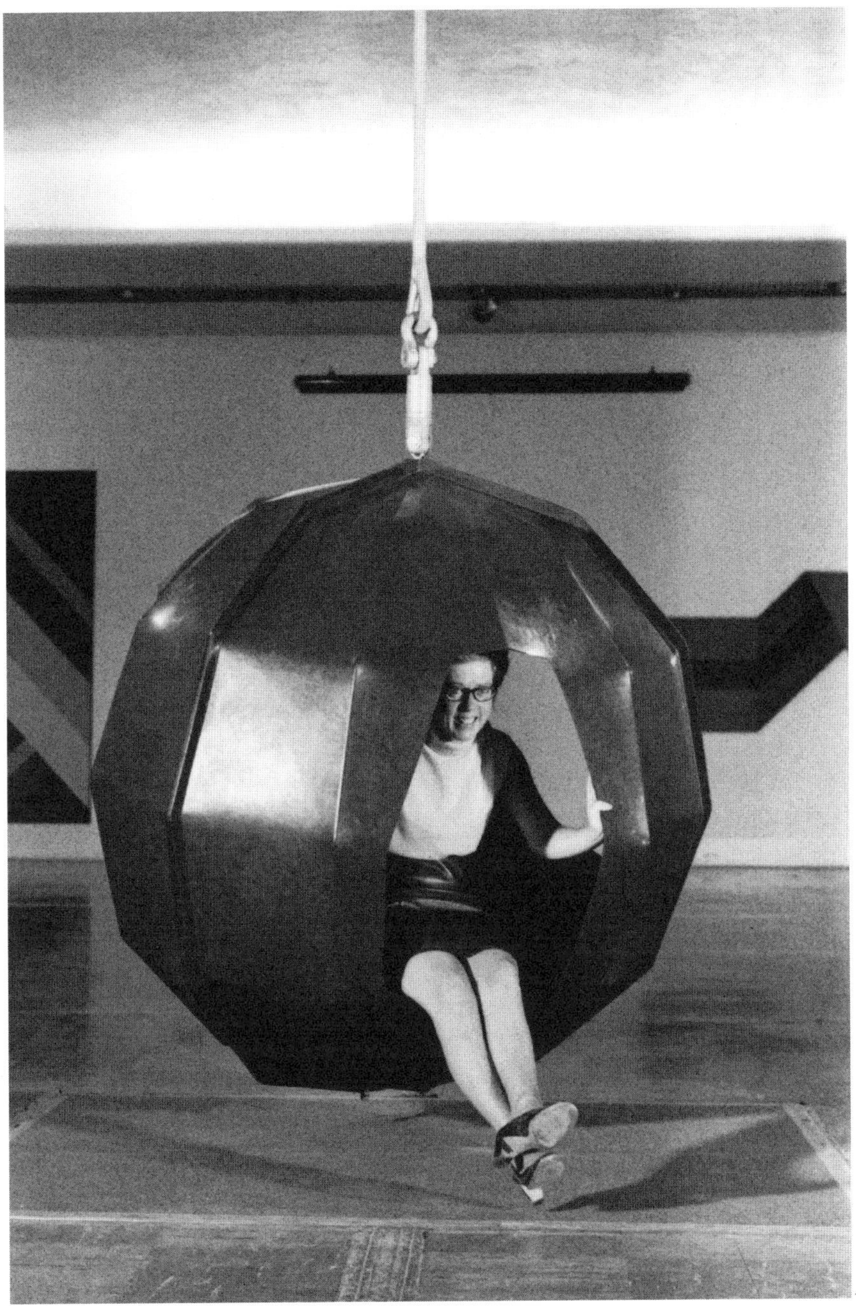

6.6 | Vancouver Art Gallery curator Doris Shadbolt sitting on an electronic sound sculpture by Dennis Vance, 1969.

Yet the level of support for experimental art spaces in the early 1970s suggests that the Canada Council relished its ability to fund new art forms both through grants to individuals – e.g., the Explorations grants introduced in 1973 – *and* to groups of artists through programs that supported the development of facilities. Nemiroff's assessment of the growth of artist-run centres in Canada documents the centrality of government funding both for the emergence of such centres and their eventual absorption into the mainstream. The secretary of state's Opportunities for Youth and Local Initiatives Program were both broad-based employment schemes exploited by artists' groups looking to build audiences for innovative art. Grants were used to renovate rented space, staff the resulting exhibition and performance venues, purchase equipment, and otherwise create communities of artists that could circumvent the normative systems and spaces of the art world. As these spaces became more established, artist-led organizations applied to the Canada Council for project grants and were able to accumulate the kinds of funds that could enable them to develop programming and build their reputations as hatching grounds for new art. The Western Front, founded in 1973 by a group of Vancouver artists who sought to establish a space for experimentation in interdisciplinary art practices, received $25,000 in funding from the Canada Council for its 1975 activities and for the purchase of materials. Winnipeg's Plug-In, founded in 1972, received its first Canada Council grant in 1973, in the amount of $11,000, and $14,000 the following year. In addition to their role in promoting experimentation, artist-run centres also provided a home for media otherwise overlooked by the larger galleries. Photographers Gallery was founded in 1971 in Saskatoon to address the Mendel's disinterest in collecting or exhibiting contemporary photography. Receiving its first Council grant of $5,000 in 1973 for the photographic study *Insight Saskatoon*, it would continue to play a significant role in fostering contemporary photographic practice with the support of regular grants from the agency.

Canada Council funding was also of central importance to art galleries across the country, the larger institutions such as the Art Gallery of Ontario receiving upwards of $200,000 in 1973 while smaller galleries like the Saskatoon Art Centre and Conservatory (a.k.a. the Mendel Art Gallery) were awarded significantly smaller amounts ($25,000 in the same year). In its assessment of its funding to art institutions as a whole, the council's annual reports emphasized the key role of art galleries in disseminating the work of Canada's contemporary artists, arguing that this work fell clearly within the agency's mandate to support individual artists in their quest for excellence. In the early 1980s, however, as the government allocation to the agency decreased and applications for grants increased, the Canada Council changed its funding format and moved away from operational funding to project funding. Under this model, all institutions – whether the larger established art galleries or the smaller artist-run centres – would submit applications for funding for specific projects that would be peer reviewed on the basis of their individual merit. The new funding model had a direct impact on public museums and galleries. In a widely circulated memo, dated 26 September 1984, council staff Edythe Goodridge and Margaret Dryden outlined the new funding structure for public museums that replaced annual grants to individual institutions with three yearly competitions in the areas of curatorial assistance (for research and travel necessary for the development of exhibitions, publications, and collections of contemporary art); exhibition assistance (for direct costs of presentation and interpretation of works in exhibitions); documentation assistance (for publications or media presentations related to exhibitions and collections); and finally, circulation assistance for galleries proposing to tour exhibitions at regional, national, or international levels. The eighteen galleries receiving annual grants would see those funds suspended until such time as the federal government's allocation increased. The primary aim of the new funding structure was to support curatorial research and investigation through juried competition "to ensure funding for the regional, national and international presentation and interpretation of the work of the contemporary artist."[79] A key component of the new structure was the emphasis on peer assessment in the allocation of funding in all its programs, a process that rewarded experimentation and rigour, and minimized the sense of entitlement of the larger public galleries who had come to expect sizeable injections of funds to their operating base on an annual basis.

Many of the major art galleries found the change from operation to project funding frustrating, particularly since the National Museums Corporation had implemented a comparable shift in its allocation of funds in 1983, removing the annual core funding grant to Associate Museums and replacing it with a project grant system. Aware of the "double dipping" of the larger organizations, the Canada Council and the NMC had earlier decided to divide their responsibilities – the latter focusing its Museum Assistance Programmes funding to exhibitions of historical objects while the Canada Council reaffirmed its commitment to contemporary art by only funding exhibitions in that area. Many organizations reacted negatively to the change in funding structure. If nothing else, the move from an annual core funding system to project funding meant that long-term planning was virtually impossible since there were no guarantees as to the level of federal government support. As an additional insult, the devolution of Canada Council funding to a competitive assessment of exhibitions (i.e., peer review) was perceived as giving the granting agency control over a museum's programming as well as its budget. As the EAG's Terry Fenton noted in 1985, the new funding structure at the Canada Council meant that the agency was effectively "playing curator of contemporary art for Canada."[80] Facing the disappearance of ongoing stable funding from federal sources, museums across the country increasingly turned to the provinces to assist with their operations.

The participation of provincial governments in museum funding had been on the mind of officials at both the NMC and the Canada Council, and became a source of contention in the late 1970s and early 1980s as federal organizations leaned on their provincial counterparts to share the burden of financing cultural matters. The NMC's *A National Museums Policy for the 80's* presented a strong argument that the responsibility for public museums in Canada could not be shouldered solely by the federal government, noting that "the national interest … is fully achieved when all levels of government divide and share responsibility for museums and act in concert."[81] Increased levels of provincial funding for culture was a key recommendation of the Federal Cultural Policy Review Committee (a.k.a. Applebaum-Hébert Committee), struck in 1980 to conduct an extensive analysis of Canadian cultural policy. Framed as the first major review of Canadian culture since the Massey Commission, the Applebaum-Hébert Committee undertook extensive consultations across the country, publishing a summary of these briefs and hearings a year before tabling its report in 1983. Responding primarily to concerns over the increased potential for ministerial intervention in the activities of agencies such as the Canada Council and the CBC, as well as the bureaucratization and centralization of government services during the 1970s, the committee's report reiterated the centrality of the arm's-length relationship between the federal government and cultural agencies. With chapters on the visual and the performing arts, writing, film production, sound recording, and the CBC, the Applebaum-Hébert report examined many of the fields considered by the Massey Commission; unlike the earlier study, however, and in line with the more market-oriented attitudes of the 1980s, the report was relatively silent on the role of the arts in building national identity, except insofar as culture was identified as an economic driver for the country on a national and international scale.

Given its concern with the bureaucratization of culture, the Applebaum-Hébert Committee was understandably critical of the National Museums Corporation, arguing that it was "no longer simply an organizational and service umbrella for the national museums; it was now also a well-funded federal cultural agency instigating national programs and providing national services."[82] Its report recommended limiting the NMC's mandate to responsibility for the four national museums, and the creation of a Canadian Heritage Council to administer the national programs. In its assessment of the National Museum Policy, the report acknowledged that the policies of democratization and decentralization had been effective in increasing the number of cultural facilities across the country and encouraging broader public interest in heritage, but that such success came at the cost of the activities of the federal institutions and their collections.[83] By shifting the NMC's attention fully to the National Museums, and earmarking separate funding as well as administrative responsibility for dissemination programs such as the Museumobiles and MAP, the Applebaum-Hébert report argued that the federal government would be better able to support the programs needed by cultural centers in the regions. In line with directions already proposed by the NMC, the Applebaum-Hébert Committee strongly endorsed greater cooperation among all three levels of government in the funding of heritage centers and materials. As it concluded from consultations across the country: "the National Museums of Canada, in pursuing the objectives of the National Programmes, has not always been as sensitive as it could have been to provincial and regional priorities, interests and standards, and has sometimes acted in a directive rather than a reactive way toward the non-national museums."[84] With its focus remaining squarely on dividing responsibility for the country's museal institutions between the NMC and the proposed Canadian Heritage Council, the Applebaum-Hébert report had little to say about regional museums or regional culture, despite receiving over 1,300 briefs and holding consultations in 18 cities across Canada. Indeed, while geography was addressed as "an important dimension of Canada's cultural diversity," regionalism was largely overlooked by a Committee predominantly concerned with the role that federal institutions – in particular government – could play in supporting the development of the arts in Canada, and specific references to cultural organizations from all parts of the country, including western Canada, were minimal.

The sheer scale of the consultations, however, meant that reaction to the Applebaum-Hébert report was widespread. Writing in *Arts Manitoba*, Christopher Dafoe noted the report's emphasis on increased funding as the solution to Canada's cultural problems; other writers were disappointed that the committee had not undertaken a thorough analysis of the state of culture in Canada in the vein of the Massey Commission; and still others considered that Applebaum-Hébert's approach to renewing Canadian cultural policy relied too heavily on a market-oriented model that was inappropriate to Canadian cultural values.[85] With a mandate to examine federal cultural policy, and having undertaken consultations across the country, the Applebaum-Hébert Committee's report was also assessed for its ability to address the experience of artists outside the centre. In a comment that echoes the words of museum directors and artists' groups throughout the twentieth century, Dafoe wrote, "During its travels between Winnipeg and Victoria, the committee was constantly reminded of Western resentment of 'centralization' in the arts. It was reminded, again and again, that Toronto [i.e., central Canada] is not the focal point of national culture."[86] Such sentiments spoke to the growing feeling among artists living outside the major centres of Toronto, Montreal, and now Vancouver that they occupied a largely peripheral status in the Canadian art world, both geographically and ideologically. However, like proponents of western Canadian exceptionalism such as Reform Party founder Preston Manning, who was becoming increasingly vocal on the political scene, such a marginal place was not necessarily a negative to be overcome. In line with broader explorations of the flexibility of identity that emerged with postmodernism, Canadian artists and writers wholly rejected the dominance of the national to explore local articulations of selfhood. Although most evident in the writing of Québécois authors, figures from the regions voiced both their frustration with the definitional power of Toronto critics and institutions to ascribe meaning to the term "Canadian" art, and sometimes sought to explore the question of identity from a regional standpoint. In the first editorial of *Border Crossings* in 1985, Robert Enright reflected on the emergence of Winnipeg as a hub of innovative artistic practice:

> One of the most exciting developments in the west of Canada in the last decade has been an acceptance of the value of *place*. The artistic brain drain to the east has stopped and artists now accept the fact that living away from the centre will not be damaging to their careers or their productivity ... What living away from the centre does is to allow relief from the relentless homogenizing tendencies of mainstream culture. In Canada, it's arguable that the most interesting cultural activity is marginal activity. The regions are part of that margin.[87]

Although the boosterish tone of this statement can be attributed to the launch of a new publication – ironically the transformation of the regional-sounding *Arts Manitoba* to the more postmodern-inflected *Border Crossings* – Enright's assertion that the strength of artistic practice comes from a sense of rootedness fits within larger discourses of globalization in which writing from the margins entails not just a critique of normative relations of power from disenfranchised peoples but the occupation of a position of power that comes from a refusal to see oneself as marginal.[88] In western Canada, as the effects of Trudeau's National Energy Program continued to feed a sense of alienation through the 1980s, there was much value in occupying a powerful position of assumed marginality, one where local interests – however they might fit within dominant political and economic interests – were ignored by federal politicians.

Interestingly, marginality was experienced to a lesser degree by art institutions that, through the influx of funds in the 1970s and early 1980s, were able to build their programming and differentiate their activities in such a way that they could carve out a place for themselves on the national and in some instances the international stage. As the National Gallery faced significant difficulties under the yoke of the NMC, museums in western Canada – especially the Vancouver Art Gallery – honed their acquisitions policies, developed innovative programming, and positioned themselves as leaders in select internationally recognized fields.[89] Of particular note during the 1980s was the Winnipeg Art

Gallery's strengthening of its Inuit art collection and the development of a more focused and active photography collection. The MacKenzie Art Gallery in Regina (the "Norman" was dropped in 1990) made a commitment to supporting the work of contemporary work by artists of Indigenous descent, a collecting focus that increased in the 1990s with the hiring of Indigenous curators such as Lee-Ann Martin and the Canada Council's Arts Acquisition Assistance program that provided matching funds for the purchase of contemporary Indigenous art. The Edmonton Art Gallery defied what it described as artistic "fashion" and actively expanded its acquisition of Canadian, American, and British formalist painters and sculptors. The Vancouver Art Gallery moved into new premises in 1983 and transformed its long-term support for photo-conceptualism into the "Vancouver School" brand that has garnered international recognition and acclaim for the artists as well as the institution.

Meanwhile, the National Gallery continued to underscore its national – and nation-building – role, but increasingly paid attention to international developments in the visual arts. Regular attempts at assessing the state of contemporary Canadian art through large-scale survey exhibitions – e.g., *Pluralities* (1980), *Songs of Experience* (1986), and the *Canadian Biennial of Contemporary Art* (1989) – were designed to permit critical reflection from the national institution on the nature of "Canadian" art during a period of shifting discourses on national identity. Each exhibition approached the question differently: *Pluralities* relied on guest curators from across the country to select what each felt to be the most significant artists working at the time; NGC acting curators Diana Nemiroff and Jessica Bradley explored the preoccupation with identity (gender and national) among Canadian artists in *Songs of Experience*; for the *Canadian Biennial of Contemporary Art*, envisioned as the first of a ten-year project to be circulated to a different regional museum every two years but cancelled due to the withdrawal of corporate sponsorship, curator Nemiroff used the metaphor of the TransCanada to map local art discourses rather than attempt a definition that would encompass the diversity of practices across the country.[90] Critics reacted to each of these exhibitions in turn, complaining about the eclectic nature of *Pluralities*, and the lack of inclusion of Quebec in *Songs of Experience*, first through a dearth of francophone artists from that province, and second due to the presence of artists using translated French texts in their work. The

Biennial was critiqued for its erasure of Newfoundland, literally in the absence of the province from the map of the country that graced the catalogue's cover, and through the inclusion of only one artist from Atlantic Canada. Battered from such critiques, the NGC refrained from organizing any more survey exhibitions, focusing instead on more thematically oriented shows such as *Land Spirit Power* (1992) that allowed for more in-depth explorations. Its commitment to Canadian art remained evident in its continued acquisition of historical and contemporary works and its public statements of its federal mandate.

The NMC, meanwhile, continued to struggle with its role and its identity as a national agency and the effects that focusing its attention on the national museums in the Capital Region might have on regional operations. With the return of Gérard Pelletier to the corporation in 1984 – this time as chairman of the Board of Trustees – the NMC's public rhetoric emphasized its commitment to serving the needs of museums across the country even as its staff was preoccupied with the construction of new buildings for the National Gallery of Canada (opening in 1988) and the Museum of Man (renamed the Canadian Museum of Civilization at its opening in 1989). The NMC's *Annual Report* for 1984–85 justified the new buildings with the argument that they would "work to fulfill a vital mandate of the National Museums Corporation, that is, the preservation and increased accessibility of Canada's cultural collections."[91] Responding to concerns that the new buildings – and the funds allocated for their construction – would limit the ability of the NMC to serve regional museums, the 1985–86 *Annual Report* reiterated that "with *operational bases* tailored to their needs, [the NGC and the CMC] will be able to exert their influence throughout the country, as they were mandated to do, through loans of exhibits, greater accessibility of collections, experiments in all museological fields, training of museum staff or dissemination of techniques – all functions that are part of their role and which their new bases of operations will finally enable them to carry out."[92] Such strong rhetoric characterized the NMC's response to the Applebaum-Hébert Committee's report, officially encapsulated in the 1984 document *After Applebaum-Hébert*, which reasserted the corporation's legitimate role to lead the federal government's national cultural activities and called for increased federal funding to permit it to more effectively carry out its national programs.

Despite such arguments, perceptions of the agency as paternalist and overly bureaucratic in its operations continued to plague the NMC, and its operations were reviewed in 1986 by the Task Force Charged with Examining Federal Policy Concerning Museums (Richard-Withrow Committee). After extensive but rapid consultations, the committee concluded that the NMC be immediately dismantled, giving each of the four federal institutions administrative autonomy as free-standing institutions with their own boards of trustees, a recommendation loudly hailed by national museums staff. Responsibility for assistance programs to non-federal museums was devolved to the minister of communications with the recommendation that such programs focus on professional development, interprovincial and international exchange, and a broader range of support to museums and exhibition centers across Canada. Despite protests from the corporation's leadership and arguments that increased funding would enable it to undertake all the national programs identified as central to maintaining the vibrancy of Canada's museums, the task force not only sounded the death knell for the corporation but questioned the very viability or logic of establishing a national museum policy in the first place. As the report queried, "The 1968 Act is ambiguous. Did Parliament intend a loose federation of four separate museums with a small central agency to provide broad policy direction from the Board of Trustees? Alternatively, did Parliament intend one integrated agency effectively controlled and managed from the centre, with four branches called 'National Museums'? Lacking guidance, through the years the Board of Trustees of the Corporation has in practice, imposed the centralist option and the results are apparent."[93]

In 1990, the Department of Communications released its Federal Museums Policy, and the accompanying Act of Parliament established each federal museum as a Crown corporation, responsible to the minister of communications. With the Museums Act, the national museums once again became the guardians of national culture, reverting to their pre-1968 roles. With new buildings for two of the four museums, the federal institutions resumed their symbolic roles as leaders of Canada's cultural development in each of their respective fields and the Associate Museums, funded by a somewhat diminished Museums Assistance Program run out of the Department of Communications, contemplated an uncertain future.

Conclusion

Over the 1970s and 1980s, the museum landscape in Canada changed dramatically. The federal government's creation of the National Museums Corporation, intended to amalgamate and give greater visibility to the nation's cultural heritage, and the subsequent establishment of the National Museum Policy, designed to make that heritage more accessible to the Canadian public by circulating it through the country, succeeded in bringing greater public attention to culture but eventually drowned in its own bureaucracy. The significant influx of funding to support the NMP was a boon to western Canadian art galleries that were able to fund much-needed expansions to existing buildings as well as support education and extension programs. The corresponding increases in both provincial and municipal funding to museums, largely the result of pressure from the federal government, were equally beneficial to galleries eager to build their national (and international) profiles. Despite such growth, the power imbalance between western Canadian art galleries and federal institutions that had characterized much of the previous eighty years continued to be felt: the national museums complained that in having to make their collections available to galleries and exhibition centres across the country, they were neglecting their own collecting and exhibiting activities; galleries in western Canada argued that under the NMP they were obligated to generate programming that conformed to the nation-building aims of the federal government, rather than attend to the development of exhibitions and activities that responded to the needs of their publics. Such opposing viewpoints could just as easily have characterized the differences in perspective between the National Gallery and the Western Canada Art Circuit in the 1950s. Yet the debate in the 1970s and 1980s was tempered by the huge investment of funds from all levels of government that resulted in greater autonomy for regional galleries. Thanks to vast influxes of money from the provinces, in addition to support from the NMP and the Canada Council, and continuing funding from municipal governments, museums outside of Ottawa were finally in a position to expand both in size and in ambition. Indeed, by the mid-1980s, western Canadian art institutions became more competitive with federal museums as they established their own programming and developed their own expertise in art-related matters; meanwhile, federal museums struggled under the NMP with both their identity as federal museums and with financial restraints. As the bureaucracy binding museums across the country began to unravel, and organizations began to envision themselves as autonomous from the constraints of the NMP, new opportunities appeared for museums, galleries, and artist-run centres and a process of renewal and differentiation began. Art museums in the centre and in the periphery could now engage in a dialogue about artistic practices, a dialogue that was as likely to be instigated from Winnipeg or Regina as it was from Ottawa.

In December 2009, the National Gallery of Canada (NGC) and the Art Gallery of Alberta (AGA) issued a joint press release announcing the inauguration of a three-year partnership between the two institutions. During that period, a gallery space in the new Art Gallery of Alberta building would be dedicated to showing exhibitions, jointly developed by curatorial staff at both institutions, but featuring works drawn from the permanent collection in Ottawa. *The National Gallery of Canada at the Art Gallery of Alberta* was presented as an opportunity for visitors to the Edmonton gallery to be able to "enjoy exceptional works of art drawn from the National Gallery of Canada's collections."[1] Announced one month prior to the opening of the AGA's new building, and framed as a key feature of its new programming, *The National Gallery of Canada at the Art Gallery of Alberta* provided ready-made programming to an institution facing the financial challenges wrought by an ambitious building plan, while simultaneously raising the national profile of a regional museum. At the same time, however, this first of what the press release described as "satellite programs" enabled the National Gallery to visibly establish a national presence by prominently featuring not only its works but also its name in a western Canadian gallery. Since 2009, similar partnerships with the National Gallery have been established at the Museum of Contemporary Canadian Art in Toronto in 2010, and the Winnipeg Art Gallery (WAG) in 2012. From the vantage point of the relationships between the NGC and western Canadian art museums that *Spaces and Places for Art* has traced, there is a certain sense of déjà vu in the creation of "The National Gallery at …" spaces and as such the program provides an ideal epilogue to the histories I have charted.

In its desire to bring objects from the national collection to the Canadian public, "The National Gallery at …" program reprises the loan exhibitions initiated by the National Gallery in 1913 that enabled arts organizations in Manitoba, Saskatchewan, Alberta, and British Columbia to offer the fine arts programming they could not deliver from their own meagre collections. Both as a service to smaller arts organizations and attempts to educate the Canadian public about art, these exhibition programs appear to share a certain paternalism – a concern over the qualities of exhibitions organized by smaller galleries and faith in the ability of the national institution to bring excellence to the regions. As this book has traced, since the beginning of the twentieth century, western Canadian art galleries have built sizeable permanent collections and developed successful exhibition programs. Indeed, over the course of writing *Spaces and Places for Art*, the Winnipeg Art Gallery celebrated its centenary in 2012; the Art Gallery of Alberta followed up its change of name with the opening of a magnificent new building in 2009; the Mendel Art Gallery announced in 2011 that it was moving to much larger facilities and changing its name to the Remai Modern Art Gallery of Saskatchewan in recognition of the significant contribution of art and funds by Saskatoon philanthropist Ellen Remai; there are ongoing discussions over new facilities for the Art Gallery of Greater Victoria; and the Vancouver Art Gallery has unveiled architectural plans and drawings for a spectacular (and not uncontroversial) new building in the heart of the city's downtown. From uncertain beginnings in the first half of the twentieth century, art institutions in western Canada appear to be if not universally thriving, then successful advocates for the visual arts in their respective communities and visible players nationally and internationally. Given this success, what do the WAG and the AGA get from their partnership with the National Gallery other than being the recipients of a steady stream of exhibitions?

By mapping the relationship between art galleries in western Canada and national institutions over the twentieth century, this book has argued that while the National Gallery has always retained its position of authority in relation to the development of art in Canada, smaller institutions in the west regularly disrupted that authority either through the organization of exhibition networks such as the Western Canada Art Circuit or through public critiques of the NGC's activities by the Federation of Canadian Artists (FCA) and the Alberta Society of Artists. Although these oppositional moments were viewed primarily as irritants by the NGC and rapidly contained through the introduction of new programs like the Extension and Exhibition Services department, their history underscores the power of organizations on the geographical periphery to critique and question the dominant point of view. This critical stance has motivated much of the writing of *Spaces and Places for Art* insofar as it has allowed me to consider two underdeveloped aspects of Canadian art history: the role of art institutions in framing Canadian art, and the place of regionalism in a discipline that has only partially addressed its nationalist aspirations. The book as a whole tackles the first point. There are few histories of art museums in Canada and this lack of critical analysis of the institutions that for better or worse determine the shape of the visual arts in this country is a major absence. Museums frame art; they mediate our engagements with objects and actively shape the narratives of artistic production that are the basis for the discipline of art history. Understanding the ideological work of museums has been the cornerstone of critical museum studies for the past thirty years, but in-depth analysis of the work of specific museums – in Canada and elsewhere – has been lacking. By going through the archives of art institutions across western Canada, reading their annual reports and board minutes, analyzing their activities, and mapping their concerns, I have highlighted the fundamental importance of art institutions to the history of art, and argued strongly for a close reading of their histories. Artists and the work they produce remain, of course, the bread and butter of the discipline, but it is only by uncovering the work of individual institutions at their most basic level that we can understand how artistic practices emerge. If this book does anything, I hope it has increased interest in the histories of museums in Canada and encouraged other scholars to engage critically with those particular histories.

In this call for the centrality of art institutions to the study of art history, I also include cultural policy as a fundamental sphere of inquiry. This is particularly relevant in Canada where, as numerous scholars have suggested, cultural history is written in and through the findings of royal commissions and task forces. More significantly, however, attending to relations between culture and the state allows for a more complex understanding of decision making at the institutional level and its effects on artistic production. As *Spaces and Places for Art* demonstrates, the fortunes of western Canadian art galleries in the 1970s and 1980s were immeasurably improved through the funding programs of the Canada Council and the National Museum Policy; of equal significance, the Massey Commission's Report failed to adequately address the needs of regional institutions in its reassertion of the centralizing role of federal institutions. Throughout this study, my goal has been to examine practices of national agencies in the management of cultural institutions, identifying how they have assessed the needs of regional galleries and mapping those institutions' responses. Attending to the validity of the perspectives of both the agencies and the funded institutions has been a central component of my approach: it's not enough to see cultural policy as the homogenous imposition of state will on cultural organizations. Art organizations across the country have largely benefitted from Canada's proclivity to "administer" culture at many levels, even as it might mean conforming to granting agencies' program criteria and participating in discourses of national identity with which they may not agree; but organizations have also been successful at manipulating programs and policies to suit their own needs. As a way of understanding negotiations of power between centralized agencies and institutions on the (geographical) periphery, the rhetoric of cultural policy as well as its implementation at the local level deserves serious consideration in any analysis of Canadian culture.

The concept of region that I identified above as an underdeveloped area of analysis in Canadian *art* history, has, in contrast, preoccupied historians of western Canada who have explored it both as a formal entity that defines geographical space and as an imagined political force that unites disparate peoples against an equally imagined centre. I have argued throughout the book that while art galleries were most immediately interested in establishing spaces for the presentation of art, they also recognized the concomitant production of place in the formation of cultural institutions in growing cities in western Canada. Museums ascribed symbolic capital to emerging centres keen to establish their economic importance and to strengthen relationships with the metropolises back east; museums quite literally put cities on the map. Until these institutions could generate their own exhibitions and acquire collections of some significance, they remained beholden to what the National Gallery of Canada could offer, thus perpetuating the centre–periphery relations that historians have long claimed characterizes the development of Canada as a nation. The assumed naturalness of the centre–periphery model has arguably underpinned the writing of Canadian art history, where the construction of a "Canadian" aesthetic has produced narratives that privilege the activities of Ottawa-Montreal-Toronto at the expense of those coming out of the regions. My reading of the archives of western Canadian art institutions confirms this bias: in the first half of the twentieth century, art galleries west of Winnipeg relied on information coming out of Ottawa, whether in the form of exhibitions, lecturers, letters from H.O. McCurry, or the contents of *Canadian Art*. By the 1940s, however, some questioned this unidirectional flow of information as can be seen in western Canadian delegates to the Kingston Artists' Conference complaining about the difficulties they faced in getting their work seen by juries for national exhibitions held in central Canada. Similar grievances emerged in the following decades and arguably continue today. Attention to the activities of western Canadian galleries is necessary, I would argue, not so much to redress absences of artists from the region in histories of Canadian art, but because knowledge of these activities enable us to think otherwise about cultural production in Canada and offer a necessary adjustment to the still-dominant national perspective of Canadian art history. Accounts of foundational events such as the Kingston Artists' Conference and the Massey Commission, for example, have been predominantly written through a central Canadian lens. By reading these events for the way they constructed an idea of "the west," I want to question the very dominance of national narratives in the writing of Canadian art history. In the wake of critiques of the discipline for overlooking questions of gender, race, and sexuality, it may appear somewhat retrograde to be asserting the value of attending to regional discourses. I would argue, however, that in tandem with these important critiques of art history, in Canada, the question of place requires considerable analysis for its ability to reveal significant biases in contemporary historiography.

In light of this discussion of the continuing relevance of thinking about centre–periphery relations in Canadian art history, how does "The National Gallery at ..." program benefit the galleries in Winnipeg and Edmonton and the local publics they have a mandate to serve? In a broader discussion of the program, the NGC's director Marc Mayer spoke to the question of audience, reiterating the National Gallery's role in presenting works from its collection to the nation: "We are not the National Gallery of Ottawa ... What's important is to keep developing the infrastructure for art in Canada."[2] Coming on the heels of arguments by artists in both Edmonton and Winnipeg that the two facilities have not made enough effort to support and present the work of local artists, the claim that a program imported from the NGC will develop the infrastructure for art in Canada suggests a literal interpretation of the term "infrastructure."

Galleries will be provided with programming, such as the *Disasters of War* print series by Goya that opened *The National Gallery at the Art Gallery of Alberta*, that will increase museum attendance but will be of little benefit to raising the profile of local artists. And despite the claim to partnership – which does entail collaboration between the two institutions in the creation and development of exhibitions – there does not appear to be a flow of exhibitions from regional galleries to the NGC. Tellingly, "The National Gallery at ..." spaces were described in the inaugural AGA press release as "satellites" of the NGC, a phrase that echoes the calls from the Federation of Canadian Artists in the 1940s for the distribution of the national collections to the regions; the resulting "branch plants," according to the FCA, giving greater public access to the NGC's holdings.

Despite the FCA's belief that such a dispersal would diminish the powerful hold the Ottawa institution had over artistic activities in the country, as "The National Gallery at ..." spaces suggest, the long arm of the NGC continues to shape activities across the country. Indeed, while the program might, in the words of the AGA press release, "build on the strong commitment of the NGC to sharing the national collections with Canadians," it also allows the national institution to assert the NGC brand through a visible occupation of space in the regions.[3] Indeed, in Edmonton and Winnipeg, the "National Gallery of Canada at ..." galleries provide an associational experience that imprints the National Gallery in the minds of visitors: first through the signage that visually marks the presence of the National Gallery outside Ottawa; and second in the viewer's physical interaction with the work in the space. Unlike the temporary loans obtained by galleries in the early twentieth century, the presence of dedicated gallery space in each host institution reinforces the National Gallery's "authorship" of "The National Gallery at ..." spaces, literally signing them as part of its national brand. In its examination of the relationship between western Canadian art galleries and federal organizations, *Spaces and Places for Art* has engaged with institutional histories, conceptions of regional identity, and implications of cultural policies in the twentieth century. As the geopolitical landscape of western Canada changes and threats to government support for culture continue to characterize the political landscape, how these art institutions face the twenty-first century will be a topic of great interest to museum scholars and Canadian art historians alike.

ILLUSTRATION CREDITS

INTRODUCTION

1 Canada, Department of Public Works, *Report of the Minister of Public Works … fiscal year ending 31 March 1914*, 65.

2 Canada, Department of Public Works, *Report of the Minister of Public Works … fiscal year ending 31 March 1918*, 158.

3 Throughout this book I will use the terms "western Canada" and "the west" to refer to the provinces of Manitoba, Saskatchewan, Alberta, and British Columbia. I do so in the full knowledge that at different times in the period under discussion these four provinces saw themselves aligned as "western Canada" and sometimes even "the west" while at others any sense of coalition or coherence was firmly repudiated. I will discuss the rhetorical mobilization of these terms in more detail further in the Introduction.

4 See, for example, Boggs, *The National Gallery of Canada* and Ord, *The National Gallery of Canada*.

5 The existing literature includes Vancouver Art Gallery, *Vancouver Art and Artists 1931–1983*; Ridell, *The MacKenzie Art Gallery*; Hughes, Morris, and Till, *Vision into Reality: Art Gallery of Greater Victoria*; Coleman, *Dreaming a Gallery*; "Celebrating a Century: A Timeline of the Winnipeg Art Gallery 1912–2012," Winnipeg Art Gallery, accessed 27 May 2014, www.wag100.ca/timeline/date:1912.

6 Friesen, "The Prairies as Region," 173.

7 Swyripa, *Storied Landscapes*, 8.

8 Friesen, "The Prairies as Region," 173.

9 Friesen, "Defining the Prairies," 23.

10 Morton, "The Bias of Prairie Politics," 150.

11 See, for example, Innis, *The Fur Trade in Canada*.

12 R.W. Hedley to H.O. McCurry, 11 July 1947, Loans, Western Canada: Western Canada Art Circuit 1945–47, box 122, file 11, NGC fonds, NGC Library and Archives.

13 Innis, "The Canadian North," cited in Buxton, *Harold Innis and the North*, 28.

14 For an in-depth analysis of the impact of the Laurentian thesis on Canadian art history see Whitelaw, "'To Better Know Ourselves,'" 8–33.

15 Careless, "'Limited Identities' in Canada," 5–12.

16 Ibid., 6.

17 Anderson, *Imagined Communities*, 4.

18 Ibid., 6.

19 Careless, "'Limited Identities' in Canada," 11.

20 Irwin, "Breaking the Shackles of the Metropolitan Thesis," 98–118.

21 Lyotard, *The Postmodern Condition*, 60.

22 Berger, *The Writing of Canadian History*, 94.

23 Innis, *The Bias of Communication*; Connor, "Harold Innis and The Bias of Communication," 274–94.

24 Berland, "Space at the Margins," 58.

25 Simmins, *Simmins Report on the Development of Art Museums*, 2:38f–38g.

CHAPTER 1

1 McCarthy, *Women's Culture*; Macleod, *Enchanted Lives, Enchanted Objects*.

2 There is little written about the Edmonton branch of the WAAC. I place the date of its demise as 1919 because that is the last mention of the Edmonton branch in the WAAC's annual reports.

3 Women's Art Association of Canada, *Annual Report of the Association and its Branches* (31 August 1918), 26.

4 On the Metropolitan Museum of Art, see Trask, *Things American*; on the Detroit Institute of Arts, see Abt, *A Museum on the Verge*; on the Portland Art Museum, see Salmony, "The Portland Museum of Art," 25–6.

5 Trudel, "Aux origines du Musée des beaux-arts de Montréal," 31–60; Lowery, "The Art Gallery of Toronto."

6 It is interesting to note the affiliation with Christian Science of the first two directors of the National Gallery and of the first director of the Edmonton Museum of Arts. This connection will be addressed in more detail in Chapter 2.

7 Buckner and Francis, Introduction to *Canada and the British World*, 7.

8 Ontario Society of Artists, *President's Annual Report 1929–30*.

9 The exhibition was held from 30 October to 1 November 1924.

10 Edmonton Museum of Arts, *Loan Exhibition Catalogue*, Palm Room, Macdonald Hotel, 1924, n.p.

11 The EMA's act of incorporation outlines the institution's mandate "to promote the knowledge and enjoyment of, and cultivation of the fine arts and to preserve historical relics."

12 "Rare Treat Awaits Public in Collection of Pictures on Exhibition in Macdonald," *The Edmonton Journal*, 30 October 1924.

13 "The Art Loan Exhibit," *The Edmonton Journal*, 31 October 1924.

14 E.L. Hill, the city's first librarian and secretary, also sat on the Board of the Edmonton Museum of Arts and proved to be very useful in negotiations with the

city regarding space and funding. During its tenure at the library, the museum displayed works in the lecture hall and opened its exhibitions to the public three days a week: Tuesday and Thursday afternoons from 12:30 p.m. to 5:00 p.m. and on Saturday from 10:00 a.m. to noon.

15 The Carnegie Corporation awarded the Edmonton Public Library a $75,000 building grant in 1913. Deciding that establishing its library operations was more important than the erection of a building, city officials deferred acceptance of the grant until the corporation wrote (in 1921) that the award could not remain outstanding indefinitely. In compliance with a new Carnegie deadline, and with the promise of an increased grant of $112,500 from the corporation if the City of Edmonton agreed to contribute $37,500, construction on the library building began in 1922. Johnson, "The Edmonton Public Library."

16 Palmer and Palmer, *Alberta: A New History*, 76–105.

17 Goyette and Roemmich, *Edmonton In Our Own Words*.

18 According to the 1932–33 *Annual Report*, attendance for the year was six thousand, which averages to about five hundred visitors per month. In 1946, the *Edmonton Bulletin* reported that attendance was one hundred persons per day "comparing favourably with museums of much larger cities in the Dominion." "Edmonton Museum of Arts Marks Its 23rd Birthday This Year," *Edmonton Bulletin*, 20 April 1946.

19 President's Report, Annual General Meeting of the Edmonton Museum of Arts, 1927, Edmonton Museum of Arts Board of Directors Minutes, box 14, vol. 1, Edmonton Art Gallery files, City of Edmonton Archives.

20 In the first of several attempts, in fall 1928 City Council allocated space for the erection of a building for the Edmonton Museum of Arts but could not get voters to approve the funds. This would occur again in 1933, 1947, and 1950.

21 Palmer and Palmer, *Alberta: A New History*, 198, 219. Palmer and Palmer characterize the appeal of the UFA's radicalism as lying in the party's combination of a utopian belief in progress based on Christian values that sought a new era of democracy that positioned itself against the corruption and greed of the old political and social system.

22 MacGregor, *Edmonton: A History*, 248.

23 Secord House was the home of Richard Secord, business partner of John A. McDougall, one of the EMA's founders.

24 "The Manitoba Society of Artists, Reasons for its Existence," reprinted in Yates, *The Manitoba Society of Artists*, 5.

25 See Berry, *Taming the Frontier*, 81–95, for a fuller discussion of the lobbying role of the Western Art Association in the establishment of the Winnipeg Art Gallery. The Winnipeg branch of the WAAC had been in existence since 1894 and had worked diligently to ensure that exhibitions of fine art and handicraft were available to Winnipeg's citizens by displaying the work of its own members and obtaining loan exhibitions from more established institutions.

26 The Industrial Bureau building was built on Main Street and Water Avenue in downtown Winnipeg as a primary exhibiting space for members of the Winnipeg Board
of Trade. During construction, an additional wing was added to provide space for
the exhibition of artworks and objects of historical interest. The Industrial Bureau
building was demolished in 1935.

27 Artibise, *Winnipeg: A Social History of Urban Growth*, 131.

28 Ibid., 133. Unfortunately, this economic prosperity would end in 1912, ironically the
year that the Industrial Bureau Exposition Building was opened. Blanchard, *Winnipeg 1912*.

29 George Wilson writing in *The Year Book of Canadian* Art (1913), cited in "Celebrating a Century: A Timeline of the Winnipeg Art Gallery, 1912–2012," Winnipeg Art
Gallery, accessed 24 January 2014, www.wag100.ca/timeline/date:1912.

30 In its document of incorporation, the Winnipeg Art Gallery and School of Art cited
as its aims "the promotion and culture of fine and applied arts and to that end to
establish and maintain in the City of Winnipeg a permanent building or buildings,
collections and exhibitions of paintings, sculpture, engravings and other works of
art, an art library and art school adequately equipped." Cited in Eckhardt, *The Winnipeg Art Gallery 1912–1962*, 4.

31 Ibid., 5.

32 The promotional brochure published to mark the auditorium's opening described
the spaces available for displays: "On the second floor are located Winnipeg's new
Museum and Art Gallery. Immediately after the opening of the Auditorium associations were organized to utilize two large exhibition halls which were prepared
for this purpose. The Museum has excellent collections representing Natural History and the history of Manitoba. The Art Gallery's collection is growing rapidly
and includes the work of some of Western Canada's foremost artists." *The Winnipeg
Auditorium*, c. 1932 (unpaginated), Winnipeg Art Gallery Archives.

33 According to Sarah Yates, FitzGerald's appointment came as a result of intense lobbying on the part of the Manitoba Society of Artists, of which Musgrove was a prominent member. With the reinvigoration of the Winnipeg Art Gallery and School in
the new Civic Auditorium, the strong relationship between that organization and
the Manitoba Society of Artists would continue for many years. Yates, *The Manitoba
Society of Artists*, 11.

34 McCann, "Urban Growth in a Staple Economy."

35 Ibid., 32–3.

36 *The Vancouver Daily News-Advertiser*, 20 January 1889, cited in Hunt, "Mutual Enlightenment in Early Vancouver," 44.

37 For the early years of the Art, Historical and Scientific Association, see Thom, "The
Fine Arts in Vancouver, 1886–1930."

38 Hunt, "Mutual Enlightenment in Early Vancouver," 88.

39 Vancouver *Province*, 13 March 1909, cited in Thom, "The Fine Arts in Vancouver," 35.

40 Information on the BC Society of Artists and on the BC Art League is taken from Thom, "The Fine Arts in Vancouver," 42.

41 Ibid., 83.

42 Disenchanted with the school and the salary reduction imposed on faculty members during the Depression, Varley and Macdonald left the Vancouver School of Decorative and Fine Arts in 1933 to form the short-lived but artistically influential British Columbia College of Arts.

43 The institution was renamed the Vancouver School of Art in 1936 and moved to larger facilities in the former Vancouver (central) High School; in 1978, the School would become the Emily Carr College of Art (now the Emily Carr University of Art and Design). See the Emily Carr University of Art and Design website, www.ecuad.ca/about/history.

44 Indeed, the loan of NGC paintings for the first EMA exhibition in 1924 had previously been on display in Vancouver and was sent on to Edmonton.

45 Henry A. Stone came to Vancouver from London, England, as the manager of the newly established Vancouver branch of Gault Bros. Ltd., a textile manufacturing and distribution firm. He was the lead donor of the Vancouver Art Gallery scheme, providing $50,000 of the promised $100,000. Ten other prominent individuals committed $5,000 each. Stone made the large donation and took on the leadership of the project as a memorial to his only son, Lieut. Horace Gordon Stone, who was killed in action in the First World War. Kevin Griffin, "An Only Son's Death Gave Birth to City's Art Gallery," *The Vancouver Sun*, 10 October 2006.

46 Thom, "The Fine Arts in Vancouver," 94–7.

47 On the early pedagogical aims of the Victoria and Albert Museum, see Burton, "The Uses of the South Kensington Art Collections"; on the Whitechapel exhibitions, see Koven, "The Whitechapel Picture Exhibitions and the Politics of Seeing."

48 Edmonton Museum of Arts, *Annual Report*, 13 October 1931.

49 Vancouver Art Gallery, *Annual Report*, 1931–32.

50 MacKenzie's collection is often described as having "begun" in 1912 when a tornado hit the city of Regina and destroyed the majority of his existing collection, forcing him to start anew. Long, "The Collector and the Collection," 28.

51 Ibid., 10.

52 Meszaros, "Visibility and Representation," 52–8.

53 Snelgrove received $3,109.06 from the Carnegie Corporation to undertake doctoral studies at The Courtauld Institute. According to H.O. McCurry's 1936 report on Carnegie- funded activities managed by the Canadian Museums Committee, Snelgrove was appointed as the [Carnegie-funded] Chair of Fine Arts at the University of Saskatchewan in 1936. "Canadian Committee on Canadian Museums Progress Report, 31 August 1936," 18, 7.4C Outside Activities/Organizations: Carnegie Corporation/Canadian Museum Association, box 291, file 1, NGC fonds, NGC Library and Archives.

54 Letter from Charles D. Kent, Chief Librarian, Regina Public Library, to H.O. McCurry, 21 January 1946, 5.14R Loans, Western Canada: Regina, Saskatchewan, box 120, file 1, NGC fonds, NGC Library and Archives. Interestingly, Kent had been assistant librarian at the London Public Library and Art Museum, an institution that was touted as a model community arts centre in the mid-1940s.

55 A new library building was opened in 1962 and was designed by Izumi, Arnott, and Sugiyama architects. It replaced a Carnegie-funded library opened in 1912. Joanne Havelock, "Regina Central Library: The Past and the Future," Friends of the Regina Public Library, Town Hall Meeting, 13 March 2012.

56 Ridell, *The Mackenzie Art Gallery*, 7–19.

57 Long, "The Collector and the Collection," 28–59.

58 Diehl, *A Gentleman from a Fading Age*, xv.

59 Harvie, first meeting of the Board of Governors of the Glenbow-Alberta Institute, 25 May 1966, cited in ibid., xxii.

60 Zimon, *Alberta Society of Artists*, 34.

61 Ibid., 28.

62 The Calgary Allied Arts Committee grew out of the Civic Centre Committee formed in the immediate postwar period to lobby for the inclusion of spaces for culture in Calgary's urban redevelopment plan. Similar organizations formed across the country in the wake of the House of Commons' Special Committee on Reconstruction and Re-establishment to urge the federal government to include culture in its postwar reconstruction plans. I discuss this in more detail in Chapter 3.

63 The Calgary Allied Arts Centre was located at Coste House until 1959 when it moved to the newly renovated Union Tractor Building; it remained there until 1969 when it ceased operations.

64 In 1960, Norah McCullough, western representative of the NGC, reported to Richard Simmins, director of extension at the NGC, that Coste House had created practice rooms upstairs and wondered if it would pose a fire hazard. "Report on Calgary Visit, October 13, 14, 15, 1960," uncatalogued Norah McCullough files, box 2, NGC Library and Archives.

65 Kaye, *Hiding the Audience*, 93–117.

66 The Saskatoon Art Association (previously the Saskatoon Art Club) was an artists' organization that held art classes and mounted exhibitions of its members' works. Many of its members were European immigrants to Canada such as Ernest Linder, Stanley Brunst, and Hilda Stewart who came to the city in the 1920s and 1930s with existing art training. Teitelbaum, *The Mendel Art Gallery*, 49.

67 "New Art Centre," *Saturday Night*, 17 June 1944.

68 "Coast to Coast in Art," *Canadian Art* 1, no. 5 (June–July 1944), 219.

69 *Nutana Collegiate Memorial Art Gallery*, ix.

70 Meszaros, "Visibility and Representation," 26–35.

71 "Art and the Community," Saskatoon *StarPhoenix*, 13 April 1949.

72 McInnes, "A Prairie Connoisseur of Art and Business."

73 Higonnet, *A Museum of One's Own*.

74 Duncan, *Civilizing Rituals*, 83.

75 Kaye, *Hiding the Audience*, 136. Such historicization of Calgary's cowboy past is invoked annually in the Calgary Stampede. See the essays in Foran, *Icon, Brand, Myth*.

76 Pitsula, "Saskatchewan's Path to Economic Development," 105–23.

77 An Address by the Honourable Mark Kearly on the Occasion of a Reception Marking the Twentieth Anniversary of the Founding of the AGGV, 20 October, 1964, AGGV Archives. The founders of the Little Centre were responding specifically to the efforts of the Island Arts and Crafts Society, whose exhibitions Emily Carr famously described as "affairs of tinkling teacups, tinkling conversation and little tinkling landscapes weakly executed in water colours." Carr, *The House of All Sorts*, 117.

78 For a history of the mansion and its transformation into the Art Gallery of Greater Victoria, see Taylor, *The Spencer Mansion*.

79 Virtually since its inception, the AGGV has been funded by contributions from the municipalities of Victoria, Saanich, Oak Bay, and Esquimalt, and served all communities through an extensive array of public programs.

80 Letter from A.H. Gibbard to Eric Brown, 25 July 1916, 5.14M Loans, Western Canada: Moose Jaw, SK, box 119, file 11, NGC fonds, NGC Library and Archives. The available facilities are described as follows: "We have in the Public Library two basement rooms unoccupied, each about 28 x 35 [feet], lighted semi-indirectly by electricity, that could be used for the purpose, or the assembly hall in the Collegiate Institute might be used. It might be possible to hang them in the lecture room and Reference room of the Public Library."

81 E.C. Warner to Eric Brown, 31 December 1920, 5.14M Loans, Western Canada: Medicine Hat, AB, box 119, file 9, NGC fonds, NGC Library and Archives.

82 Letter from Mrs E.S. Bolton to Secretary National Art Galleries [*sic*], 6 November 1922, 5.14B Loans, Western Canada: Brandon, MB, box 118, file 2, NGC fonds, NGC Library and Archives.

83 *Brandon Art Club Twenty-Fifth Anniversary Souvenir Booklet* [1932], Winnipeg Art Gallery Archives.

84 Letter from Mrs D.R. Doig to H.O. McCurry, 30 April 1950, 5.14B Loans, Western Canada: Brandon, MB, box 118, file 2, NGC fonds, NGC Library and Archives.

85 H.O. McCurry to L.B. Stibbs, Principal Kelowna Junior High School, 18 March 1937, 5.14K Loans, Western Canada: Kelowna, BC, box 119, file 5, NGC fonds, NGC Library and Archives.

86 The Third International Art Show catalogue, 22 to 31 May 1950, 5.14K Loans, Western Canada: Kelowna, BC, box 119, file 5, NGC fonds, NGC Library and Archives.

87 The Brandon Art Club became the Brandon Allied Arts Council in 1959 and found space for studios and exhibitions. The organization opened a permanent art gallery and studio in 1989 and renamed itself the Art Gallery of Southwestern Manitoba. The current gallery moved to the abandoned Eaton's store in the Town Centre Mall

in 2000. Art Gallery of Southwestern Manitoba, "History," accessed 31 May 2013, www.agsm.ca/history.

88 Hubbard, "A Climate for the Arts," 99.

89 This was not the intended use of the Carnegie funds, but the EMA's financial records show that they addressed chronic financial shortfalls by channelling whatever Carnegie monies were left over towards operating costs. It should be noted that the director, Maud Bowman, was rarely paid for her work and that in some years Carnegie money was used to pay her an honorarium. In 1935, for example, she received $150 for her work, and nothing in 1936. H.O. McCurry to E.H. Hill, 24 August 1936, 7.4C Outside Activities/Organizations: Carnegie Corporation, Alberta, Edmonton Museum of Arts, vol. 1, box 291, file 7, NGC fonds, NGC Library and Archives.

90 The amount was increased to $1,000 in 1953. Minutes of the Council of the Edmonton Museum of Arts, 12 May 1953, box 14, book 5 (1951–54), Edmonton Art Gallery Files, City of Edmonton Archives.

91 This is John O'Brian's argument in the wonderfully named essay "Where the Hell is Saskatchewan and Who Is Emma Lake?"

92 Excerpt of letter from W.S. Lloyd, Minister of Education to the Lieutenant Governor in Council, 3 February 1948, published in the first Annual Report of the SAB, cited in *The Saskatchewan Arts Board Collection*, 8.

93 McCullough's official title was secretary, but her role was effectively that of the director of the organization as she travelled throughout the province meeting with artists and cultural organizations, liaised with government officials, and orchestrated the SAB's dealings with other cultural organizations, such as the National Gallery and the WCAC.

94 See *The Saskatchewan Arts Board Collection*.

95 Cultural Development Act, Alberta Legislature, 1946 session, Chapter 9, cited in Kaasa, "History of the Cultural Development Branch and Division from 1946 to 1981."

96 Kelly, *For the Arts*, 17.

97 Ibid., 19.

98 "Coast to Coast in Art," 71.

99 Ostrower, *Trustees of Culture*, 24.

100 The Vancouver Art Gallery formed its Ladies Auxiliary in 1943, the Edmonton Museum of Arts' Women's Committee was established in 1944, the Art Gallery of Toronto created a Women's Committee in 1945, and both the Winnipeg Art Gallery and the Art Association of Montreal formed Women's Committees in 1948. The work of these organizations is the subject of my next research project "Beyond the Gift Shop: Volunteer Women as Guardians of Culture in North American Art Museums."

101 Scoles, "The Winnipeg Show."

102 In its first report to the membership in 1945, the Women's Committee of the Edmonton Museum of Arts reported that it had raised $500. By 1974, it was regularly

contributing upwards of $50,000 significantly increasing the gallery's ability to acquire works of art. On the role of women's committees in the acquisition of artworks for museums' permanent collections, see Logan, "Acquiring Authority at the Art Gallery of Ontario and the Agnes Etherington Art Centre" and Whitelaw, "From the Gift Shop to the Permanent Collection."

103 These photographs no longer appear to be in the collection (they have no accession number).

104 Purchase and Acceptance Committee Report, 17 June 1943, Vancouver Art Gallery Council Minutes, 12 May 1941 to 28 April 1946, VAG fonds, VAG Archives.

105 According to Sarah Stanners, Stone was the final arbiter in decisions on purchases, despite Scott's more obvious expertise. Scott's comments on the VAG president's taste underscore a cautiousness and aesthetic conservatism that would significantly affect the nature of the gallery's collection. Stanners, "Going British and Being Modern," 56.

106 "The Founder's Collection," 6.

107 In addition to her examination of the VAG, Stanners traces the acquisition of British art by the Art Gallery of Ontario and the Beaverbrook Art Gallery.

108 Stanners, "Going British and Being Modern," 70.

109 Finlay, "Identifying with Nature," 43–59.

110 "The Founders' Collection," 6.

111 This was the phrase used by council president W.H. Malkin when the bequest was announced in the gallery's 1946–47 *Annual Report*.

112 Jack Shadbolt was also a member of the board from 1946 to 1948.

113 These exhibitions would be discontinued in 1951 through a change in exhibition policy that excluded non-juried group exhibitions as well as exhibitions of existing groups or societies.

114 Shadbolt, "A Report on Art Today in British Columbia," 4.

115 The Group of Seven consistently sent their works to western Canada in the belief that such exhibitions would encourage collecting in the region. Hill, *The Group of Seven: Art for a Nation*, 29.

116 The Southam brothers were quite generous to the Edmonton Museum of Arts, donating a total of six works to the institution between 1928 and 1931.

117 Boutilier, *Inspirational*, 43–4.

118 Boutilier notes that Southam's purchase of *Landscape Under a Stormy Sky* (1888) in 1929 was the first Van Gogh to be acquired by a Canadian collector. Southam capped his acquisition of modern European art with the purchase of Picasso's *Fruit Dish* (1908–09) in 1940. Ibid., 12, 15.

119 Long, "The Collector and the Collection," 30.

120 Ibid., 39.

121 Harper, Introduction to *The Ernest E. Poole Foundation Collection*, n.p.

122 Teitelbaum, *The Mendel Art Gallery*, 9, 11.

CHAPTER 2

1 The Canadian Academy of Arts was established in 1879 with the support of Canada's governor general, the Marquis of Lorne, and held its first exhibition on 6 March 1880; the "Royal" designation was approved in July 1880. Hill, "To Found a National Gallery," 2.

2 National Gallery, London, formed in 1824; National Gallery of Scotland, Edinburgh, formed in 1859; Alte Nationalgalerie, Berlin, opened in 1874.

3 Duncan and Wallach, "The Universal Survey Museum," 449–50.

4 National Gallery of Canada, *Annual Report*, 1920–21, 7.

5 Trudel, "Aux origines du Musée des beaux-arts de Montréal," 31–62.

6 Boutilier and Maréchal, *William Brymner*.

7 Brooke, *Discerning Tastes*.

8 Jackson, *A Painter's Country*, 14–15.

9 Ottawa *Daily Free Press*, 10 March 1888, cited on the National Gallery's website, "Our History, Pre 1900s," accessed 20 May 2013, www.gallery.ca/en/about/pre-1900.php.

10 Boggs, *The National Gallery of Canada*, 5. Boggs is not completely dismissive of Taylor. She notes that in his 1890 report to the minister of public works, the curator complained about the condition of the gallery, the manner of heating, and suggested that an extension be built at the back or to the side of the Fisheries building to better accommodate the collection.

11 Ibid., 1. "The Years of Obscurity" is the title of the chapter devoted to the first years of the NGC: 1880–1907.

12 Report of the Committee of the Privy Council approved by the Governor General on 3 April 1907, excerpted in the National Gallery of Canada, *Annual Report*, 1920–21, 22.

13 For an examination of Walker's role in the arts in Canada, see Marshall, "Sir Edmund Walker, Servant of Canada." Walker also had a lengthy association with the Royal Ontario Museum. He was chair of its Board of Trustees from 1912 to his death in 1924, but his campaign to establish a natural history museum in Toronto went back to 1893 when he was a member of the University of Toronto's Board of Trustees.

14 Brown, *Breaking Barriers*, 17.

15 Canada, Department of Public Works, *Report of the Minister of Public Works … fiscal year ending 31 March 1912*, 60.

16 *National Gallery of Canada Act*, 1913.

17 Canada, Department of Public Works, *Report of the Minister of Public Works … fiscal year ending 31 March 1913*, 61.

18 An indication of how contentious the gallery's actions were perceived to be is evident in the question raised by members of Parliament about the effectiveness of the gallery's leadership and calls for the resignation of director Eric Brown. See Hill, "The National Gallery, a National Art, Critical Judgement and the State," 64–83.

19 Zemans, "Establishing the Canon," 8.

20 Eric Brown to A.H. Gibbard, Moose Jaw Public Library, 20 February 1917, 5.14M Loans, Western Canada: Moose Jaw, SK, box 119, file 11, NGC fonds, NGC Library and Archives. A subsequent letter from Gibbard to Brown notes that the postcards were on display in the library Reading Room but that the public was not interested in purchasing any. Gibbard to Brown, 15 July 1918.

21 The National Gallery of Canada, *Annual Report*, 1928–29, 15.

22 John Huff to H.O. McCurry, 13 June 1933, cited in Zemans, "Establishing the Canon," 21.

23 Zemans, "Envisioning Nation" and "Sampson-Matthews and the NGC."

24 J. Henry Standforth (Canadian Industrial Exhibition Association of Winnipeg) to Eric Brown, 5 June 1912, 5.14W Loans, Western Canada: Winnipeg, MB, box 123, file 7, NGC fonds, NGC Library and Archives; James Adam (Honorary Secretary of the Edmonton Exhibition Association) to Eric Brown, 19 March 1913, Correspondence with NGC binder 1, box 11, Edmonton Art Gallery files, City of Edmonton Archives.

25 Eric Brown to Sir Edmund Walker, 26 June 1912, 5.14W Loans, Western Canada: Winnipeg, MB, box 123, file 7, NGC fonds, NGC Library and Archives.

26 Canada, Department of Public Works, *Report of the Minister of Public Works… fiscal year ending 31 March 1914*.

27 Canada, Department of Public Works, *Report of the Minister of Public Works… fiscal year ending 31 March 1915*, 61.

28 Ibid.

29 Minutes of the 14th meeting of the Board of Trustees, 29 May 1917, 9.21B Board of Trustees – Minutes – vol. 1 (1913–1922), box 343, file 6, NGC fonds, NGC Library and Archives.

30 Buxton and Acland, *American Philanthropy and Canadian Libraries,* 3. Between 1901 and 1917, 125 libraries were built in Canada with Carnegie Corporation funding. Grants were awarded to any community willing to pledge an equivalent of 10 percent of the amount provided by Carnegie. The corporation spent a total of $2,559,660 on library buildings in Canada, mostly in Ontario. No Carnegie libraries were built in the province of Quebec. Even in towns, such as Moose Jaw, where Carnegie funding was not obtained, a stone edifice had been erected as a library. In its initial correspondence with the National Gallery concerning a loan, Moose Jaw's chief librarian, A.H. Gibbard, sent a photograph of the exterior of the public library to demonstrate the fireproof quality of the building (see Fig. 1.15).

31 National Gallery of Canada, *Annual Report*, 1935–36, 7.

32 National Gallery of Canada, *Annual Report*, 1934–35, 8.

33 Eric Brown to A.H. Gibbard, Moose Jaw Public Library, 14 November 1919, 5.14M Loans, Western Canada: Moose Jaw, SK, box 119, file 11, NGC fonds, NGC Library and Archives.

34 The 1920–21 *Annual Report* of the National Gallery describes the rearrangement of the galleries: a sculpture court added on the ground floor of the east wing of

the building, and the second, third, and fourth floors organized in order to create fifteen galleries for paintings and prints. The east wing was also separated from the rest of the museum building through the addition of fireproof partitions that had the extra benefit of enabling the gallery to control the heating and ventilation of its rooms. A new entrance was also planned for the gallery on Elgin Street to further distinguish it from the National Museum next door. National Gallery of Canada, *Annual Report*, 1920–21, 11.

35 The 1922–23 *Annual Report* summarizes the situation: "These loans entail a very large amount of work at the National Gallery before they can be despatched [*sic*]. The wear and tear on frames necessitates constant overhauling and a considerable amount of actual replacement. The extremely variable climate and the far from perfect handling by railways and individuals necessitates equally incessant and expert attention to the pictures themselves" (21).

36 Eric Brown to A.H. Gibbard, Moose Jaw Library, 26 March 1925, 5.14M Loans, Western Canada: Moose Jaw, SK, box 119, file 11, NGC fonds, NGC Library and Archives.

37 National Gallery of Canada, *Annual Report*, 1927–28, 18–19.

38 National Gallery of Canada, *Annual Report*, 1930–31, 11.

39 National Gallery of Canada, *Annual Report*, 1920–21, 10. It should be understood that "native" refers here to "Canadian" rather than Indigenous art.

40 Report from H.O. McCurry to Eric Brown [1922], 9.9R Reports (by H.O. McCurry) Travel Meetings (Miscellaneous Correspondence), box 355, file 2, NGC fonds, NGC Library and Archives.

41 After MacKenzie's death in 1936, Robert Newton, president of the University of Alberta, was the next western Canadian representative on the Board of Trustees, serving from 1947 to 1953. The region's representation was expanded with the appointment of Vancouver-based Lawren Harris in 1950, Winnipeg-based John A. MacAulay in 1951, and Edmonton-based Dorothy (Bobby) Dyde in 1952.

42 Minutes of the 41st meeting of the Board of Trustees, 2 July 1927, 9.21B Board of Trustees – Minutes – vol. 2 (1923–1932), box 343, file 7, NGC fonds, NGC Library and Archives.

43 "Ottawa Official's Visit Cheers Lovers of Art," *The Edmonton Journal*, 28 October 1931.

44 "National Gallery Achieves Importance In Half a Century," *The Edmonton Journal*, 20 September 1930.

45 "More Space for Art Museum," *The Edmonton Journal*, 17 February 1931.

46 Paikowsky, "'From Away'"; McTavish, *Defining the Modern Museum*.

47 T.W. Fripp Letter to the Editor, *The Vancouver Sun*, 11 February 1930, 1, cited in Thom, *The Fine Arts in Vancouver*, 153.

48 H.O. McCurry, "Report on Western Trip August 18th to September 24th 1930," 3. Appended to Minutes of the 48th meeting of the Board of Trustees, National Gallery of Canada, 3 July 1930, 9.21B Board of Trustees – Minutes – vol. 2 (1923–1932), box 343, file 7, NGC fonds, NGC Library and Archives.

49 Minutes of the 48th meeting of the Board of Trustees, National Gallery of Canada, 3 July 1930.

50 W.G. Constable, *Report on the National Gallery of Canada*, 1931, 36, 9.9R Correspondence, Misc. box 355, file 4, NGC fonds, NGC Library and Archives.

51 Dawn, *National Visions, National Blindness*, 55–115.

52 National Gallery of Canada, *Annual Report*, 1926–27, 9.

53 National Gallery of Canada, *Annual Report*, 1930–31, 9.

54 Minutes of the 46th meeting Board of Trustees, National Gallery of Canada, 29 May 1929, 9.21B Board of Trustees – Minutes – vol. 2 (1923–32), box 343, file 7, NGC fonds, NGC Library and Archives.

55 National Gallery of Canada. *Annual Report*, 1930–31, 11.

56 Ibid., 12.

57 Cholette, "The Beleaguered Biennials," 23. *The Annual Exhibition of Canadian Painting* became a biennial exhibition in 1955 with the idea that the greater time lag between exhibitions would allow for an increased choice of works and the time to produce an illustrated catalogue.

58 From an original amount of $100,000 in 1913, the government's annual appropriation to the National Gallery fell to $20,000 in 1920–21, was back to $100,000 in 1923–24, fell to between $30,000 and $40,000 during the Depression and the war years, and then rose again to $295,977 by 1951 when the passing of a new National Gallery Act established a separate purchase account (over $100,000 in 1951) and moved responsibility for the gallery to the Department of Citizenship and Immigration. The National Gallery of Canada, *Annual Report*, 1951–52, 33. The purchase account amount of $100,000 is worth almost $905,000 in 2014 dollars; in comparison, parliamentary appropriations to the NGC in 2013–14 totalled $47.2 million of which $8 million was allocated to acquisitions. NGC, *National Gallery Summary of Corporate Plan for 2014–15 to 2018–19*.

59 Alicia Boutilier examines this relationship in *Inspirational: The Collection of H.S. Southam*.

60 The details of Carnegie and Rockefeller support to higher education in Canada can be found in Brison, *Rockefeller, Carnegie and Canada*, and Buxton and Acland, *American Philanthropy and Canadian Libraries*.

61 Brison, *Rockefeller, Carnegie, and Canada*, 28.

62 Ibid., 123. The survey was supervised by Richard F. Bach, then associate in industrial arts and later to become dean of education and extension of the Metropolitan Museum of Art in New York City.

63 Anderson, Introduction to *Carnegie Corporation: Program in the Arts 1911–1967*, 3.

64 Panayotidis, "The Department of Fine Art at the University of Toronto, 1926–1945"; Reichwein, "Holiday at the Banff School of Fine Arts."

65 Paikowsky, "'From Away,'" 42.

66 Jubin, *Carnegie Corporation: Program in the Arts 1911–1967*, 36–7.

67 Countries covered within this survey include Sri Lanka (Ceylon), Federated Malay States, Straits Settlement, West Indies, Bermuda, Guyana, Hong Kong, Fiji, British North Borneo, and Malaysia.

68 Miers and Markham, *A Report on the Museums of Canada to the Carnegie Corporation of New York*, 30. The report follows these statistics with the statement that funding of museums in London and New York total over $5 million each and that the annual budgets of both the British Museum and the Field Museum in Chicago is double the total amount of money spent on museums and galleries in Canada.

69 Ibid., 18.

70 Ibid., 3: "Comparatively little has been done by the provincial governments or the municipalities to provide a museum service, and in the matter of art the three provinces are even worse provided."

71 McCurry to Keppel, 25 April 1931, 7.4C Outside Activities/Organizations: Carnegie Corporation – General file 1, box 290, file 1, NGC fonds, NGC Library and Archives.

72 Brown to Keppel (undated – likely May 1932) quoting excerpts from Lismer's report of his tour, 7.4C Outside Activities/Organizations: Carnegie Corporation – General file 1, box 290, file 1, NGC fonds, NGC Library and Archives.

73 As Brison notes, the two major cultural institutions in Toronto (the Art Gallery of Toronto and the Royal Ontario Museum) were shut out of the committee despite intense lobbying on the parts of Massey and Webster to appoint W.T. Currelly and Dymond Jenness. McCurry's initial selection of Massey to serve on the CMC was the result of the latter's membership on the board of directors of both the AGT and the Royal Ontario Museum, which McCurry felt recognized the status of those institutions while failing to place any undue competition on the stature of the National Gallery. Brison, *Rockefeller, Carnegie and Canada*, 127–8.

74 Ibid., 125.

75 Keppel to Massey, 12 June 1934, 7.4C Outside Activities/Organizations: Carnegie Corporation – General file 1, box 298, file 1, NGC fonds, NGC Library and Archives.

76 Paikowsky, "'From Away,'" 55–8.

77 The following excerpt of a letter from Bowman to McCurry, dated 9 July 1938, indicates the nature of much of the correspondence between the two: "It is practically impossible for us to carry on without some outside help and I will do anything to help get it. The work here is shaping up and more people are interested than ever before. We feel that we cannot afford to drop the educational work. We can keep the Gallery open and have special exhibitions but the other needs some help. I have every confidence in what you say and will gladly be guided by what you suggest. Please do not think I mean to be a bother, but really I do not know what to do for the best." 7.4C Outside Activities/Organizations: Carnegie Corporation, Alberta, Edmonton Museum of Arts, vol. 1, box 291, file 7, NGC fonds, NGC Library and Archives.

78 McCurry to Bowman, 9 July 1936, 7.4C Outside Activities/Organizations: Carnegie Corporation, Alberta, Edmonton Museum of Arts, vol. 1, box 291, file 7, NGC fonds, NGC Library and Archives.

79 *Progress Report on Educational Activities Supported by the Carnegie Corporation*, National Gallery of Canada, 14 April 1945, 7.4C Outside Activities/Organizations: Carnegie Corporation, Canadian Museum Association, vol. 1, box 291, file 1, NGC fonds, NGC Library and Archives.

80 R.W. Hedley to H.O. McCurry, 28 July 1943, 7.4C Outside Activities/Organizations: Carnegie Corporation, Alberta, Edmonton Museum of Arts, vol. 1, box 291, file 7, NGC fonds, NGC Library and Archives.

81 Jasen, "Mind, Medicine, and the Christian Science Controversy in Canada, 1888–1910," 11.

82 Douglas Ord has examined the importance of Eric Brown's adherence to Christian Science on his work at the National Gallery. Ord's focus on the National Gallery precludes a broader investigation of the national and international networks that Christian Science might have enabled. This is in distinct contrast to the research undertaken on the impact of theosophy on artists in Canada. Ord, *The National Gallery of Canada.*

CHAPTER 3

1 The Law Reform Commission of Canada wrote in 1977, "it is significant that much of the history of Canada could be interpreted through the work of commissions of inquiry." *Commissions of Inquiry* (Ottawa: Minister of Supply and Services Canada, 1977), 11, cited in Bradford, "Writing Public Philosophy," 137. In 1995, Jody Berland stated, "It would not be stretching the truth very far to say that the first texts in Canadian cultural studies were written by royal commissions." "Marginal Notes on Cultural Studies in Canada," 515.

2 Bradford, "Writing Public Philosophy," 136.

3 Tippett, *Making Culture: English-Canadian Institutions and the Arts before the Massey Commission.*

4 Berland, "Nationalism and the Modernist Legacy"; Dowler, "The Cultural Industry Policy Apparatus"; Druick, "International Cultural Relations as a Factor in Postwar Cultural Policy."

5 Canada, Federal Cultural Policy Review Committee, *Report of the Federal Cultural Policy Review Committee.*

6 Canada, Royal Commission on National Development in the Arts, Letters and Sciences, *Report*, 271.

7 Boutilier, *A Vital Force: The Canadian Group of Painters.*

8 McKay, "Canadian Political Art in the 1930s," and Carney, "Modern Art, the Local, and the Global, c. 1930–1950."

9 Catherine Mastin argues that despite most Group of Seven members painting scenes of western Canada, these works were rarely exhibited in the west, so collectors in the region tended to buy paintings with Algoma and Georgian Bay subjects. Mastin, "East Views West: Group Artists in the Rocky Mountains," 61. On the reproduction programs of the National Gallery, see Zemans, "Establishing the Canon."

10 Sicotte, "À Kingston, il y a 50 ans, la conférence des artistes Canadiens."

11 Nurse, "Artists, Society, and Activism."

12 The Wartime Information Board would not get off the ground until September 1942, by which time Cloutier was no longer affiliated with the program. Documentary filmmaker and founding head of the National Film Board, John Grierson, was named the Wartime Information Board's general manager. Potter, *Branding Canada*, 79–81.

13 See Bell, "The Welfare of Art in Canada," v, for more on the series of conferences on Canadian–American affairs held on alternate years at Queen's University.

14 Hudson, "Art and Social Progress: The Toronto Community of Painters," 108. Hudson specifically states that the Carnegie's establishment of the Chair in Fine Arts at the University of Toronto was the result of being assured that the first holder of the position, John Alford, supported Carnegie's humanistic views. Alford was one of the invited speakers to the Kingston Conference and his speech was reprinted in the October/November 1941 issue of *Maritime Art*.

15 Wallace had been the principal of the University of Alberta between 1928 and 1936 and was at the helm of Queen's University from 1936 to 1951. He was also a member of the Canadian Museums Committee.

16 Frances Smith notes that there was a considerable amount of correspondence between Biéler and Keppel, between Biéler and Wallace, as well as between the National Gallery's McCurry and both Keppel and Wallace, suggesting that the Corporation wanted to maintain as much control as possible over the event. Such involvement evolved easily out of the Carnegie's existing influence through the Canadian Museums Committee, which also had Wallace on its board, as well as its sponsorship of other cultural initiatives in Canada, including the establishment of the Banff School of Fine Arts; programs at both Queen's University and the University of Alberta during Wallace's time as president; and Walter Abell's tenure as professor of fine art at Acadia University. Smith, *André Biéler*, 179–213.

17 Brison, "The Kingston Conference, the Carnegie Corporation and a New Deal for the Arts in Canada," 505.

18 Smith, *André Biéler*, 179.

19 *Kingston Conference Proceedings*, 5.

20 Bell, "The Welfare of Art in Canada"; Nurse, "'A Confusion of Values'"; Niergarth, "'Missionary for Culture.'"

21 *Kingston Conference Proceedings*, 14.

22 Ibid., 16.

23 Ibid.

24 Ibid., 17.

25 The motion initially was addressed to McGill only but was subsequently amended to include all Canadian universities. *Kingston Conference Proceedings*, 111–12.

26 Ibid., 104.

27 Ibid., 106.

28 Abell, "Conference of Canadian Artists," 3.

29 F.B. Taylor to Lawren Harris, 21 July 1944, Federation of Canadian Artists papers, Queen's University Archives.

30 As part of the terms of this sponsorship, a copy of *Canadian Art* was sent to all FCA members, continuing a practice established in late 1942 by *Maritime Art*. In an editorial praising the "cooperative arrangement" between *Maritime Art* and the FCA, Walter Abell informed readers that it would "bring the magazine additional readers and resources, assisting us to improve our pages and thus benefitting all our readers. It will provide Federation members with a Canadian art magazine, at the same time extending the message of the Federation beyond its own membership. We trust that in the course of time other such cooperative links may develop to unite for common purposes all those who have at heart the welfare of art in Canada." Abell, "Cooperation or Conflict?," 35–6.

31 Lawren Harris to the membership of the FCA, undated [summer 1945], Federation of Canadian Artists Papers, Queen's University Archives.

32 Lawren Harris to members of the Saskatoon Art Association, 11 February 1945, Federation of Canadian Artists papers, Queen's University Archives.

33 Nurse, "Artists, Society and Activism," 8.

34 For a detailed discussion of the war petition, see Nurse, "Artists, Society and Activism," 9–11.

35 Harris, "The Function of an Art Gallery"; Harris, "The Federation, the National Gallery and a New Society."

36 Kuffert, *A Great Duty*, 69.

37 Dorise Nielson cited in Wood, "A National Program for the Arts in Canada," 93.

38 See, for example, "Through similar government encouragement Canada, with her vast natural resources, could achieve a proud culture as well as a unique world position in industrial development and export." "Brief Concerning the Cultural Aspects of Canadian Reconstruction" [hereafter "Artists' Brief"], 3, 7.4R Outside Activities/ Organizations: Reconstruction and Re-establishment, Cultural Aspects of (file 1), box 20, file 1 (Outside Activities/Organizations), NGC fonds, NGC Library and Archives.

39 Ibid., 5.

40 Wood's essay called for the inclusion of the arts in all future urban planning; the encouragement of handicraft cooperatives and the stimulation of original design in industry; the establishment of a national theatre; extension of the King's Printer's services to make available the many musical and literary works lying unpublished; and increasing the dissemination of all cultural works through appropriate channels.

41 Wood, "A National Program for the Arts," 127.

42 "Artists' Brief," 7.

43 Ibid., 5.

44 Harris, "The Federation, the National Gallery, and a New Society," 126.

45 Ibid., 126, 127.

46 Harris writes, "We need centralization only for purposes of assembly and distribution. The need now is for the National Gallery to make itself more and more into an efficient distributing agency for works of art of all kinds, from various crafts, prints and posters to the finest pictures it possesses, and a distributing centre of educational material and personnel and an administrator of as many small branch galleries and exhibition rooms as possible from the Atlantic to the Pacific. In this way, it can greatly increase its service to the Canadian people, but only in this way." Ibid., 127.

47 Harris, "Reconstruction through the Arts," 186.

48 Taylor to Harris, 21 July 1944, Federation of Canadian Artists papers, box 1, Queen's University Archives.

49 Harris, "Reconstruction through the Arts," 186.

50 See, for example, the following statement from the brief: "Central Institutions and Services [sic] which function throughout the whole fabric of Canadian cultural life should have greatly expanded facilities, and new institutions should be initiated for services not now available." "Artists' Brief," 8.

51 Elizabeth Wyn Wood discusses the process of writing the brief and getting it in front of the committee in "Art Goes to Parliament," 41–2.

52 William Arthur Deacon, "The Arts in Canada Speak out before Parliamentary Committee," *Globe and Mail*, 24 June 1944.

53 Qtd. in "An Acorn on Parliament Hill," 17.

54 Qtd. in "Regional Support Promised for Community Art Centres," 39.

55 Statement from the Winnipeg Art Gallery Association, qtd. in ibid., my emphasis.

56 Cited in "An Acorn on Parliament Hill," 16.

57 Minutes of the Council of the Edmonton Museum of Arts, 4 April 1946, box 14, book 3 (1942–1947), Edmonton Art Gallery Files, City of Edmonton Archives.

58 Minutes of the Council of the Edmonton Museum of Arts, 11 February 1947, box 14, book 3 (1942–1947), Edmonton Art Gallery Files, City of Edmonton Archives.

59 Report of the Director, Minutes of the Council of the Edmonton Museum of Arts, 8 February 1947, box 14, book 3 (1942–1947), Edmonton Art Gallery files, City of Edmonton Archives.

60 MacGregor, *Edmonton*, 283.

61 While he was in London, Hedley participated in a conference with curators from Windsor, Ingersoll, and London to discuss the creation of an art circuit much like the Western Canada Art Circuit, which Hedley had established a year earlier. See Chapter 4.

62 R.W. Hedley, "Report on the Trip to Ottawa, Montreal, Toronto, London and Chicago Art Galleries," Minutes of the Council of the Edmonton Museum of Arts, 9 October 1945, 5, box 14, book 3, Edmonton Art Gallery files, City of Edmonton Archives.

63 Crouch, "A Community Art Centre in Action," 22–8.

64 National Gallery of Canada, *Annual Report*, 1943–44, 5.

65 Heath, *Uprooted: The Art and Life of Ernest Lindner*, 70–81.

66 The editors of *Canadian Art* emphasized the usefulness of the Junior League, arguing that "their co-operation would be invaluable to any group setting out to pave the way for implementation of the program suggested to the government in the artists' brief." "Community Art Centres: A Growing Movement," 63.

67 Jackson, *The Junior League*, 102.

68 Community Arts Council of Vancouver, *Brief to the Royal Commission on National Development in the Arts, Letters and Sciences*.

69 Canada, Royal Commission on Dominion-Provincial Relations (Ottawa, 1940), 2:80, cited in Smiley, "The Rowell-Sirois Report, Provincial Autonomy, and Post-War Canadian Federalism," 55.

70 From the Order in Council, PC 1786, 8 April 1949, reprinted in Canada, Royal Commission on National Development in the Arts, Letters and Sciences, *Report*, xii.

71 Although the commission was officially tasked with examining "national development in the arts, letters and sciences," in both the briefs presented to the commissioners and in the report itself, the arts and letters – i.e., culture – received much more attention than the sciences, which were arguably already well served through the National Research Council, in place since 1916. In press coverage and in general parlance, the commission was often referred to as the "culture commission."

72 These were the terms *The Canadian Forum* stated were used to describe the groups who presented briefs to the commission. "Fine Arts in the West," 1.

73 Dowler, "The Cultural Industries Policy Apparatus," 337.

74 "Unwanted" is the key phrase here: as many writers have noted, American culture was perfectly acceptable to the commissioners (and indeed many of the organizations who presented briefs) if it was considered suitable. Radio broadcasts from the Metropolitan Opera, for example, were viewed as valuable American imports, where soap operas were not. See Charland, "Technological Nationalism."

75 Canada, Royal Commission on National Development in the Arts, Letters and Sciences, *Report*, 15–16. This section continues this line of argument with the statement, "But for American hospitality we might, in Canada, have been led to develop educational ideas and practices more in keeping with our way of life."

76 The report's emphasis on geography was picked up by many critics at the time; see Eggleston, "Canadian Geography and National Culture."

77 Canada, Royal Commission on National Development in the Arts, Letters and Sciences, *Report*, 11–12.

78 Friesen, "Space and Region in Canadian History," 20.

79 Litt, *The Muses, the Masses, and the Massey Commission*.

80 Canada, Royal Commission on National Development in the Arts, Letters and Sciences, *Report*, 77.

81 Ibid., 83.

82 See, for example, the concluding statement of report's chapter on galleries: "In all our dealings with local galleries we were much impressed by the enthusiasm with

which they were operating under very difficult conditions, and by their determination to increase and develop their activities ... The many helpful suggestions and criticism offered are evidence of the keen interest which has been developed in painting and the related arts through the joint efforts of the National and the local galleries" (86).

83 Ibid.

84 Saskatoon Archaeological Society, "Brief" cited in ibid., 12.

85 "A Good Museum for Every City," *The Edmonton Journal*, c. February 1949, Edmonton Art Gallery Newspaper Clippings (1925–1954) file, Edmonton Art Gallery files, Edmonton City Archives.

86 "National Gallery Service Scored," *Calgary Herald*, 2 November 1949.

87 Brief of the Regina Art Association, Incorporated, to the Royal Commission on National Development in the Arts, Letters and Sciences, 5.

88 "National Gallery Service Scored," *Calgary Herald*, 2 November 1949.

89 While the Canadian Museums Committee, discussed in Chapter 2 and directed by H.O. McCurry, identified which art museums should receive funding for their art education activities, the funding came from the Carnegie Corporation.

90 Andrew, "The Canada Council," 297.

91 Canada Council, *Annual Report*, 1958–59, 17.

92 In 1958–59 purchase awards were awarded to the Vancouver Art Gallery, which used the funds to purchase works by Harold Town, Tony Urquhart, and Herbert Gilbert; to the Winnipeg Art Gallery for the purchase of paintings by Jacques de Tonnancour, Alistair Bell, Don Jarvis, George Swinton, Harold Town, John Hatcher, and Kelly Clark; and to the Art Gallery of Toronto to acquire works by Albert Jacques Franck, Peter Haworth, J.W.G. Macdonald, and Doris McCarthy. Awards to the London Public Library and Art Museum, the Montreal Museum of Fine Arts, and the Art Gallery of Greater Victoria were to follow. Canada Council, *Annual Report*, 1958–59, 22.

93 Canada Council, *Annual Report*, 1959–60, 19.

94 Peter Dwyer, "Some Present Problems of Subsidy," an address to the delegates to Seminar '65, 20 January 1965, published in the *Annual Report* of the Canada Council, 1964–65, 91.

95 Canada Council, *Annual Report*, 1966–67, 19.

CHAPTER 4

1 The gallery at Regina College was little more than a series of rooms holding Norman MacKenzie's 1936 bequest of paintings and funds for a new gallery. The Norman MacKenzie Art Gallery opened in 1953 in a new building that also housed the college's art department. Librarian Marjorie Dunlop devoted exhibition space in the Regina Public Library in 1948, eventually establishing a gallery in the new Regina Public Library building erected in the late 1950s.

2 "Constitution of Western Art Gallery Committee" (n.d., c. 3 June 1944), 5.14W Loans, Western Canada: Western Canada Art Circuit, vol. 1, box 122, file 11, NGC fonds, NGC Library and Archives.

3 "Suggested Agenda for Conference June 3rd, 1944. At Edmonton," 5.14E Loans, Western Canada: Edmonton Museum of Arts, vol. 3, box 119, file 1, NGC fonds, NGC Library and Archives.

4 The National Gallery's *Annual Report* of 1942–43 notes, "The services of the National Gallery to other parts of Canada have been widely recognized by art authorities as being unique. Nowhere else in the world has a national art institution developed such a widespread and effective system of loan exhibitions, lectures and other means of supporting new and growing galleries and associations" (9).

5 Letter from McCurry to Hedley, 30 April 1945, 5.14W Loans, Western Canada: Western Canada Art Circuit (1945–47), box 122, file 11, NGC fonds, NGC Library and Archives.

6 Paikowsky, "'From Away,'" 36–72.

7 Maritime Art Association constitution, cited in Paikowsky, "'From Away,'" 50.

8 For a full list of member organizations, see Brayley, "A Regional Agency," 23.

9 McCurry to Abell, 2 November 1934, quoted in Paikowsky, "'From Away,'" 50.

10 Walter Abell to H.O. McCurry, 23 September 1935, quoted in Brayley, "A Regional Agency," 51. Other members of the Maritime Art Association would write the commentaries for exhibitions, including Elizabeth McLeod, head of the Art School at Mount Allison University, and Saint John artist Lillian Clarke.

11 Maritime Art Association website, Gail and Stephen A. Jarislowsky Institute for Studies in Canadian Art, Concordia University, accessed 25 September 2015, maa.concordia.ca.

12 Paikowsky, "'From Away,'" 52.

13 The list of exhibitions available to circuit members in 1949–50 was attached to the WCAC's brief to the Massey Commission.

14 The members of the WCAC in 1949 were the Winnipeg Art Gallery, the Brandon Art Association, the Regina Public Library, the Saskatoon Art Centre, the Moose Jaw Public Library, Prince Albert City Hall (under the auspices of the Federation of Canadian Artists), Coste House (Calgary Allied Arts Centre), the Edmonton Museum of Arts, the University of Alberta, the Medicine Hat Art Association, the Nelson (BC) Art Association, the Vancouver Art Gallery, the University of British Columbia Art Gallery, the Victoria Arts Centre, and the Kimberley Art Association.

15 "Western Canada Art Circuit – Classification of Galleries and Centres," c. 1953, 5.14W Loans, Western Canada: Western Canada Art Circuit, vol. 4, box 122, file 14, NGC fonds, NGC Library and Archives.

16 Letter from Hedley to McCurry, 11 July 1947, 5.14W Loans, Western Canada: Western Canada Art Circuit (1945–47), box 122, file 11, NGC fonds, NGC Library and Archives.

17 A.Y. Jackson to H.O. McCurry, 30 August 1947 (excerpt), 5.14W Loans, Western Canada: Western Canada Art Circuit (1945–47), box 122, file 11, NGC fonds, NGC Library and Archives.

18 "Rules Regarding the Art Exhibition from the Four Western Provinces to Travel Throughout Eastern Canada" (n.d., c. 1945), 5.14E Loans, Western Canada: Edmonton Museum of Arts, vol. 3, box 119, file 1, NGC fonds, NGC Library and Archives.

19 I have found no evidence that this exhibition came to fruition.

20 Jerrold Morris to A.F. Key, 23 March 1950, 5.14W Loans, Western Canada: Western Canada Art Circuit (1950–51), box 122, file 13, NGC fonds, NGC Library and Archives.

21 See Western Ontario Regional Circuit file (list of members and exhibitions, 1958–59), 5.13W Loans, Ontario, box 117, file 5, NGC fonds, NGC Library and Archives.

22 See 5.13N Northern Ontario Art Association, Loans, Ontario, box 110, file 17, NGC fonds, NGC Library and Archives. In 1957, its members were the Noranda Art Guild, the Kapuskasing Art Club, the Porcupine Art Club (Timmins), the Kirkland Lake Arts Club, the New Liskeard Art Club, the Haileybury Art Club, the North Bay Arts and Letters Club, the Algoma Art Club (Sault Ste Marie), the Blind River Art Club, the Parry Sound Art Club, the Burkes Falls Art Club, and the Huntsville Art Club. The Northern Ontario Art Association is still in existence and continues to promote the fine arts to communities in Northern Ontario.

23 "The Regina Conference: A Meeting of the Art Exhibiting Centres and Circulating Agencies of Western Canada at the Norman Mackenzie Art Gallery, Regina, 12 and 13 April 1958," (Report), 10, 7.4R Outside Activities/Organizations: Regina Conference, box 325, file 1, NGC fonds, NGC Library and Archives.

24 Pearse to Jarvis (undated, summer 1956), 7.4V Vancouver Conference (1956), Outside Activities/Organizations, box 325, file 3, NGC fonds, NGC Library and Archives.

25 Chaired by Hamilton S. Southam, the National Gallery's Board of Trustees in 1952 consisted of Jean Chauvin (Montreal), Dorothy (Bobby) Dyde (Edmonton), Charles P. Fell (Toronto), Ross Flemington (Sackville), Lawren Harris (Vancouver), John A. MacAulay (Winnipeg), Cleveland Morgan (Montreal), and Jean Raymond (Montreal).

26 Cholette, "The Beleaguered Biennials." Annual exhibitions of contemporary Canadian art were held between 1926 and 1933; the practice was re-established in 1953 but changed to a biannual format in 1955 until 1967. The National Gallery regularly purchased works from these juried exhibitions for their permanent collection.

27 Limbos-Bomberg, "The Ideal and the Pragmatic," 37–65. Limbos-Bomberg examines in detail the debate between Harris and McCurry over how to determine the number of artists from each region, as well as the composition of the regional juries. She records the final distribution of works as follows: Maritime provinces, 11; Quebec, 16; Ontario, 18; Prairie provinces, 16; British Columbia, 16.

28 Minutes, 77th meeting of Board of Trustees, 15–16 October 1952, 4.4B Board of Trustees – Minutes – vol. 4 (1950–52), box 343, file 9, NGC fonds, NGC Library and Archives.

29 Letter from Harris to McCurry, 23 January 1953, 9.2H NGC – Trustees, Harris, Lawren (vol. 2) (1953–58), box 339, file 4, NGC fonds, NGC Library and Archives.

30 Minutes, Annual Meeting of the Western Canada Art Circuit, 21–22 May 1949, 5.14W Loans, Western Canada: vol. 2, box 122, file 12, NGC fonds, NGC Library and Archives.

31 J.K.B. Robertson, Memorandum for Mr McCurry, 19 July 1949, 5.14W Loans, Western Canada: Western Canada Art Circuit, vol. 2, box 122, file 12, NGC fonds, NGC Library and Archives.

32 Elaborating on the WCAC's brief to the Massey Commission, Key argued that the exhibitions sent to western Canada were often of poor quality and badly packed. Western Canada Art Circuit, "Brief Submitted to Vancouver Meeting – August 15–18, 1956," 3, 7.4V Outside Activities/Organizations: Vancouver Conference (1956), box 329, file 4, NGC fonds, NGC Library and Archives.

33 Horrall, *Bringing Art to Life*.

34 Letter of invitation sent to delegate to the Vancouver Conference, March 1956, 7.4V Outside Activities/Organizations: Vancouver Conference (1956), box 329, file 4, NGC fonds, NGC Library and Archives.

35 There was some disagreement over how the appointments would be made and the number of regional directors. Clare Bice of the London Regional Art Gallery, for example, suggested that an artist could be hired and paid $4,000 a year for three-quarters-time work; the remainder of the time being available for his [*sic*] art practice. Minutes/Transcript, "The National Gallery Conference, Vancouver BC," 21, 7.4V Outside Activities/Organizations: Vancouver Conference (1956), box 329, file 4, NGC fonds, NGC Library and Archives.

36 Untitled brief attached to letter from A.F. Key to Alan Jarvis, 5 May 1955, 5.14W Loans, Western Canada: Western Canada Art Circuit, vol. 6, box 123, file 1, NGC fonds, NGC Library and Archives.

37 Ibid.

38 Letter from Binning to Jarvis, 14 May 1956, 7.4V Outside Activities/Organizations: Vancouver Conference (1956), box 329, file 1, NGC fonds, NGC Library and Archives.

39 Minutes/Transcript, "The National Gallery Conference, Vancouver BC," 3, 7.4V Outside Activities/Organizations: Vancouver Conference (1956), box 329, file 4, NGC fonds, NGC Library and Archives.

40 Ibid., 2.

41 McCullough files, NGC Library and Archives.

42 National Gallery of Canada. *Annual Report*, 1956–57, 36.

43 McCullough, "A Living Art," 375.

44 McCullough remarks that there are approximately eighty-five institutions in Canada where exhibitions are shown, including universities, libraries, and art clubs as well as "galleries proper." Ibid., 376.

45 Ibid., 375.

46 I use the term "erstwhile" as the 1957 meeting of the WCAC ended in some disarray and no board was officially elected. Key had been director up to that point and

despite numerous pleas to the membership that he be relieved of his duties, he retained the title of circuit director and continued to advocate on the circuit's behalf from that position.

47 Simmins to McCullough, 13 March 1958, 7.4R Outside Activities/Organizations: Regina Conference (1958), box 325, file 1, NGC fonds, NGC Library and Archives.

48 Ibid.

49 Jarvis to Binning, 16 May 1956, 7.4V Outside Activities/Organizations: Vancouver Conference (1956), box 329, file 4, NGC fonds, NGC Library and Archives.

50 The institutions represented at the conference were the Kelowna Art Exhibits Association, the Vernon Art Association, the Prince Rupert Art Club, the Vancouver Art Gallery, the Kitimat Art Association, the Art Gallery of the University of British Columbia, the Vancouver Community Arts Council, the Okanagan Regional Library, the Western Canada Art Circuit, Coste House, the Provincial Institute of Technology and Art (Calgary), the Calgary Allied Arts Council, the Cultural Branch of the Province of Alberta, the Community Art Club Medicine Hat, the Lethbridge Allied Arts Council, the Department of Art of the University of Alberta, the Edmonton Art Gallery, the North Central Saskatchewan Regional Library (Prince Albert), the University of Saskatchewan Library, the Department of Art of the University of Saskatchewan, the Regina Public Library, the Norman MacKenzie Art Gallery, the Saskatoon Art Centre, the Saskatchewan Arts Board, the School of Art University of Manitoba, the School of Architecture University of Manitoba, the Brandon Art Club, and the Winnipeg Art Gallery.

51 This is the long title given to the Minutes of the Regina Conference. 7.4R Outside Activities/Organizations: Regina Conference 1958, box 325, file 1, NGC fonds, NGC Library and Archives.

52 In other words, the Southern Ontario Art Association, consisting of the art galleries in London, Windsor, and Hamilton, and Hart House in Toronto.

53 All quotes and information taken from the Minutes of the Regina Conference. 7.4R Outside Activities/Organizations: Regina Conference 1958, box 325, file 1, NGC fonds, NGC Library and Archives.

54 Ibid., 2.

55 Ibid., 41.

56 Ibid., 51.

57 Minutes of the Regina Conference, 58, 7.4R Outside Activities/Organizations: Regina Conference 1958, box 325, file 1, NGC fonds, NGC Library and Archives. The exhibition was *Some Contemporary Painters of Quebec.*

CHAPTER 5

1 Letter from Sir Kenneth Clark to C.P. Fell, 3 November 1954, cited in Horrall, *Bringing Art to Life,* 236.

2 The controversy relates to Jarvis's commitment to purchase two paintings from the Prince of Lichtenstein without the approval of Treasury Board, based on previous

purchases made by McCurry. These events are chronicled in Horrall, *Bringing Art to Life*, 282–98, and Ord, *The National Gallery of Canada*, 157–70.

3 "H.O. McCurry, Servant of the Arts," 118–22. In 1944, Frederick Taylor of the Federation of Canadian Artists characterized McCurry as "first and always a civil servant" in a letter to Lawren Harris. Taylor to Harris, 21 July 1944, FCA Papers.

4 Bennett, *The Birth of the Museum*, 17–57.

5 Hirzy, "The AAM after 72 Years," 44–8.

6 Minutes, Annual General Meeting of the Winnipeg Art Gallery Association, 15 March 1950, Board of Governors, Bound Records, Minute Series, MB 2.10, Winnipeg Art Gallery/Winnipeg Art Gallery Association fonds, Winnipeg Art Gallery Archives.

7 Teather, "The Museum Keepers," 33.

8 In 1930, the NGC's Board of Trustees proposed Constable along with Sir Campbell Stuart, KBE and Robert Wallace (president of the University of Alberta) to form a committee of experts to advise the National Gallery. Stuart declined the offer and the decision was made to shelve the committee idea and to instead have Constable undertake an unofficial survey of the National Gallery's activities when he was next in Canada, in the summer of 1931. Minutes of the 49th meeting of the Board of Trustees, 31 October 1930, 9.21B Board of Trustees – Minutes – vol. 2 (1923–32), box 343, file 7, NGC fonds, NGC Library and Archives.

9 "Canadian Committee on Canadian Museums, Progress Report," 31 August 1936, 15, 7.4C Outside Activities/Organizations: Carnegie Corporation/Canadian Museum Association, box 291, file 1, NGC fonds, NGC Library and Archives.

10 Alfred Bailey became assistant director at the New Brunswick Museum in Saint John in 1935; Alice Johannsen was hired by McGill's Redpath Museum, becoming assistant curator in 1942; and Donald Taylor was named head of the museum at the University of Alberta in 1935.

11 Gordon Snelgrove, for example, was given funding to enroll in the PhD program in art history at The Courtauld. After completing his dissertation on late seventeenth- and early eighteenth-century English painting, he was appointed chair of fine arts at the University of Saskatchewan.

12 Constable, "Training for Museum Work," 277.

13 "Canadian Committee on Canadian Museums, Progress Report," 22.

14 Ibid., 23. At the time, McCullough was working with Arthur Lismer in the Art Gallery of Toronto's children's education program.

15 McTavish, *Defining the Modern Museum*, 129–52.

16 National Gallery of Canada, *Annual Report*, 1935–36, 11.

17 "The Canadian Museums Association, Proposed Constitution and By-laws," 14 July 1939, 7.4C Outside Activities/Organizations: Carnegie Corporation/Canadian Museums Association, box 291, file 1, NGC fonds, NGC Library and Archives.

18 "Organization of Canadian Museums Association," 2.

19 The Canadian institutions were the Art Association of Montreal, the National Gallery of Canada, the National Museum of Canada, and the Royal Ontario Museum.

20 "Report of Second Annual Meeting," *Canadian Museums Association Bulletin* 2, no. 2 (no date, October 1949), 6. Interestingly, this suggestion was made by Martin Baldwin, director of the Art Gallery of Toronto.

21 McCurry, "Canadian Museums and the Future," 3.

22 Minutes of the Board of Governors Meeting, 14 October 1949, Board of Governors, Bound Records, Minutes Series, MB 2.10, Winnipeg Art Gallery Association/Winnipeg Art Gallery fonds, Winnipeg Art Gallery Archives.

23 Duncan, "Harvard's 'Museum Course,'" in particular the copy of the three-page syllabus for Sachs's course, 3–5.

24 Ibid., 3.

25 Morris left the VAG in 1956 to become chief curator of the San Francisco Museum of Art. He joined the Laing Galleries in Toronto in 1957 before opening his own gallery of contemporary Canadian and international art on the sixth floor of an office building in Toronto in 1962.

26 Simmins was hired as the curator of the Norman MacKenzie art collection at Regina College and as assistant professor of art history at Regina College. The Norman MacKenzie Art Gallery was established as an autonomous entity with the construction of separate quarters in 1953.

27 Minutes of the Board of Governors Meeting, 31 August 1950, Board of Governors, Bound Records, Minutes Series, MB 2.10, Winnipeg Art Gallery Association/Winnipeg Art Gallery fonds, Winnipeg Art Gallery Archives.

28 Minutes of the Board of Governors Meeting, 30 March 1953, Board of Governors, Bound Record, Minutes Series, MB 2.9, Winnipeg Art Gallery Association/Winnipeg Art Gallery fonds, Winnipeg Art Gallery Archives. The minutes of this meeting also note that Eckhardt is "not a communist or a nazi," allaying any unspoken concerns of members in hiring a foreign national.

29 Ibid.

30 MacGillivray came to Edmonton from the London Regional Art Gallery and Library in 1961. He was appointed director of the EAG after both Ron Bloore and Ted Godwin turned down the position.

31 The phrase "museum man" was in regular use at the period. Paul J. Sachs prepared his students in his museum course at Harvard by giving them the following instructions: "As a museum man, considering your museum, think of the object in the light of 'Do I like it? … Is it an object I should like for my museum?'" Qtd. in Duncan, "Harvard's 'Museum Course,'" 9. H.O. McCurry also discussed the "museum man" in correspondence with members of various museum boards.

32 Also notable are the roles played by Norah McCullough, first as the secretary of the Saskatchewan Arts Board and then as Western Liaison Officer for the NGC; Leona Collins, director of the Saskatoon Art Centre; and Marjorie Dunlop, chief librarian of the Regina Public Library and the force behind the regular programming of art exhibitions at that institution.

33 Teather, "Professionalism and the Museum," 305.

34 "Mandate/Mission," Canadian Art Museum Directors' Organization website, accessed 20 January 2014, www.camdo.ca/blog/?page_id+829.

35 Rathbone, "On Collecting," 34.

36 Eckhardt, catalogue essay in Winnipeg Art Gallery, *The Eckhardts in Winnipeg*, 14.

37 Report of the Director, Annual General Meeting, 15 May 1956, Winnipeg Art Gallery Association/Winnipeg Art Gallery fonds, MB 3.5, Winnipeg Art Gallery Archives.

38 John A. Russell, *The Concept of the New Winnipeg Art Gallery Building* (Winnipeg: WAG, 1967), n.p., qtd. in Keshavjee, "Introduction: Modified Modern," 21.

39 Similar arrangements occurred in Windsor and Victoria, and it must be remembered that the Art Museum of Toronto was formed thanks to the donation of The Grange, the family home of Hariette Smith. Coste House in Calgary, which housed the Calgary Allied Arts Centre among other cultural organizations, was also a former residence.

40 *Winnipeg Free Press*, April 1955.

41 Memo from Jerrold Morris to Council members of the Vancouver Art Gallery, 2 February 1951, 1, Building Extension Committee, Fundraising (1950–51), box, 112, Jerrold Morris Files, VAG fonds, VAG Archives.

42 Ibid.

43 Ibid., 6.

44 "Vancouver Will Now Build Canada's Most Modern Art Gallery," 128.

45 McCullough, "The Norman MacKenzie Art Gallery," 224.

46 Flaman, Howlett, and Ring, *Character and Controversy*.

47 The minutes of Council Meeting of 13 October 1964 describe McLanathan as "an expert in museum planning who is now devoted full time to museum consulting and writing. Mr. Johnson was closely associated with Mr. McLanathan in the building of the museum in Utica." Minutes of the Council of the Edmonton Museum of Arts, 13 October 1964, box 14, books 9–10 (1962–64), Edmonton Art Gallery Files, City of Edmonton Archives.

48 Journalist Virgil Hammock quoting Pierre Théberge, assistant curator of Canadian art at the NGC: "[he] told me that it was the finest gallery building in Canada, period. And I believe him." "Our New Gallery Needs Art to Match," *The Edmonton Journal*, 6 December 1968. For a discussion of Edmonton as a centre of modernist art practices, see Whitelaw, *Thinking Through Modernism*.

49 Keshavjee, *Winnipeg Modern*, 17.

50 "Beautiful but Bare," 14.

51 The classifications for exhibiting spaces in western Canada are given in "Western Canada, Categories for Exhibiting Centres," June 1958, appended to the Minutes of the Regina Conference, 7.4R Outside Activities/Organizations: Regina Conference 1958, box 325, file 1, NGC fonds, NGC Library and Archives.

52 In 1960, Eckhardt was able to secure an exhibition of paintings and drawings by Vincent Van Gogh organized by the Montreal Museum of Fine Arts that was also shown at the National Gallery and the Art Gallery of Toronto; and Winnipeg was

one of six stops of the *Tutankhamun Treasures* exhibition in 1964. However, neither exhibition was held in the Winnipeg Art Gallery. Instead, larger and more secure premises were obtained nearby.

53 A new building for the Regina Public Library, designed by the firm of Izumi, Arnott, and Sugiyama, opened in 1962 and included an art gallery; as outlined in Chapter 1, the Saskatoon Art Centre was absorbed into the Mendel Art Gallery with the erection of the new building in 1964.

54 A notice in the *Canadian Museums Association Bulletin* remarked that the projected series of forty-one booklets would "constitute an official textbook for museum and art gallery workers." *Canadian Museums Association Bulletin* 6, no. 4 (1953): 5.

55 Director's Report to the Board of Governors, 24 November 1950, Winnipeg Art Gallery Association/Winnipeg Art Gallery fonds, MB 2.10, Winnipeg Art Gallery Archives.

56 Greg Spurgeon, personal communication, 16 July 2012.

57 Breuer, "What Museum Directors Expect of Registrars," 10.

58 Long, "The Collector and the Collection," 48.

59 Roger Boulet, *Art Gallery of Greater Victoria – Plan for Development*, Submitted to the Board of Trustees of the Art Gallery of Greater Victoria, 1 May 1979, Art Gallery of Greater Victoria Archives, 50.

60 Bowen, "Picture Gallery Home."

61 Report of the Selection and Exhibition Committee, 11 March 1952. Minutes of the Council of the Edmonton Museum of Arts, box 14, book 5 (1951–54), Edmonton Art Gallery Files, Edmonton City Archives.

62 Minutes of Exhibition Committee, 11 December 1953, Winnipeg Art Gallery Association/Winnipeg Art Gallery fonds, MB 3.6, Winnipeg Art Gallery Archives.

63 Eckhardt, Introduction to *Selected Works from the Winnipeg Art Gallery Collection*, 4–5.

64 Guthe and Guthe, *The Canadian Museum Movement*, 27.

65 Amendment 18, By-laws of the Edmonton Museum of Arts, Minutes of the Council of the Edmonton Museum of Arts, 23 January 1953, box 14, book 5 (1951–54), Edmonton Art Gallery Files, City of Edmonton Archives.

66 Cox, *Pictures*, 7.

67 Ibid., 5.

68 Ronald Bloore to Peter Friedgut, 16 June 1961, cited in Long, "The Collector and the Collection," 46.

69 Long, "The Collector and the Collection," 49, 53.

70 Ibid., 54.

71 At this time there was no other institution in the city with a mandate to preserve Edmonton's history, apart from the University of Alberta, which had been steadily acquiring objects for its collections, albeit in a highly eclectic and departmentalized manner. The Provincial Museum (now the Royal Alberta Museum) only opened in

1967, leaving the EMA with major responsibility for the collection and display of historical artifacts.

72 Bush pilot Leigh Brintnell and C.W. Mather, one of the first photographers to work in Edmonton, were two recorded donors of objects of Indigenous expressive culture to the Edmonton Museum of Arts.

73 "In the larger Emily Carr Gallery a small display of Indian masks and other works of art which influenced the artist could be built up in the middle of the room, and would not in any way interfere with the pictures themselves or distract from them." Jerrold Morris, Memo to Council members, 2 February 1951, 3, Building Extension Committee, Fundraising 1950–51, Jerrold Morris Files, box 112, Vancouver Art Gallery fonds, Vancouver Art Gallery Archives.

74 Russell, "Aboriginal Art," 80–5.

75 Rushing, "Marketing the Affinity of the Primitive and the Modern."

76 It is somewhat ironic that just as the Edmonton Art Gallery was getting rid of its Inuit collection, Inuit art was making significant inroads into the North American art market and becoming a staple of museum gift shops across the country. See Whitelaw, "From the Gift Shop to the Permanent Collection," 105–23.

77 See comment in the Report of the Selection and Exhibition Committee in October 1956 regarding the recommendation that the EAG accept a gift of First Nation–made objects from Madaline King: "that the gift be received with the understanding that it be included in our present collection of Indian material and that should the Provincial Government inaugurate a museum for such material that these artefacts be presented to them at that time." Report of the Selection and Exhibition Committee, 3 October 1956, Minutes of the Council of the Edmonton Museum of Arts, box 14, book 6 (1955–57), Edmonton Art Gallery Files, City of Edmonton Archives.

78 Toronto collector and Picture Loan Society founder Douglas Duncan left works to galleries and universities across the country upon his death in 1968; Robert Laidlaw used profits from his father's lumber company to establish a philanthropic foundation that included support for cultural institutions. His donations – including a Tom Thomson sketch – followed shortly after Bobby Dyde was appointed to the EMA's board and were likely due to a personal connection to her; gallerist Max Stern made extended loans to several Canadian museums and galleries in exchange for storage in the late 1960s. From the late 1960s to his death in 1987, Stern gifted several significant works by such artists as Emily Carr and Goodridge Roberts to the EAG. Barwick, *Pictures from the Douglas M. Duncan Collection*; Gilbert and Zemans, *Making Change: Fifty Years of the Laidlaw Foundation*; Moreault, *Max Stern: Montreal Dealer and Patron*.

79 See Alfoldy, *Crafting Identity*, for an analysis of museums' and galleries' attitudes towards fine art craft in Canada.

80 For a discussion of the National Gallery's photography collection, see Thomas, "The National Gallery of Canada."

81 Kunard and Payne, "Writing Photography in Canada," 237.

CHAPTER 6

1 Canada, An Act to establish a corporation for the administration of the National Museums of Canada, 16 Elizabeth II, Chapter 21, 21 December 1967.
2 Canada, *House of Commons Debates*, 30 November 1967, 4913.
3 Sheppard, *Special Report on the Cultural Policy*.
4 Babaian, *CMST Origins*, 12.
5 While establishment of a multiculturalism directorate increased the recognition of the diversity of the Canadian population, it also reduced definitions of "culture": to narrow ethnic forms and activities that could be more easily assimilated into a liberal view of national identity and unity. For a discussion of the history and effects of Canada's multiculturalism policy, see Bissoondath, *Selling Illusions*; and Mackey, *House of Difference*.
6 See, for example, Bennett, "Useful Culture"; Barnett, "Culture, Government and Spatiality"; and Throsby, *The Economics of Cultural Policy*.
7 Robertson, *Policy Matters*.
8 Canada, Royal Commission on Government Organization, Preface to *Summary of the Glassco Commission Report*, n.p.
9 O'Neal, "Reorganizing Government."
10 Mallory, "The Lambert Report," 517–18.
11 Berton, *1967: The Last Good Year*; Whitelaw "'To Better Know Ourselves.'"
12 It must be remembered that education is a provincial responsibility; the federal government's incursions into support for educational activities has remained at the level of capital and research funding only, as can be seen in the history of the Social Sciences and Humanities Research Council and its relationship to the Canada Council.
13 Babaian, *Making Do*.
14 For a more in-depth discussion of the powers of the secretary-general and the NMC's Board of Trustees, see Ord, *The National Gallery of Canada*, 247–77.
15 The 1952 act replaced the original act establishing the National Gallery in 1913.
16 National Gallery Act, paragraph 23, section 1, 1952.
17 "Former Director Critical of National Museum Bill," *Ottawa Citizen*, 24 April 1967.
18 Boggs, "The National Gallery," 17.
19 Senate Standing Committee on Finance, May 1967, qtd. in Ord, *The National Gallery of Canada*, 234.
20 Archie F. Key, "Travelling Museums – A New National Concept," *Calgary Herald*, 23 May 1972.
21 "Reorganization of the National Museums of Canada," *CMA Gazette* 2, no. 4 (1968): 2.
22 "'National Museums' Act Now Law: Proclamation Expected Shortly," *CMA Gazette* 2, no. 2 (1968): 1.

23 The Canadian Museums Association was awarded $54,000 to expand its national program of training seminars for Canadian museum employees in 1972–73, the first year that such a grant was awarded. "First Funds Granted Under New Policy," CMA *Gazette* 6, no. 5/6 (1973): 15. In 1978 it received core funding of $100,000 a year plus $110,000 for training assistance; in 1979, the NMC allocated $170,000 in core-funding assistance and $72,900 for training. Ian Clark to George MacBeath, 8 February 1980, vol. 6, box 94, NMC fonds, Library and Archives Canada.

24 Pelletier, "Museums and the National Heritage," 12.

25 Pelletier, "A New Policy for Museums," 12.

26 National Museums of Canada, *Annual Report*, 1974–75, 5.

27 The National Loan Collection was never implemented because many art galleries opposed the proposal because of the potential harm to objects in their collections, and those institutions that were in favour of the program could not agree on who would coordinate it.

28 Pelletier, "A New Policy for Museums," 4–5.

29 National Museums of Canada, *The National Museum Policy*, 1.

30 Pelletier, "A New Policy for Museums," 4.

31 Ibid.

32 Reflecting on his decision to announce the policy in Calgary, Pelletier later wrote, "Pourquoi-pas, me disais-je, faire cette fleur à une ville de l'ouest canadien, dans une province où l'on se plaint amèrement du fait que toute nouvelle politique, culturelle ou autre, est immanquablement annoncée dans une ville de l'est?" Pelletier, *L'Aventure du pouvoir*, 261. (I asked myself, why not give this gift to a city in western Canada, in a province that bitterly complains that all policy announcements, cultural or other, are invariably announced in an eastern Canadian city?)

33 Pelletier, "A New Policy for Museums," 4.

34 Pelletier, *L'Aventure du pouvoir*, 24–8.

35 Ostry, *The Cultural Connection*, 115; Axworthy and Trudeau, *Towards a Just Society*.

36 Pelletier, *L'Aventure du pouvoir*, 25.

37 Lebovics, *Mona Lisa's Escort*, 124–9.

38 Pelletier to Boggs, 24 January 1972, Museum Assistance Programmes (Consultative Committee) – Associate Museums, Director's Office, box 82, NGC fonds, NGC Library and Archives.

39 France established a ministry of cultural affairs in 1959.

40 See Paquin, *Art, public et société*.

41 Lebovics, *Mona Lisa's Escort*, 109.

42 The following statement from the National Gallery's *Annual Review* for 1972–73 fully illustrates the bureaucratic encumbrance produced by the National Museum Policy: "At the same time that financial management was transferred to the Corporation of the National Museums of Canada, the management of personnel was transferred to the Department of the Secretary of State. Although the constantly changing members of the staff in the Secretary of State's Personnel Administration Branch have been helpful, another layer of bureaucracy has been inserted between

the Gallery and Treasury Board (for classification of positions) and the Gallery and the Public Service Commission (for their staffing). The complications are many and should not be detailed here. It is sufficient to note that, after an analysis of the administration of the Corporation of the National Museums of Canada for its Board of Trustees, an independent consultant recommended that the Gallery have an administrative officer on the level of an assistant director to be responsible for finance, personnel, Installations, and the Registrar. But implementation of this recommendation would require additional positions and the agreement of the Board." National Gallery of Canada, *Fifth Annual Review 1972–73*, 52–3. The *Annual Review* was a publication instituted by Boggs in 1968 to give the gallery an autonomous voice outside the NMC's comprehensive *Annual Report*.

43 See Ord, *The National Gallery of Canada*, for a detailed discussion of this period of the National Gallery's history.

44 The appropriation fund question was particularly frustrating under the National Museums Corporation, because as a Crown corporation, the NMC had to return to the public purse any government appropriations that hadn't been used within two years. This made any long-term planning, or "saving up" for important acquisitions virtually impossible.

45 National Museums of Canada, *Annual Report*, 1972–73, 5.

46 National Museums of Canada, *Annual Report*, 1973–74, 4.

47 National Gallery of Canada, *Fifth Annual Review 1972–73*, 65.

48 The Associate Museums in western Canada were the Winnipeg Art Gallery, the Manitoba Museum of Man and Nature, the Norman MacKenzie Art Gallery, the Western Development Museum, the Mendel Art Gallery, the Glenbow-Alberta Institute, the Edmonton Art Gallery, the Provincial Museum and Archives of Alberta, the Vancouver Centennial Museum, the Vancouver Art Gallery, the Art Gallery of Greater Victoria, and the British Columbia Provincial Museum.

49 Director's Report to the Annual General Meeting of the Winnipeg Art Gallery, 21 June 1973, Board of Governors, Bound Records, Minutes Series, MB 6.2, Winnipeg Art Gallery Association/Winnipeg Art Gallery fonds, Winnipeg Art Gallery Archives.

50 Ibid.

51 Council Minutes of the Vancouver Art Gallery, 12 April 1973 and 20 September 1973, Vancouver Art Gallery Archives.

52 National Museums of Canada, *Annual Report*, 1972–73, Appendix II. Note: this includes $48,600 to the McBride Museum in Whitehorse, the designated National Exhibition Centre in the Northwest Territories.

53 National Museums of Canada, *Annual Report*, 1972–73, 5.

54 Simmins, *The Simmins Report on the Associate Museum System in Canada*, 99.

55 Ibid., 102.

56 Report of the Consultative Committee on National Museum Policy, Meeting of 10 and 11 March 1975, Board of Trustees Meeting, 17, 18, and 19 March 1975, box

72, National Museums of Canada Corporation, NMC fonds, Library and Archives Canada.

57 Simmins, *Simmins Report on Associate Museums*, 113, emphasis in original.

58 National Museums of Canada, *Annual Report*, 1975–76, 3.

59 Ibid., 4.

60 Ibid.

61 Ibid.

62 The budget of the Edmonton Art Gallery, for example, increased from $184,743 in 1970 to $1,141,224 in 1980. Edmonton Art Gallery, *Annual Report* 1971, n.p.; Edmonton Art Gallery, *Annual Report* 1980, 15.

63 Duncan Cameron to Ian Christie Clark, 4 September 1978, vol. 1, box 35, NMC fonds, Library and Archives Canada.

64 "The Edmonton Art Gallery Mandate" document produced for Future Directors Workshop for Board of the EAG c. 1985, Edmonton Art Gallery Board of Governors files.

65 Boulet, *Plan for Development*, 67.

66 Simmins, *Simmins Report on Associate Museums*, 77.

67 Ibid.

68 "Museum II," quoted in ibid., 123. All museum directors and staff interviewed for Simmins's report were kept anonymous.

69 Ibid., 139.

70 National Museums of Canada, *Annual Report*, 1978–79, 3.

71 National Museums of Canada, *A National Museums Policy for the 80's*, 5.

72 Greater consultation between the federal and provincial governments around issues of culture was noted in the 1980–81 *Annual Report* of the NMC, which reported on meetings of the ministers responsible for culture and historical resources in 1979 and 1980: "Previously, federal-provincial consultations had been viewed as bilateral interchange. The creation of a committee of four D[eputy] M[inister]s of Culture representing the Provinces and the federal DM of Communications (the Four Plus One Committee) has provided an ongoing multi-level forum for federal-provincial consultation" (4). As part of these meetings, a working group on museums was formed to discuss, among other issues, an indemnification plan for major inter-provincial and international travelling exhibitions.

73 The National Museum of Man was still sharing cramped quarters in the Victoria Memorial Museum Building with the National Museum of Nature; the National Gallery was still languishing in the office building on Lorne Street it had occupied since 1960 as a "temporary" solution to a permanent home.

74 National Museums of Canada, *Annual Report*, 1981–82, 5.

75 Boulet, *A Plan for Development*, 28.

76 Nemiroff, "A History of Artist-Run Spaces in Canada"; Wallace, *Whispered Art History*.

77 Canada Council, *Annual Report*, 1967–68, 34.

78 Ed Varney interviewed by Diana Nemiroff, June 1983, cited in Nemiroff, "A History of Artist-Run Spaces in Canada," 120.

79 Edythe Goodridge and Margaret Dryden, Canada Council, to Keith de Bellefeuille-Percy, National Museums Corporation, 26 September 1984, National Programmes – Grants – General, box 64, NMC fonds, Library and Archives Canada.

80 Edmonton Art Gallery, Summary of Program Grants and Project Grants for the Board of Governors of the Edmonton Art Gallery, 3 June 1985, Edmonton Art Gallery files.

81 National Museums of Canada, *A Museums Policy for the 80's*, 25.

82 Canada, Federal Cultural Policy Review Committee, *Report of the Federal Cultural Policy Review Committee*, 126.

83 Ibid., 118.

84 Ibid.

85 McCormack, "Culture and the State."

86 Dafoe, "Applebert West," 12.

87 Enright, "The Fine Art of Border Crossing," 9.

88 This idea is thoroughly developed – albeit in a wholly different context – by Dipesh Chakrabarty in *Provincialising Europe*.

89 On the VAG's turn to internationalism, see Harris, "Of Rauschenberg, Policy and Representation at the Vancouver Art Gallery."

90 For an analysis of two such exhibitions, see Whitelaw, "Statistical Imperatives."

91 National Museums of Canada, *Annual Report*, 1984–85, 8.

92 National Museums of Canada, *Annual Report*, 1985–86, 10 (emphasis in original).

93 Canada, National Museums Task Force, *Report and Recommendations of the Task Force Charged with Examining Federal Policy Concerning Museums*, 19.

EPILOGUE

1 National Gallery of Canada, "National Gallery Embarks on New Partnership with the Art Gallery of Alberta," press release, 16 December 2009, http://www.gallery.ca/en/about/237.php. At the time of writing, the partnership continues to thrive.

2 National Gallery of Canada, "National Gallery of Canada and the Museum of Contemporary Canadian Art Forge a New Partnership," press release, 9 November 2010, http://www.gallery.ca/en/about/240.php.

3 National Gallery of Canada, "National Gallery Embarks on New Partnership with the Art Gallery of Alberta."

BIBLIOGRAPHY

ARCHIVAL SOURCES

Art Gallery of Greater Victoria Archives
    Art Gallery of Greater Victoria fonds
City of Edmonton Archives
    Edmonton Art Club fonds
    Edmonton Exhibition fonds
    Edmonton Museum of Art files
Library and Archives Canada
    Dorothy Reynolds Dyde fonds
    Norah McCullough papers
    Harry Orr and Dorothy McCurry fonds
    National Museums of Canada Corporation fonds
National Gallery of Canada Archives
    Norah McCullough fonds
    National Gallery of Canada fonds
Queen's University Archives
    Federation of Canadian Artists fonds
University of British Columbia Archives
    Western Canada Art Circuit collection
Vancouver Art Gallery
    Vancouver Art Gallery fonds
Winnipeg Art Gallery
    Brandon Art Club files
    Winnipeg Art Gallery/Winnipeg Art Gallery Association fonds

PRIMARY AND SECONDARY SOURCES

Abell, Walter. "Conference of Canadian Artists: An Editorial." *Maritime Art* 2, no. 1 (1941): 2–3.
– "Cooperation or Conflict?" *Maritime Art* 3, no. 2 (1942/43): 35–6.

Abt, Jeffrey. *A Museum on the Verge: A Socioeconomic History of the Detroit Institute of the Arts, 1882–2000*. Detroit: Wayne State University Press, 2001.

"An Acorn on Parliament Hill." *Canadian Art* 1, no. 6 (1944): 15–18.

Alfoldy, Sandra. *Crafting Identity: The Development of Professional Fine Craft in Canada*. Montreal and Kingston: McGill-Queen's University Press, 2005.

Anderson, Benedict. *Imagined Communities: Reflections on the Origin and Spread of Nationalism*. Rev ed. New York: Verso Press, 1991.

Anderson, Florence. Introduction to *Carnegie Corporation: Program in the Arts 1911–1967*, by Brenda Jubin, 1–10. New York: Carnegie Corporation of New York, 1968.

Andrew, G.C. "The Canada Council: A National Necessity." *Queen's Quarterly* 61 (Autumn 1954): 291–303.

Art Gallery of Alberta. *Capital Modern: A Guide to Edmonton Architecture and Urban Design 1940–1969*. Edmonton: Art Gallery of Alberta, 2007. Exhibition catalogue.

Art Gallery of Southwestern Manitoba. "History." Accessed 31 May 2013. www.agsm.ca/history.

Artibise, Alan F.J. *Winnipeg: A Social History of Urban Growth 1874–1914*. Montreal and London: McGill-Queen's University Press, 1975.

Ayre, Robert. "The Press Debates the Massey Report." *Canadian Art* 9, no. 1 (1951): 25–30; 36–8.

– "Report of the Royal Commission on National Development in the Arts, Letters and Sciences." *Canadian Art* 8, no. 4 (1951): 145–9.

Axworthy, Thomas S., and Pierre Elliott Trudeau, eds. *Towards a Just Society: The Trudeau Years*. Markham, ON: Viking, 1990.

Babaian, Sharon. *Making Do: The Early Years of the Canada Science and Technology Museum*. Ottawa: Canada Science and Technology Museum, n.d. Accessed 8 September 2016. http://cstmuseum.techno-science.ca/en/the-early-years-of-the-canada-science-and-technology-museum.php.

Barman, Jean. "A British Columbian View of Regions." *Acadiensis* 35, no. 2 (2006): 144–56.

Barnett, Clive. "Culture, Government and Spatiality: Reassessing the 'Foucault Effect' in Cultural-policy Studies." *International Journal of Cultural Studies* 2, no. 3 (1999): 369–97.

Barwick, Frances Duncan. *Pictures from the Douglas M. Duncan Collection*. Toronto and Buffalo: University of Toronto Press, 1975.

"Beautiful but Bare." *Time* (Canadian edition) 92, no. 50 (13 December 1968): 14.

Bell, Michael. "The Welfare of Art in Canada." In *The Kingston Conference Proceedings: A Reprint of the Proceedings of the 1941 Kingston Artists' Conference*, iii–xxxiv. Kingston, ON: Agnes Etherington Art Centre, 1991.

Bennett, Tony. *The Birth of the Museum: History, Theory, Politics*. London: Routledge, 1995.

– "Useful Culture." *Cultural Studies* 6, no. 3 (1992): 395–408.

Berger, Carl. *The Writing of Canadian History: Aspects of English-Canadian Historical Writing Since 1900*. 2nd ed. Toronto: Toronto University Press, 1986.

Berland, Jody. "Marginal Notes on Cultural Studies in Canada." *University of Toronto Quarterly* 64, no. 4 (1995): 514–25.

– "Nationalism and the Modernist Legacy: Dialogues with Innis." In *Capital Culture: A Reader on Modernist Legacies and the Value(s) of Art*, edited by Jody Berland and Shelley Hornstein, 14–38. Montreal and Kingston: McGill-Queen's University Press, 2000.

– "Space at the Margins: Colonial Spatiality and Critical Theory After Innis." *Topia* 1 (Spring 1997): 55–82.

Berry, Virginia. *Taming the Frontier: Art and Women in the Canadian West 1880–1920*. Winnipeg and Calgary: Winnipeg Art Gallery and Bayeux Arts Inc., 2005.

Berton, Pierre. *1967: The Last Good Year*. Toronto: Seal Books, 1998.

Bissoondath, Neil. *Selling Illusions: The Cult of Multiculturalism in Canada*. Toronto: Penguin, 1994.

Blanchard, Jim. *Winnipeg 1912: Diary of a City*. Winnipeg: University of Manitoba Press, 2005.

Boggs, Jean Sutherland. "The National Gallery." *artscanada* 26, no. 128/129 (1969): 14–18.

– *The National Gallery of Canada*. Toronto: Oxford University Press, 1971.

Borys, Stephen, ed. *Winnipeg Art Gallery: Guide to the Collection*. Winnipeg: Winnipeg Art Gallery, 2010.

Boulet, Roger. *Plan for Development*, submitted to the Board of Directors of the Art Gallery of Greater Victoria, 1979.

Boutilier, Alicia. *A Vital Force: The Canadian Group of Painters*. Kingston: Agnes Etherington Art Centre, 2013. Exhibition catalogue.

– *Inspirational: The Collection of H.S. Southam*. Hamilton: Art Gallery of Hamilton, 2009.

Boutilier, Alicia, and Paul Maréchal. *William Brymner: Artist, Teacher, Colleague*. Kingston: Agnes Etherington Art Centre, 2010.

Bowen, Ruth. "Picture Gallery Home." *Saturday Night*, 10 December 1955.

Bradford, Neil. "Writing Public Philosophy: Canada's Royal Commissions on Everything." *Journal of Canadian Studies* 34, no. 4 (1999/2000): 136–67.

Brayley, Katharine. "A Regional Agency: Maritime Art Association Programming from 1935 to 1945." MA thesis, Concordia University, 2010.

Breuer, Alice Putnam. "What Museum Directors Expect of Registrars." *The Museum News* 18, no. 20 (1941): 9–11.

"Brief on the Eleven Points on Cultural Policy as it Applies to Museums, as Stated by the Secretary of State." *CMA Gazette* 5, no. 3 (1971): 5–12.

Brison, Jeffrey D. "The Kingston Conference, the Carnegie Corporation and a New Deal for the Arts in Canada." *American Review of Canadian Studies* 23, no. 4 (1993): 503–22.

– *Rockefeller, Carnegie, and Canada: American Philanthropy and the Arts and Letters in Canada*. Montreal and Kingston: McGill-Queen's University Press, 2005.

Brooke, Janet. *Discerning Tastes: Montreal Collectors 1880–1920*. Montreal: Montreal Museum of Fine Arts, 1989. Exhibition catalogue.

Brown, F. Maud. *Breaking Barriers: Eric Brown and the National Gallery*. Ottawa: Society for Art Publications, 1964.

Buckner, Phillip, and R. Douglas Francis, eds. *Canada and the British World: Culture, Migration and Identity*. Vancouver: UBC Press, 2006.

Burley, David. "Winnipeg's Landscape of Modernity, 1945–1975." In *Winnipeg Modern: Architecture, 1945–1975*, edited by Serena Keshavjee, 29–85. Winnipeg: University of Manitoba Press, 2006.

Burton, Anthony. "The Uses of the South Kensington Art Collections." *Journal of the History of Collections* 14, no. 1 (2002): 79–95.

Buxton, William, ed. *Harold Innis and the North: Appraisals and Contestations*. Montreal and Kingston: McGill-Queen's University Press, 2013.

Buxton, William, and Charles Acland. *American Philanthropy and Canadian Libraries: The Politics of Knowledge and Information*. Montreal: Graduate School of Library and Information Studies and the Centre for Research on Canadian Cultural Industries and Institutions, McGill University, 1998.

Calgary Herald. "National Gallery Service Scored." 2 November 1949.

Canada. *An Act to establish a corporation for the administration of the National Museums of Canada*. 16 Elizabeth II, Chapter 21. 21 December 1967.

– *National Gallery Act*, 1952.

Canada Council. *Annual Reports*, 1957–90.

– Advisory Arts Panel. *The Future of the Canada Council*. Ottawa: Canada Council, 1979.

– "Twenty Plus Five: A Discussion Paper on the Role of the Canada Council in the Arts After the First Twenty Years and Over the Next Five." Canada Council, Ottawa, 1977.

Canada, Department of Public Works. *Report of the Minister of Public Works on the works under his control for the fiscal year ending 31 March 1912*. Ottawa: King's Printer, 1912.

– *Report of the Minister of Public Works on the works under his control for the fiscal year ending 31 March 1913*. Ottawa: King's Printer, 1913.

– *Report of the Minister of Public Works on the works under his control for the fiscal year ending 31 March 1914*. Ottawa: King's Printer, 1914.

– *Report of the Minister of Public Works on the works under his control for the fiscal year ending 31 March 1915*. Ottawa: King's Printer, 1915.

– *Report of the Minister of Public Works on the works under his control for the fiscal year ending 31 March 1918*. Ottawa: King's Printer, 1918.

Canada. *House of Commons Debates*. 30 November 1967.

Canada, Federal Cultural Policy Review Committee. *Report of the Federal Cultural Policy Review Committee*. [Applebaum-Hébert Report]. Ottawa: Information Services, Department of Communications, 1982.

Canada, National Museums Task Force. *Report and Recommendations of the Task Force Charged with Examining Federal Policy Concerning Museums*. Ottawa: Department of Communications, 1986.

Canada, Royal Commission on Government Organization. *Summary of the Glassco Commission Report*. Regina: Saskatchewan Budget Bureau, 1963.

Canada, Royal Commission on National Development in the Arts, Letters and Sciences [Massey Commission]. *Report*. Ottawa: King's Printers, 1951.

Careless, J.M.S. "'Limited Identities' in Canada." In *Contemporary Approaches to Canadian History*, edited by Carl Berger, 5–12. Toronto: Longman, 1987.

Carney, Lora Senechal. "Modern Art, the Local, and the Global, c. 1930–1950." In *The Visual Arts in Canada: The Twentieth Century*, edited by Anne Whitelaw, Brian Foss, and Sandra Paikowsky, 99–120. Don Mills, ON: Oxford University Press, 2010.

Carr, Emily. *The House of All Sorts*. Vancouver: Douglas & McIntyre, 2004.

Celebrating a Century: A Timeline of the Winnipeg Art Gallery, 1912–2012. Accessed 24 January 2014. www.wag100.ca/timeline/date:1912

Chakrabarty, Dipesh. *Provincialising Europe: Postcolonial Thought and Historical Difference*. Princeton: Princeton University Press, 2000.

Charland, Maurice. "Technological Nationalism." *Canadian Journal of Political and Social Theory* 10, no. 1 (1986): 196–220.

Cholette, Katie. "The Beleaguered Biennials." *RACAR: Revue d'art canadienne/Canadian Art Review* 35, no. 2 (2010): 21–34.

"Coast to Coast in Art." *Canadian Art* 1, no. 5 (1944): 219.

Coleman, Helen "Bubs." *Dreaming a Gallery: Saskatoon's Mendel Art Gallery in History and Memory*. Saskatoon: Mendel Art Gallery, 2015.

Coleman, Laurence Vail. *Manual for Small Museums*. New York and London: G.P. Putnam and Sons, 1927.

– *The Museum in America: A Critical Study*. Washington, DC: American Association of Museums, 1939.

"Community Art Centres: A Growing Movement." *Canadian Art* 2, no. 2 (1944–45): 62–3; 77; 85.

Community Arts Council of Vancouver. *Brief to the Royal Commission on National Development in the Arts, Letters and Sciences*, 1949.

Conn, Steven. *Museums and American Intellectual Life, 1876–1926*. Chicago: University of Chicago Press, 1998.

Connor, Edward. "Harold Innis and The Bias of Communication." *Information, Communication and Society* 4, no. 2 (2001): 274–94.

Conrad, Margaret. "Regionalism in a Flat World." *Acadiensis* 35, no. 2 (Spring 2006): 138–43.

Constable W.G. "Training for Museum Work." *Museums Journal* 33 (November 1933): 273–9.

Cox, Trenchard. *Pictures: Handbook for Museum Curators*. Part D: Art, Sections 1 & 2. London: The Museums Association, 1956.

Crouch, Richard E. "A Community Art Centre in Action." *Canadian Art* 2, no. 1 (1944): 22–8.

Dafoe, Christopher. "Applebert West: Half-Baked or Paradise?" *Arts Manitoba* 3, no. 2 (1983): 12–15.

Dawn, Leslie. *National Vision, National Blindness: Canadian Art and Identities in the 1920s.* Vancouver: UBC Press, 2007.

Deacon, William Arthur. "The Arts in Canada Speak Out Before Parliamentary Committee." *The Globe and Mail*, 24 June 1944.

Diehl, Fred M. *A Gentleman from a Fading Age: Eric Lafferty Harvie.* Calgary: Devonian Foundation, 1989.

Dowler, Kevin. "The Cultural Industry Policy Apparatus." In *The Cultural Industries in Canada: Problems, Policies and Prospects*, edited by Michael Dorland, 328–45. Toronto: Lorimer, 1996.

Druick, Zoë. "International Cultural Relations as a Factor in Postwar Cultural Policy: The Relevance of UNESCO for the Massey Commission." *Canadian Journal of Communication* 31, no. 1 (2006): 177–95.

Duncan, Carol. *Civilizing Rituals: Inside Public Art Museums.* New York: Routledge, 1995.

Duncan, Carol, and Alan Wallach. "The Universal Survey Museum." *Art History* 3, no. 4 (1980): 448–69.

Duncan, Sally Anne. "Harvard's 'Museum Course' and the Making of America's Museum Profession." *Archives of the American Art Journal* 42, no. 1/2 (2002): 2–16.

Duval, Paul. "Canadian Arts Council." *Canadian Art* 3, no. 4 (1946): 166–8.

Eckhardt, Ferdinand. Introduction to *Selected Works from the Winnipeg Art Gallery Collection.* Winnipeg: Winnipeg Art Gallery, 1971.

– *The Winnipeg Art Gallery 1912–1962: An Introduction to the History, the Activities and Collection.* Winnipeg: Civic Auditorium, 1962.

Edmonton Art Club. *The Changing Picture: 65 Years of the Edmonton Art Club.* Edmonton: Edmonton Art Gallery, 1986. Exhibition catalogue.

Edmonton Art Gallery. *Annual Reports*, 1931–90.

Edmonton Bulletin. "Edmonton Museum of Arts Marks its 23rd Birthday This Year." 20 April 1946.

The Edmonton Journal. "The Art Loan Exhibit." 31 October 1924.

– "Mayor Bury Formally Opens New Home of Museum of Arts." 16 November 1927.

– "More Space for Art Museum." 17 February 1931.

– "National Gallery Achieves Importance In Half a Century." 20 September 1930.

– "Ottawa Official's Visit Cheers Lovers of Art." 28 October 1931.

– "Rare Treat Awaits Public in Collection of Pictures on Exhibition in Macdonald." 30 October 1924.

Edmonton Museum of Arts. *Loan Exhibition Catalogue.* Palm Room, Macdonald Hotel, 1924.

Eggleston, Wilfrid. "Canadian Geography and National Culture." *Canadian Geographic Journal* (December 1951): 254–73.

Elder, Alan, and Ian Thom, eds. *A Modern Life: Art and Design in British Columbia 1945–1960*. Vancouver: Vancouver Art Gallery, 2004. Exhibition catalogue.

Enright, Robert. "The Fine Art of Border Crossing." *BorderCrossings* 4, no. 4 (1985): 9.

Felske, Lorry W., and Beverly Rasporich. "Challenging Frontiers." In *Challenging Frontiers: The Canadian West*. Calgary: University of Calgary Press, 2005.

Ferguson, Barry, and Robert Wardhaugh. "'Impossible Conditions of Inequality': John W. Dafoe, the Rowell-Sirois Royal Commission, and the Interpretation of Canadian Federalism." *The Canadian Historical Review* 84, no. 4 (2003): 1–19.

"Fine Arts in the West." *The Canadian Forum* 31, no. 367 (1951): 1.

Finlay, Karen. "Identifying with Nature: Graham Sutherland and Canadian Art, 1939–1955." *RACAR: Revue d'art canadienne/Canadian Art Review* 21, no. 1/2 (1994): 43–59.

"First Funds Granted under New Policy." *CMA Gazette* 6, no. 5/6 (1973).

Flaman, Bernard, Jeff Holett, and Dan Ring. *Character and Controversy: The Mendel Art Gallery and Modernist Architecture in Saskatchewan*. Saskatoon: Mendel Art Gallery, 2004. Exhibition catalogue.

Foran, Max, ed. *Icon, Brand, Myth: The Calgary Stampede*. Edmonton: Athabasca University Press, 2008.

Friesen, Gerald. *The Canadian Prairies: A History*. Toronto and London: University of Toronto Press, 1987.

– "Defining the Prairies: or, Why the Prairies Don't Exist." In *Toward Defining the Prairies: Region, Culture and History*, edited by Robert Wardhaugh, 13–28. Winnipeg: University of Manitoba Press, 2001.

– "The Prairies as Region: The Contemporary Meaning of an Old Idea." In *River Road: Essays on Manitoba and Prairie History*, 165–82. Winnipeg: University of Manitoba Press, 1996.

– "Space and Region in Canadian History." *Journal of the Canadian Historical Association* 16, no. 1 (2005): 1–22.

Fuglem, Terri. "Manitoba Mod: The Work of Gustavo da Roza II." In *Winnipeg Modern: Architecture, 1945 to 1975*, edited by Serena Keshavjee, 221–8. Winnipeg: University of Manitoba Press, 2006.

Gilbert, Nathan, and Joyce Zemans, eds. *Making Change: Fifty Years of the Laidlaw Foundation*. Toronto: ECW Press, 2001.

Griffin, Kevin. "An Only Son's Death Gave Birth to City's Art Gallery." *The Vancouver Sun*, 10 October 2006.

Goyette, Linda, and Carolina Jakeway Roemmich. *Edmonton in Our Own Words*. Edmonton: University of Alberta Press, 2004.

Guthe, Carl E., and Grace M. Guthe. *The Canadian Museum Movement*. Ottawa: Canadian Museums Association, 1958.

Hammock, Virgil. "Our New Gallery Needs Art to Match." *The Edmonton Journal*, 6 December 1968.

Harper, J. Russell. Introduction to *The Ernest E. Poole Foundation Collection: An Exhibition of Canadian Painting*. Edmonton: The Edmonton Art Gallery, 1966. Exhibition catalogue.

Harris, Lawren. "The Federation, the National Gallery and a New Society." *Maritime Art* 3, no. 4 (1943): 126–7.

– "The Function of an Art Gallery." *Vancouver Art Gallery Bulletin* 10, no. 2–10, no. 6 (April 1942–February 1943).

– "Reconstruction through the Arts." *Canadian Art* 1, no. 5 (1944): 185–6; 224.

Harris, Steven. "Of Rauschenberg, Policy and Representation at the Vancouver Art Gallery: A Partial History 1966–1983." MA thesis, University of British Columbia, 1985.

Hartle, Douglas G. "The Report of the Royal Commission on Financial Management and Accountability" (The Lambert Report). *Canadian Public Policy* 3 (Summer 1979): 366–82.

Havelock, Joanne. "Regina Central Library: The Past and the Future." Friends of the Regina Public Library, Town Hall Meeting, 13 March 2012.

Heath, Terrence. *Uprooted: The Art and Life of Ernest Lindner.* Saskatoon: Fifth House, 1983.

Higonnet, Anne. *A Museum of One's Own: Private Collecting, Public Gift.* Pittsburgh: Periscope Publishing, 2009.

Hill, Charles C. "To Found a National Gallery: The Royal Canadian Academy of Arts, 1880–1913." *National Gallery of Canada Journal* 36 (6 March 1980): 1–8.

– *The Group of Seven: Art for a Nation.* Toronto: McClelland and Stewart, 1995. Exhibition catalogue.

– "The National Gallery, a National Art, Critical Judgement and the State." In *The True North: Canadian Landscape Painting 1896–1939*, edited by Michael Tooby, 64–83. London: Barbican Art Gallery/Lund Humphries, 1992. Exhibition catalogue.

Hill, Kate. *Culture and Class in English Public Museums, 1850–1914.* Aldershot: Ashgate, 2005.

Hirzy, Ellen C. "The AAM after 72 Years." *Museum News* 56, no. 5 (1978): 44–8.

"H.O. McCurry, Servant of the Arts." *Canadian Art* 12, no. 3 (1955): 118–22.

Horrall, Andrew. *Bringing Art to Life: A Biography of Alan Jarvis.* Montreal and Kingston: McGill-Queen's University Press, 2009.

Hubbard, R.H. "A Climate for the Arts." *Canadian Art* 12, no. 3 (1955): 99–105; 139.

Hudson, Anna. "Art and Social Progress: The Toronto Community of Painters." PhD diss., University of Toronto, 1997.

Hughes, Mary Jo, Michael Morris, and Barry Till. *Vision into Reality: Art Gallery of Greater Victoria Early Years, 1951–1973.* Victoria: Art Gallery of Greater Victoria, 2009.

Hunt, Alfred Ian. "Mutual Enlightenment in Early Vancouver, 1886–1916." PhD diss., University of British Columbia, 1987.

Innis, Harold. *The Bias of Communication*. Toronto: University of Toronto Press, 1951.

– *The Fur Trade in Canada: An Introduction to Canadian Economic History*. Rev. ed. Toronto: University of Toronto Press, 1956.

Irwin, Robert. "Breaking the Shackles of the Metropolitan Thesis: Prairie History, the Environment and Layered Identities." *Journal of Canadian Studies* 23, no. 3 (1997): 98–118.

Jackson, A.Y. *A Painter's Country*. Toronto: Clarke, Irwin and Co., 1958.

Jackson, Nancy Beth. *The Junior League: 100 Years of Volunteer Service*. New York: Association of Junior Leagues International Inc., 2001.

Jasen, Patricia. "Mind, Medicine, and the Christian Science Controversy in Canada, 1888–1910." *Journal of Canadian Studies* 32, no. 4 (1997/98): 5–22.

Jenson, Jane. "Commissioning Ideas: Representations and Royal Commissions." In *How Ottawa Spends, 1994–95: Making Change*, edited by Susan Phillips, 39–69. Ottawa: Carleton University Press, 1994.

Johnson, Percy. "The Edmonton Public Library: An Architectural History of a Carnegie Library Building." MA thesis, Concordia University, 1994.

Jubin, Brenda. *Carnegie Corporation: Program in the Arts 1911–1967*. New York: Carnegie Corporation of New York, 1968.

Kaasa, Walter. "History of the Cultural Development Branch and Division from 1946 to 1981." Provincial Archives of Alberta. Typescript.

Kaye, Frances W. *Hiding the Audience: Viewing Arts and Arts Institutions on the Prairies*. Edmonton: University of Alberta Press, 2003.

Kelly, Paula. *For the Arts: A History of the Manitoba Arts Council*. Winnipeg: Manitoba Arts Council, 1995.

Keshavjee, Serena. "Introduction: Modified Modernism." In *Winnipeg Modern: Architecture, 1945–1975*, edited by Serena Keshavjee, 18–27. Winnipeg: University of Manitoba Press, 2006.

Keshavjee, Serena, ed. *Winnipeg Modern: Architecture, 1945–1975*. Winnipeg: University of Manitoba Press, 2006.

Key, Archie F. *Beyond Four Walls: The Origins and Development of Canadian Museums*. Toronto: McClelland and Stewart, 1973.

– "Travelling Museums – A New National Concept." *Calgary Herald*, 23 May 1972.

The Kingston Conference Proceedings: A Reprint of the Proceedings *of the 1941 Kingston Artists' Conference*. Introduction by Michael Bell. Biographical Notes by Frances K. Smith. Kingston: Agnes Etherington Art Centre, 1991.

Korneski, Kurt. "Minnie J.B. Campbell, Reform, and Empire." In *Prairie Metropolis: New Essays on Winnipeg Social History*, edited by Esylit W. Jones and Gerald Friesen, 18–43. Winnipeg, University of Manitoba Press, 2009.

Koven, Seth. "The Whitechapel Picture Exhibitions and the Politics of Seeing." In *Museum Culture: Histories, Discourses, Spectacles*, edited by Daniel J. Sherman and Irit Rogoff, 22–48. Minneapolis: University of Minnesota Press, 1994.

Kuffert, Leonard B. *A Great Duty: Canadian Responses to Modern Life and Mass Culture 1939–1967*. Montreal and Kingston: McGill-Queen's University Press, 2003.

Kunard, Andrea, and Carol Payne. "Writing Photography in Canada: A History." In *The Cultural Work of Photography in Canada*, edited by Carol Payne and Andrea Kunard, 231–44. Montreal and Kingston: McGill Queen's University Press, 2011.

Lebovics, Herman. *Mona Lisa's Escort: André Malraux and the Reinvention of French Culture*. Ithaca, NY: Cornell University Press, 1999.

Limbos-Bomberg, Nathalie. "The Ideal and the Pragmatic: The National Gallery of Canada's Biennial Exhibitions of Canadian Art, 1953–1968." MA thesis, Carleton University, 2000.

Li, Peter S. "People of the Land: Population Changes in Saskatchewan." In *Perspectives of Saskatchewan*, edited by Jene M. Porter, 1–12. Winnipeg: University of Manitoba Press, 2008.

Litt, Paul. *The Muses, the Masses, and the Massey Commission*. Toronto: University of Toronto Press, 1992.

Logan, Catherine. "Acquiring Authority at the Art Gallery of Ontario and the Agnes Etherington Art Centre: Canadian Women and the Cultural Volunteer Experience." MA thesis, Carleton University, 1997.

Long, Timothy. "The Collector and the Collection." In *The Mackenzie Art Gallery: Norman Mackenzie's Legacy*, edited by W.A. Riddell, 28–59. Regina: The Mackenzie Art Gallery, 1990.

Long, Timothy, and Stephen King, eds. *The Vaults: Art from the MacKenzie Art Gallery and the University of Regina Collections*. Regina: University of Regina Press, 2013.

Lowery, Susan. "The Art Gallery of Toronto: Pattern and Process of Growth, 1872 to 1966." MA thesis, Concordia University, 1985.

Lyotard, Jean-François. *The Postmodern Condition: A Report on Knowledge*. Manchester: Manchester United Press, 1984.

MacGregor, J.G. *Edmonton: A History*. 2nd ed. Edmonton: Hurtig Publishers, 1975.

Mackey, Eva. *The House of Difference: Cultural Politics and National Identity in Canada*. Toronto: University of Toronto Press, 2002.

Macleod, Dianne Sachko. *Enchanted Lives, Enchanted Objects: American Women Collectors and the Making of Culture 1800–1940*. Berkeley: University of California Press, 2008.

Mallory, J.R. "The Lambert Report: Central Roles and Responsibilities." *Canadian Public Administration* 22, no. 4 (1979): 517–29.

"Mandate/Mission." *Canadian Art Museum Directors' Organization*. Accessed 20 January 2014. www.camdo.ca/blog/?page_id+829.

Marshall, Barbara Ruth. "Sir Edmund Walker, Servant of Canada." MA thesis, University of British Columbia, 1971.

Mastin, Catherine. "East Views West: Group Artists in the Rocky Mountains." In *The Group of Seven in Western Canada*, edited by Catherine Mastin, 33–61. Toronto: Key Porter Books; Calgary: Glenbow Museum, 2002. Exhibition catalogue.

McCann, L.D. "Urban Growth in a Staple Economy: The Emergence of Vancouver as a Regional Metropolis, 1886–1914." In *Vancouver: Western Metropolis*, edited by L.J. Evenden. Victoria: University of Victoria, 1978.

McCarthy, Kathleen D. *Women's Culture: American Philanthropy and Art, 1830–1930.* Chicago: University of Chicago Press, 1991.

McCormack, Thelma. "Culture and the State." *Canadian Public Policy* 10, no. 3 (1984): 267–77.

McCullough, Norah. "A Living Art." *Food for Thought* 18, no. 8 (1958): 357–9.

– "The Norman MacKenzie Art Gallery and the School of Art, Regina College." *Canadian Art* 15, no. 3 (1958): 224–5.

McCurry, H.O. "Canadian Museums and the Future." *Canadian Museums Association Bulletin* 2, no. 1 (1949): 2–6.

McInnes, Graham. "A Prairie Connoisseur of Art and Business." *Saturday Night*, 25 September 1948.

McKay, Ian. "The Liberal Order Framework: A Prospectus for a Reconnaissance of Canadian History." *Canadian Historical Review* 81, no. 4 (2000): 617–51.

– "A Note on 'Region' in Writing the History of Atlantic Canada." *Acadiensis* 29, no. 2 (2000): 89–101.

McKay, Marilyn. "Canadian Political Art in the 1930s: 'A Form of Distancing.'" In *The Social and the Real: Political Art of the 1930s in the Western Hemisphere*, edited by Alejandro Anreus, Diana L. Linden, and Jonathan Weinberg, 71–94. University Park: Pennsylvania State University Press, 2006.

McTavish, Lianne. *Defining the Modern Museum: A Case Study of the Challenges of Exchange.* Toronto: University of Toronto Press, 2013.

Mendel Art Gallery. *From Regionalism to Abstraction: Mashel Teitelbaum and Saskatchewan Art in the 1940s.* Saskatoon: Mendel Art Gallery, 1991. Exhibition catalogue.

Meszaros, Cheryl. "Visibility and Representation: Saskatchewan Art Organizations Prior to 1945." MA thesis, Queen's University, 1990.

Miers, Sir Henry A., and S.F. Markham. *A Report on the Museums of Canada to the Carnegie Corporation of New York.* Edinburgh: T. and A. Constable Ltd., 1932.

Moreault, Michel. *Max Stern: Montreal Dealer and Patron.* Montreal: Montreal Museum of Fine Arts, 2004. Exhibition catalogue.

Morton, W.L. "The Bias of Prairie Politics." In *Contexts of Canada's Pasts: Selected Essays of W.L. Morton*, 149–60. Toronto: MacMillan, 1980.

National Gallery of Canada. *Annual Reports of the Board of Trustees* for the fiscal years 1920–21 to 1967–68.

– *Annual Reviews* for the fiscal years 1968–90.

– *National Gallery Summary of Corporate Plan for 2014–15 to 2018–19 and Operating and Capital Budgets for 2014–15.* Accessed 24 August 2016. https://www.gallery.ca/documents/planning%20and%20reporting/2014-15-NGC-Corporate-Plan-Summary-ENG.pdf

"'National Museums' Act Now Law: Proclamation Expected Shortly." *CMA Gazette* 2, no. 2 (1968): 1.

National Museums of Canada. *After Applebaum-Hébert*. Ottawa: National Museums of Canada, 1984.

– *Annual Reports* for the fiscal years 1969–89.

– *The National Museum Policy: A Programme for Canadian Museums.* Ottawa: Queen's Printer, 1972.

– *A National Museums Policy for the 80's: Preliminary Statement of Intent and Brief to the Federal Cultural Policy Review Committee.* Ottawa: National Museums of Canada, 1981.

Nemiroff, Diana. "A History of Artist-Run Spaces in Canada, With Particular Reference to Véhicule, A Space and the Western Front." MA thesis, Concordia University, 1985.

"New Art Centre." *Saturday Night*, 17 June 1944.

Nickle Arts Museum. *Calgary Modern 1947–1969*. Calgary: Nickle Arts Museum, 2000. Exhibition catalogue.

Niergarth, Kirk. "'Missionary for Culture': Walter Abell, *Maritime Art* and Cultural Democracy, 1928–1944." *Acadiensis* 36, no. 1 (2006): 3–28.

Norman MacKenzie Art Gallery. *The Saskatchewan Arts Board Collection.* Regina: Norman MacKenzie Art Gallery, 1978. Exhibition catalogue.

Nurse, Andrew. "Artists, Society, and Activism: The Federation of Canadian Artists and the Social Organization of Canadian Art." *Southern Journal of Canadian Studies* 4, no. 1 (2011): 1–24.

– "'A Confusion of Values': Artists and Artistic Ideologies in Modern Canada, 1927–1952." MA thesis, Queen's University, 1991.

Nutana Collegiate Memorial Art Gallery: Permanent Collection. With introductory essay by Donna Volden, Saskatoon: Nutana Collegiate, 1995.

O'Brian, John. "Where the Hell is Saskatchewan and Who Is Emma Lake?" In *The Flat Side of the Landscape, The Emma Lake Artists' Workshop: Essays*, edited by John O'Brian, 13–19. Saskatoon: Mendel Art Gallery, 1989. Exhibition catalogue.

O'Neal, Brian. "Reorganizing Government: New Approaches to Public Service Reform." *Government of Canada: Political and Social Affairs Division.* January 1994. Accessed 3 June 2011. http://dsp-psd.pwgsc.gc.ca/Collection-R/LoPBdP/BP/bp375-e.htm#%2811%29end.

Ontario Society of Artists. *President's Annual Report 1929–30.* Accessed 21 January 2010. http://www.ccca.concordia.ca/history/osa/english/references/1930-rpt.html.

Ord, Douglas. *The National Gallery of Canada: Ideas, Art, Architecture.* Montreal and Kingston: McGill-Queen's University Press, 2003.

Order in Council. PC 1786, 8 April 1949. Reprinted in Canada, Royal Commission on National Development in the Arts, Letters and Sciences. *Report.* Ottawa: King's Printer, 1951.

"Organization of Canadian Museums Association." *Canadian Museums Association Bulletin* 1, no. 1 (1948): 1–2.

Ostrower, Francie. *Trustees of Culture: Power, Wealth and Status on Elite Arts Boards.* Chicago: University of Chicago Press, 2002.

Ostry, Bernard. *The Cultural Connection: An Essay on Culture and Government Policy in Canada.* Toronto: McClelland and Stewart, 1978.

Ottawa Citizen. "Former Director Critical of National Museum Bill." 24 April 1967.

Ottawa Daily Free Press. 10 March 1888. Cited on the National Gallery of Canada's website. "Our History, Pre 1900s." Accessed 20 May 2013. www.gallery.ca/en/about/pre-1900.php.

Owram, Doug. *Promises of Eden: The Canadian Expansionist Movement and the Idea of the West, 1856–1900.* Toronto: University of Toronto Press, 1992.

Paikowsky, Sandra. "'From Away': The Carnegie Corporation, Walter Abell and American Strategies for Art in the Maritimes from the 1920s to the 1940s." *Journal of Canadian Art History* 23 (2006): 37–72.

Palmer, Bryan. *Canada's 1960s: The Ironies of Identity in a Rebellious Era.* Toronto: University of Toronto Press, 2008.

Palmer, Howard, and Tamara Palmer. *Alberta: A New History.* Edmonton: Hurtig Publishers, 1990.

Panayotidis, E. Lisa. "The Department of Fine Art at the University of Toronto, 1926–1945: Institutionalizing the 'Culture of the Aesthetic.'" *Journal of Canadian Art History* 25 (2004): 100–22.

Paquin, Jean. *Art, public et société: L'expérience des Maisons de la culture de Montréal.* Montréal: Les Éditions Hurtubise HMH Ltée, 2006.

Pelletier, Gérard. *L'Aventure du pouvoir, 1968–1975.* Montréal: Stanké, 1992.

– "Museums and the National Heritage: A Cultural Policy." *CMA Gazette* 5, no. 1 (1971): 10–17.

– "A New Policy for Museums." *CMA Gazette* 6, no. 2 (1972): 3–13.

Perry, Adele. "Whose World Was British? Rethinking the 'British World' from an Edge of Empire." In *Britishness Abroad: Transnational Movements and Imperial Cultures,* edited by Kate Darian-Smith, Patricia Grimshaw, and Stuart Macintyre, 133–52. Melbourne: University of Melbourne Press, 2007.

Pitsula, James M. "Saskatchewan's Path to Economic Development." In *Perspectives of Saskatchewan,* edited by Jene M. Porter, 105–23. Winnipeg: University of Manitoba Press, 2008.

Potter, Evan H. *Branding Canada: Projecting Canada's Soft Power through Public Diplomacy.* Montreal and Kingston: McGill-Queen's University Press, 2009.

Rathbone, Perry. "On Collecting." *Canadian Art* 17, no. 1 (1960): 34, 48.

Read, Robyn. "Eric Harvie: Without and Within Robert Kroetsch's *Alibi.*" In *The West and Beyond: New Perspectives on an Imagined Region,* edited by Alvin Finkel, Sarah Carter, and Peter Fortna, 375–96. Edmonton: Athabasca University Press, 2010.

"Regional Support Promised for Community Centres." *Canadian Art* 2, no. 1 (1944): 38–9.

Reichwein, PearlAnn. "Holiday at the Banff School of Fine Arts: The Cinematic Production of Culture, Nature and Nation in the Canadian Rockies, 1945–1952." *Journal of Canadian Studies* 39, no. 1 (2005): 49–73.

"Reorganization of the National Museums of Canada." CMA *Gazette* 2, no. 4 (1968): 2.

"Report of Second Annual Meeting." *Canadian Museums Association Bulletin* 2, no. 2 (1949): 6.

Ridell, W.A. *Cornerstone for Culture: A History of the Saskatchewan Arts Board from 1948 to 1978.* Regina: Saskatchewan Arts Board, 1979.

Ridell, W.A., ed. *The Mackenzie Art Gallery: Norman Mackenzie's Legacy.* Regina: The Mackenzie Art Gallery, 1990.

Robertson, Clive. *Policy Matters: Administrations of Art and Culture.* Toronto: YYZ Books, 2006.

Russell, Bruce Hugh. "Aboriginal Art." In *Quebec and Canadian Art: The Montreal Museum of Fine Arts' Collection*, edited by Jacques Des Rochers, 80–5. Montreal: Montreal Museum of Fine Arts, 2011.

Rushing, W. Jackson. "Marketing the Affinity of the Primitive and the Modern: René d'Harnoncourt and 'Indian Art of the United States.'" In *The Early Years of Native American Art History*, edited by Janet Berlo, 191–236. Seattle: University of Washington Press, 1992.

Salmony, Alfred. "The Portland Museum of Art." *Parnassus* 19, no. 5 (1937): 25–6.

Schafer, D. Paul. *A Cultural Survey of British Columbia.* Presented to the British Columbia Centennial Fund, British Columbia Government, January 1972.

Scoles, Diane. "The Winnipeg Show 1955–1970: Local and National Significance." MA thesis, University of Victoria, 1995.

Shadbolt, Jack. "A Report on Art Today in British Columbia." *Canadian Art* 4, no. 1 (1946): 4–7; 45.

Sheppard, Gordon. *Special Report on the Cultural Policy and Activities of the Government of Canada.* Ottawa: Government of Canada, 1966.

Sicotte, Hélène. "À Kingston, il y a 50 ans, la conférence des artistes Canadiens: Débat sur la place de l'artiste dans la société." *Journal of Canadian Art History* 14, no. 2 (1990): 28–47.

Simmins, Richard B. *The National Exhibition Centres: A First Study.* 2 vols. Ottawa, National Museums Canada, 1975.

– *Simmins Report on Art Gallery Development in Canada.* 2 volumes. Ottawa: Canada Council, 1969.

– *The Simmins Report on the Associate Museum System in Canada.* Ottawa: National Museums Canada, 1977.

Smiley, D.V. "The Rowell-Sirois Report, Provincial Autonomy, and Post-War Canadian Federalism." *Canadian Journal of Economics and Political Science* 28, no. 1 (1962): 54–69.

Smith, Frances K. *André Biéler: An Artist's Life and Times.* Rev. ed. Richmond Hill, ON: Firefly Books, 2006.

Spurgeon, David. "A Bright New Image for Our 'Stuffy' Museums." *Ottawa Journal*, 1 March 1969.

The StarPhoenix (Saskatoon). "Art and the Community." 13 April 1949.

Stanners, Sarah. "Going British and Being Modern in the Visual Art Systems of Canada, 1906–1976." PhD diss., University of Toronto, 2009.

Stolow, Nathan. "Conservation Policy and the Exhibition of Museum Collections." *Journal of the American Institute for Conservation* 16, no. 2 (1977): 12–20.

Swyripa, Frances. *Storied Landscapes: Ethno-Religious Identity and the Canadian Prairies.* Winnipeg: University of Manitoba Press, 2010.

Taylor, Robert Ratcliffe. *The Spencer Mansion: A House, a Home and a Museum.* Victoria: Touchwood Editions, 2012.

Teather, J. Lynne. "The Museum Keepers: The Museums Association and the Growth of Museum Professionalism." *Museum Management and Curatorship* 9 (1990): 25–41.

– "Professionalism and the Museum." In *The Museum: A Reference Guide*, edited by Michael Steven Shapiro with Louis Ward Kemp, 299–327. Westport, CT: Greenwood Press, 1990.

Teitelbaum, Matthew. *The Mendel Art Gallery: Twenty-Five Years of Collecting.* Saskatoon: Mendel Art Gallery, 1989. Exhibition catalogue.

Thom, William Wiley. "The Fine Arts in Vancouver, 1886–1930." MA thesis, University of British Columbia, 1969.

Thomas, Ann W. "The National Gallery of Canada." *History of Photography* 20, no. 2 (1996): 171–80.

Throsby, David. *The Economics of Cultural Policy.* Cambridge: Cambridge University Press, 2010.

Tippett, Maria. *Making Culture: English-Canadian Institutions and the Arts before the Massey Commission.* Toronto: University of Toronto Press, 1990.

Tooby, Michael, ed. *The True North: Landscape Painting 1896–1939.* London: Barbican Art Gallery / Lund Humphries, 1992.

Trudel, Jean. "Aux origines du Musée des beaux-arts de Montréal: La fondation de l'Art Association of Montreal en 1860." *Journal of Canadian Art History* 15, no. 1 (1992): 31–62.

Trask, Jeffrey. *Things American: Art Museums and Civic Culture in the Progressive Era.* Philadelphia: University of Pennsylvania Press, 2012.

Vancouver Art Gallery. *Annual Reports*, 1931–1990.

– "The Founder's Collection." *Souvenir Catalogue.* Vancouver: Vancouver Art Gallery, 1931. Exhibition catalogue.

– *Souvenir Catalogue.* Vancouver: Vancouver Art Gallery, 1931. Exhibition catalogue.

– *Vancouver Art and Artists 1931–1938.* Vancouver: Vancouver Art Gallery, 1983. Exhibition catalogue.

"Vancouver Will Now Build Canada's Most Modern Art Gallery." *Canadian Art* 6, no. 3 (1949): 128.

Waiser, Bill. "Our Shared Destiny? Saskatchewan in 1905 and 2005." *Acadiensis* 35, no. 2 (2006): 157–62.

Wallace, Keith, ed. *Whispered Art History: Twenty Years at the Western Front.* Vancouver: Arsenal Pulp Press, 1993.

Wardhaugh, Robert. *Mackenzie King and the Prairie West.* Toronto: University of Toronto Press, 2000.

Watson, Scott. "Art in the Fifties: Design, Leisure and Painting in the Age of Anxiety." In *Vancouver Art and Artists 1931–1938.* Vancouver: Vancouver Art Gallery, 1983. Exhibition catalogue.

Whitelaw, Anne. "From the Gift Shop to the Permanent Collection: Women and the Circulation of Inuit Art." In *Craft, Community and the Material Culture of Place and Politics, 19th–20th Century,* edited by Janice Helland, Beverly Lemire, and Alena Buis, 105–23. Aldershot: Ashgate Press, 2014.

– "Professional/Volunteer: Women at the Edmonton Art Gallery, 1923–1970." In *Rethinking Professionalism: Essays on Women and Art in Canada, 1850–1970,* edited by Kristina Huneault and Janice Anderson, 357–79. Montreal and Kingston: McGill-Queen's University Press, 2012.

– *Thinking through Modernism: Edmonton, 1965–1985.* Edmonton: Art Gallery of Edmonton, 2008. Exhibition catalogue.

– "'To Better Know Ourselves': J. Russell Harper's *Painting in Canada: A History."* *Journal of Canadian Art History,* 26, no. 1 (2005): 8–33.

– "Statistical Imperatives: Representing the Nation in Exhibitions of Contemporary Art." *Topia* 1 (Spring 1997): 22–41.

Williamson, Moncrieff. "An Art Gallery Worthy of Victoria." *Canadian Art* 15, no. 2 (1958): 138.

Winnipeg Art Gallery. *The Eckhardts in Winnipeg: A Cultural Legacy.* Winnipeg: Winnipeg Art Gallery, 2007. Exhibition catalogue.

– *Selected Works from the Winnipeg Art Gallery.* Winnipeg: Winnipeg Art Gallery, 1971. Exhibition catalogue.

Women's Art Association of Canada. *Annual Report of the Association and its Branches.* Toronto: Women's Art Association of Canada, 31 August 1918.

Wood, Elizabeth Wyn. "Art Goes to Parliament." *Canadian Art* 2, no. 1 (1944): 3–5, 41–2.

– "A National Program for the Arts in Canada." *Canadian Art* 1, no. 3 (1944): 93–5; 127–8.

Yates, Sarah. *The Manitoba Society of Artists: A History.* Winnipeg: Manitoba Society of Artists, 1992.

Zemans, Joyce. "The Canon Unbound." *Journal of Canadian Art History* 25 (2004): 151–79.

– "Envisioning Nation: Nationhood, Identity and the Sampson-Matthews Silkscreen Project: The Wartime Prints." *Journal of Canadian Art History* 19, no. 1 (1998): 6–51.
– "Establishing the Canon: Nationhood, Identity and the National Gallery's First Reproduction Program of Canadian Art." *Journal of Canadian Art History* 16, no. 2 (1995): 7–35.
– "Sampson-Matthews and the NGC: The Post-War Years." *Journal of Canadian Art History* 21, nos. 1 and 2 (2000): 96–140.
Zimon, Kathy E. *Alberta Society of Artists: The First Seventy Years.* Calgary: University of Calgary Press, 2000.

224, 254–6; *Report on the Development of Art Galleries in Canada*,
147–8
Canadian Art, and Harris–Wood
debate, 128–30; and move to
National Gallery, 155; and relationship to the Federation of Canadian
Artists, 123, 130–1, 291n30; and
western Canada, 107, 269
Canadian art: as collecting area, 3, 4,
69–70, 146; exhibitions of, 25–6, 41,
93, 95, 166; and National Gallery,
18, 80–6, 97–8, *102–3*, 140–1,
170, 260–1, 296n26; and Norman
MacKenzie Art Gallery, 219; as part of
loan exhibitions, 87–8; and Vancouver Art Gallery, 66–8; and western
Canada, 113–14; and Winnipeg Art
Gallery, 217; and women's committees, 40–1, 64, 68
Canadian art history, 97, 267–9
Canadian Broadcasting Corporation
(CBC), 130, 138, 139, 155, 168, 256–7
Canadian Museums Committee (CMC),
75, 104–7, 116, 288,n73, 290n15,
294n89; and museum training program, 189, 191–3
Canadian Museum of Civilization. *See*
National Museum
Canadian Museums Association (CMA),
169, 193–4, 198, 214, 232, 305n23
Carnegie Corporation, 39, 94, 99–101,
139, 154, 155–6, 282n89; and
Canadian Museums Committee, 41,
75, 99–110, 155, 185, 189–92, 279n53,
294n89; and funding for libraries in
Canada, 27, *27*, 35, *55*, 85, 277n15,
285n30; and Kingston Conference,
114–16, 119–20; and sponsorship
of children's art classes, 59, *59*, 75,
96, 110

cataloguing, 214–22, 233–4; and the
Art Gallery of Greater Victoria,
215; and the Edmonton Art Gallery,
216–17, 219; and the National Gallery
of Canada, 214–15; and the Norman
MacKenzie Art Gallery, 215; and the
Winnipeg Art Gallery, 196, 214, 217
centralization: and government
services, 228, 256; and National
Gallery, 129, 170–2, 173, 292n46;
and National Museums Corporation,
238, 258; of power in Canada, 12, 18,
20, 72
centre–periphery, 10–14, 19, 72, 75, 119,
264, 268, 269
Christian Science, 109, 276n6, 289n82
civilizing values of museums, 37–8, 62,
72, 132–3
Coleman, Laurence Vail, 189–90, 198
collecting, 39, 43, 46, 49–50, 283n115;
and the Edmonton Art Gallery, 210,
216–17; and the National Gallery, 74,
215; and the Norman MacKenzie Art
Gallery, 260; and the Vancouver Art
Gallery, 66–8; in western Canada,
65–71; and the Winnipeg Art Gallery,
68, 217–18, 220–2, 259–60. *See also*
Harvie, Eric; MacKenzie, Norman;
Mendel, Frederick, and Southam,
H.S.
collections (development of), 3–5,
39, 58, 69, 71, 90–1, 94, 150–1, 157,
219–23, 266, 302n71
collections management, 214–17, 233,
246
Collins, Leona, 48, 108, 300n32
community art centres, 123, 125–6,
130–7, 166, 171, 237
Conference of Canadian Artists
(Kingston Conference), 114–21, *118*,
290n16; effects of recommendations,

Mendel Art Gallery, 25; buildings,
201, 206–7, *208, 209,* 266, 302n53;
funding, 241–2, 254; and patronage
of Frederick Mendel, 49–50. *See also*
Saskatoon Art Centre

Mendel, Frederick, 6, 46, 49–53, 71

Miers, Henry, 101, 190. *See also Report
on the Museums of Canada*

Montreal Museum of Fine Arts (MMFA),
183, 214, 217, 252, 294n92. *See also*
Art Association of Montreal

Moose Jaw, and establishment of
permanent collection, 90, 110; and
requests for loan exhibitions, 3, 54–5,
84, *86,* 87, 92; spaces for exhibitions,
25, *55,* 57–8, 81, 158, 281n80; and
Western Canada Art Circuit, 156. *See
also* Gibbard, A.H

Morris, Jerrold: as director of Vancouver Art Gallery, 196, 300n25; display
strategies at Vancouver Art Gallery,
203–6, 303n73; and Western Canada
Art Circuit, 161–2

Mulcaster, Wynona, 71, *124*

museum architecture, 199–214. *See also*
International modernism

Museum Assistance Programmes
(MAP), 243–5, 255–6

"museum man," 182, 185, 194, 198–9,
300n31

museum training, 101, 106, 189–99;
and National Museum Policy, 244–5,
305n23. *See also* Canadian Museums
Committee; Harvard museum course

Museumobiles, 234, 238, 239, 243,
246, 257

Museums Association (UK), 101, 190–1,
214, 218

museums, ideological work of, 15, 73–4,
267–8

Musgrove, Alexander: as director of
Winnipeg Art Gallery, 32–3, 118–19,

195, 278n33; receiving funds from
the Canadian Museums Committee,
191–2

nation building, and the Artists' Brief,
127–8, 131, and Canada Council,
144–6; and Massey Commission,
62, 111–12, 142–4; and National
Gallery, 7, 74–5, 260–1; and National
Museum Policy, 232–8

National Exhibition Centres, establishment of, 224, 233, 238; funding,
243–4, 249

National Film Board, 130, 131, 290n12

National Gallery Act (1952), 230,
304n15

National Gallery of Canada Act (1913),
3, 79–80, 110

National Gallery of Canada (NGC): at
the Art Gallery of Alberta, 265–6,
269–70; and Carnegie Corporation,
99, 103–8; circulating exhibitions
84–92, *84,* 165–70; and classification
of Canadian galleries, 212–14;
criticism of, 129–31, 142–3, 150–1;
directors' tours of western Canada,
92–6; founding of, 73–4, 79–81;
juried exhibitions of Canadian
art, 95–9, 165–7; lecturers, 96–7,
103–4, *104;* and nation building, 7,
18, 74–5, 260–1; and paternalism,
170–1; and professionalization,
187–99; Regina conference, 173–6,
181–3; reproduction programs, 81–2;
Vancouver conference, 168–73, 296;
at the Winnipeg Art Gallery, 265–6,
269–70

National Museum, 77, *78, 79,* 101;
and accessibility, 142–3. *See also*
Canadian Museum of Civilization

National Museum of Man. *See* National
Museum